Creating a
Forest Garden

CREATING A
FOREST GARDEN

WORKING WITH NATURE TO GROW EDIBLE CROPS

MARTIN CRAWFORD

green books

First published in 2010 by

GREEN BOOKS
Foxhole, Dartington
Totnes, Devon TQ9 6EB
www.greenbooks.co.uk

Reprinted 2010 and 2012 with minor amendments

Design & layout
Stephen Prior

Photographs by Martin Crawford and
Joanna Brown www.jozart.co.uk
(see page 6 for credits)

Illustrations by Marion Smylie-Wild
www.marionsmylie.co.uk

Printed in the UK by Butler Tanner & Dennis
Text printed on Arctic Matt

Disclaimer
Many things we eat as a matter of course – potatoes,
beans, rhubarb, sorrel (to name but a few) – are all
toxic to some degree if not eaten in the right way, at
the right time and with the right preparation. At the
time of going to press, the advice and information in
this book are believed to be true and accurate, and if
plants are eaten according to the guidance given here
they are safe. However, someone, somewhere is allergic
to almost anything, so if you are trying completely
new plants to eat, try them in moderation to begin with.
The author and the publishers accept no liability for
actions inspired by this book.

ISBN 978 1 900322 62 1

Cover and preliminary page images
Front cover: Top left: redcurrants (*Ribes rubrum*). Top
centre: hazelnuts (*Corylus avellana*). Top right: plum
(*Prunus domestica*) 'Purple Pershore'. Bottom: ramsons
(*Allium ursinum*). *Back cover:* Top: heartnuts (*Juglans
ailantifolia* var. *cordiformis*). Centre: honey bee on apple
blossom. Bottom: new shoot of fishpole bamboo (*Phyllostachys aurea*). Page 1: snowbell tree (*Halesia carolina*).
Page 2: autumn olive (*Elaeagnus umbellata*). This page:
hawthorn (*Crataegus pinnatifida* var. *major*) 'Big Golden
Star'. Page 8: cones of stone pine (*Pinus pinea*).

Acknowledgements

The journey that has culminated in this book has relied on many authors and innovators, but in particular I would like to acknowledge Miguel Altieri, Ken Fern, Masanobu Fukuoka, Robert Hart, Dave Jacke, J. Russell Smith and Eric Toensmeier.

Thanks to the Dartington Hall Trust for making land available for my forest garden and agroforestry experiments.

Thanks to Justin West for his useful comments and feedback on the manuscript, and for his challenging questions in the forest garden.

Thanks to Marion Smylie-Wild for her line drawings and to Joanna Brown for her photos.

Picture credits

All photographs in this book were taken in Martin Crawford's forest garden in Dartington. All are by Martin Crawford except those on the following pages, which are by Joanna Brown.
4/5, 12, 16, 24, 26, 27, 40, 49, 50, 76, 88, 97, 98, 107, 117, 119 bottom left, 122 top left, 131, 141, 146, 158 top right, 159, 172, 178, 183, 185, 191 top right, 194, 211 bottom left, 212, 213, 217 bottom right, 224 bottom right, 229, 236, 237, 243, 247, 252 bottom right, 253, 254, 269 bottom left, 276, 287, 290, 296, 302, 305, 307, 320. Front cover: top left & top right. Back cover: middle left.

*To Sandra, without whom none
of this would have happened*

Contents

Foreword

In 1992, in the middle of my Permaculture Design course, about twelve of us hopped on a bus for a day trip to Robert Hart's forest garden, at Wenlock Edge in Shropshire. On arrival we were greeted by the short, somewhat eccentric Mr Hart himself, who had pioneered the concept of temperate forest gardening, and who lived a rather lonely existence in what was in effect a lean-to shed in an advanced state of dilapidation, surrounded by, and seemingly sustained by, his forest garden. He seemed to live for the visits of other people to his garden – an extraordinary three-dimensional jumble of trees and shrubs, many of which I had never heard of before.

In spite of his advancing years, a forest garden tour with Robert Hart was like a tour of Willy Wonka's chocolate factory with Mr Wonka himself. "Look at this!" "Try one of these!" Every tree had a story about how he had heard of it, where it came from and why he had planted it. There were very few fruits there that I recognised. Little berries, warty knobbly things, delicious-looking colourful fruits, odd-looking objects vaguely recalled from Elizabethan fruit books – a riot of colour, shape and texture. I was surrounded by Robert's diet, hung from wildly different trees and shrubs. Here, he felt at home. Me, I felt bewildered, yet profoundly intrigued. There was something extraordinary about this garden, something that touched many of those who made the pilgrimage to Wenlock Edge. As you walked around the garden, and as you lay under the trees eating your sandwiches once the tour had finished, an awareness dawned that what surrounded you was more than just a garden. It was, like that garden that Alice in *Alice in Wonderland* can see only through the door she is too big to get through, a tangible taste of something altogether new and wonderful, yet also instinctively familiar.

This seeming riot of plants and trees, when explained, proved to be an intelligently designed, three-dimensional food system, based on perennial plants, which offered a whole new way of imagining agricultural systems. Above all, it created an extraordinary space – with height, with colour, with scents and wildlife – yet one in which one instinctively felt at home. Perhaps what Hart created was the closest to what we imagine the Garden of Eden as being. I remember being taken with the idea of a garden one could get lost in.

After Hart's death, the garden was lost to the world as a working model. Over subsequent years his books, as well as the taste of what was possible that people had gained from their visits to Wenlock Edge, acted as an inspiration for thousands of such gardens around the world. Using Robert's books, and then Patrick Whitefield's *How to Make a Forest Garden*, people began trying to replicate Hart's garden – many of them, as Dave Jacke and Eric Toensmeier discovered when researching their *Edible Forest Gardens* books, replicating Hart's mistakes as much as his successes.

Martin Crawford was one of those early visitors to Hart's forest garden, and since then has made the single most extraordinary contribution to our understanding of what makes a forest garden actually work. For many years, as a permaculture teacher, I have been in awe of Martin's work. Here is a man who, virtually singlehandedly, runs a demonstration forest garden, a larger research site, a mail-order business, training courses and tours, and publishes a quarterly journal. I have subscribed to *Agroforestry News* for many years, and whenever I meet other teachers we always rave about Martin's work and its extraordinary potential.

When, in 2005, I moved to Devon, just up the road from Martin, I was struck by how few people had heard of his work, which is so respected internationally. With his appearance in Rebecca Hosking's film *A Farm for the Future*, and now with this book, Martin's vision of what food production in this country could look like, and indeed needs to be like, is starting to spread. Not before time. The challenge we need to grapple with is nothing less than this: how do we transform everything we do, including the systems by which we feed ourselves, in such a way that at the end of each day we have locked more carbon into the ground than we have emitted? To say that this calls for a rethink of many basic assumptions is to greatly understate the magnitude of the challenge. One of the key questions for farming is how to move it towards something that is diverse, robust, perennial, based not on tilling the soil but on building soil instead, and able to draw up its own nutrients and lock up carbon. It is such systems that Martin has both researched and developed, and he is an unrivalled source of knowledge on the subject.

I have waited a long time for this book, and I am delighted that you finally hold it in your hands. It is the distillation of many years of Martin's work, and it offers a toolkit for forest gardeners; both novices and old hands. When I am asked to articulate a vision for the future, that vision contains urban agriculture, localised food systems, local markets and so on, but always agroforestry – whether as urban fruit and nut tree plantings or as intentionally designed and abundant large-scale agroforestry. What I always point out to people is that these things are not fanciful and somehow Utopian; rather they are all things one can see working already in different places – Martin's demonstration forest garden on the Dartington Estate in Devon being one of the key examples. The power of Martin's work is not just that it offers a vision of an abundant, post-fossil-fuel farming system, but also that it offers research to back that up, the tools for designing it, the models and even the plants themselves. And now, the definitive manual. Once one has tasted the potential of what Martin suggests in this book, one cannot look at food production in the same way again. I have nothing but the deepest gratitude for Martin's work.

Rob Hopkins

Introduction

Forest gardens are complex systems. Creating your own forest garden can seem overwhelming: there are so many things to think about at the same time. In this book I have tried to split the process up to make it all more manageable, using a step-by-step structure.

Thus, just as forest gardens themselves can be thought of as layered systems, with plants at different heights, I have treated the design of the top (canopy) layer, the middle (shrub) layers and the lower (perennial or ground-cover) layers separately. More often than not these layers are planted at different times, so it is quite easy to look at them in isolation. Remember, though, that the layers are linked (see 'guilds', page 196) and that nothing in a forest garden is really growing in isolation.

The forest garden lush in summer.

How to find your way around the book

Most people start their forest gardens by designing and planting the trees first, then moving on to shrubs and lower plants, so that is the order I have used in this book. However, even the latter stages of design – clearings and paths – have a bearing on the early stages, so I highly recommend that you read through the whole book before you start the design process.

A large number of plants is described in the book. Wherever possible I have used both Latin and common names, and the index contains both to make them easy to find. Species are organised primarily by their use (common tree fruits, tree nuts/seeds, etc.) and then by Latin name.

In the descriptions of plants, where there is no relevant information then the category is missed out – for example 'Secondary uses' is not included if there are no such uses known.

Next to the name of each plant, a pictorial key indicates important information, as in the example here:

> Deciduous/Evergreen: D
> Zone (*Hardiness zone*): 4
> Sun/shade preference: ◯
> Shade tolerance: ◖
> Performance rating: ✓✓
> Fertility: SF   Flowers (*Flower colour*): Yellow
> Cover (*Ground-cover rating*): ✓✓✓

Deciduous/evergreen

D indicates a deciduous woody plant or a herbaceous perennial that dies down to roots in winter.
E indicates an evergreen plant.
SE indicates a semi-evergreen plant.

Hardiness zone

The zone number given for a plant gives an indication of its hardiness. Zones 1 to 9 indicate the minimum average winter temperatures that a plant can tolerate – hence a plant hardy to zone 5 (say) can be grown in zones 5 and upwards. Devised in the USA, the hardiness zone system is most useful in continental climates, where zone maps indicate what zone a location is in. In the USA, subdivisions of each numbered zone are sometimes used, hence zone 5b, etc. Note that a given species may exhibit a hardiness range if it is adapted to growing in different areas.

In the UK the system does not work quite so well, because here the cooler summers must also be taken into account – sometimes new growth is either insufficient or does not harden off, which can also affect plant survival over winter. However, the zone is a useful indicator of winter hardiness.

Most of the UK is classed as zone 8, with upland areas as zone 7 and areas adjacent to coasts, especially in the south, as zone 9. But the microclimate you create in your garden can move your hardiness zone rating one higher – so if in theory you are in a zone 8 area, in a well-sheltered garden you may be able to grow zone 9 species. Another complication is that the hardiness of a species may vary with where it originates from, with provenances further north leading to hardier plants.

Hardiness zone maps for Europe and North America can be found online, for example at http://en.wikipedia.org/wiki/Hardiness_zone.

ZONE NUMBER	AVERAGE MIN TEMP (°C)	AVERAGE MIN TEMP (°F)
1	Below -46	Below -50
2	-46 to -40	-50 to -40
3	-40 to -34	-40 to -30
4	-34 to -29	-30 to -20
5	-29 to -23	-20 to -10
6	-23 to -18	-10 to 0
7	-18 to -12	0 to 10
8	-12 to -7	10 to 20
9	-7 to -1	20 to 30

Sun/shade preference

This indicates the light conditions a plant really prefers and will thrive in. Note that this is for British conditions – in lower latitudes with hotter, sunnier summers (for example, north-eastern USA) then you should assume that slightly shadier conditions are preferred than are indicated. Likewise, in higher latitudes with cooler summers (for example, Norway and Sweden) assume that slightly sunnier conditions are preferred. Soil moisture also has an effect on light tolerance; generally, in moister soils woodland plants will tolerate more sun than in dry soils.

○ Prefers full sun conditions
◑ Prefers light shade (about 50 per cent or 4-5 hours of full sun per day)

◑ Prefers moderate shade (about 20 per cent or an hour or two of direct sun per day)
● Prefers fairly deep shade (no direct sun but some indirect light)

Shade tolerance

This indicates the shadiest conditions that a plant will grow happily in and persist. This is for British conditions, and the same modifications for other latitudes apply as for sun/shade preference, left.

○ Does not tolerate shade
◑ Tolerates light shade (about 50 per cent or 4-5 hours of full sun per day)

◗ Tolerates moderate shade (about 20 per cent or an hour or two of direct sun per day)

● Tolerates fairly deep shade (no direct sun but some indirect light)

●● Tolerates deep shade beneath evergreen trees and shrubs

Performance rating

This indicates how well the plant performs in a forest garden. In other words, it is an indication of how well it grows and crops.

✓ Fair
✓✓ Good
✓✓✓ Very good
✓✓✓✓ Excellent

Fertility

If the plant is a fruiting plant, an indication is given here of its fertility.

SF Self-fertile. One plant will fruit happily by itself.

PSF Partially self-fertile. One plant by itself will fruit, but will produce more fruit, and usually larger fruit, with cross-pollination with another plant, which needs to be a different variety.

SS Self-sterile. One plant by itself will not fruit; cross-pollination with a different variety is essential.

M/F There are male and female plants, and both are needed for fruiting (i.e. the plant is dioecious). Usually one male plant will pollinate several females in the vicinity.

Flower colour

This indicates the normal colour(s) of the flowers. If the flower colour of the species can vary then a list of colours with commas indicates different possibilities. An '&' indicates that the different colours appear on the same flower. Note that ornamental varieties of some species mentioned in this book have been bred with many different flower colours in addition to those listed here.

Ground-cover rating

For perennial and ground-layer plants, this indicates how well a dense planting covers the ground and excludes weeds.

✗ Poor ground cover

✓ Fair ground cover. Will probably need weeding in spring and summer.

✓✓ Good ground cover. May need occasional weeding, particularly in spring.

✓✓✓ Very good ground cover. Pretty weed-proof.

METRIC AND IMPERIAL VALUES

Values throughout the book are given in metric, with imperial conversions for lengths, weights and temperature. Other metric-to-imperial conversions are as follows:

$1m^2$ = 1.2 sq yards
1 hectare = 2.5 acres
1 litre = 1.75 pints (UK); 2.1 pints (USA)
100 litres = 22 gallons (UK); 26 gallons (USA)

Part 1
How forest gardens work

Quince (*Cydonia oblonga*).

Chapter 1

Forest gardens

What is a forest garden?

A forest garden is a garden modelled on the structure of young natural woodland, utilising plants of direct and indirect benefit to people – often edible plants. It may contain large trees, small trees, shrubs, herbaceous perennials, herbs, annuals, root crops and climbers, all planted in such a way as to maximise positive inter-actions and minimise negative interactions, with fertility maintained largely or wholly by the plants themselves.

The plants in a forest garden are mainly perennial, which gives the system its long-term nature. Many of the plants used are multipurpose; they may have a main function or crop but will very often also have a number of other uses. Plants are also mixed to a large degree, so there are few large blocks or areas of a single species, and each species is grown close to many others in ways that are mutually beneficial.

A forest garden is in fact a carefully designed and main-tained ecosystem of useful plants (and perhaps animals too). The self-fertilising nature comes from the use of nitrogen-fixing plants and other plants that are particularly good at raising nutrients from the subsoil, and from the very efficient nutrient cycling that develops in a forest-like system. The soil is maintained in peak condition by being covered by plants at most times, and garden health is boosted by the use of plants that attract predators of likely pests, and plants that reduce disease problems. Diversity is important too: high diversity almost always increases ecosystem health.

The term 'forest garden' may imply something large and extensive, which is not necessarily the case – forest gardens can be cultivated on any scale, from a small back garden to a field, or several fields. 'Woodland garden' can sometimes be the same thing. Unfortunately, in our culture, 'forest' or 'woodland' implies a denser, darker collection of trees, which is not the case in a forest garden, as you'll see.

Although the history of forest gardens in the UK and North America is short – forest gardening in the UK has developed only in the last 25 years – there is a much longer history of two-storey systems of food production: for example, plum orchards with rows of soft fruit between; hazelnut orchards with alleys of vegetables between; and undergrazed orchards using large fruit trees.

Apricot (*Prunus armeniaca*) and cabbage palm (*Cordyline australis*) in my forest garden.

In many parts of the world, forest gardens are called home gardens, for they adjoin or surround people's

A typical Chinese forest garden. Fruit trees and shrubs are interplanted with narrow timber trees and underplanted with bamboo, vegetables and medicinal plants.

homes. Scientists call these gardens 'multistrata systems'. There are thousands of square miles of such gardens, particularly in tropical Asia and Africa, Central America and temperate and subtropical China.

In Chinese forest gardens, high timber trees such as poplar and elm are usually integrated with other crops – something that is less likely to be seen in the UK and North America, where the growing of timber has been 'professionalised' by foresters. Chickens and ducks are also often included in forest gardens in China, where these gardens have been found to have significant economic, social and ecological benefits.

ROBERT HART

The term 'forest gardening' was coined by Robert Hart in the 1980s. Robert experimented with his own 500m² garden in Shropshire, England, creating one of the first forest gardens in Britain.

With little horticultural knowledge, Robert created a productive garden that supplied much of his food. However, trees were planted much too close together – the temptation being to try to fit too many into a small area, leaving the understorey dark, damp and fairly unproductive. There was little in the way of overall planning, with a pretty random spread of species. Few nitrogen-fixing plants were used, and mulch materials were imported into the garden every year to suppress weeds and maintain fertility.

On my visits to Robert in the 1990s, we sat in his shack-like home and chatted while mice ran merrily around the skirting boards. Robert was keen for others to take up the baton, and in no doubt that his experiment could and should be improved upon and extended. That, indeed, has been part of what I have tried to do at the Agroforestry Research Trust since 1990.

Robert's writings remain inspirational, not so much as a how-to-do-it but rather as a mixture of biography, philosophy and historical folklore.

The benefits of forest gardening

People grow forest gardens for different reasons, and, whereas most intensive annual vegetable plots are pretty similar, every forest garden is different because they are designed around the needs and requirements of their users. The following are some of the reasons why forest gardens are cultivated.

Working with the land instead of against it

In a moist temperate climate, the climax vegetation is woodland or forest – i.e. if you do nothing to a piece of land, it will eventually become a forest; the forces of nature are actively moving the land towards woodland. The further your agricultural or horticultural system is from woodland, the more energy it takes to maintain and the more disturbed and distant the system is from a long-term sustainable biological state. So arable fields or annually cultivated ground take the most energy; pasture less; orchard systems still less. Natural woodland takes no human energy to maintain – it looks after itself.

Forest gardens lie between orchard systems and natural woodland, and form some of the lowest-energy-input systems for producing useful products.

Japanese persimmon (*Diospyros kaki*).

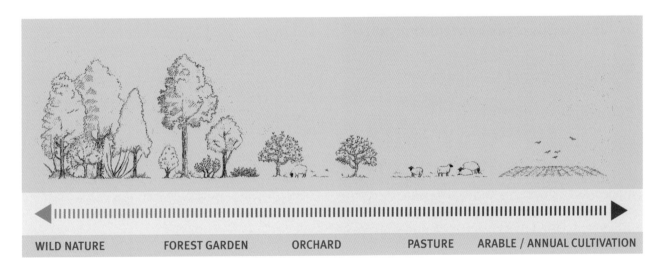

| WILD NATURE | FOREST GARDEN | ORCHARD | PASTURE | ARABLE / ANNUAL CULTIVATION |

Less energy to maintain	More energy to maintain
More resilient	Less resilient
High diversity	Low diversity
High interconnectedness	Low interconnectedness
Low/zero maintenance	High maintenance
Low/negative greenhouse gas emissions	Medium-to-high greenhouse gas emissions

Low maintenance and high efficiency

A forest garden will contain a mixture of trees, shrubs, perennial and annual plants. It can certainly also contain annual vegetables, but mostly the ground tends to be covered with ground-covering herbaceous perennial plants of direct or indirect use. Trees and shrubs need little maintenance apart from occasional pruning.

An important part of forest gardening is to try to keep most of the soil covered with plant growth or plant matter at all times; this keeps the soil in good condition, which in turn benefits all the other plants. In annual plant gardens, a large part of the maintenance is spent on weeding, whereas in a forest garden there is little space or opportunity for weeds to establish, and weeding is minimal. In a forest garden there tends to be masses of plant growth, with few gaps between plants, and sometimes one plant has to be cut back to give others room, whereas in 'traditional' gardening, plants are spaced with bare ground beneath – ideal for weed infestations and guaranteed to increase maintenance time.

Fruits of the strawberry tree (*Arbutus unedo* f. *rubra*).

The biological efficiency of any agricultural system is defined as the ratio of energy outputs over energy inputs; it is not the same as output or yield. Because forest gardens are low-input systems this makes them highly efficient. In terms of outputs, they range from low to high, depending on the design. Tree-based systems can certainly yield as much as arable fields – just look at an apple orchard.

Wide range of products

Forest gardens are designed around the requirements of their users, and can yield a wide variety of products, including fruits, nuts, seeds, vegetables, salad crops, herbs, spices, firewood, mushrooms grown on logs, poles and canes, tying materials, basketry materials, medicinal herbs, dye plants, soap plants, honey from bees, sap products, etc.

High nutritional value

There is plenty of evidence to show that crops from perennial plants tend to be more nutritious than similar crops from annual plants. The more extensive and perennial nature of the root system of perennial plants must account for much of the benefit, for these plants can exploit the soil space more efficiently than annual plants and thus accumulate higher quantities of minerals.

Resilience to climate extremes

Forest-based systems are the most resilient in the face of weather extremes. The structure and diversity of a forest garden ensures good resilience, for example to the impacts of climate change – some of which will be more extreme weather conditions.

Biologically sustainable

The sustainability of forest gardens comes from their diversity and the complex web of below- and above-ground interactions between species. Forest gardens in the tropics have been in existence for over twelve thousand years. Agricultural scientists rarely study them because of their complexity – it is difficult enough to model two species growing together; to model the 100 or 200 species that most forest gardens contain is quite beyond reductionist science methods.

Aesthetically beautiful

Forest gardens are very beautiful places, irrespective of whether aesthetic objectives were part of the design process. When you are in a forest garden it does not feel like a 'normal' cultivated garden – it feels somehow wilder, more jungle-like in places, less managed, less interfered with. In an age where so many people do not perceive themselves as living close to nature, forest gardens can reconnect them to an abundant nature in a way that visits to nature reserves cannot – for we are all participants in nature and consumers of the food and other materials that nature provides.

Although most plants used in forest gardens have direct or indirect uses for people, they can often be ornamental too; and, of course, plants can be included purely for ornament if desired.

COMMON SHOWY ORNAMENTALS WITH EDIBLE USES	
Canopy trees and shrubs	
Amelanchier spp.	Juneberries
Cercis siliquastrum	Judas tree
Cornus kousa	Chinese dogwood
Cornus mas	Cornelian cherry
Crataegus spp.	Hawthorns
Elaeagnus x *ebbingei*	
Rhus typhina	Stag's horn sumach
Shrubs	
	Bamboos
Chaenomeles spp.	Flowering quinces
Fuchsia spp.	Fuchsias
Mahonia spp.	Oregon grapes
Phormium tenax	New Zealand flax
Rosa rugosa	Apple rose
Herbaceous perennials	
Camassia quamash	Quamash
Campanula spp.	Bellflowers
Centranthus ruber	Red valerian
Hemerocallis spp.	Day lilies
Hosta spp.	Hostas
Lathyrus spp. (climbers)	Sweet peas
Polygonatum spp.	Solomon's seals
Sedum spectabile	Ice plant
Viola spp.	Violets
Annuals	
Calendula officinalis	Pot marigold
Lunaria annua	Honesty
Tropaeolum majus	Nasturtium

Environmentally beneficial

Forest gardens have lots of environmental benefits. They sequester carbon dioxide in the soil and in the woody biomass of the trees and shrubs. Greenhouse gas emissions are negligible. By keeping the soil covered and the soil structure in good condition, forest gardens are excellent at storing water after heavy rains and preventing flooding and erosion. They can shelter buildings, reducing energy use for heating. They are also excellent for wildlife (some of which may become pests of course!); the complex three-dimensional structure and the diversity of plants (whether native or non-native) provides many niches for insects and small animals. A recent invertebrate study in our own forest garden found a higher diversity of species in the forest garden than in a planted native woodland of the same age – perhaps indicating that diversity of plant species is more important than their origin.

Cardoon (*Cynara cardunculus*).

Commercial potential

Most forest gardens in the world have a commercial element to them, even if it is just one or two crops from fruit trees – for example a bumper crop of apples or mangoes. To exploit a forest garden on a more serious commercial scale than that, certain features should be introduced during the design stage (see Chapter 9, page 92) – particularly a limit to the diversity (for example, 300 species would be too complex to manage efficiently) and

changes to the positioning of species to make harvesting more efficient.

SUMMARY: THE BENEFITS OF FOREST GARDENING

- Working with the land instead of against it
- Low maintenance and high efficiency
- A wide range of products yielded
- Resilience to climatic extremes and changes of weather
- Biologically sustainable
- Environmentally beneficial
- Aesthetically beautiful
- Some commercial possibilities

Common questions about forest gardens

The following are some of the main questions people ask about forest gardening.

Is it permaculture?

No. It is sometimes one element of permaculture and people sometimes mistakenly call it permaculture. Permaculture is a design system formulated by Bill Mollison and David Holmgren in the 1970s. Originally meaning 'permanent agriculture', it has broadened in concept to encompass all aspects of sustainable living, including building design, energy use, etc. To avoid confusion, I don't call my forest garden 'permaculture'; I just stick to 'forest garden'.

How productive is a forest garden?

This question is often asked by people who assume that the understorey of a forest garden is going to be as shady as that of a natural mature forest. If that were so, there would be little that could be grown productively beneath the trees. However, a forest garden in temperate climates must be designed with a very open, broken tree canopy to allow plenty of light to reach plants beneath trees to increase productivity.

Is forest gardening the same as gardening in a forest?

No. An established forest usually has close-growing trees that do not allow for much light beneath for other plants. There is little that you can grow in a productive and useful sense beneath the trees in a temperate climate. A forest can be converted into a forest garden, but this usually entails extensive thinning and replanting.

Do you have to eat weird and disgusting unusual crops?

This question needs untangling! As I've mentioned, you cannot grow most of the common annual vegetable crops in shade beneath trees, though they can be incorporated into a forest garden where there is good light. So you will probably want to grow some more unusual crops in the understorey layers. And in the tree/shrub layers you may well want to grow unusual crops such as almonds, bamboos, mulberries, persimmons, etc., all of which are delicious! Everybody's palate is different, but none of the edible plants I talk about in this book are disgusting, though some have strong flavours, which I will note.

In books or databases of useful plants, a number of the plants listed as 'edible' may be so only in an emergency or famine situation, and not be particularly pleasant. So try to find a personal assessment of a plant before you use it.

Orpine (*Sedum telephium*), a lovely salad leaf.

Damselfly by the forest garden pond. Damselflies and dragonflies are beneficial predators.

Chapter 2

Forest garden features and products

Key features of forest gardens

The features found in most forest gardens throughout the world are as follows.

Young forest mimicry

The garden is maintained in a state akin to a young or mid-succession-stage woodland. This is to allow good levels of light right down to ground level, which is necessary to grow productive plants there. In tropical climates, where the sun energy reaching plants can be seven or eight times that in temperate climates, more shading can be allowed; on the other hand, gardeners designing forest gardens in Canada or Scandinavia must be extra careful to give good tree spacing.

Young woodland also often contains nitrogen-fixing trees and shrubs, which are pioneer species, establishing quickly and improving soil and environmental conditions for other trees to follow. These same nitrogen fixers are extremely useful fertility providers in a forest garden, and good light levels are necessary to sustain them.

Vertical layers of plants

Since a forest garden is a three-dimensional structure, the different plants used can be subdivided into different vertical layers of growth. These layers may be separate from one another in places, and in other places they may overlap or intermingle. Also, trees can be treated as shrubs if they are pruned, coppiced or grown on dwarfing rootstocks – as in the case of some fruits – and then may fit into a shrubby layer.

Forest gardens will contain some or all of the following layers.

Smooth-sheathed bamboo (*Phyllostachys vivax*) behind coppiced alder (*Alnus glutinosa*).

- **Medium-to-large canopy trees over about 10m (33')
  high**. These are usually not harvested annually as they are too inaccessible; they are more likely to be either timber trees (as in a typical Chinese forest garden) or trees to benefit other plants, for example a nitrogen-fixing tree. The most common large canopy tree I use in my forest garden is Italian alder (*Alnus cordata*), for nitrogen fixation. Small forest gardens are more likely to miss out this layer altogether.

- **Small trees and large shrubs up to 4-9m (13-30')
  high**. In small gardens this is likely to be the uppermost canopy layer. Most fruiting species come into this layer, as do medicinal trees, coppiced trees, nitrogen-fixing trees, etc. Crops from this layer are accessible and productivity can be very high. Some tree crops can be treated as shrubs when coppiced: for example, I have several coppiced lime trees (*Tilia* spp.) in my garden for the excellent edible leaves.

PLANT DIVERSITY AND DIET

Sceptics of forest gardening usually assume that the understorey is as dark as that in an established forest and therefore is fairly unproductive. They would be correct if that were so – but I emphasise that a temperate forest garden must be planned to let light through to the understorey. A huge range of edible plants can be grown in such situations. Food diversity is good for wildlife, soil, the environment and people.

It does seem to be unhealthy – both for the environment and people – to subsist on only a couple of dozen food crops, as do most people in 'developed' countries today. Look at some of our closest relatives in the animal kingdom, the apes, and you'll find that it is common for 200-300 different species or more to be included in the diet. Most tropical forest gardens – some of which have been around for thousands of years – contain at least 150 species, often many more. Harvesting a dozen plants for a meal instead of one almost inevitably means more harvesting work, but if the dozen plants are perennial then there is a great saving of time raising plants, weeding, etc.

- **Shrubs up to 3m (10') high.** Many bush fruit species come into this layer as well as smaller nut and seed producers, more nitrogen fixers, etc. Examples include redcurrant (*Ribes rubrum*) and blueberries (*Vaccinium* spp.).

- **Herbaceous perennials and evergreen plants**, which may range from a few centimetres in height to 3m (10'). This merges with the ground-covering layer (see below) and is sometimes part of it. There are numerous perennial crops – edible, medicinal, dye plants, etc. – in this layer. Unfortunately, most of the last few thousand years of plant breeding and selection have focused on annuals, so there are few well-known perennial edibles. There are, however, many excellent edible perennials suitable for this layer: examples include globe artichoke (*Cynara cardunculus* Scolymus Group), cardoon (*Cynara cardunculus*) and sea kale (*Crambe maritima*).

- **Ground-cover plants and creepers**. These are usually shade-tolerant perennials or low creeping shrubs; sometimes spreading plants that in other circumstances may be regarded as weeds! Evergreen plants are more efficient in terms of soil protection, but there are many herbaceous plants of use too. The main function of many plants in this layer may not be for harvesting (though that may be a secondary use); rather they are there to protect the soil and keep the soil structure in good condition, thus aiding all the other plants growing in the garden. In small gardens, there are likely to be more plants of direct use in the perennials /evergreen layer, and fewer ground-covers of indirect use, whereas in larger gardens, where there is an excess of space for perennial crops, more ground-covers

are likely. Favourite ground-covers in our forest garden include Nepalese raspberry (*Rubus nepalensis*) and apple mint (*Mentha suaveolens*).

New Zealand flax (*Phormium tenax*) with soapwort (*Saponaria officinalis*) and horse mint (*Mentha longifolia*).

- **Climbers, perennial or shrub**. These span the layers, potentially reaching high into the canopy. They are usually introduced only when they have something to climb up (obvious really!). Examples include hop (*Humulus lupulus*) and grapes (*Vitis* spp.) Most have an aerial crop, though some, for example yams (*Dioscorea* spp.) have a root crop. Climbing shrubs usually need a pruning strategy to keep them low: the Romans grew grapes 15m (50') up poplar trees that were used as vine supports, but they had slaves to pick them. Your children may be one option!

- **The underground layer**. Root crops can be included (obviously the soil has to be dug to harvest them), for example scorzonera (*Scorzonera hispanica*), which is a perennial root crop. Fungi too grow mainly underground and are a vitally important part of the forest garden, as they are of forests and other ecosystems generally; some have edible mushrooms too. Chapter 21, 'Fungi in forest gardens', describes the importance and uses of fungi in more detail.

People spaces are important in forest gardens.

Two categories of food plants that need special design features if they are to be included are low-growing carbohydrate foods and most conventional annual vegetables. Carbohydrates are high-energy foods and require a lot of sun energy to manufacture: you cannot grow them in much shade. Tree-based carbohydrates, e.g. sweet chestnut, are easily incorporated into forest gardens, but if you want to grow your own supply of potatoes, wheat, oats, etc. then you need to either allow for a sunny clearing within the forest garden, or grow them elsewhere. If you look at agriculture where forest gardens are popular, usually people will grow a carbohydrate staple crop on a field scale in addition to growing all the more interesting foods in a forest garden.

Conventional annual vegetables are also mainly sun-demanding; they originate from the Mediterranean, seashore, Central America, etc., and have long been bred in full sun conditions. Apart from a few leafy vegetables such as Swiss chard, most will do poorly in shade, though some can take partial shade. So if you want annual

vegetables, they too will need a sunny clearing where they can get plenty of light.

Careful optimisation of tree density

Planning for the correct tree density to allow light through to the lower layers to grow what you want is one of the more critical parts of the design process.

Design for maximum inter-species interaction

This means, basically, trying not to group together the same or closely related species more than you have to. The more that species can be mixed, the more resilient the system and garden. This is mainly because pests and diseases cannot move from plant to plant so easily. However, sometimes, for example when cross-pollination is required, similar species do need to be close. This is just one of many compromises that have to be made in the design and implementation of a forest garden.

Diversity

The higher the diversity, the more resilient and productive the forest garden system usually is. This is because different species rarely share the same pests and diseases, and different species utilise different ecological niches (e.g. root and aerial space) to maximise the efficient use of available resources.

But what is a 'diverse enough' garden? Well, most forest gardens you find in other parts of the world typically have 100-200 different species growing in them. Even in a small garden there is not much chance of getting to those numbers, but 50 or so species should be achievable and will still yield many of the benefits of a forest garden. Larger gardens should easily be able to accommodate 100 species. My forest garden in Dartington, which is just over 2 acres in size, has about 500 species.

Edges where light levels are higher

Nearly all forest gardens will have edges where light levels are higher – either the boundary of the garden (unless it borders woodland), the sides of wide paths, or the boundary of a clearing or near a building – but many of the benefits of a forest garden in terms of microclimate still apply. At these edges there are opportunities for growing plants that need extra sun and heat.

Most of the soil is not annually cultivated

Since most crops in a forest garden are perennial, they don't need replanting every year (though of course perennials don't last forever, so occasional replanting is not ruled out). Leaving the soil undisturbed is very beneficial for the soil structure and the soil flora and fauna (in particular mycorrhizal fungi), and is consequently very beneficial for all the plants growing in it.

Areas of annual crops can, of course, be grown in cultivated soil, though most annual vegetables can be grown in no-dig beds quite successfully.

The soil surface is mainly covered with plant growth

This again is to benefit the soil structure, and therefore all the plants that grow in it. In regions such as the UK, where winter rainfall can wash out lots of nutrients from bare soil, it is important that the soil is covered, even in winter. Evergreen plants are good, but herbaceous plants can also be good by leaving a thick mulch of dead stems over the soil surface. Annual cropping areas can be sown with overwintering green manures.

Fertility is largely or wholly maintained by plants themselves

Many gardeners know about using short-lived green manures to improve soil fertility but, apart from clovers, few perennials have been traditionally utilised in the same way. In a forest garden, most of the nitrogen fixation used for fertility needs to take place in the tree and shrub layers, because perennial nitrogen fixers such as clover are not very shade tolerant.

Some plants, know as mineral accumulators, are particularly good at scavenging for certain nutrients in the soil or subsoil, and bring some of them up into the topsoil layers where they can be used by other plants. Comfreys (*Symphytum* spp.) are well-known examples.

Sometimes a clearing will be desired to grow annual crops

Clearings are only feasible in moderate-sized forest gardens – in very small gardens there is not enough space between trees. A clearing may have many purposes, including the growing of annual sun-demanding crops, a pond, or just a place to sit or play.

Siberian purslane (*Claytonia sibirica*) and wild strawberry (*Fragaria vesca*) cover the ground well.

Squash, an annual vegetable, in the forest garden.

SUMMARY: THE KEY FEATURES OF FOREST GARDENS

- They mimic young forests in structure
- They have several vertical layers of plants
- Tree density is optimised
- Inter-species interactions are maximised
- There is high diversity
- They usually have edges where light levels are higher
- Most of the soil is not cultivated
- The soil surface is covered with plant growth
- Fertility is mostly maintained by plants
- Clearings are possible in larger gardens

crop. Potatoes could easily be grown in a sunny clearing, but it isn't worth trying to grow a grain in a forest garden. However, there are alternatives: sweet chestnuts, for example, are very similar in composition to rice, and have been used as a 'tree grain' in the past. With the right varieties they are very productive too!

Spice crops such as Nepalese pepper (*Zanthoxylum armatum*) are easy to grow in a forest garden.

The main products of a forest garden

As already mentioned, the one thing that it is difficult to produce from a forest garden is a low-growing staple carbohydrate crop – for example potatoes or an annual grain

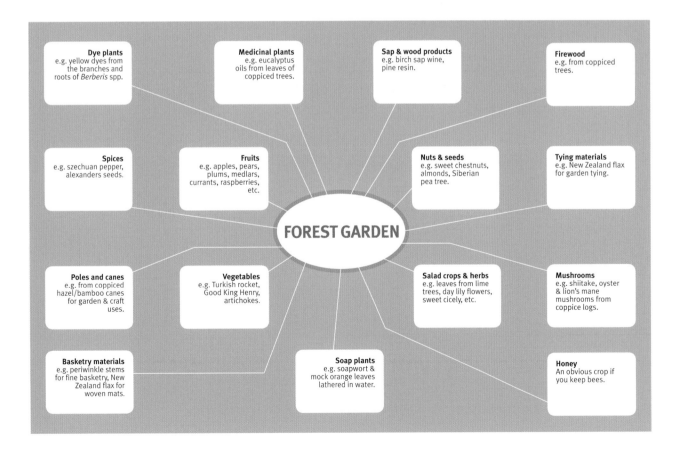

Dye plants
e.g. yellow dyes from the branches and roots of *Berberis* spp.

Medicinal plants
e.g. eucalyptus oils from leaves of coppiced trees.

Sap & wood products
e.g. birch sap wine, pine resin.

Firewood
e.g. from coppiced trees.

Spices
e.g. szechuan pepper, alexanders seeds.

Fruits
e.g. apples, pears, plums, medlars, currants, raspberries, etc.

Nuts & seeds
e.g. sweet chestnuts, almonds, Siberian pea tree.

Tying materials
e.g. New Zealand flax for garden tying.

FOREST GARDEN

Poles and canes
e.g. from coppiced hazel/bamboo canes for garden & craft uses.

Vegetables
e.g. Turkish rocket, Good King Henry, artichokes.

Salad crops & herbs
e.g. leaves from lime trees, day lily flowers, sweet cicely, etc.

Mushrooms
e.g. shiitake, oyster & lion's mane mushrooms from coppice logs.

Basketry materials
e.g. periwinkle stems for fine basketry, New Zealand flax for woven mats.

Soap plants
e.g. soapwort & mock orange leaves lathered in water.

Honey
An obvious crop if you keep bees.

Plants for small gardens

If you have only a small garden, you might find the choice of plants described in this book rather overwhelming. To aid you in plant selection I have made a shortlist below of species I consider 'most valuable' (which is subjective, of course). This means they should be reliable in cropping, not too large, not too likely to annoy your neighbours, etc. Full details of these species are given in Chapters 11, 13 and 15.

Tree fruits

Apple (*Malus domestica*) – on M26 and MM106 rootstocks
Plums, greengages, bullaces and damsons (*Prunus domestica* and *P. insititia*) – on Pixy rootstocks
Pears (*Pyrus* spp.) – on Quince C rootstock
Medlar (*Mespilus germanica*)
Sweet cherry (*Prunus avium*) – on Gisela rootstock
Hawthorns (*Crataegus* spp.)
Mulberries (*Morus* spp.)

Tree nuts

Almond (*Prunus dulcis*)
Hazels (*Corylus* spp.)
Siberian pea tree (*Caragana arborescens*)

Other edible tree crops

Lime trees (*Tilia* spp.) – coppiced
Pepper trees (*Zanthoxylum armatum, Z. schinifolium* and *Z. simulans*)
Snowbell tree (*Halesia carolina*)

Nitrogen-fixing trees

Bayberries (*Myrica* spp.)
Wattles (*Acacia* spp.)

Fruiting shrubs

Apple rose (*Rosa rugosa*)
Blackberries and hybrid berries (*Rubus* spp.)
Blackcurrant (*Ribes nigrum*)
Blueberries (*Vaccinium* spp.)
Flowering quinces (*Chaenomeles* spp.)
Gooseberry (*Ribes uva-crispa*)
Goumi (*Elaeagnus multiflora*)
Japanese wineberry (*Rubus phoenicolasius*)
Jostaberry (*Ribes* x *culverwellii*)
Raspberry (*Rubus idaeus*)
Redcurrant (*Ribes rubrum*)
Saskatoon (*Amelanchier alnifolia*)
Worcesterberry (*Ribes divaricatum*)

Other shrub crops

American elder (*Sambucus canadensis*)
Bamboos (*Phyllostachys* spp., *Pleioblastus* spp., *Pseudosasa japonica*, *Semiarundinaria* spp. and *Yushania* spp.) – with root barrier
Bay (*Laurus nobilis*)
Beech (*Fagus sylvatica*) – trimmed small
Bog myrtle (*Myrica gale*)
Japanese pepper (*Zanthoxylum piperitum*)
Mountain flax (*Phormium colensoi*)
New Zealand flax (*Phormium tenax*)
Northern bayberry (*Myrica pensylvanica*)
Sage (*Salvia officinalis*)

Nitrogen-fixing shrubs

Bog myrtle (*Myrica gale*)
Broom (*Cytisus scoparius*)
Goumi (*Elaeagnus multiflora*)
Northern bayberry (*Myrica pensylvanica*)

Low-growing, 'base layer' herbaceous perennials

Bird's foot trefoil (*Lotus corniculatus*) 'Plenus' (also N-fixing)
Dwarf comfrey (*Symphytum ibericum*)
Creeping bramble (*Rubus pentalobus*)
Nepalese raspberry (*Rubus nepalensis*)
Ramsons (*Allium ursinum*)
Siberian purslane (*Claytonia sibirica*)
Strawberries (*Fragaria* spp.)

Other herbaceous perennial crops

Babington's leek (*Allium ampeloprasum* var. *babingtonii*)
Bowles's mint (*Mentha* Bowles's mint)
Chicory (*Cichorium intybus*)
Chinese artichoke (*Stachys affinis*)
Comfreys (*Symphytum* spp.)
Day lilies (*Hemerocallis* spp.)
Fennel (*Foeniculum vulgare*)
Fuchsia (*Fuchsia magellanica*)
Globe artichoke (*Cynara cardunculus* Scolymus Group)
Good King Henry (*Chenopodium bonus-henricus*)
Hostas (*Hosta* spp.)
Jerusalem artichoke (*Helianthus tuberosus*)
Lemon balm (*Melissa officinalis*)
Mallows (*Malva* spp.)
Mitsuba (*Cryptotaenia japonica*)
Multiplier onions and Egyptian onions (*Allium cepa* var.)
Oregano (*Origanum vulgare*)
Peppermint (*Mentha* x *piperita*)
Perennial brassicas (*Brassica oleracea*)
Red valerian (*Centranthus ruber*)
Rhubarbs (*Rheum* spp.)
Sea beet (*Beta vulgaris* subsp. *maritima*)
Sedums (*Sedum* spp.)
Solomon's seals (*Polygonatum* spp.)
Sorrels (*Rumex* spp.)
Sweet cicely (*Myrrhis odorata*)
Sweet peas (*Lathyrus* spp. – climbers) (also N-fixing)
Turkish rocket (*Bunias orientalis*)
Violets (*Viola* spp.)
White clover (*Trifolium repens*) (also N-fixing)

Feverfew (*Tanacetum parthenium*).

Chapter 3

The effects of climate change

Most rational people accept that the evidence for climate change caused by human behaviour is so strong now that there is no real argument to be made against it.

Science cannot ever be 100-per-cent sure of the truth of anything; nevertheless, when the probability becomes high enough, common sense says that the issue is decided. Personally, I have absolutely no doubt about the facts behind climate change or that it is happening – fast. In fact, it appears to be happening faster than most scientists expected.

Part of the problem about getting climate change taken seriously is the small numbers involved – after all, a degree centigrade sounds very little, as do a few centimetres of sea-level rise. However, to put this into perspective, a 1°C (1.8°F) rise in the UK is equivalent to around a 160km (100 mile) shift southwards.

Climate change is not just starting now, either: it has been going on for a long time, speeding up dramatically in the last 50 years. Although average world temperatures have risen only some 0.7°C (1.3°F) over the 50 years to 2007, the temperatures at latitudes nearer to the poles have risen much more. In the UK, annual average temperatures have increased over the 45 years to 2006 by 0.8-1.8°C (1.4-3.2°F); the higher figure in the south-east, the lower in the north-west. This corresponds to a southwards shift of climate of 130-290km (80-180 miles), *which we have already experienced since 1960*.

And climate change is still accelerating. At the time of writing, greenhouse gas emissions have increased by 35 per cent since the Kyoto Protocol was signed: the world is still not taking the issue seriously enough. Even if greenhouse gas emissions were stopped today, there would be several decades of climate warming in the pipeline. Just maybe, emissions will start to be controlled by 2020 or 2030, but we will still have global warming until 2050 at least.

In the UK, warming temperatures is one of the lesser problems we face in terms of land use – people who welcome warming temperatures because they like Mediterranean conditions just don't realise what is going to hit them. It is not gradually changing conditions that will cause big problems – it is the extremes of wind, rain and heat. Furthermore, as global temperatures rise there is an increasing but unknown risk of sudden sharp increases in the rate of climate change. If the human population is determined (and lucky) enough we won't reach this point. If we do then your forest garden might just keep you alive.

Climate changes expected in the UK over the next 40 years

The following predictions are derived from the Met Office publication *UKCIP08: The climate of the UK and recent trends*. Like all science, of course, such predictions for the future cannot be expected to be completely accurate. However, there seems little disagreement that most of the below is unavoidable.

Temperature

- Temperatures will continue to rise, perhaps starting to tail off by 2040 if emissions are seriously curbed in the next decade.
- Further increases of around 2°C (3.6°F) above 2010 temperatures are likely for much of the UK by 2050.
- By 2050, southern England is expected to have a climate similar to Bordeaux in France in 1960; Wales to mid-west France in 1960; northern England and southern Scotland to northern France in 1960; and northern Scotland to Wales in 1960.

The temperature changes that have already occurred in the UK are highlighted by the Met Office map below.

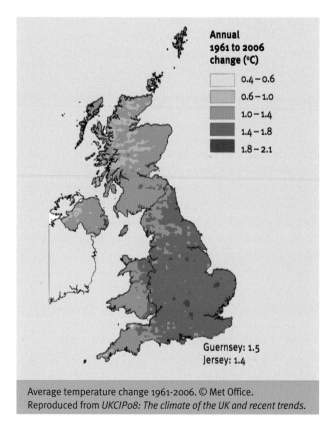

Annual 1961 to 2006 change (°C)

	0.4 – 0.6
	0.6 – 1.0
	1.0 – 1.4
	1.4 – 1.8
	1.8 – 2.1

Guernsey: 1.5
Jersey: 1.4

Average temperature change 1961-2006. © Met Office.
Reproduced from *UKCIP08: The climate of the UK and recent trends*.

Diurnal effects

- Nights will warm more than days in winter.
- Days will warm more than nights in summer.

Sea levels

- Sea levels will continue to rise by some 40-60cm (16-24") by 2050.
- The risk of coastal flooding will increase significantly.

The Gulf Stream

- The scientific consensus is that this is unlikely to fail this century.
- Some weakening is expected, which is included in climate models.
- By the time that failure is likely, global warming will outweigh an overall drop in north-west European temperatures from year 2000 levels.

Rainfall

- Overall, there will be little change in annual rainfall totals.
- It will be drier in summer (30 per cent less in the south-east by 2050), wetter in winter.
- There will be more intense rain events and flooding.

Relative humidity

- This will decrease throughout the year, with a greater decrease in summer than in winter.

Cloud cover

- This will decrease significantly in summer (thus solar radiation will increase).
- There will be a slight increase in winter.

Wind

- Overall there will be little change in average wind speeds.
- There will be stronger winds in southern and central Britain in winter.
- There will be more severe storms and extreme events.

Soil moisture

Soil moisture levels are related to rainfall, temperature, evaporation, wind speeds and solar radiation.

- All areas will show a decrease in soil moisture in summer and autumn, with up to a 30-40 per cent decrease in south-east England expected by 2050.
- Winter soil moisture levels are likely to be similar to those at present (with higher winter rainfall offset by higher temperatures and evaporation, etc.).

Frost

- There has been a steady decline in the average number of frosts in the UK over the last 50 years, as can be seen from the Met Office map opposite.
- The number of frosts will continue to decline.

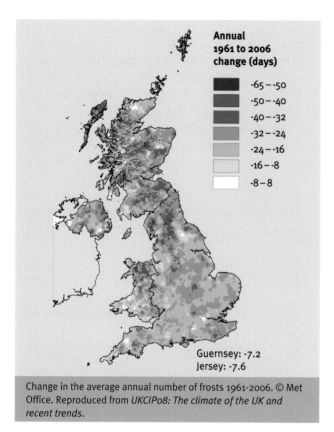

Annual 1961 to 2006 change (days)

- -65 – -50
- -50 – -40
- -40 – -32
- -32 – -24
- -24 – -16
- -16 – -8
- -8 – 8

Guernsey: -7.2
Jersey: -7.6

Change in the average annual number of frosts 1961-2006. © Met Office. Reproduced from *UKCIP08: The climate of the UK and recent trends*.

Thermal growing-season length

The growing season is the period of time each year during which plants can grow.

- This will extend by 50-80 days by 2050; the lesser amount in Scotland, the higher in England, especially the south-east.

The effects of climate changes on plants and gardens

The main impacts on growing conditions of the expected climate changes in the UK are outlined below. Although it is plant responses to changing averages that are relevant here, bear in mind that it is likely to be the extreme climate conditions, rather than rising averages, that will have the biggest impacts on cultivated plants – e.g. drought conditions, temperatures in excess of 40°C (100°F), hurricane winds, etc.

Forest gardens are an obvious response to these threats to garden stability and ultimately food security. Suscepti-

bility to drought is minimised, owing to the soil being in prime condition with high levels of organic matter from being kept covered, and owing to having a perennial-based system. Susceptibility to pests and diseases is minimised by means of the diversity of plants and by designing for a more complex system of plant inter-dependency than is the norm in gardens.

Carbon dioxide

Increased carbon dioxide levels will have a small fertilising effect on plants, potentially leading to increased growth, perhaps by 10-20 per cent (especially in already fast-growing plants), and higher yields of crops (fruits, etc.) – but *only* if all other factors remain favourable. In reality, this fertilising effect may well be offset by dry or drought conditions in summer.

Temperature

Similarly, the increased temperatures expected in the UK will generally be beneficial for plant growth – but again, only if other factors are favourable.

Growing season

The growing season is lengthening by two days per year in southern England, and by one day per year in northern Scotland. Leafing and flowering times of plants are generally becoming earlier in spring, and growth ceases later in autumn. However, different plants are responding in different ways – for example, in response to a 1°C (1.8°F) rise, almond flowering has advanced by nine days and hazel by only four days.

Dormancy

Dormancy is explained in more detail later in this chapter (see page 37).

The number of chilling hours (number of hours in winter under 7.2°C/45°F – see page 37) in the UK has already reduced by 10-20 per cent (250-500 hours) since 1960. Chilling hours are reducing as the climate warms by about:

- 15 hours/year (150 hours/decade) in the south
- 11 hours/year (110 hours/decade) in the Midlands

- 10 hours/year (100 hours/decade) in Scotland.

So by 2050 the likely reduction of chilling hours (from present levels) is 400-650 hours.

Fruit trees and bushes that do not get enough chilling are likely to become less productive, with fruiting increasingly erratic. Already, commercial blackcurrant growers are experiencing poor crops after mild winters, caused by abnormal flower development.

'Local' varieties of fruit tree, e.g. apples selected or bred in parts of the UK over the past centuries, tend to have chill requirements near to the average chill available (if they needed less chilling they would leaf out or flower very early and be susceptible to frost damage, and thus fruit erratically; if they needed more chilling then they would rarely get enough, and so flower poorly and also fruit erratically). But because chilling hours are reducing fast – by 1 per cent a year in the south – 'local' varieties will become steadily less well adapted in the areas where they are traditionally grown.

So we will need to gradually switch from local well-adapted varieties to varieties that need less chilling, usually from a more southerly region. In particular this applies to apple, blackcurrant, blueberry (northern), cherry (sweet and sour), gooseberry, grape, hazel, pear, plum, raspberry, redcurrant and walnut.

Native trees will also be affected by the lack of chilling combined with higher temperatures and drought conditions. Some, where they are currently towards the north of their range, may cope well (e.g. lime trees, *Tilia* spp.) while others, currently towards the south of their range, may suffer badly (e.g. birches, *Betula* spp.). This may have a bearing on your species choice if you want to integrate a coppiced fuel crop in your forest garden.

Frost

Despite earlier leafing, there should be less frost damage to spring flowers and leaves, simply because of the declining numbers of frosts.

Drought

Increasing temperatures will mean drier soils and faster breakdown of soil organic matter. Sandy and well-drained soils will become more difficult to manage. Measures to safeguard and maintain organic matter in soils will become paramount, including mulching, maintaining plant cover in all seasons, and no-cultivation methods. Forest gardens should cope well in these respects.

Irrigation will also become increasingly vital to cope with summer droughts. Collecting winter rain – of which there is not likely to be a lack – for use in summer should be high on the list of priorities during the design process.

Pests

Insects can respond to climate change more rapidly than plants. Whereas climate zones are moving north by about 70km (44 miles) per decade (or upwards in altitude by 70-100m/230-330' per decade), plants are moving north by about 6km (4 miles) (with large variations) per decade (or upwards by 6m/20' per decade), and insect ranges are moving north by 15-70km (9-44 miles) per decade, with insect pests from mainland Europe moving north and west into the UK.

Insect life cycles are beginning earlier in the season, with birds hatching only slightly earlier. This 'decoupling' of timings between pests and predators will become an increasingly serious problem both in 'natural' ecosystems and in cultivated gardens and farms. For example, if the normal caterpillar food source for a predator (be it a bird, ladybird, etc.) is not present because it hatched earlier and has already become a moth, then the predator may find other food, or experience a population crash. The knock-on effects of either could be serious.

Most pest control in gardens happens entirely naturally without our having to do anything, but we are heading for a situation where insects that have not been pests before could suddenly and unpredictably become pests because of a predator population crash.

Some glasshouse pests, e.g. the red spider mite, will become a serious problem outside (although the biological controls we presently use inside may also be used outside in the future). Pests that produce many generations in a season, e.g. aphids, spider mites and thrips, and those controlled by winter cold, will become a bigger problem as a result of warmer winters.

Diseases

Warmer wet winters will:

- favour the spread of diseases that need water to spread, such as the *Phytophthora* species of mostly root-attacking fungi
- favour a wide range of bark- and wood-invading fungi that are able to overcome tree defences during dormancy
- allow greater survival of overwintering diseased material and disease inoculum (spores or fungi). These diseases then onset and spread more quickly as the growing season begins in spring.

Drier, warmer summers will favour diseases such as powdery mildew and rusts, which spread in dry conditions; will possibly stress trees and leave them more susceptible to diseases; but will reduce the incidence of diseases that need moist conditions during the growing season, such as apple scab and apple canker.

Diseases too are moving their ranges northwards. Perhaps the most serious threat is the outbreak of new diseases that have evolved through hybridisation of disease forms that were previously isolated from one another. There have already been some cases of this happening on non-valuable plants – alder phytophthora has killed 15 per cent of alder trees in the UK, and horse chestnut bleeding canker has killed many of the horse chestnut trees in Holland in a few years. If a new virulent disease started killing wheat or potatoes at that rate we would really be in trouble.

The problems of new pests and diseases may be more difficult to manage by organic methods.

SUMMARY: THE MOST SERIOUS CLIMATE CHANGE IMPACTS ON CULTIVATED PLANTS

- Drought and water shortages in summer
- Insect pests moving north
- Previously naturally controlled insects becoming pests in an unpredictable manner
- Diseases moving north
- New virulent and unpredictable diseases

Dormancy

Most perennials (including trees) in the UK have annual growth cycles with three phases:

- a rest period, during which active growth has ceased; the plant appears inactive but in fact there is high internal activity, with the plant producing flower and leaf initials in readiness for rapid spring growth
- a waiting period, during which the plant waits until temperatures are warm enough to start active growth
- an active growth period, which is eventually halted by a combination of shortening day lengths, lower light levels and cooler temperatures in autumn.

The rest and waiting periods together constitute the dormant period.

A period of low 'chilling' temperatures (most effective at 0-5°C/32-41°F) is required during the dormant period before a plant can resume normal active growth. Chilling also reduces the response time for bud burst in spring when temperatures warm.

If chilling is inadequate, the development and/or expansion of leaf and flower buds (and thus fruiting) may be impaired.

Chilling requirements are usually measured as an accumulation of hours of temperature below a threshold (usually 7.2°C/45°F), called 'chilling hours'.

The number of chilling hours required varies widely between species and also between cultivars, as shown in the table overleaf.

It also depends on winter weather, particularly minimum temperatures, so can vary widely from location to location – it will be significantly higher in a frost pocket compared with a nearby hillside, for example. The warmest winter regions – south-west England and coastal areas around most of England – currently average about 1,600 chilling hours per annum. The Midlands and East Anglia average 2,000-2,500 hours; Wales similarly apart from the mountains. Northern England averages 2,500-2,800 hours, Scotland 2,500-3,000 hours and Northern Ireland about 1,900 hours.

CROP		CHILLING REQUIREMENTS (HOURS)	
		Lowest	Highest
Actinidia deliciosa	Kiwi	600	850
Asimina triloba	Pawpaw	1,000	1,800
Carya illinoinensis	Pecan	650	1,550
Castanea spp.	Chestnuts	300	700
Citrus spp.	Citrus	0	0
Corylus spp.	Hazels	850	1,700
Cydonia oblonga	Quince	50	450
Diospyros kaki	Japanese persimmon	50	450
Ficus carica	Fig	50	500
Fragaria spp.	Strawberries	50	300
Juglans regia	Walnut	400	1,550
Malus domestica	Apple	800	1,750
Morus spp.	Mulberries	300	500
Prunus armeniaca	Apricot	300	1,000
Prunus avium	Cherry (sweet)	500	1,450
Prunus cerasus	Cherry (sour)	600	1,500
Prunus domestica	Plum / gage	700	1,750
Prunus dulcis	Almond	50	700
Prunus persica	Peach / nectarine	375	1,200
Prunus salicina	Japanese plum	600	1,600
Pyrus communis	Pear	600	1,500
Pyrus pyrifolia and *P. ussuriensis*	Asian pears	300	750
Ribes nigrum	Blackcurrant	1,200	2,500
Ribes rubrum	Redcurrant	800	1,500
Ribes uva-crispa	Gooseberry	800	1,500
Rubus fruticosus	Blackberry	350	600
Rubus idaeus	Raspberry	800	1,800
Vaccinium australe and *V. corymbosum*	Blueberries (northern)	800	1,250
Vaccinium ashei and *V. darrowii*	Blueberries (southern)	200	400
Vitis spp.	Grapes	400	1,650

LOCAL VARIETIES

Most fruit varieties bred or discovered in the UK have chilling requirements at the top end of the range shown in the table opposite. Already, however, the south of England is experiencing problems with a lack of chilling. The winter of 2006/7 was exceptionally mild, and here in Devon we had around half of the average winter chilling; as a result crops such as blackcurrants and walnuts leafed out extremely late and fruited poorly. These problems will extend further north and be exacerbated in the south in the next few decades. The only sensible response is to start to plant lower-chill varieties, e.g. from France or warmer-winter regions; so in Wales, for example, consider planting south-west English varieties of apples.

I'm all in favour of local production of food, reducing the miles food travels, but it is now a mistake to hold on romantically to old 'local' varieties of fruit where they originated. The realities of climate change give us no choice but to adapt. Traditional varieties can still be of great use, but further north (or higher up in altitude) rather than at their original sites.

Honey bee on apple blossom.

Chapter 4

Natives and exotics

This topic can cause heated debates between ecologists and gardeners! My perspective on it, as you will see, is very much at the liberal end of the scale. However, bear in mind that this is mostly a British perspective, and that in other parts of the world where there is a much less disturbed ecosystem remaining, the arguments may differ.

What are natives and what are exotics?

This is not such a simple question to answer as it may seem. Some definitions of a native plant are as follows.

'A plant that lives or grows naturally in a particular region without direct or indirect human intervention.' The United States National Arboretum, www.usna.usda.gov/Gardens/glossary.html.

'Any plant that occurs and grows naturally in a specific region or locality.' The Garden Helper, www.thegardenhelper.com/dictionary.html.

'A plant that is naturally found in an area.' (As opposed to plants that people introduce into an area.) Public Broadcasting Service (PBS), www.pbs.org/kqed/oceanadventures/glossary/.

'. . . one that occurred naturally and has existed for many years in an area. These plants can be trees, flowers, grasses or any other plant.' Wikipedia, en.wikipedia.org/wiki/Native plant.

From these definitions you can see that plants introduced by other animals to a new area are 'allowed' as native but those introduced by humans (deliberately or not) are not. This is an example of the all-too-common attitude of the last few centuries, of humans being separated off from

the natural world as though they are not a part of it. Just look where that has led us!

So, botanists and ecologists come up with a list of what is considered native, and everything else is an exotic. But the real world isn't quite like that: seeds are moving all the time, even if you discount human intervention. A storm can blow seeds hundreds of miles, across oceans, with no problem. And birds, of course, can fly thousands of miles on their migration routes, carrying seeds both internally with the food they have eaten, and externally on their legs, feet and feathers.

The truth is there can be no fixed list of native plants, even for an island. I prefer to think of 'spheres of nativeness' radiating out from a region, where 'nativeness' is not a yes/no but more of a sliding scale.

New plants are always arriving into an ecosystem and always have done (ecosystems did not just occur fully formed). Some arriving plants, which can be called opportunistic, produce many seeds or runners in the hope that there will be a disturbance they can exploit, and some may lack the natural controls (pests or diseases) that will keep the plant numbers in balance in an ecosystem. These are the plants that some in the conservation movement like to call 'invasive', 'aggressive', 'over-running', etc. Such language I believe to be inappropriate when applied to plants – which do not have evil intentions – and in its worst forms becomes eco-fascism.

Now, nobody wants to introduce a plant that is going to cause all sorts of problems for that locality, but these things must be considered in context. New opportunistic species arriving into an ecosystem often take 300-500 years to achieve a balance; until then the ecosystem is disturbed. Eventually a pest or disease evolves that controls the new plant.

People are not very good at looking ahead 300 or 500 years, but in botanical time this is a mere blink. So this, with the combination of low risk (500 years of plant species importation into the UK, of some 40,000 species, has led to a few species considered 'a problem'), explains my fairly relaxed attitude.

Of course, plant ranges moving northwards because of climate change adds another dimension to how 'native' needs to be reassessed. Having said all that, there are some plants I would never introduce, for example known toxic plants such as poison ivy.

HOW IMPORTANT IS NATIVE?

I frequently get asked about native and non-native plant issues when I show people around my forest garden in Devon. As well as outlining some of the above points, I find it useful to remind people to look over the fields of this country – what would they see? Wheat, barley, maize, lucerne, apple trees, potatoes, hybrid grazing grasses, peas, beans, pear and plum trees, sweet chestnuts, walnuts – none of which are native plants.

Biodiversity in the UK is relatively low, and a forest garden made of native plants would be hard-pressed to feed you. Sloes, wild haws and wild service tree berries, with wild garlic and ground elder beneath, would give you a few meals. Hunter-gatherers here would have supplemented them with whatever wild meat they could catch. The food available would have supported only a small human population. I see little point in growing such a native forest garden, which would produce such a limited crop for the gardener: if you want a wildlife forest then plant a native forest!

I rather agree with David Holmgren (one of the founders of permaculture) in that, as a general rule, useful plants from elsewhere that increase local self-reliance and efficiency of growing systems should be welcomed.

New shoots of greenwax golden bamboo (*Phyllostachys viridiglaucescens*).

Chapter 5

Emulating forest conditions

It is worth looking at how conditions are different within forests (compared with open gardens) before starting to design a garden, as this can give lots of clues and ideas about what sorts of plants will be happy where.

Shade

The amount of shade beneath a forest canopy is the most limiting factor for lower plants. In a closed canopy forest (where the canopies of large trees are touching and there are few gaps letting light through), very little light energy reaches the ground in temperate latitudes, and few productive and useful plants can be grown. This is why I emphasise that a temperate forest garden is *not* a closed canopy forest; it is more like a young establishing forest where there are plenty of gaps between trees and shrubs to allow light in. This is one of the main differences between temperate and tropical forest gardens – in tropical regions there may be eight times as much sun energy, and even below a fairly closed canopy there is enough energy to grow many other crops.

Under a closed deciduous canopy, most plant growth below the trees occurs in spring, before the trees are fully in leaf, with very little growth occurring in summer and autumn. This can often be seen in natural forests, where for example there may be an explosion of growth of bluebells, wild garlic and other bulbs in late winter and spring, which can virtually vanish by late summer.

The shade experienced by lower plants is mainly controlled by the density of the tree canopy above – which is largely controlled by the tree spacing, and also by the density of foliage in individual trees. Trees such as rowan (*Sorbus aucuparia*) and black locust (*Robinia pseudoacacia*) have small leaves that allow quite a lot of light energy to filter through them – up to 40 per cent by my own measurements. Other trees with larger leaves may allow much less light energy to filter through – for example, about 5 per cent in the case of lime trees (*Tilia* spp.).

The height of the crown of taller trees is also an important factor. Raising the canopy of the tallest trees by pruning

Different tree densities control the shade beneath and determine what can be grown there.

off lower side branches is a good strategy for increasing the amount of light energy reaching plants in the vicinity and beneath – bearing in mind that this would not neces- sarily be a good idea for trees with crops that need hand harvesting. Raising the canopy of some trees also physi- cally allows more space beneath for other plants.

By raising the height of the tree canopy, more light is available beneath.

Humidity

Air humidity is higher beneath trees and in forests. The leafmould holds water like a sponge, and lower plants transpire moisture, much of which is trapped inside the forest by the canopy. Also the airflow is limited by shelter effects and the air is more turgid. Any streams or ponds make it even more moist.

Most woodland perennials require humid conditions to thrive (no surprises there), but this can pose problems when establishing a forest garden from a bare field / garden or pasture site, which initially lacks the extra humid conditions desired. It might be necessary to wait to introduce woodland perennials until trees are large enough, after several years. Your regional climate also has an influence here – in the west of Britain, the weather is much moister and humidity is higher: here, less tree cover is required for woodland perennials to thrive than in the drier east of the country.

Temperature

Air temperatures within forests are moderated – they are usually cooler in summer and warmer in winter, compared with an open site. This has implications in a forest garden: for example, species needing warm conditions to thrive must be sited carefully where they will get maximum sun. Because of cooler autumn temperatures, new woody growth may harden off more slowly and if it does not harden off completely it may be more at risk of cold weather damage in winter. The risk is offset by the fact that winter temperatures are slightly warmer inside forests.

Trees and shrubs slow airflow within forests, preventing chilling winds, which are often more damaging than mere cold temperatures. They also often prevent light frosts from reaching the ground on cold nights.

Soil temperatures are also moderated by the insulating leafmould layer, which keeps the soil cooler in summer and warmer in winter.

Soil moisture

Trees transpire copious amounts of water in summer, making competition for soil water intense in periods of dry weather. Different tree species extend their roots to different distances – the extent of which varies not only with species but also with soil type. In sandy well-drained soils, roots will usually extend further than in heavy clay soils. Most trees will have a concentration of feeder roots below the drip line of the canopy (i.e. directly beneath the edge of the canopy), but the roots may go much further. One of the most competitive native British trees in terms of roots is the ash (*Fraxinus excelsior*), whose roots can go laterally twice the distance of the tree's height. In others, such as Italian alder (*Alnus cordata*), the roots tend to go 35-40 per cent of the tree's height in outward growth. Coniferous tree roots tend to go rather less distance than deciduous tree roots. A robust and resilient forest garden planting scheme should plan for summer water competition beneath and near to trees and shrubs.

The summer moisture distribution in the soil near a tree also depends on the density of the canopy.

Rain distribution beneath trees. The deciduous tree with thin canopy (left) allows a much more even distribution of rain through to the soil than the dense evergreen tree (right).

The main factors to take into account in a planting scheme are as follows.

• Dense and evergreen trees tend to shed rain mostly around the outside (drip line) of the tree, with the inner circle of soil getting very dry in dry summer conditions.

• Deciduous trees with thinner canopies allow some rain to percolate through the canopy and land on the soil under the tree, so they tend to have a more even soil-moisture distribution.

• Some rain also runs down the branches and eventually the main trunk of trees.

Another factor to consider, where there are gaps between trees, is that more rain falls on the windward side of trees in leaf (usually the south-west side in Britain). This is because the rain does not fall vertically, but at an angle with the wind.

This situation is likely to occur in a forest garden where there are gaps between trees, leading to moister soil areas to the south-west of the tree and drier areas to the north-east. Note that if local conditions (e.g. a valley) cause prevailing winds to be different, then the areas of moistness and dryness will be slightly different.

Rain distribution near trees. If the rain mainly falls during windy periods, the soil will be wetter on one side than the other.

REGAINING A FOREST CULTURE

In the UK we seem to have forgotten that, if left to itself, most of the country would naturally be covered with forest or parkland-like scattered trees. Because the forest cover has been low for so long we have lost the cultural attachment and comfort of being part of a forest – a culture that still exists in many other parts of Europe. Personally I feel like a forest being, and feel much more integrated with nature when in a forest or a forest garden than on open ground.

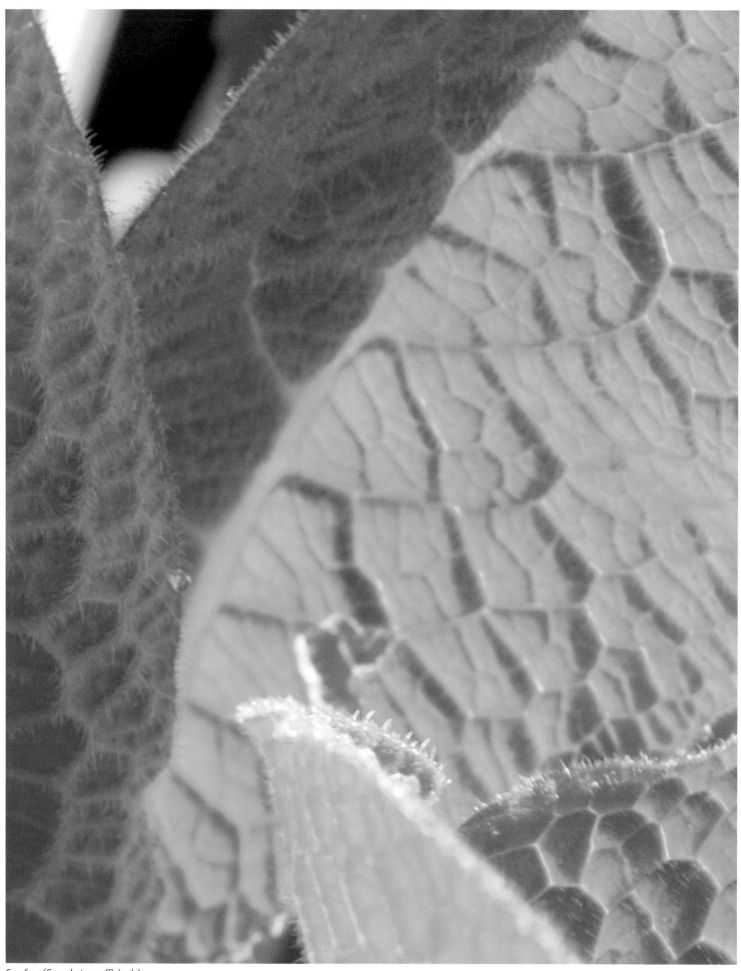

Comfrey (*Symphytum officinale*).

Chapter 6

Fertility in forest gardens

Natural forests do not need feeding – that is obvious. They just grow: trees flower and fruit, and smaller plants usually survive any browsing damage from insects and animals.

In fact natural forests do get inputs of nutrients, notably nitrogen. These come from a variety of sources – bird and animal droppings, soil-dwelling nitrogen-fixing bacteria, nitrogen-fixing plants (in a woody situation these are usually trees and shrubs), and from atmospheric deposition of nitrogen – this is greater where there is pollution with chemicals such as oxides of nitrogen from burning fossil fuels. Sustainable sources of all plant nutrients also come from natural mineralisation processes of rock and soil, greatly aided by fungi.

Forest gardens may be modelled on natural young forests, but we usually want a greater yield from them than that available from natural forests, and that means we have to plan for feeding certain plants with extra nutrients to replace those harvested.

Different plants need different nutrients

The types of plant in a forest garden can be divided into four groups, according to their demands for nutrients.

- Undemanding, lightly cropping unimproved (i.e. un-bred) fruits, for example hawthorn species (*Crataegus* spp.) or salal (*Gaultheria shallon*); and lightly cropped perennials, for example Good King Henry (*Chenopodium bonus-henricus*) or lime trees for leaves (*Tilia* spp.). These plants should gain enough nutrients from normal processes and do not usually require extra feeding.

- Moderately cropping fruiting plants, e.g. currants (*Ribes* spp.). These are likely to require a source of

potash (potassium) and small amounts of nitrogen to maintain good fruiting.

Redcurrant (*Ribes rubrum*) needs potash but only a little nitrogen.

- Heavily fruiting plants, e.g. chestnuts (*Castanea* spp.), hazels (*Corylus* spp.), walnut (*Juglans regia*), blackberry (*Rubus fruticosus*), apple (*Malus domestica*), apricot (*Prunus armeniaca*), medlar (*Mespilus germanica*), mulberries (*Morus* spp.), peach and nectarine (*Prunus persica*), pears (*Pyrus* spp.) and plum (*Prunus domestica*), along with managed bamboos and heavily cropped perennials. These will require extra sources of nitrogen and potassium in particular to sustain productivity.

- Annual vegetables. These require very high fertility to yield the kinds of crops we expect from them. These species have been bred over many years to respond to high levels of nitrogen and potassium in the soil and grow to large sizes accordingly. They require in the order of three to four times as many inputs as the heavily fruiting plants mentioned above, which is difficult to supply without annual additions of compost, manure or other fertiliser. This level of fertility is rarely found in nature, for with it come the associated problems of reduced diversity, excessive growth and, as a result, pests, diseases, etc. But it is partly because of the huge yields of annual vegetables that can be achieved with high fertility and maintenance that the huge human population is (just about) sustained. Don't get me wrong – I am not advocating abandoning all annual vegetables; indeed I grow small patches of them in my forest garden. But bear in mind that the unnatural fertility they require has lots of consequences in terms of maintenance needed, pests and diseases attracted, leaching of excess nutrients into groundwater and so on.

The following tables list nutrient demands for the main common trees and shrubs.

Walnuts (*Juglans regia*) need plenty of nitrogen and potassium to thrive.

TREE FERTILITY CATEGORIES		
Heavy cropping / most nutrient-demanding	**Moderate cropping**	**Undemanding / least nutrient-demanding**
BAMBOOS	*Amelanchier* spp. JUNEBERRIES	*Corylus avellana* HAZEL (for poles)
Castanea spp. CHESTNUTS	*Arbutus unedo* STRAWBERRY TREE	*Drimys* spp. WINTER'S BARK
Citrus spp. CITRUS	*Crataegus* spp. HAWTHORNS	*Ficus carica* FIG
Corylus spp. FILBERTS	*Halesia carolina* SNOWBELL TREE	*Pinus* spp. PINES (for nuts)
Corylus spp. HAZELNUTS	*Myrica* spp. BAYBERRIES	TREES FOR LEAF CROPS AND COPPICE
Cydonia oblonga QUINCE	*Prunus avium* and *P. cerasus* CHERRIES (SWEET AND SOUR)	
Diospyros spp. PERSIMMONS	*Sambucus* spp. ELDERS	
Juglans regia WALNUT	*Sorbus* spp. ROWANS, WHITEBEAMS AND SERVICE TREES	
Malus spp. APPLES	*Zanthoxylum* spp. PEPPER TREES	
Mespilus germanica MEDLAR		
Morus spp. MULBERRIES		
Prunus armeniaca APRICOT		
Prunus domestica PLUM / GAGE		
Prunus insititia DAMSON / BULLACE		
Prunus persica PEACH / NECTARINE		
Pyrus spp. PEARS		

SHRUB FERTILITY CATEGORIES		
Heavy cropping / most nutrient-demanding	**Moderate cropping**	**Undemanding / least nutrient-demanding**
Ribes nigrum BLACKCURRANT	*Cephalotaxus* spp. PLUM YEWS	*Juniperus* spp. JUNIPERS
Ribes uva-crispa GOOSEBERRY	*Cornus mas* CORNELIAN CHERRY	SHRUBS FOR LEAF CROPS
Rubus fruticosus BLACKBERRY	*Cornus* spp. DOGWOODS	
	Decaisnea fargesii BLUE BEAN	
	Diospyros lotus DATE PLUM	
	Myrica gale and *M. pensylvanica* BOG MYRTLE AND NORTHERN BAYBERRY	
	Ribes rubrum REDCURRANT	
	Rhus spp. SUMACHS	
	Rubus idaeus RASPBERRY	
	Xanthoceras sorbifolium YELLOWHORN	
	Zanthoxylum piperitum JAPANESE PEPPER	

Supplying nutrients sustainably

Traditional organic gardening relies on home-made compost to feed annual vegetables and other plants, and you can certainly do the same in a forest garden if you want and can collect enough matter to make compost. You can also import fertility in the form of manure to compost, etc. However, I prefer to forest garden in a way where most or all of the nutrients required are grown on site – a closed-loop system. Ultimately no system of gardening or farming is sustainable if it relies heavily on the import of fertility.

The tables overleaf list the average amounts of both on-site and some more sustainable imported fertility materials that are required to sustain cropping of different types (see tables opposite and above for the groups of plant types). Some materials can provide both nitrogen and potassium, the two main nutrients that need to be supplied.

The tables (overleaf) show approximately how much of the fertility-enhancing material is required per square metre of the plant in question. For trees and shrubs, their area should be taken as the plan area of the canopy (i.e. $3.14 \times R^2$, where R is the radius), so, for example, a five-metre diameter tree has a canopy plan area of $3.14 \times 2.5 \times 2.5 = 19.6m^2$. An easy way of calculating the canopy area is to square the diameter and subtract 20 per cent.

When applying any fertilisers – whether comfrey, urine or other materials – to trees or shrubs, they are best applied in a circle around the drip line beneath the canopy.

Nitrogen

The best way to supply nitrogen into a forest garden system is by the use of nitrogen-fixing plants. By using these plants, which in a forest garden are mostly trees or shrubs (rather than low herbaceous perennials such as clovers, which are not very shade-tolerant), extra nitrogen makes its way into the nitrogen fixer itself, and then in time into the soil in the vicinity and wider afield, where it can be used by other plants. The drawback (if such it is) is that the nitrogen fixer requires space of its own to grow and thrive; however, it may have other uses, for example it may be an edible fruiting or a bee-attracting plant. Even annual vegetable production can be sustained by growing a nitrogen-fixing green manure every third year or so. For me, the sustainability benefits of using nitrogen fixers easily outweigh any yield loss from a reduced area of crop.

Nitrogen-fixing trees and shrubs fix nitrogen at similar rates to the better-known herbaceous perennials such as clovers and trefoils. The nitrogen makes its way into the soil via leaf fall (the leaves are higher in nitrogen than those of other plants), fine root turnover and beneficial fungi. Most of it is insoluble and adds to the nitrogen reservoir in the soil that is gradually made available to other plants. The use of nitrogen fixers is expanded on later in this chapter (see page 59).

NITROGEN SUPPLY TO SUSTAIN CROPPING				
		Annual requirement		
Supply of nitrogen	**Nitrogen (N) content**	**Moderate croppers: 2g/m². Amount of N supply per m² =**	**Heavy croppers: 8g/m². Amount of N supply per m² =**	**Annual vegetables: 28g/m². Amount of N supply per m² =**
Nitrogen fixer in full light	10g/m²	0.2m²	0.8m²	3m²
Nitrogen fixer in part shade	5g/m²	0.4m²	1.6m²	6m²
Human urine	5.6g/pee	Half a pee	1.5 pees	5 pees
Manure	6g/kg	0.3kg	1.3kg	4.5kg
Compost	5g/kg	0.4kg	1.6kg	5.5kg
Comfrey mulch (single cut)	0.5g per cut	4 cut plants	16 cut plants	60 cut plants
Fresh seaweed	2g/kg	1kg	4kg	14kg

EXAMPLE OF NITROGEN REQUIREMENT AND SUPPLY

An apple tree (on a vigorous rootstock) grows to a diameter of 6m (20'). The plan of the canopy has an area of about 3.14 x 3m x 3m = 28.3m².

As a heavy cropper this tree, when in full production, will require around 8g/m² of nitrogen, i.e. about 28.3 x 8 = 226g nitrogen during the growing season.

This equates to about 22m² of nitrogen-fixing plant (supplying about 10g/m²), which could be a 5m (16') diameter alder tree just to the north of the apple. It could also equate to about 40 pees – a little over one per week through the growing season.

METRIC TO IMPERIAL CONVERSIONS

1kg = 2lb 3oz; 10g = 0.35oz
1m² = 1.2 sq yards
1m = 3'3"

Wild lupin (*Lupinus perennis*) is a perennial nitrogen fixer.

Potassium

Potassium is more difficult to provide from on-site sources than nitrogen. Potassium is particularly important in thickening cell walls (thus controlling pests and diseases), and in the formation of flowers and fruits. Most soils contain plentiful potassium, but almost all of it is insoluble and made available only by weathering processes.

POTASSIUM SUPPLY TO SUSTAIN CROPPING				
		Annual requirement		
Supply of potassium	Potassium (K) content	Moderate croppers: 3g/m². Amount of K supply per m² =	Heavy croppers: 10g/m². Amount of K supply per m² =	Annual vegetables: 37g/m². Amount of K supply per m² =
Human urine	7g/pee	Half a pee	1.5 pees	5 pees
Manure	4.2g/kg	0.75kg	2.5kg	9kg
Compost	6.7g/kg	0.5kg	1.5kg	5.5kg
Comfrey mulch (single cut)	10g per cut	One-third of a cut plant	1 plant	4 plants
Seaweed meal	22g/kg	135g	0.5kg	1.7kg
Wood ash	80g/kg	40g	125g	0.5kg

EXAMPLE OF POTASSIUM REQUIREMENT AND SUPPLY

Saskatoon (*Amelanchier alnifolia*), one of the juneberries, is a lovely large fruiting shrub with fruits that taste quite like blueberries. It grows to a diameter of about 2m (6'6"), so its canopy has an area of 3.14 x 1m x 1m = 3.14m. It comes in the moderate cropping group and thus has a potassium demand of about 3g/m², so a fully grown cropping bush will have a demand of about 3.14 x 3 = 9.4g potassium per year in the growing season.

This is easily achieved from a mulch of comfrey leaves from just one comfrey plant, or alternatively a couple of pees or 120g wood ash.

Phosphorus

Phosphorus levels in soils are generally very stable, and normal weathering processes usually make enough available for growth and heavy cropping. Most chemical fertilisers that are sold contain quite superfluous amounts of phosphorus. Several of the materials listed in the nitrogen and potassium tables here contain phosphorus: wood ash contains high amounts, while manure, compost, seaweed and human urine all contain moderate amounts.

Useful sources of fertiliser

There are some very readily available sources of fertiliser in a forest garden: comfrey, which is one of the easiest on-site sources of nutrients to grow, and human wastes.

Urine

Human urine is a valuable source of fertiliser. It really is too valuable to waste. You can pee in situ – this is the ideal, but it is easier and more socially acceptable for men than women! And if your garden is overlooked by other houses then privacy is an issue. Collecting urine in buckets, etc. is all very well in principle but it can rapidly become smelly and disgusting. You'll want to be selective in where you apply urine – for example, obviously not on a low-growing leaf crop. Urine does not need diluting before applying.

A useful side-effect of regular use of urine in the garden is that it is likely to repel a number of animal pests, including deer and rabbits.

As for human manure, this too is a valuable source of fertility, but at the moment it remains a step too far for most folk to install composting toilets. For those that do, the compost is best used as a mulch around fruit trees, not near to any low-growing plants that are to be eaten, to avoid potential contamination.

Comfrey

Cut comfrey is an excellent mulch, degrading fast and supplying nitrogen and potassium. I use it a lot. Comfrey plants can be cut once or twice a year without having to particularly feed them, but they can be cut four or five times a year if they are fed, for example with urine.

Comfrey (*Symphytum* spp.) beneath a plum tree. The root system of a deep-rooted accumulator such as comfrey competes very little with that of a fruit tree.

Nutrient budgets

Rather than try to work out the nutrient requirements for each individual cropping plant and try and apply it individually, it is much easier to work out rough requirements for the whole system – the entire forest garden – and then try to make sure that you have enough sources to cover this.

Russian comfrey (*Symphytum* x *uplandicum*) 'Bocking 14' produces masses of leaf material.

The actual allocation of nutrients to each plant can partly be addressed in the design – for example, by the placement of nitrogen-fixing plants, and of comfrey mulch – but in a functioning semi-mature forest garden you will find that as long as there are enough nutrients around, they will automatically get allocated to the plants that need them. This occurs because of the network of mycorrhizae that form in time beneath a perennial plant system. These symbiotic fungi are critical parts of a healthy wild or agro-ecosystem. Mycorrhizae scavenge for hard-to-find nutrients, passing these on to plants, but they also move nutrients around from areas of surplus to areas of shortage – so they will move nitrogen from areas of soil where there is plenty (under nitrogen fixers, for example) to areas of demand (heavily cropping fruit trees, for example).

Example nutrient budget (1)

This example is one I have applied to our forest garden in Dartington.

Nitrogen requirements
Areas of high demand:

Trees – 670m² of heavy-cropping, demanding plants.
Shrubs – 800m² of heavy-cropping, demanding plants.

1,470m² of heavy-cropping plants fully cropping equates to a nitrogen demand of about 11.8kg per year (1,470m² x 8g of nitrogen/m²).

Area of moderate demand:
2,800m² of trees, shrubs and herbaceous perennials with a moderate nitrogen demand equates to a nitrogen demand of about 5.6kg per year (2,800m² x 2g of nitrogen/m²).

So the total nitrogen demand will be about 17.4kg of N per year.

Nitrogen supply

Human urine (about 1.5 pees per day)	3kg
Cut comfrey – 4,000 cuts	2kg
N-fixing trees in sun – 610m²	6.1kg
N-fixing shrubs in sun – 300m²	3.0kg
N-fixing shrubs in part shade – 400m²	2.0kg
N-fixing herbaceous perennials in part shade – 200m²	1 kg
	17.1kg of N

Potassium requirements
Areas of demand:

Trees – 670m² of heavy-cropping, demanding plants.
Shrubs – 800m² of heavy-cropping, demanding plants.

1,470m² of heavy-cropping plants fully cropping equates to a potassium demand of about 14.7kg per year (1,470m² x 10g of potassium/m²).

Area of moderate demand:
2,800m² of trees, shrubs and herbaceous perennials with a moderate potassium demand equates to a potassium demand of about 8.4kg per year (2,800m² x 3g of potassium/m²).

So the total potassium demand will be about 23.1kg of K per year.

Potassium supply

Human urine	3.8kg (1.5 pees per day)
Cut comfrey – 2,000 cuts	20kg
	23.8kg of K

Don't worry about getting the figures in a nutrient budget exactly right. All the figures in the tables on pages 54 and 55 are averages and will vary up and down with a host of variables. The important thing to ensure sustainability in nutrients is that there is a rough balancing of demand and supply.

Note that the requirements listed in this nutrient budget are for fully grown trees, shrubs and lower plants. The requirements may not reach these levels for fifteen or twenty years in the case of some trees. So there is plenty of time to amend the design or add in patches of fertilising plants such as comfrey at a later stage if you find that there is a shortage of nutrients in later years.

Example nutrient budget (2)

If you want to have a sustainable nitrogen supply almost entirely from nitrogen-fixing plants, then it is best to plan for these in the canopy space. As a general rule a total of about 25-30 per cent area of nitrogen fixers is enough, though if you have mostly heavily cropping plants with a high nitrogen demand then this may rise to 40 per cent.

So if you had as crop trees:
2 apple trees (MM106 rootstock)
2 plum trees (St Julien rootstock)
1 pear tree (Quince A rootstock)
then the total area of these is about 47m² and they will have a total nitrogen demand when fully cropping of about 376g.

If you also had planted two autumn olive (*Elaeagnus umbellata*), growing to a combined area of about 40m², these would supply around 400g nitrogen per year, so that should be plenty, assuming they were well placed amongst the other trees so that their canopy edge (and hence their root system) was near all the other trees.

You would still have to grow or find potassium sources of about 470g per year. This could be, for example, a mixture of comfrey and wood ash (about 30 comfrey plants to cut and mulch with, and 2kg of wood ash).

COMPOST

You might notice that I don't go into the making and use of compost in this chapter. There is a fallacy that it is essential to make compost to be able to grow food crops. If you look at the annual vegetable crops that most people rely on nowadays, they have been bred over centuries to respond to very high levels of soil fertility (actually unnaturally high, for such high fertility is rarely found in nature). The plant's response is to grow quickly, grow large, and be susceptible to pests and diseases because of the high nitrogen levels in the plant itself. So if you want to grow a lot of annual vegetables you need to feed the soil a lot too, and compost is good for this. However, if most of the crops you are growing do not require such high-fertility soil, then you rarely need quantities of high-nutrient feed such as compost or manures.

Soil pH

Calcium is essential for cell division and root tip growth, and determines the soil pH (acidity or alkalinity – a low pH is acid; a high pH is alkaline) – which also determines the availability to plants of other nutrients.

- Nitrogen availability is best at pH 6.0-8.0.
- Potassium availability is best above pH 6.0.
- Phosphorus availability is best at pH 6.5-7.5.
- Most other minerals are freely available at pH 5.5-7.0.
- Earthworms start to decline when pH is under 5.0.

Thus, quite often an apparent shortage of nutrients is in fact caused by the soil being too acid (below about pH 5.5) or too alkaline (above about pH 7.5).

Most trees and shrubs are happy in soil of pH 5.5-7.0. The ideal is 6.0-6.5. Legumes prefer neutral acidity/alkalinity (pH 7.0). Ericaceous plants (e.g. blueberries) need very acid soil (pH 5.5 or less).

The topsoil pH is mainly determined by the underlying rock type – chalk and limestone usually lead to alkaline soils. In areas of heavy rainfall, acidification naturally occurs – quickest in cultivated soils; much slower in forest soils.

Farmers and gardeners, usually cultivating crops annually, regularly apply lime to correct acid soils. Even orchards need occasional liming. In a forest garden, it is quite likely that liming will be required, at least at the beginning of the garden's life. But as the garden matures, nutrient cycling becomes more and more efficient – the network of many different types of roots and mycorrhizal hyphae tap nutrients before they can be washed out of the topsoil. When I started my forest garden I assumed that this process may take many years, but I have found that the soil pH has stabilised after seven to eight years, and I don't think I will need to lime much at all from now on.

If you do need to lime, which is quite likely at the outset of a project, the quantity of calcium (lime) needed to amend the soil pH depends on the type of soil – sandy soils need most, clay soils need least to increase the pH a given amount. I would advise getting a soil analysis to begin with, which will tell you lots of other useful things. This will often give recommended amounts of 'CaO' needed. CaO is calcium oxide, or quicklime, and lime is never applied in this form, so you need to convert the amount of CaO given into a weight of product, e.g. limestone, to apply. A material such as ground limestone is given a CaO value of 56 per cent, meaning that 1kg of ground limestone is 56 per cent as effective as 1kg of CaO. Thus, if you were recommended to apply 500g/m² of CaO, this would translate to 500 x (100/56) = 893g of ground limestone.

There is no ecologically sound source of liming material that I know of. Sources used today are mostly dug out of quarries (limestone and dolomite) or dredged off the sea floor (calcified seaweed).

Wood ash has some liming value but you'd need to burn acres of trees to get enough. In medieval times in Britain, lime was used in the form of marl, which is a type of alkaline clay subsoil – hence the remnants of marl pits dotted around the countryside. Even this is not really sustainable. But in a forest garden situation, where hopefully you will only ever need to lime once or twice, the environmental impact is pretty small, and outweighed in time by the benefits of the garden!

Bear in mind that there may be areas of the forest garden that you want to leave unlimed, so you can grow acid-loving plants there such as blueberries, cranberries, salal, etc.

Calcium sources

The following sources take about two years to achieve full effect.

	CaO value	
Calcified seaweed	44%	+ many trace elements
Dolomite	34%	+ magnesium
Ground limestone	56%	

To give an example: in my forest garden, to raise the pH from 5.7 to 6.0, a soil analysis advised I needed to apply 60g/m² of CaO. This is equivalent to 60 x (100/44) = 136g/m² of calcified seaweed. For the total area of about 8,000m² this was just over a ton of material to broadcast, which I did by hand, refilling a bucket, taking a day or so.

Nitrogen fixation in plants

Nitrogen gas (N_2) constitutes four-fifths of the world's atmosphere – a virtually inexhaustible supply. Yet very few plants and no animals can assimilate nitrogen in its free form. Nitrogen is, however, the essential constituent of the proteins necessary for cell protoplasm, and all organisms are dependent on it being available in a form that they can utilise.

Most plants obtain their nitrogen from the mineralisation of soil organic matter and plant residues, and living organisms and ecosystems are organised to obtain *and preserve* usable nitrogen. The modern use of synthetic nitrogen fertilisers is fraught with long-term dangers (depleting soil nitrogen reserves, pollution of groundwater, rivers and lakes), and the fertilisers themselves will become increasingly expensive through increasing energy costs.

Biological nitrogen fixation, particularly of the symbiotic type, plays a crucial ecological role in maintaining adequate nitrogen reserves in the plant world. Two groups of plants in particular, the **legumes** (**rhizobial** plants) – for example black locust (*Robinia pseudoacacia*) and white clover (*Trifolium repens*) – and **actinorhizal** plants – for example autumn olive (*Elaeagnus umbellata*) and bog myrtle (*Myrica gale*) – can thrive with only a minimal supply of nitrogen in the soil. These plants, through the agency of specific bacteria (mostly *Frankia* and *Rhizobium* genera), which invade the root hairs and establish a mutually beneficial association inside their root swellings (nodules), can convert free air nitrogen into fixed nitrogen for eventual plant protein assimilation and storage. These select groups of plants have thus obtained an evolutionary advantage over most other living organisms. Root infection and nodule development of both actinorhizal and legume symbioses are similar: the infection occurs via the penetration of deformed root hairs by bacteria, or by the bacteria gaining entry to the root through intercellular spaces.

Ecologically, most legumes and actinorhizal plants are pioneer species on open, nitrogen-poor sites. They improve the soil and enable the succession towards scrub or forest to begin. As shading of them increases, they decline. Since they are pioneers, there is scope for them to easily become naturalised and become somewhat weedy in the agricultural landscape – for example, oleaster (*Elaeagnus angustifolia*) is regarded as a weed by some in western North America. Several actinorhizal plants persist as understorey plants in open forest stands – for example, evergreen *Elaeagnus* species and bayberries (*Myrica* spp.), and these plants are generally more shade tolerant than the legumes.

Factors affecting nitrogen fixation

There are a number of factors that affect the efficiency of nitrogen fixation.

- Temperature: this depends on the bacteria species and the host plants; for example, 4-6°C (39-43°F) is adequate for broad bean (*Vicia faba*), whereas 18°C (64°F) or more is necessary for most subtropical and tropical species.

- Seasonality: for most species, fixation rates rise rapidly in spring from zero, to a maximum by late spring / early summer, which is sustained until late summer, then they decline back down to zero by late autumn. In evergreen species, N-fixation occurs throughout the winter provided the soil temperatures do not fall too low.

- Soil pH: the legumes are generally less tolerant of soil acidity than actinorhizal plants, which is reflected by *Rhizobium* species being less acid tolerant than *Frankia* species. So, for example, the clovers (*Trifolium* spp. with *Rhizobium* bacteria) do not tolerate very acid soils, while alders (*Alnus* spp. with *Frankia* bacteria) do.

Of the actinorhizal plants, alders and bayberries (*Myrica* spp.) are most acid tolerant.

- Availability of nitrogen in the soil: if nitrogen is abundant and freely available, N-fixation is usually much reduced, sometimes to only 10 per cent of the total that the N-fixing plants use.

- Moisture stress: in droughts, bacterial numbers decline; they generally recover quickly, however, when moisture becomes available again. Some species (usually actinorhizal), for example common alder (*Alnus glutinosa*) and bog myrtle (*Myrica gale*), are adapted to perform well in waterlogged conditions.

- Light availability: N-fixation is powered via sunlight and thus will be reduced in shady conditions. For most N-fixing plants, which are shade sensitive, N-fixation rates decline in direct proportion to shading, i.e. 50 per cent shading leads to 50 per cent of the nitrogen fixed. The relationship for N-fixing species that are not so shade sensitive is not so clear – they may well continue to fix significant amounts of nitrogen in shade.

Nitrogen availability and contributions

Nitrogen from N-fixers is made available to other plants by three main natural methods.

- Litterfall, which is high in nitrogen.

- Root turnover (and leaching from roots), which is now believed to be a significant contributor to nitrogen flow, returning at least as much as litterfall does. Fine roots are grown annually on most plants (including woody ones) and these die off each year, releasing nutrients into the soil.

- Mycorrhizal fungi. These are symbiotic fungi that form an association with plant roots – nearly all plants form such associations. Where there is an established mycorrhizal mat (typically under trees with the soil not cultivated and not heavily fertilised), the fungi can move nutrients around, and will move nitrogen from areas of the soil where it is in high amounts (e.g. under/around nitrogen-fixing plants) to areas where it is lacking (i.e. under/around demanding plants), sometimes moving it several tens of metres.

In addition to these methods, interventions can aid the liberation of nitrogen, for example regular coppicing or pruning, with the prunings left to decompose on the soil floor or shredded and used as a mulch. When nitrogen-fixing trees or shrubs are coppiced or heavily pruned, the prunings (particularly small branches) contain significant amounts of nitrogen, which are gradually liberated into the soil if left on the surface. There is no problem with 'nitrogen robbery' (nitrogen being drawn from the soil to degrade the material) if branches are scattered without being shredded, although if they are shredded this is a potential temporary problem.

The use of nitrogen fixers to supply essential nitrogen to enable other plant growth has several advantages over the use of ordinary fertilisers.

- The supply of nitrogen is more regular and continues over a longer time.
- There is less leaching and loss to the air of the nitrogen.
- Nitrogen fixers also increase soil organic matter.

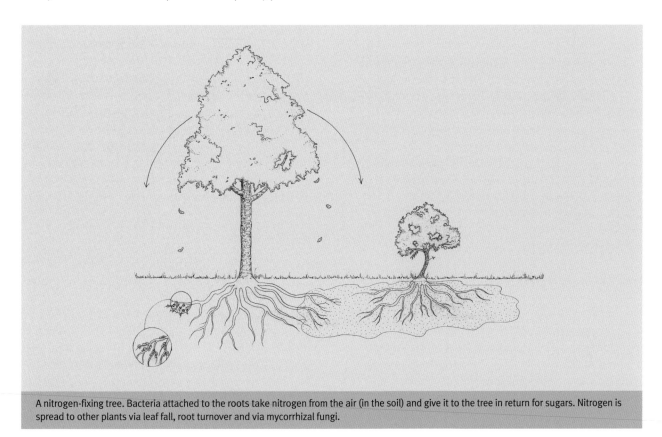

A nitrogen-fixing tree. Bacteria attached to the roots take nitrogen from the air (in the soil) and give it to the tree in return for sugars. Nitrogen is spread to other plants via leaf fall, root turnover and via mycorrhizal fungi.

Other uses of nitrogen-fixing plants

Nitrogen-fixing plants may have a number of other uses in addition to supplying nitrogen to the system.

Mineral accumulation

Many nitrogen fixers are excellent mineral accumulators, as befits their role as pioneer plants that improve soil conditions for future successions of plants. They achieve this by finding mineral sources in the subsoil with their deep taproots, and raising the minerals so gained to their upper parts, which may be eaten or die off in winter, releasing their minerals into the soil or food chain.

There is also increasing evidence that accumulated minerals may leach out of the roots into the surrounding soil, where the root systems of other plants may be able to utilise them. A second method of accumulation is via mycorrhizal associations, where phosphorus and other nutrients are made available to the plants via these symbiotic fungi.

Windbreaks

Several nitrogen fixers are excellent windbreak trees, for example:

- Siberian pea tree (*Caragana arborescens*) – very good in continental climates and produces good edible seeds and young pods

- *Elaeagnus* spp. – for example autumn olive (*E. umbellata*), which is a great bee-attracting and fruiting plant.

- Sea buckthorn (*Hippophae rhamnoides*) – very good in salt winds and again a great fruiting plant.

Maritime exposure (salt spray) is tolerated by several other nitrogen-fixing species as well (for example the evergreen *Elaeagnus* and the sea buckthorns – *Hippophae* spp.), making them suitable for coastal windbreaks.

Bee attraction

A large number of legumes are excellent bee (honey) plants – from herbaceous perennials such as clovers (*Trifolium* spp.) and vetches (*Vicia* spp.) to trees such as the black locust (*Robinia pseudoacacia*). Some of the actinorhizal plants, particularly the *Elaeagnus* family, are also great bee plants.

Soil improvement

Nitrogen-fixing plants can increase soil organic matter levels near them by up to 20 per cent via their leaf litter and fine-root turnover. Soil organic matter is the primary storage medium for soil nitrogen, and an increase in it improves soil tilth, mineral levels, water retention, soil porosity and aeration, and soil structure. There is now evidence that N-fixing understorey plants can recycle greater amounts of phosphorus in litter than non N-fixers, and thus influence phosphorus cycling on sites where this mineral is in limited supply.

Disease prevention

Another effect of N-fixing plants often found, notably with alders, is the suppression of fungal diseases. The reasons are not clear, but the alders may release substances from their roots that suppress these disease fungi, and the increased nitrification of soils may encourage pests of the fungi.

Edible crops

Many of the legumes and actinorhizal plants, because they are pioneer plants, synthesise various toxins that are held in the aerial parts of the plant to deter animals from browsing on them. However, others, for example in the pea (*Pisum*) and bean (*Phaseolus*) genera, are not poisonous and many have edible seeds and leaves, while others, for example sea buckthorn and *Elaeagnus* spp., have edible fruits.

Plants for nitrogen fixation

The tables opposite list the main useful plants to include in your forest garden for nitrogen fixation – trees, shrubs and herbaceous perennials, and those that are suitable for sun or shade and as overstorey trees. There are also many more such plants than those listed here. Particularly if you are outside of the UK, there may be many other possible plants to use in your forest garden. For a full listing of useful nitrogen-fixing plants please refer to my book *Nitrogen-Fixing Plants for Temperate Climates* (details in Resources section).

Recommended nitrogen fixers for shady locations

Most N-fixing plants are pioneer species, which are quite sun-demanding: they are at home in the canopy of a forest but often disappear from the understorey when shaded. The most shade tolerant (some even tolerating deep shade) are listed opposite (top). Trees larger than the general canopy can be coppiced at intervals to ensure that other trees are not shaded. Similarly, large N-fixing shrubs in the understorey can be kept under control by trimming when they get too large. Such trimmings, etc. should be left on the soil floor or chipped and used as a mulch if possible to ensure the return of nutrients (note that with chipping there may be a temporary nitrogen robbery from the soil while the chips decompose). The following are recommended for use in the UK and North America, where, unless noted otherwise, they are known to nodulate (i.e. form working symbioses) successfully.

Nitrogen fixers tolerating full shade

These species tolerate conditions where they receive 0-2 hours of exposure to sun per day in summer.

NITROGEN FIXERS THAT TOLERATE FULL SHADE	
Small trees / large shrubs	**Herbaceous perennials**
Elaeagnus x ebbingei (evergreen)	Apios americana GROUNDNUT
Elaeagnus pungens (evergreen)	

Nitrogen fixers tolerating part shade

These species can tolerate conditions where they receive 2-6 hours of exposure to sun per day in summer.

NITROGEN FIXERS THAT TOLERATE PART SHADE				
Large/medium trees (coppiced or trimmed)	**Small trees / large shrubs (may be coppiced or trimmed)**	**Medium/small shrubs**	**Herbaceous perennials**	**Annuals**
Alnus glutinosa COMMON ALDER	Alnus sinuata SITKA ALDER	Elaeagnus multiflora GOUMI	Glycyrrhiza echinata RUSSIAN LIQUORICE	Amphicarpaea bracteata HOG PEANUT
Alnus rubra RED ALDER	Alnus viridis GREEN ALDER	Myrica pensylvanica NORTHERN BAYBERRY	Glycyrrhiza glabra LIQUORICE	Lathyrus odoratus SWEET PEA
	Elaeagnus angustifolia OLEASTER		Gunnera magellanica GUNNERA	Medicago lupulina BLACK MEDICK
	Elaeagnus glabra (evergreen)*		Gunnera tinctoria CHILEAN RHUBARB	
	Elaeagnus umbellata AUTUMN OLIVE		Lathyrus latifolius EVERLASTING PEA (climber)	
	Myrica californica CALIFORNIAN BAYBERRY (evergreen)*		Lathyrus sylvestris WOOD PEA (climber)	
	Myrica cerifera WAX MYRTLE (evergreen)		Lathyrus tuberosus EARTHNUT PEA	
			Lotus corniculatus BIRD'S FOOT TREFOIL	
			Lotus uliginosus GREATER BIRD'S FOOT TREFOIL	
			Trifolium repens WHITE CLOVER	
			Vicia sylvatica WOOD VETCH (climber)	

* These species are hardy only in mild areas of the UK.

Recommended overstorey nitrogen fixers

It is a good idea to utilise some of the high tree layer, or overstorey, of the forest garden for nitrogen-fixing trees. The trees can be high-pruned, with the side branches taken off as they grow, to maximize the amount of light that gets though beneath them. Making partial use of the high tree layer in this way is good, because it is not very suitable for growing crops that need picking (carting long ladders around in a forest garden is not much fun), and also because the leaf fall from high nitrogen-fixing trees is well spread when it drops, thus spreading the fertiliser around the garden well.

Suitable trees tend to be upright and more conical in form than rounded.

OVERSTOREY NITROGEN FIXERS		
Species		**Comments**
Alnus cordata	Italian alder	One of my favourites, more tolerant of dry summer conditions than most alders. Nice conical form. I have this dotted all around my forest garden. Great in windbreaks too.
Alnus rubra	Red alder	Very fast-growing, the fastest of all the alders. Likes moist soil. Good in wind-breaks too.
Hippophae salicifolia	Himalayan sea buckthorn	Thorny like ordinary sea buckthorn but larger and an upright tree. Likes moderate to well-drained soil. Fruits round and similar to European sea buckthorn. Can sucker.
Robinia pseudoacacia	Black locust	Conical and fast, but thorny and can sucker. Likes moderate- to well-drained soil. A good bee plant. One of the few good tree legumes for temperate climates. Thin canopy allows lots of light through.

Recommended nitrogen fixers for sunny / good light locations

Most nitrogen-fixing plants do best in sunny conditions, so in good light conditions you have the largest choice of species to use.

Trees and shrubs
For sunny or lightly shaded forest garden sites there are lots of nitrogen-fixing shrubs and small trees that might earn their place – many more than are shown in the table opposite, which lists the best species. The legumes tend to need better drainage than the actinorhizal plants (the latter includes alders, elaeagnus, bayberries and sea buckthorn).

Black locust (*Robinia pseudoacacia*).

TREE & SHRUB NITROGEN FIXERS FOR GOOD LIGHT CONDITIONS		
Species		**Comments**
Alnus sinuata	Sitka alder	Good as a green manure tree; can be pruned or coppiced regularly.
Alnus viridis	Green alder	Good as a green manure shrub; can be pruned or coppiced regularly.
Amorpha fruticosa	False indigo	Contains insect repellent chemicals and is a source of dyes. Formerly used as a spice but may not be wholesome. Susceptible to wind damage.
Caragana arborescens	Siberian pea tree	Slow-growing in temperate climates but bears good edible small pods and seeds. Also a bee plant.
Cytisus scoparius	Broom	A great pioneer legume, worth putting in at the start of a forest garden. It will probably die out after 10-15 years as shade increases. A great bee plant with many other uses.
Elaeagnus angustifolia	Oleaster	Fast, good in windbreaks. A poor fruiter in the UK in my experience.
Elaeagnus x *ebbingei*		Evergreen shrub, good in windbreaks. Bears a very early ripening fruit in spring if pollinated.
Elaeagnus multiflora	Goumi	A lovely summer-fruiting plant, with flowers loved by bees. Cherry-sized fruits borne well when pollinated.
Elaeagnus umbellata	Autumn olive	One of my favourites, a fast-growing, bushy, beautiful shrub; a great early-spring bee plant and produces masses of excellent fruits. Good in windbreaks.
Genista tinctoria	Dyer's greenweed	Lots of medicinal and dye uses, and a good bee plant too.
Hippophae rhamnoides	Sea buckthorn	Thorny and suckering, so can sometimes become troublesome. When pollinated, bears masses of nutritious acid fruits, quite slow to harvest.
Lespedeza bicolor	Bush clover	A pretty shrub with flowers loved by bees. Many minor uses.
Lupinus arboreus	Tree lupin	Evergreen shrub, great for bees. Not very hardy in much of the UK, and needs a well-drained soil.
Myrica cerifera	Wax myrtle	Evergreen and easy to grow, leaves and fruits can be used as flavourings; fruits are covered in wax, which can be used to make aromatic candles, etc.
Myrica gale	Bog myrtle	A nice spice shrub to grow in boggy and wet conditions.
Myrica pensylvanica	Northern bayberry	A smaller version of *M. cerifera* with the same uses.
Ulex europaeus	Gorse	Very prickly! I would not recommend planting it, but if it is naturally growing on site then it is doing useful work and protects young trees against browsing pretty well.
Wisteria spp.	Wisterias	Well-known climbing shrubs used ornamentally. Few uses, but a good bee plant. Could be grown up larger trees.

Herbaceous perennials

Herbaceous nitrogen fixers may be harder to fit into a forest garden because of the decreasing light at ground level. Most are legumes and need reasonable drainage.

A few, including some of those in the table below, are shade tolerant (see table on page 63), but where there is good light and only light shade, the following are worth considering.

HERBACEOUS PERENNIAL NITROGEN FIXERS FOR GOOD LIGHT CONDITIONS		
Species		**Comments**
Apios americana	Groundnut	A twining climber, so plant it near a shrub to clamber up. Produces nice starchy edible tubers.
Astragalus glycyphyllos	Milk vetch	Leaves used medicinally, good bee plant.
Glycyrrhiza echinata	Russian liquorice	Roots used for food and medicine.
Glycyrrhiza glabra	Liquorice	Roots used for food, medicine and more!
Gunnera magellanica	Gunnera	Likes moist soil and has edible peeled leaf stems (like rhubarb). Not a legume or actinorhizal plant.
Lathyrus latifolius (climber)	Everlasting pea	A tendril climber, good to interplant with other perennials that it can clamber up. A good bee plant. Pods/peas edible in small amounts (see page 283).
Lathyrus sylvestris (climber)	Wood pea	As for *L. latifolius*.
Lathyrus tuberosus	Earthnut pea	As for *L. latifolius*, but it also produces an edible starchy tuber free of toxic substances.
Lotus corniculatus	Bird's foot trefoil	Great bee and wildlife plant.
Lotus uliginosus	Greater bird's foot trefoil	Great bee and wildlife plant.
Lupinus perennis	Wild lupin	Likes acid soil. A good bee plant and source of dyes. Seeds not edible.
Trifolium pratense	Red clover	Great bee plant with edible leaves and flowers.
Trifolium repens	White clover	Great bee plant with edible leaves and flowers.

Mycorrhizal fungi

Mycorrhizae are structures that develop where certain fungi colonise the tissues of fine plant roots. The fungi help to find and supply hard-to-find minerals to the plant in return for carbohydrates and other substances such as vitamins. This mutually beneficial relationship is called symbiotic or a symbiosis.

These types of fungi are an essential part of a healthy forest garden and, it is becoming clear, of all healthy eco-systems. Mycorrhizal fungi will always eventually turn up, but there are various methods of encouraging them, which are described in Chapter 21 (page 310).

Part 2

Designing your forest garden

Red valerian (*Centranthus ruber*).

Chapter 7

Ground preparation and planting

How you prepare the ground prior to starting any planting rather depends on the speed at which you are planting the forest garden. For smaller gardens it is quite possible to try to plant the whole gamut of species – trees, shrubs, herbaceous perennials, etc. – at the same time over one winter: in this case you need weed-free bare soil at the outset, which will mean that you have either just cultivated the area or have sheet-mulched it to kill off existing growth (see pages 72-73 for more on sheet-mulching). Of course, a third option is to use herbicides, but that is something I do not recommend because of their detrimental effect on the soil fauna, amongst other things. Apart from one or two shockers – for example bindweed (*Convolvulus* spp.) and horsetail (*Equisetum* spp.) – most perennial weeds can be killed off very successfully by the use of sheet-mulching.

Most folk plant their forest gardens over a number of years, which usually makes more sense. In this case there is no requirement to start with bare weed-free soil.

Compacted ground

Whatever time span you are using to plant your forest garden, before you do any planting it is worth investigating the soil. I've already mentioned soil acidity and how to correct it (see Chapter 6, page 58), but soil structure is another important factor. If you've acquired a piece of agricultural land, then more likely than not the soil structure will be in poor condition. This is because regular tractor cultivation, as well as grazing by sheep or cattle, often results in a compacted layer of soil, called a 'soil pan'. This layer, often just below the top 15-20cm (6-8") of topsoil, will slow and restrict plant root growth – just where you want all your tree and shrub roots growing down deep. It is well worth trying to do something about

compacted ground like this, even in a garden situation. There are two options for breaking up compacted ground prior to planting your forest garden.

1. Physically break up the compacted layer. In a small garden this might mean digging to a spade's depth and then wiggling a garden fork down into the soil beneath, or even going over the area with a metal pike, making holes every 10cm (4") or so. On a larger and field scale, the best way to break up compacted soil pans is to hire an agricultural contractor with a subsoiling attachment on a tractor. These attachments have long vertical tines, sometimes vibrating, which are pulled through the soil, ripping through the compacted layer without turning the soil over.

2. Grow a deep taprooted green manure for a year (or even longer) and let the plant roots break through the compacted layer. This requires cultivated ground of course, to sow the green manure seeds into in spring. Even one year of growth of these deep-rooted plants will significantly improve soil conditions for what follows. Some of the best plants to break up soil pans are docks and sorrels (*Rumex* spp.) and dandelions (*Taraxacum officinale*), but I wouldn't normally recommend you plant these deliberately as they will be troublesome to remove! (However, next time you see a field of docks think of it as natural soil restoration in action!) It is better to sow annual or biennial sun-loving plants, which will not persist for long in the forest garden even if they do self-seed. They need to be fast-growing and cover the ground quickly to avoid too many weed seeds germinating. If they are nitrogen-fixing as well then they will in effect inject nitrogen into the soil for the plants that follow to use. The table overleaf shows some of the possibilities.

DEEP-ROOTED GREEN MANURES			
Species		**Annual or biennial**	**Nitrogen-fixing?**
Borago officinalis	Borage	Annual	
Fagopyrum esculentum	Buckwheat	Annual	
Lupinus angustifolius	Blue lupin	Annual	N-fixing
Medicago lupulina	Black medick	Biennial	N-fixing
Phacelia tanacetifolia	Phacelia	Annual	
Raphanus sativus	Fodder radish	Annual	
Trifolium incarnatum	Crimson clover	Annual	N-fixing
Trifolium subterraneum	Sub clover	Annual	N-fixing

Most of these species will grow in most soils, though the clovers and lupin dislike really acid soil. Cheap bulk seed is not available for all these species, so for larger areas concentrate on buckwheat, blue lupin, trefoil, fodder radish and the clovers. Seed of these is cheap even for an acre of land. You can mix several species together too, rather than just sowing one, which should giving better coverage and a more resilient cover. See Chapter 16 for recommended sowing rates.

Soil types

If the soil tends to an extreme in any way – very acid, very alkaline, very sandy or very heavy clay – then now is the time to try to improve conditions if possible, before planting too much.

Acid

Very acid soil conditions are usually corrected by liming (see page 58, Chapter 6). If you don't want to lime then you will be quite limited as to which fruiting and other useful plants you can grow. Species tolerant of very acid conditions include the Ericaceae family (blueberries, cranberries, *Gaultheria* spp.), the strawberry tree (*Arbutus unedo*), pines (*Pinus* spp.), yews (*Taxus* spp.), rowans, whitebeams and service trees (*Sorbus* spp.) and hawthorns (*Crataegus* spp.).

Alkaline

Very alkaline soil conditions are difficult to correct. They are usually caused by an underlying alkaline rock type – chalk or limestone. In the past, acids were sometimes used but were very harmful to soil fauna and didn't last long in any case. You will probably just have to put up with it and grow tolerant species, which include Siberian pea tree (*Caragana arborescens*), redbuds (*Cercis* spp.), Cornelian cherry (*Cornus mas*), hazel (*Corylus avellana*), hawthorns (*Crataegus* spp.), beech (*Fagus sylvatica*), junipers (*Juniperus* spp.), holm oak (*Quercus ilex*), black locust (*Robinia pseudoacacia*), elders (*Sambucus* spp.), rowans, whitebeams and service trees (*Sorbus* spp.) and yews (*Taxus* spp.).

Sandy

Very well-drained (sandy) soils may make establishment of trees and other plants more difficult – irrigation may be essential – and fruiting trees will probably need ongoing irrigation in summer. For this type of soil, take all measures to improve humus levels to increase water retention. Add any kind of bulk organic matter you can get hold of. When planting trees, try to maximise the chances of the right mycorrhizae being present (see page 310, Chapter 21), as these will reduce water stress.

Clay

Very heavy (clay) soils again may make establishment more difficult – they are often too wet to plant in winter. As with well-drained soils, take all measures to improve humus levels. If the soil is waterlogged for more than a week or so in winter, consider installing drainage. Perforated plastic drainage pipe is fairly cheap from agricultural stores, and a herringbone pattern of 60cm (2')-deep drainage trenches can be dug by hand on a small scale or quickly with a mini-digger. A fall of 1 in 100 is ideal (i.e. a 1cm fall per metre). The drainage pipe is laid at the bottom, optionally wrapped in landscape fabric to slow the rate of silting up, and the trenches backfilled.

Mulching

Whether you are planting trees (and perhaps shrubs) into bare ground or into grass, pasture or other low plant growth, they should be initially mulched. The mulch has two main functions.

- It reduces or eliminates weed competition with the young tree. Grasses are the most competitive plants, especially for soil moisture. Trees without competition can grow up to twice as fast in their early years as those with no weed control.

- It helps slow the loss of soil moisture during summer and maintains better soil conditions for tree roots.

In the case of planting into pasture or grasses, or amongst other low plants, the mulch needs to kill off an area of these plants at the same time as the tree is establishing. A sheet mulch should kill grasses in three to four months, though perennials may take longer to kill.

Try to mulch to a minimum diameter of a metre for each tree. Foresters often use a circle of herbicide around each tree to achieve some of the same benefits.

Materials for mulching newly planted trees

Many different materials can be used for mulching newly planted trees, some of which are free and others of which must be bought. The options are as follows.

For mulching trees planted into bare-soil sites
The best mulch to use is something bulky of organic origin that does not contain many weed seeds.

- Chipped bark is good (often available cheaply from local timber mills), but avoid chipped wood unless it's well composted for a few years, as this may result in nitrogen robbery (see page 75).

- Straw is good if you can get it in small bales – use 10cm (4") wedges as they come off the bale – though rodents will like to live in your mulch. Avoid hay – it has too many weed seeds.

- Grass mowings are good – apply in thin layers of 3-4cm (1.2-1.6") and top up as required.

- Other possibilities may depend on what you have available nearby: chopped bracken is good, as is hop waste, often freely available from small breweries. Loose organic mulches should not be piled too high against the trunk of trees, as this can cause canker diseases and encourage vole damage to bark – a few centimetres is fine, but if more than this I would advise using a tree guard to keep the mulch from the trunk.

- Home-made compost is not recommended, because it is too good a seed bed for airborne weed seeds; neither is manure, unless the soil is of poor fertility – trees do not generally need feeding in their early years.

- You can also use any of the options overleaf for planting trees into grass on bare-soil sites.

In the foreground, woven ground-cover fabric mulch. In the background the same mulch has been removed to expose clean soil for planting.

For mulching trees planted into pasture, grass, etc.
You need a solid layer of something laid on top of the ground around the tree, which the existing plants can't grow through. This solid material will also need securing so it doesn't blow away. Possible options include the following.

- Bought tree-mulch mats. These may be made out of different materials.

  › Black polythene – cheap, effective and short-lived (1-2 years). Can be secured by pushing edges into the ground with a spade. Impermeable to water, but rain will infiltrate from the edges for a 1m (3')-wide mat.

  › Woven ground-cover-type fabric – more expensive, effective, permeable and long-lived (7-8 years; can be removed and reused at least once). Can be secured by pushing edges into the ground with a spade.

  › Flax or hemp matting – even more expensive, biodegradable and short-lived (1 year). May need weighing down to stop weeds underneath pushing it up.

- Thick card from packaging boxes, etc. You'll need at least two thicknesses of card – a folded box is usually sufficient for a year. If you have access to a large local supply then this is a good (and free) option. The card will need weighing down to stop it blowing away in gales. Pieces of card need overlapping by 5cm (2") to stop weeds growing through gaps.

Flax matting.

- Newspapers. These can be used in the same way as card. Use a whole newspaper thickness to last a year. It may need weighing down. Chemicals in newspaper inks biodegrade quickly, so you need not be too concerned by coloured inks.

- Old carpet. Wool carpets can be cut up into squares and used like matting mulch mats. Backing fibres are often nylon and will need to be removed at some stage after the wool has biodegraded. Modern carpets will have been impregnated with fire-resistant chemicals, which can leach into the soil. If they are old then the chemicals will probably have gone, but if they are quite new then I would advise against using them.

Solid materials that need weighing down – paper, card and often fibre-based mats – can be weighted with branches, stones (less effective) or an organic loose mulch of the type described for bare-soil sites.

Sheet-mulching

If you are planting out a forest garden over several years, then prior to planting ground-covers and herbaceous perennials the ground must be cleared of low vegetation. Few herbaceous plants will establish well if there are still grasses and other weeds growing and competing with them.

Most often, a sheet mulch will be used on the ground between and under the trees/shrubs already planted, though there are other options, as follows.

- Cultivation. On a small garden scale, ground can be hand-cultivated. On a larger scale, if there is enough ground between trees for machinery then machine cultivation is possible, although it will be tricky because of irregular tree spacing – and of course the ground cannot be cultivated too close to existing trees.

- Using livestock. Chickens at a high enough density will remove almost all vegetation: a chicken 'tractor' (moveable ark) could be moved around as areas are cleared; this is suitable for smaller areas. Geese will also clear most vegetation if their density is high enough, without damaging most trees. Some kind of electric fencing might be needed to keep them in a small enough area for it to be cleared. Pigs will dig out most vegetation but will also dig up small trees, so you would need to use electric fencing carefully to protect them.

- Herbicides. I personally do not like herbicides – even so-called 'safe' ones do damage the soil fauna, and soil health is the number-one priority in any sustainable land-use system.

Sheet mulches are easy to use but are not always aesthetically pleasing. However, they are temporary and they do a good job. I think it is worth using them for their great benefits.

The materials to use for a sheet mulch are the same as those used for solid mulches around trees (see opposite): thick card, newspaper, carpet, black plastic (either the sort made specifically for mulching or you can reuse discarded silage bags, etc.), permeable woven plastic or hemp/flax matting. Larger areas of them are obviously needed than when mulching around trees. The plastic mulches and hemp/flax matting are available in rolls, which makes their use much easier. If you do use a roll of mulch and there are trees/shrubs in the way, you'll have to cut slits or holes for them and lay the mulch around them.

I have mulched up to 600m² a year during the establishment of my forest garden, mostly using woven black plastic mulch. Large areas of mulch like this can be weighed down with branches, etc. or pinned down with ground-cover pegs or 'staples' made of wire. Using oil-based plastics at all in the garden somewhat compromises sustainable practice, but in this case I think it is justified. If you don't like the look of them you can cover them with a few centimetres of loose chipped bark or similar organic materials. Latterly I have also been using flax and hemp matting as a sheet mulch.

A sheet mulch needs to be down at least 6 months, and preferably 12 months to kill off dandelions, docks, couch grass, etc. I always move my sheet mulches in winter, leaving them down a year. When they are moved, the soil underneath is loose, friable and 99-percent weed free: there may be a few tiny docks just surviving, which can be pulled out by hand with their remaining thin roots. There are also usually a lot of mouse trails – I have a healthy mouse population! I don't mind this because, amongst other things, old mice holes are a great habitat for wild bees, such as bumble bees.

If the soil is not very fertile, then before you put down a sheet mulch you can put down any fertility-building materials: compost, animal manure, organic materials, etc. Just spread these on the ground and put the sheet mulch over the top. While the grasses/weeds are being killed, worms will take down a lot of the fertilising materials, as well as dead plant matter, into the soil and so improve the soil structure and fertility.

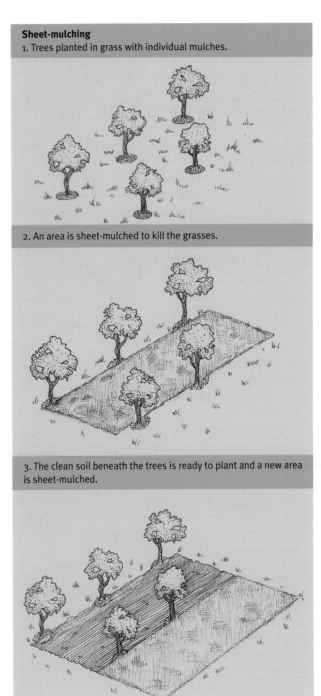

Sheet-mulching
1. Trees planted in grass with individual mulches.

2. An area is sheet-mulched to kill the grasses.

3. The clean soil beneath the trees is ready to plant and a new area is sheet-mulched.

Sheet mulches, and similar mulches around individual trees, can lead to strong weed growth at the edge of the mulch where it meets existing grass, etc. These grasses and other weeds exploit the fine soil conditions under the edges of the mulch to grow faster than normal, so you might find that this growth needs cutting or strimming more often than other grass areas.

Planting

Trees and shrubs are supplied by nurseries as bare-rooted (i.e. dug up in the dormant winter season and supplied only then) or pot-grown (when they can potentially be supplied all year around), whereas smaller herbaceous and other perennials tend to be mostly pot-grown. While pot-grown plants would appear to give you the advantage of a longer planting season, I mainly advocate planting in the dormant season. In particular, planting pot-grown trees and shrubs in the spring or summer leaves them very prone to drought stress and they will usually require watering in dry spells during the growing season for the first year at least. Bare-rooted trees or shrubs planted in early-to-mid winter rarely need watering the following season.

In the UK and similar mild-temperate climates, the optimum planting times are as follows.

- Most trees, shrubs and ground-covers are best planted in autumn or early-to-mid winter (September/October to January).

- Ground-cover plants and herbaceous perennials may be better planted in spring with a loose organic mulch. In winter, birds can disturb a lot of the loose mulch, leaving gaps where spring-seeding weeds can get in.

- Tender trees and shrubs may be better planted in spring (March to April) to avoid low winter temperatures when they are small. Most tender trees and shrubs become hardier after a few years.

Provided winter conditions aren't too harsh, autumn or early winter planting is preferable because the soil is still warm, and roots (even of dormant plants) will usually grow for a while. This helps the establishment of the plant, especially in a dry spring.

In areas where winters are colder, and the ground often frozen in winter, spring planting tends to be the norm.

When planting trees and shrubs, make sure you dig a large enough planting hole. None of the roots should be squashed up or bent to fit them in the hole. Sprinkle in mycorrhizal inoculant if required, or dip the roots in a mycorrhizal root dip if you have made one (see page 310 for details), then refill the hole with the soil you took out. Unless the soil is very poor do not add extra materials to it.

Ground-covers/perennials too can be mulched at the planting stage if you want. This has the advantages of less weeding while they establish, and better soil conditions, especially in a dry first spring or summer; also, the mulch provides a good habitat for beetles and other beneficial insects. The disadvantages are the extra work involved, good conditions for slugs and snails, and perhaps more expense. I have tried both methods in my forest garden, and decided that if the perennials/ground-covers are going to cover the soil quickly (within 8 weeks, say) then a loose mulch isn't worth it; otherwise it is. But everybody will have a different view.

If you decide to mulch newly planted perennial/ground-cover plants, plant first and put the mulch around the plants afterwards. There are many options as to what mulch to use, as follows – weed-free materials are not so critical as when mulching around trees, as most germinating weeds should be outcompeted by the perennial plants already establishing.

- Leaves (on a sheltered site).

- Leafmould (i.e. rotted leaves – likely to have weed seeds).

- Chopped bracken – cut in late spring (before spores are released) and apply thickly. Chop into 10-20cm (4-8") pieces if possible, or put through a shredder. Bracken is high in nitrogen and potassium.

- Grass mowings – apply in thin layers up to 4cm (1.6") thick. Can be topped up from time to time. This is a good source of nutrients.

- Mushroom compost (organic is advised – non-organic will have lots of insecticide residues). This is often alkaline, and is a good source of nutrients.

- Garden compost. (Likely to have weed seeds.)

- Farmyard manure (rotted) – apply in spring. (May have weed seeds.)

- Chipped bark – coarse better than fine as it is not such a good seedbed for weeds. A layer 2.5cm (1") thick suffices for 1 year. At this thickness, 100 litres covers 4m².

- Chipped wood – well composted.

- Straw (on a sheltered site) – though may encourage rodents. Non-organic straw may contain all sorts of chemicals, including hormonal ones, which affect plants.

- Commercial waste products – tea leaves / coffee grounds / hop waste, etc. (Best on a sheltered site.)

Wood shavings or sawdust are not recommended, as they result in 'nitrogen robbery' – nitrogen being drawn from the soil to degrade them, resulting in a deficiency.

A planting sequence using perennial and annual plants

1. Clean soil beneath trees in autumn after removal of sheet mulch.
2. White mustard (*Sinapsis alba*) sown as a short-term ground cover in autumn. It has been interplanted with small oregano (*Origanum vulgare*) plants, which are dormant.
3. The mustard flowers in spring. Oregano (barely visible) is only just starting to grow beneath the mustard.
4. By summer the mustard is full height.
5. By the following spring, the mustard has vanished and the ground cover is pure oregano.
6. The oregano makes a thick cover.

PLANTING TIMES ARE FLEXIBLE

I often lapse from best practice regarding planting time. I always aim to do my planting in late autumn or early winter, but very often it gets delayed until late winter or early spring. For me this is because I grow a lot of plants to sell and everybody else wants their plants in autumn! When the spring turns out moist with plenty of rain then the delay makes no difference and I 'get away with it', but when the spring turns dry and hot then extra watering is entailed and I curse myself for not planting in the winter!

New shoots of giant Solomon's seal (*Polygonatum commutatum*).

Chapter 8

Growing your own plants

Most folk thinking about making a forest garden will already be growing some of their own plants. Growing plants is fun and interesting – even more so for trees, shrubs and herbaceous perennials, which most people do not start off themselves. Seed is relatively cheap, and some of the rarer species may be available only as seed.

Seed-grown plants are almost always genetically different from their parents. This can be a good and a bad thing. Genetic diversity is generally good for a plant. However, if we want a good fruiting tree then this cannot be guaranteed by growing a seed from a good fruiting tree; what you get depends very much on the genetics of the tree and how highly bred it has been.

With apples, for example, they have been so highly bred with back crosses of various different crab species for disease resistance, etc. that the chances of getting a tree from seed with fruit as nice as the mother tree is quite small and not really worth trying unless you are prepared to grow thousands of seedlings. You are better off buying a grafted tree of a known variety.

With a species such as heartnut (*Juglans ailantifolia* var. *cordiformis*), about half of the seedlings from a good fruiting tree will have fruits (nuts) as good, or better, than the mother tree, so it makes much more sense to use the seeds to grow your own trees.

In containers or in the ground?

It is far better to grow most plants that are started from seed in controlled conditions inside a greenhouse or polytunnel, using containers and a specific seed compost. This is for several reasons.

- A lot of seed of perennial and woody species is slow to germinate. Sown in soil they are likely to be overrun by weed growth before they even appear above the soil surface.

- Tree and shrub seed in particular is a favourite food of rodents such as mice, rats and squirrels. It is very difficult to defend small areas of sown seeds outside against these pests. Birds also often try to dig up seeds to eat. Mice can still be a problem inside a tunnel or greenhouse, however – I put sown large seeds on suspended shelves hanging from the frame of my polytunnel.

- Seed sown in autumn is even more vulnerable to rodent attack. Seeds of many woody and herbaceous perennial species require a period of cold conditions (see page 37) and germinate best after an autumn sowing or a spell of cold, moist conditions provided by other means.

Large-scale forest tree nurseries – which grow millions of trees per year – do use outdoor seedbeds, but in these cases the large area is more easily defended against rodents and is netted against birds when necessary.

Hardwood cuttings (see page 82) taken in winter can often be planted straight into soil outside.

Seed and potting composts

Seed compost

A seed compost should have a fine texture, to ensure good contact with small seeds, and be free draining, to prevent seeds from dying of lack of oxygen, but doesn't need to contain a large supply of nutrients because the seedlings won't be left in it for very long. Although you can make your own seed compost from a mixture of garden compost, good soil and perhaps leafmould, I do not recommend it for growing woody and perennial species. This is because home-made composts inevitably contain numerous weed seeds, which will cause a lot of both work and confusion – the latter because you will be endlessly wondering if the seed leaves just emerging are a weed or the seeds you are trying to grow.

A bag of seed compost is inexpensive and goes a long way. I use an easily available organic compost based on composted green waste, and add in a little vermiculite for drainage.

Maidenhair tree (*Ginkgo biloba*) and heartnut (*Juglans ailantifolia* var. *cordiformis*) seedlings in Rootrainers.

Potting compost

Potting composts are a bit more complicated. Remember that you are trying to mimic good soil: the compost should hold on to nutrients and release them slowly; similarly for water; and it should steadily release nutrients to promote growth over a long period.

Trees and shrubs in particular, but often also herbaceous perennials, need to be grown for at least a whole season before they will be sturdy enough to plant out. This is a problem because most commercially available potting composts (organic or otherwise) contain only enough nutrients for a couple of months – fine for growing vegetable plants for planting out, for example, but if used

without supplementary feeding then the results are ill-looking and poorly developed plants.

I make up my own potting compost, starting with the same commercial organic compost as for making seed compost. To improve drainage and to act as a buffer (i.e. holding on to water and nutrients, releasing them slowly) I add vermiculite, but perlite would do the job too. Vermiculite is the result of heating a naturally occurring ore resembling mica; perlite is a heat-expanded natural volcanic glass.

Because our nursery is on a small commercial scale, I add a slow-release fertiliser with trace elements that releases nutrients gradually over a whole season. This is not organic and is a compromise, but I have experimented for several years with organic alternatives and never achieved plants as healthy as those cultivated with the non-organic variety. Organic ingredients added to compost mixtures (e.g. bonemeal, fishmeal, etc.) release their nutrients erratically and mimic soil badly. Another alternative is to feed with a home-made liquid fertiliser (e.g. nettles and comfrey soaked in water for 4-5 days), but this is a soluble fertiliser and subject to the same problems as soluble chemical fertilisers in terms of short action span, and a lot of the nutrients wash straight through the compost.

I also give all my container plants a boost about once a month from midsummer to autumn, by spraying or feeding with a dilute seaweed solution. This contains many micro-nutrients and ensures that plants remain healthy.

If you are growing only a few plants then you can certainly make your own compost from a mixture of soil and garden compost, although for more than a few plants you are unlikely to have enough spare compost and soil for this. Drainage is often a problem in such composts, and well-composted bark or leafmould can help. You'll almost certainly need to feed with liquid feeds of some sort for much of the season.

The final ingredient I use in my potting compost mix is a mixture of mycorrhizal spores. Mycorrhizae are fungi that form symbiotic relationships with plants; they do this with most plants but are especially important for trees and shrubs. When the root–fungi symbiosis is established there are numerous benefits for the plant, and I think it is well worth trying to maximise the chances of establishment by adding dry spores of suitable fungi species to the compost mix. I buy in the spores for composts, but there are other ways of introducing mycorrhizae at planting time that are free (see page 310, Chapter 21).

A few species require an especially acid seed and potting compost; these are mostly members of the Ericaceae family, which includes cranberries and blueberries. Unless you have acid materials to hand then these are best grown using a bought ericaceous compost, adapted as described above.

Stratification

Some seeds (for example, those of many of the common vegetables we grow) are not dormant. These do not require any treatment but can be sown in warm temperatures in the spring and should germinate straight away.

Seeds of many species of tree and shrub – as well as many herbaceous perennials – are dormant and require a period of stratification before they will germinate. Stratification is subjection to cold, moist conditions, sometimes preceded by a period of warm, moist conditions. Basically, the seeds are expecting to go through a winter and germinate in the spring. Without the cold conditions they will not germinate at all.

Sowing outside in the ground would obviously give such seeds the cold they require, but you'll probably lose most of the seed to rodents. If you have a reliably cold winter then one option is to sow in a pot or seed tray in autumn. Cover the pot or tray over with a slate or something else to keep birds and rodents out, and leave it to experience outside temperatures over the winter. In spring, bring it into a greenhouse or polytunnel where you can protect the seeds as they germinate.

Stratification in bags

Different species need different lengths of stratification (see Appendix 1 for more details). Work backwards from a suitable spring date (March in the south of England, or April further north) to find when to start the stratification. So, for example, a plant that needs 3 months should be put into stratification in late December for sowing in late March.

- Mix four parts moist (not wet) silver sand (a coarse, well-draining sand) with one part seed by volume,

place in a well-labelled plastic bag, and put into a fridge or outside over winter in a rodent-proof bin with a lid. Here in the south-west of England we don't always get a cold enough winter for outside stratification to work well, so I usually put my seeds in the fridge. Make sure the fridge temperature is 1-5°C (34-41°F).

- As spring approaches, start checking for germination inside bags in the fridge or in seed trays that are still covered. Sometimes seeds will start germinating before you expect in cold conditions, and they need sowing quickly if so.

Once the stratification period is over, seeds mixed with sand can be sown, and those already sown in seed trays or pots should be brought into warmer conditions to aid germination and survival of seedlings. Seeds that didn't require any stratification can be sown now too.

Stratification for longer periods

Quite a few species need a period of warmth followed by cold. These are usually seeds that naturally ripen in early summer and expect to germinate the following spring. Prepare these seeds as for cold stratification, but allow them to experience ambient summer/autumn temperatures before giving them cold temperatures from late autumn onwards.

Some tree and shrub seeds can take more than a year to germinate – for example Cornelian cherry (*Cornus mas*), hawthorns (*Crataegus* spp.) and yews (*Taxus* spp.). These need to go through one or more warm–cold–warm cycles before they will germinate. The easiest strategy for these is to sow them after a winter of stratification, but make sure you don't throw the seed away if it doesn't germinate the first year!

Scarification

Some seeds, mostly from the legume family, need special treatment before they will germinate. These seeds of pioneer species expect to germinate after a fire. You don't have to try burning them though – to scarify them (which means making the seed coat more permeable to water), put them in a jar and pour on near-boiling water. Allow them to soak in the cooling water for 24 hours, then sow them.

Cleaning fruit for sowing

If you harvest fruits with the aim of sowing the seeds inside, then the fruit flesh must be removed as this usually containers germination inhibitors. With some fruits, e.g. *Chaenomeles* spp., you can just cut the fruit open and get the seeds out easily. Other more juicy fruits may be processed by several methods.

- Crushing and washing.

- Using a blender. Mix one part fruit with two parts water by volume in a blender and carefully blend to remove all the flesh from the fruits. Only use this method for hard-seeded fruits, e.g. hawthorns (*Crataegus* spp.). After blending, the seeds will sink and the flesh should float or be suspended, so you can separate the seeds quite easily by pouring off the water and pulp, refilling the container with water and pouring it off again until the seeds are clean.

- Immersing in water and allowing natural fermentation to separate off the fruit pulp – but be careful the seeds don't drown by being in water for too long.

Sowing

Containers for sowing

I am very economical with the space used for sowing seeds. This is partly because I grow a lot of species, often several hundred, and partly because I transplant seedlings at a very young age, so they don't need much space. I use standard seed trays, filling them with seed compost first, then subdividing the top layer with old plant labels side-on so I can sow six, eight or even ten species in one seed tray.

A rough rule of thumb I use is that seeds under about 6mm (0.25") across are fine to sow in a seed tray, but any larger than that should be sown in a deeper container. This is because the fast-growing taproots on larger seeds can too-easily get broken when transplanting. The smaller seeds are sown in trays with about 4cm (1.6") depth of seed compost, and most should be covered by a similar depth of compost as the seeds' width. An exception is very fine dust-like seed (e.g. *Campanula* spp.) or very light tree seeds (e.g. birches; *Betula* spp.), which should be sown on the surface of an already-moistened compost and left uncovered.

The seeds in seed trays may take weeks or months to germinate, so I keep the trays covered, usually with another empty seed tray upside down over the top. (Alternatively, a layer of grit can be used over the seeds.) If you don't cover the trays or compost then you'll get a layer of algae, moss and liverworts growing on the compost surface, which can interfere with germination of small seeds. Surface-sown seed, however, often needs some light to germinate, so I will often give these a few hours of light every now and again by removing the covers. Water all seed trays from time to time (every 4-5 days is usually fine).

Temperature

Warmth speeds germination, and you want your tree seeds germinating in spring, not in August when they probably won't survive the next winter. Most of my seed trays go on to a home-made heated bench kept at about 21°C (70°F) in the spring. Heated benches are quite easy to make – you need some sort of bench to start with (old office desks can work well), and the warmth is provided by flexible heating cables embedded in a layer of sand.

Pest protection

You need to keep the seed trays away from rodents, so up on a bench is a good first stage of protection, although like me you may need to use mouse traps temporarily in spring to further protect your valuable seed.

Checking for germination

Seed trays that are covered need checking every 2-3 days in spring for germination. When seedlings are emerging they can either be potted up immediately (treat them with care as they are fragile at this stage) or the seed tray can be left uncovered for a few days, enabling the seedlings to grow a little before transplanting.

Large seeds

Large seeds, for example chestnuts (*Castanea* spp.), oaks (*Quercus* spp.) and the walnuts (*Juglans* spp.), should be sown straight into deep containers where they can be grown for most of the season. These species have deep taproots that often grow 10-15cm (4-6") deep before any shoot growth occurs.

Chestnuts and oaks are best sown in autumn, and will start putting down roots almost immediately. These seeds do not store very well and become less viable as they dry out. Keep them well off the ground so mice can't dig them up.

Transplanting and care

Rootrainers are kept off the ground, using bricks and wooden batons, so roots are air-pruned and become well branched.

Containers

I usually transplant tree and shrub seedlings into deep-cell containers called 'Rootrainers'. These create an excellent branched root system by encouraging the roots out of a hole at the bottom of the container and into the air, where the root tip dies, causing a much better-branched root system inside the container and helping to prevent any circling roots. This means the tree will transplant well and have excellent stability in future life – spiralling roots can lead to poor anchorage. Round pots I try to avoid, but if planting a tree or shrub that has been in a round pot I cut vertically through any circling roots by making five or six cuts with a knife, 1cm (0.4") deep into the compost around the rootball.

For herbaceous perennials I use Rootrainers too, but also round and square pots as the stability issue is not important.

Seedling pests and diseases

Young seedlings are at risk of attack from slugs and snails, so take precautions. One advantage of growing in deep-cell containers is that these have to be raised off the ground on wooden batons to take advantage of the air pruning of roots. Thus slugs and snails have a disadvantage to start with.

In cool damp weather, damping-off diseases (caused by a number of fungi) can kill seedlings. Typically you will see a seedling flopped over, with the stem near soil level shrivelled and brown. Improve airflow and provide warmth if you can. If attacks are bad then consider starting your seed sowing a little later when the weather is warmer.

Two other pests can be serious whenever a fair number of plants are grown in containers. One is the compost fly, whose tiny larvae can burrow into compost and eat plant roots. I keep their numbers under control by using yellow sticky traps (basically a piece of yellow plastic with a non-drying glue on both sides, to which the flies stick). These traps also catch aphids, but larger predatory insects (bees, etc.) do not get stuck. I put these up in May and replace them with a second batch in late July.

The other pest, vine weevil, is potentially serious. The weevil itself takes semicircular bites out of the edges of plant leaves – a useful tell-tale sign – but does not cause much damage itself. The larvae are the problem: white with brownish-red heads, they can devour plant roots and grow several centimetres long. Whereas most nurseries use insecticides in composts against vine weevils, there is a very good biological control I use, which is a naturally occurring nematode. This comes as a powder that is mixed with water and watered on to the surface of compost in containers. The nematode parasitises the vine weevil larvae, killing them.

If your tree seedlings start to grow and then stop in summer, looking poorly, then they may be lacking the mycorrhizal fungi that they require to grow properly. This is often the case with pine trees (*Pinus* spp.) grown from seed. The best solution is to scrape up a little pine litter and surface soil from beneath an established pine tree and sprinkle it on to the compost around the seedlings. The seedlings will soon become inoculated and start growing again.

When to plant out

First-year growth of trees and shrubs from seed can be up to 40-50cm (16-20"), though some will be only 10-15cm (4-6") – it varies a lot by species and growing conditions. A height of 40-50cm is just about OK for planting out, but at less that this height it is advisable to grow on the plant for another year. Very small trees are too easily swamped by weeds or damaged by pests. Pot them up during the winter following sowing, using a larger deep container and fresh compost.

Growing from cuttings

A small number of trees and shrubs take easily from cuttings in the winter (hardwood cuttings). More can be propagated from cuttings taken in the summer (softwood or semi-ripe cuttings), though this is more difficult and can require some equipment. Most trees and shrubs that root from cuttings grow into healthy vigorous trees, but with some species, notably conifers, it matters where you take the cuttings from – those from upright shoots grow upright, while those from horizontal shoots may never grow into a normal upright plant.

Hardwood cuttings

These are cuttings of ripened wood. In the UK they are usually taken in late autumn, but they can be taken any time from autumn through to early spring. The cuttings are taken of shoots of diameter 0.6-1.5cm (0.4-0.6"), with the lower cut just beneath a bud and the top cut just above a bud, and an overall length of 15-30cm (6-12"). Place the cutting straight into the soil if possible, leaving 5cm (2") or so above ground. The warm soil in late autumn greatly aids callusing, which precedes rooting. Keep the young cuttings weeded the following season as they grow; if you are taking a lot of cuttings, then planting through a sheet mulch can vastly reduce the weeding required. See Appendix 1 for suitable species for hardwood cuttings.

Softwood and semi-ripe cuttings

These are usually taken in June or July using new-season growth. The lower leaves are removed and very often plant hormones are required to promote rooting, in the form of either a hormone rooting powder or liquid, or a home-made willow rooting liquid (see box opposite).

These cuttings require a well-drained compost (50 per cent compost, 50 per cent vermiculite or perlite is ideal), bottom heat (a heated bench or propagator at 21-25°C/70-77°F) and a humid atmosphere. Commercially the latter is created with a misting unit, but on a small scale you can enclose an area or individual pots with a plastic tent made of plastic bags or sheeting, which maintains a moist atmosphere inside. When cuttings show signs of rooting, gradually normalise conditions by lowering the heat and reducing the humidity to harden off the young plants. Very often they will need some care over their first winter and should be kept under cover until the following spring. See Appendix 1 for suitable species for softwood cuttings.

Other propagation methods

Root cuttings

A few trees and other perennials can be propagated from root cuttings – short sections of root replanted. Comfreys (*Symphytum* spp.) are known for being propagated like this, and one tree that can be propagated this way is the black locust (*Robinia pseudoacacia*).

WILLOW ROOTING LIQUID

It is easy to make this hormone rooting liquid to use for cuttings.

1. Harvest some fresh willow and remove the leaves.
2. Chop stems into 1cm (0.4")-long pieces and soak in water for 24 hours.
3. Remove the stems.
4. The resulting water is the hormone rooting liquid. To use, soak the rooting end of the cuttings in it for an hour or two before placing into compost.

Layering

Most trees and shrubs can also be propagated by simple layering – pegging down a branch to the ground or into a pot. Rooting can take a year or more.

Stool layering

Hazel trees are usually propagated this way, but it is not the easiest technique. A mother plant is coppiced to the ground in winter, and the young shoots that grow in the spring are earthed up. They are encouraged to root by girdling with copper wire (which does not rust) before being earthed up. In the autumn the rooted shoots are removed and planted out.

Propagating herbaceous perennials

Normal round or square pots are completely adequate for herbaceous perennials, although I often use the same deep-cell containers as I do for trees.

From seed

Many perennials are easy from seed, and various perennials can also be propagated easily from cuttings. For example, the mint family (*Mentha* spp.) takes easily from summer

cuttings placed in water – they will soon form roots and can then be potted up.

Some perennials are fast-growing enough that it is possible to start plants off in early spring and plant out in the summer. However, I much prefer to start perennial propagation a little later and plant in winter at the same time as trees and shrubs. Planting in summer can succeed in a wet season, but in a dry season (and with climate change we are likely to get many more of these) you will be forever watering to keep the poor plants alive – I don't recommend it.

Layering

Some useful perennials, e.g. the strawberry family (*Fragaria* spp.) and the ground-cover raspberries (*Rubus* spp.), are easy to propagate by layering – just lay the trailing stem into a pot and out again, and cover the stem with compost. If you are going to need a lot of plants then you can set up your own layering bed, by planting permanent mother plant(s) whose stems are layered each year and removed once rooted.

Division

Many perennials can be propagated by division: cutting an existing clump into several parts, usually with a spade in spring, and replanting each part.

One more point of note about propagating herbaceous perennials: make sure you allow enough space in your propagating area. For most underplanted perennials in a forest garden, between five and twelve plants are required per square metre of planting – so you may need lots of plants! Allow 1m² of propagating space per 50 plants grown for a full season.

Grafting trees and shrubs

Grafting fruit trees is a long-established method of propagating true-to-name varieties. Among other things, it means that rootstocks of different vigour can be selected to grow trees of different sizes. It is possible to grow some varieties of apples and plums on their own roots (usually by air layering) – and own-rooted fruit trees are claimed to be healthier, longer-lived and have tastier fruit than grafted trees. However, there are some distinct disadvantages to having fruit trees on their own roots, namely that: 1) you lose any advantage of root-disease resistance and soil tolerance of the rootstock; and 2) you lose any dwarfing effect of a rootstock, leading to a large tree needing regular pruning that takes many years to start fruiting. These disadvantages mean that, for most people, grafted fruit trees are a better choice.

A GRAFTED TREE

To produce a grafted tree, a piece of wood from the variety you want (the *scion*) is attached to another piece of wood with roots (the *rootstock*). They are attached so that the union (where they meet) heals and the plant grows as one.

Rootstocks have been bred for most common fruit trees for their disease resistance to soil-borne diseases, tolerance of different soil conditions, and vigour (which controls how big the combined tree grows).

Usually, scions of fruit trees are grafted on to a young (1-2-year-old) rootstock. So apples can be grafted on to MM106, M26, M27, etc., pears are grafted on to quince A, quince C or wild pear; plums are grafted on to Myrobalan, St Julien or Pixy, and so on.

Sometimes wild seedlings or established trees can be converted into a productive fruit tree. Thus hawthorns (*Crataegus* spp.) can be grafted with medlar or sometimes apple or pear; and wild plum species (*Prunus* spp., including blackthorn, *P. spinosa*) can often be grafted with plum.

The main types of graft used to produce fruit trees on a rootstock are:

- a whip-and-tongue graft, which is made in late winter or early spring on to a dormant rootstock

- chip budding in summer, made on to a growing rootstock.

Grafting usually requires a knife with a very sharp, preferably straight, cutting edge, so take care – it is easy to cut yourself. Becoming good at knife grafting is largely a matter of practice, and you can practise on any bits of branchwood available.

Whip-and-tongue grafting

This is undertaken on shoots of 5-15mm (0.2-0.6") diameter.

1. Cut or buy scionwood in December or January. The scionwood is the previous season's growth from the tree of the variety you want, e.g. 'Bramley's Seedling'

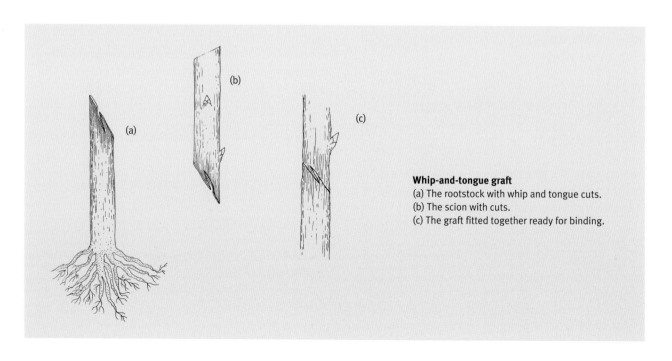

Whip-and-tongue graft
(a) The rootstock with whip and tongue cuts.
(b) The scion with cuts.
(c) The graft fitted together ready for binding.

apple. This needs be cut when fully dormant. Some tree nurseries sell graftwood, and it can also be obtained from the National Fruit Collection at Brogdale.

2. Store scionwood in plastic bags in a fridge – it must be kept dormant until grafting time. Make sure it is dry when put into bags, otherwise it may rot.

3. Buy rootstocks if required. These are young bare-rooted plants of the rootstock variety (e.g. MM106, Pixy, etc.). These can be bought from some fruit tree nurseries.

4. Graft under cover on rootstocks from February to April (February to May in cold winter climates).

5. On the scion, make a first long sloping cut, 2.5-5cm (1-2") long. Make this cut away from you for safety. This is the whip cut. The scion should ideally have two to four buds, but if you are short of scionwood one bud will often suffice.

6. Make a second cut on the scion, starting a third of the way down the sloping cut, and cutting in almost parallel to the sloping cut. This cut is made towards the hand holding the scion, so do it slowly and carefully. This is the tongue cut.

7. Make identical cuts on the rootstock, where the diameter of it is the same as that of the scion where cut.

8. Fit the two tongues together and the graft will hold together.

9. Wrap the graft with tape to stop it drying out and to give it some extra structural support while it heals. I use biodegradable grafting tape but you can use plastic tape, insulation tape, masking tape or even strips of plastic bag. Tie or stick the tape to stop it unravelling.

10. Some species require warmth at the graft for it to heal. Others, such as apples, don't. Plums prefer 20°C (68°F) or so, while chestnuts and walnuts need it even warmer. Warmth can be provided by using a hot grafting pipe.

The grafted plant is then potted up or planted out in a temporary position for a year or two before planting in its final position. If a non-biodegradable grafting tape has been used, this must be slit by midsummer to prevent constriction of the graft.

Commercial nurseries sometimes use hand-operated grafting machines to make cuts on the rootstock and scion, ensuring a good fit. Grafting pliers (see page 88) can also be used.

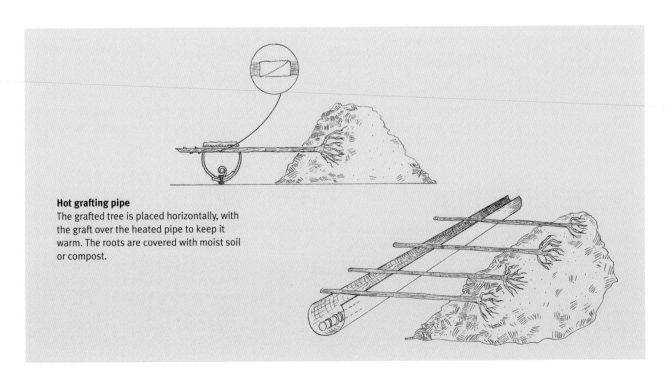

Hot grafting pipe
The grafted tree is placed horizontally, with the graft over the heated pipe to keep it warm. The roots are covered with moist soil or compost.

Chip budding

Chip budding is undertaken in July or August.

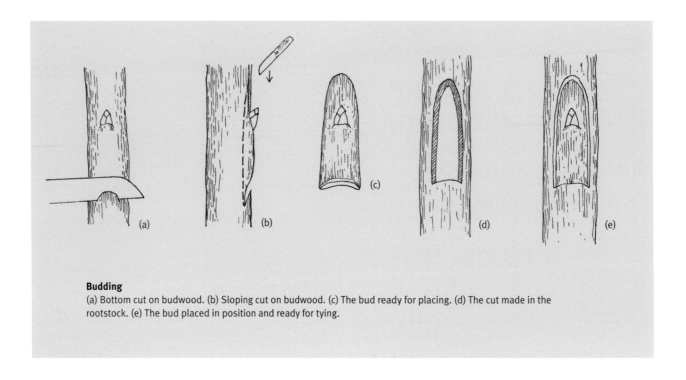

Budding
(a) Bottom cut on budwood. (b) Sloping cut on budwood. (c) The bud ready for placing. (d) The cut made in the rootstock. (e) The bud placed in position and ready for tying.

1. Cut or buy budwood of the variety you want. This is a fresh growing shoot and is very susceptible to drying out – budding should take place within hours of cutting budwood if possible. As soon as you obtain budwood, cut off any leaves, allowing a small piece of stalk to remain, then store it cool and moist.

2. You must have a rootstock already growing, usually in the ground but it could be in a pot. This will normally be 60-90cm (2-3') high. Cut off any low branches up to a height of 30cm (1') flush to the trunk to give good access.

3. Cut the 'chip' out of the rootstock. Lean over the rootstock and make a cut into the wood about 15cm (6") above soil level about 5mm (0.2") deep. Then make a second, sloping cut, starting 2.5-5cm (1-2") above the first cut. Cut downwards to meet the first cut. Remove the chip.

4. Cut out an identical chip from the budwood where the diameter is ideally the same as the rootstock where the chip has been cut. Choose a suitable small viable bud beneath one of the leaf stalks and make the short cut about 1.2cm (0.5") below it and the sloping cut a similar height above it. Hold the chip by the leaf stalk to avoid touching the wood.

5. Place the budwood chip into the rootstock. If the stock bark is thicker than the budwood bark then a margin of the stock rind should be left visible around the bud. Tie with biodegradable grafting tape or a budding rubber.

6. The bud sometimes starts growing in late summer but more often remains dormant until the following year.

7. In the winter following budding, cut back the rootstock to just above the budding.

8. The next season the bud should grow vigorously, giving a tree ready to plant out in its final position 16-18 months after the budding operation.

Grafting on to existing trees

Existing fruit trees can be regrafted to a different variety (or more than one), and wild trees can be grafted in spring to become a fruit tree. Cleft grafting is the simplest method to use. So hawthorn (*Crataegus monogyna*) can be grafted with pear or medlar, whilst blackthorn (*Prunus spinosa*) can be grafted with plum.

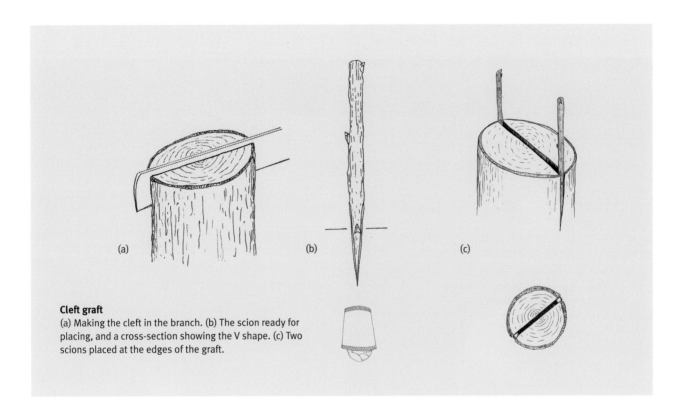

Cleft graft
(a) Making the cleft in the branch. (b) The scion ready for placing, and a cross-section showing the V shape. (c) Two scions placed at the edges of the graft.

1. Cut or obtain graftwood of the variety you want in December/January and store it in the fridge.

2. Do the grafting in late April or early May in the UK; if possible when a spell of warm weather is forecast. It is fine if the tree is already coming into leaf.

3. Cut off the top of the tree or several main branches back to stubs. The best diameter to cleft graft is 4-7.5cm (1.6-3"), so this will usually determine where to cut.

4. For each branch to be grafted, make a cleft down the centre of the branch. The split should avoid side branches (existing or removed), as you want it straight. I use a billhook to make the cleft, hitting it with a hammer, but any tough bladed implement can be used. The cleft needs to go 7-10cm (3-4") down into the branch.

5. Remove the billhook from the cleft and jam in a large flat-headed screwdriver in the centre of the cleft. You'll use this to lever open the cleft to insert the graftwood.

6. Cut two pieces of graftwood. On each, you need to make two long sloping cuts, about 5cm (2") long, not quite parallel, so in cross section there is a V shape. Each piece should have 3-4 good buds on it.

7. At each side of the cleft, insert the graftwood with the point of the V on the graftwood inwards. The aim is to line up the inside edge of the outer bark of the graftwood (very thin bark) with the inside edge of the outer bark of the branch (often quite thick), so the graftwood is often recessed into the cleft. Use the screwdriver to lever open the cleft to insert the graftwood, then remove it when finished.

8. Wax over or tape over the whole cut face of the branch, as well as down the branch to cover the cleft splits.

9. If the grafts take, they will start growing within 2 to 3 weeks and grow vigorously. The point of doing two grafts per branch is insurance as much as anything – if both take then one can be cut out if necessary. Because the whole root system of the tree is already in place, fruiting will usually start within a year or two.

Cleft-grafting hawthorn
1. Newly made cleft grafts on a hawthorn (*Crataegus monogyna*) rootstock.
2. Four months later, new grafted shoots of *Crataegus arnoldiana* are growing vigorously.

GRAFTING PLIERS

Getting good at grafting with a knife is a matter of practice – you can always practise on fresh-cut twigs at any time of the year. It took me several years to get proficient, and then I discovered that there is a fantastic low-technology tool called grafting pliers, which takes most of the skill out of grafting but which makes the process faster and more successful even for a proficient grafter! So now I do most of my whip-and-tongue grafting using the pliers, though I still use a knife for grafts of a very small diameter.

Flower of apple rose (*Rosa rugosa*).

Chapter 9

First design steps

Most people start with a clear site (usually grass or pasture) for their forest garden. Some, however, start with a woodland, and in this case, although the steps described in Chapter 7 are still followed, the process is obviously different in places.

Finding land

Forest gardens are being grown on everything from tiny back gardens to 5-acre fields. If you don't have a garden to convert, one low-cost option is to start a forest garden on one or more allotments. Some allotment rules discourage the planting of trees, so check them out carefully first!

Many folk want to start a rural forest garden on a field site, which necessitates buying a small piece of land. There are plenty on the market, but competition is fierce and land prices in Britain are spiralling upwards alarmingly. Small pieces of pasture can reach £5-7,000 or more per acre in some regions. You can search for land on estate agents' websites easily these days.

The financial crises in recent years have made small pieces of land even more attractive to own. If banks cannot be relied on to keep saved capital safe, then what can be? The answer is real physical earth, of course. Unfortunately this means that land prices in Britain continue to rise. Owning a piece of land is also the ultimate safety net, should things start to go awry in a Lovelockian future of runaway climate change.

FOREST OR FIELD?

Forestry land is always cheaper to buy than pasture or arable land (though it is biologically more valuable!), but starting from a forest to create a forest garden is more work than starting with a bare field site.

Land is cheaper in unpopulated hilly and highland areas (for example, in Wales and Scotland), but be aware that such areas often have poor-quality soil and growing conditions.

Land and farms are still much cheaper in France, Spain and other European countries. However, the further you get into regions with hot Mediterranean summers, the more difficult it is to grow a fully layered forest garden of the type this book is concerned with: the dry summer soil conditions cannot support the lush growth of perennials that we expect in the UK unless you irrigate.

In terms of orientation, a south-facing slope is ideal; west-facing is second best. There is more advantage to plants from a west-facing slope than an east-facing slope, because the temperatures are higher in the afternoons and so photosynthesis works better then than in the mornings. As a general rule, every degree of slope south (compared with a level site) increases your growing season by two days, and every degree of slope north decreases it by two days. So a 10° south slope gives you an extra 20 days of growing season (valuable for any late-ripening crops), whereas a 10° slope north loses you 20 days of growing season, which will make it difficult to grow even late-ripening apples.

Before you buy a piece of land, it is worth doing soil tests, even rudimentary ones. If the pH or soil type is extreme in any way (very acid, very sandy, very clay or very alkaline) it will create extra work and may be quite limiting.

Land in Britain is often sold at auctions, and in this case you need to make sure you have the money available immediately.

Finally, in our overcrowded and over-regulated island, there are planning complications with field sites. 'Gardens' (implication: ornamental gardens) are deemed a change of use from agricultural/forestry land and require planning permission. However, 'agroforestry' does not, and forest gardens are better described to officialdom as 'intensive agroforestry systems' or 'underplanted orchards'.

What are your aims?

Ask yourself: what crops do you want from the garden? Every forest garden is unique and should be designed around your individual requirements. If you don't like apples, then don't include apple trees in your design just because everybody else does! Think about when you want crops – All year round? Mainly in spring and autumn? In your design you can plan for most crops to be available when you want them.

Bear in mind that large fruit trees can give lots of fruit that needs using in a very short time. If you think that having 100kg (22lb) of fresh plums within a week or two will either be too much for you to ever eat or too much to process, then think twice about planting large standard plum trees. Having said that, fruit that is not picked off a tree will usually fall to the ground or be eaten by birds, etc.; our Western culture tends to think of this as a waste, but what is wasted? If it has taken little work to grow then little human effort has been wasted. The fruit is recycled by moulds, bacteria or animals and the goodness remains within the closed-loop forest garden system. In many other cultures where forest gardens are numerous, it is common for some fruit or other edible trees to be regarded as 'insurance' crops – hardly harvested at all in some years, when perhaps more desirable crops yield well or when there is not time to harvest, but in other years harvested avidly. Just because a plant yields a crop that does not mean we are obliged to harvest 100 per cent of it. The one drawback of not harvesting 'improved' fruits such as apples, pears and plums is that diseases can build up on mummified fruits in the tree (see page 324, Chapter 22).

Make lists of what you want, divided into trees, shrubs, herbaceous perennials, etc. You will have to work out the space required by trees in the canopy layer (see pages 147 to 150, Chapter 12), and until you do so you won't know whether you can comfortably fit in all the trees on your list. The tree layer is the one to concentrate on first, and if you are intending to underplant over a number of years then you probably won't need definitive shrub and perennial lists at the outset.

Flowering quinces (*Chaenomeles* spp.) are valuable fruiting shrubs.

In medium- or large-sized forest gardens there is usually an excess of space allowed for aromatic herbs and herbaceous perennials. This all depends, of course, on how intensively you want to utilise the lower layers, but realistically, people who want to grow a forest garden hardly want a market garden growing beneath the trees. In small gardens (under a few hundred square metres), the ground-cover layers are likely to be used more intensively, simply because of the shortage of space, which means that some planting strategies (as described on pages 94-96) may be ruled out. In larger forest gardens there tends to be plenty of space beneath the woody layers, and it may be completely appropriate to have large patches of plants such as the *Rubus* ground-covers, or aromatic herbs such as mints, which are not cropped intensively but nevertheless have important system functions such as protecting the soil and encouraging beneficial insects.

Commercial requirements necessitate specific design components. Most temperate forest gardens to date have not been commercial, with the exception of occasional heavy crops being sold. If commercial aims are important then some compromises have to be made in the design process: for example, tending and harvesting of plants needs to be more efficient, so plants of the same type may have to be put close together rather than being more scattered; the latter being more ecologically sound. As you'll find out, the design of a forest garden in fact involves a whole series of sometimes conflicting principles, and compromises have to be made along the way.

There may also be other requirements to bear in mind through the design process. Perhaps the garden is to have an educational function (or may even be at a school), in which case the issues of prickly plants and poisonous plants has to be tackled. On the latter point, I must say that in the UK we seem to have a very unfortunate culture of being afraid of plants and mushrooms unless we are informed of their safety. Very few plants can cause serious illnesses, and most that do so taste disgusting and would not voluntarily be eaten by children!

How much time and energy do you have?

The establishment of a forest garden takes time: there is no way around that, and even when it is fully established time will be needed – it will never be a do-nothing garden.

Based on my experience in my 2.1-acre forest garden in Dartington, I have tried to give estimates of the time required for the design, establishment, maintenance and harvesting from a forest garden. The actual time needed will vary, depending on the number of time-demanding crops that are grown. The estimated times (see below) are per year and per 100m² of forest garden. So for a 500m² garden, multiply by five.

Design

- It is really difficult to put a figure on how long the design takes. This is largely due to my recommendation that you keep the design 'on the go' for several months, perhaps only coming back to it for a few minutes from time to time. It probably takes at least two hours per 100m²; sometimes much more.

Establishment

- Initial windbreak or hedge planting: very variable, and of course this may not be required at all sometimes. A windbreak may take a day per 100m (330') to plant and mulch.

- Tree (and possibly shrub) planting in the first year or two: the pacing or measuring out to make sure of correct positions may take as long as the actual planting itself. Allow 1 hour per 100m² to be planted.

- Plant raising (especially herbaceous perennials) in spring: a forest garden usually requires large numbers of plants to be planted out in the perennial/ground-cover layer and, unless money is no object, you'll probably want to grow at least some of them yourself. This is a good reason for spreading out the under-planting over a number of years. Allow 2-3 days per 100m² of perennials to raise.

- For planting and mulching in autumn and winter of perennial layers, allow 2-3 days per 100m² of planting.

Maintenance and harvesting

- Maintenance time is extremely variable, depending very much on what you plant. High-maintenance plants include tender fruits, highly trained trees, self-seeding annuals and annual vegetables. Weeding will always be required from April to August, but not outside those times in my experience. Allow ¼ -1 day per 100m² over the spring and summer.

- Again, harvesting time is very variable and different in every forest garden. Allow ½ to 1+ days per 100m² over the year.

What is your budget?

For most people, the desire is to get trees planted as soon as the design is finalised. This means buying in trees of about 60-200cm (2'-6'6") height, some of which may be quite expensive (particularly varieties of fruit and nut tree, and bamboos, which all require specialised propagation). Another option would be to try to graft trees yourself, but apart from apples, which are fairly easy, you might find results of other fruits patchy, and nuts are really difficult to graft. So grafting your own trees may be a false economy and delay you for several years, although if your budget is small then you may have no option.

Some trees and shrubs – generally the more unusual fruiting trees and trees for other uses – are fairly easy to grow from seed, and a few are easy from cuttings if you can source them. Many perennials too can be grown from seed or cuttings. You'll need to organise a propagation area, growing containers, compost, watering, etc. if you are going to grow a reasonable number of your own plants.

Other initial costs include any tree protection, fencing against pests such as rabbits (which costs about £1 per metre) and mulches. Sheet mulches are an important part of most people's implementation of a forest garden, and the biodegradable hemp or similar mulches, as well as the permeable plastic kind, are not cheap – alternatives such as scrap cardboard are cheaper if you can access a free source.

Collecting information and mapping your site

Try to become aware, if you are not already, of various aspects of the site:

- the local climate
- slopes
- microclimates – frost pockets, existing shady areas and areas exposed to wind
- soil types – wet or dry areas, pH and drainage (get a soil analysis)
- any natural water supply
- any existing plants you might want to retain.

It is essential to make a large-scale map of the site. By large-scale I mean 1:100 or 1:200. A garden or small field site can be measured by pacing (find the average length of your pace by taking ten paces and measuring that, and dividing by ten). Garden and field shapes usually appear on property deeds and it is easy to get these enlarged by repeated photocopying until they are at a suitable scale. Get several copies made of your large-scale map.

On the map, mark on slopes, shady areas, exposed areas, soil variations, existing trees and hedges and so on.

These will all be useful when you are trying to place trees and other plants in the design.

Planting span and succession stages

Converting land to a forest garden can be undertaken by planting up everything in one year, or doing it over several years.

Single-year planting involves planting trees, shrubs and ground-cover layers all at once. This type of planting has a number of limitations.

- It is really suitable only for smaller areas – under about 500m².
- It usually requires weed-free bare ground ready for planting.
- It usually requires a reasonably sheltered site.
- It requires a lot of plants to be planted in a single season.

My forest garden at three years old. In the early years a forest garden is very open and sunny!

Bear in mind that in the early stages, the lower layers will be receiving lots of light – which means that shade-loving plants may not be happy!

Converting a piece of land into a forest garden by planting over a number of years is much more common. This type of implementation has a number of advantages.

- It is suitable for small and larger areas.

- It spreads the work and money needed. There isn't a fixed time span for planting a forest garden – planting could take 2 years, 10 years or longer.

- It normally involves planting hedges and/or canopy trees in the first year or two, then later shrubs and ground-cover layers.

- It does not require weed-free ground or a sheltered site to start with. Hedge plants, canopy trees and shrubs can be planted into existing pasture or grass and then mulched with a light impermeable material. The trees establish as the grasses under the mulch rot. Of course, for almost all ground-layer plants, the existing grasses will have to be killed off (e.g. by sheet-mulching) before your plants are planted. Only a few low plants – for example Chinese bramble (*Rubus tricolor*) – can outcompete grasses.

- It allows shade to develop before shade-loving plants are introduced. In a single-year planting, the initial ground layers will have to be sun-tolerant, and some may need replacing as the shade increases; this replanting may be avoided by planting later.

- However, it will require the existing ground cover (most commonly grass or pasture) to be controlled until it is replaced. This usually means mowing or strimming the existing grass, etc. between trees once a month or so during the growing season. Alternative grass control by grazing is possible only in the early stages, and then only with good tree protection. Not controlling the existing cover is not a good idea if you want to productively underplant your forest garden – uncut grasses grow long, make large clumps, seed everywhere and will be invaded by brambles within a couple of years, all of which will cause more work in clearing to underplant than mowing in the first place.

After seven years trees are having a significant impact.

If you start off with a bare field site, or a pasture that you cultivate by ploughing and harrowing, then another option is to sow a relatively long-lived green manure crop, for example lucerne (*Medicago sativa*) or white clover (*Trifolium repens*), which should persist for several years before becoming weedy. Trees and shrubs are planted into the green manure and mulched as for grass. The green manure itself should not need any maintenance for several years, and is killed off in sections to replant with ground-layer plants. If the green manure starts getting weedy or seeds too much then it will need mowing or strimming as for grass. Transitional ground-covers like these are discussed in more detail in Chapter 16 (see pages 256-260).

White clover (*Trifolium repens*) is a good long-term green manure.

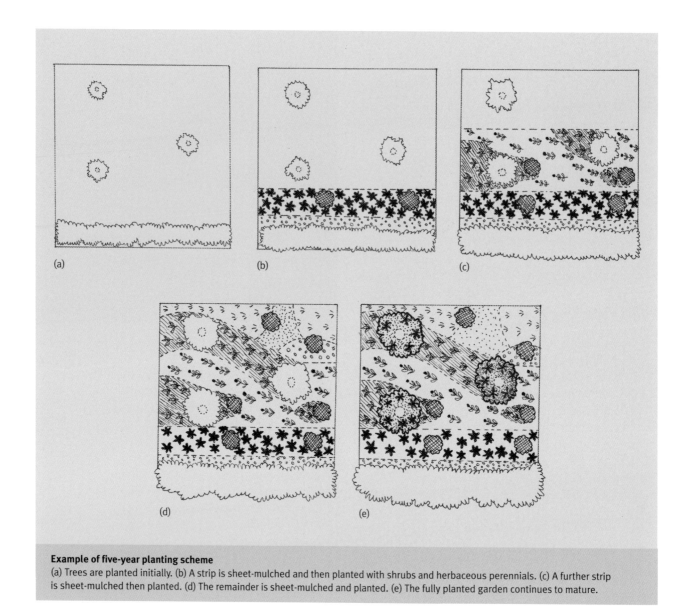

Example of five-year planting scheme
(a) Trees are planted initially. (b) A strip is sheet-mulched and then planted with shrubs and herbaceous perennials. (c) A further strip is sheet-mulched then planted. (d) The remainder is sheet-mulched and planted. (e) The fully planted garden continues to mature.

A forest garden created over several years goes through several stages, which can be likened to succession stages in a natural ecological system. For several years, while there is a good amount of light (assuming you are starting with an open field site), some of the area can be used, if desired, for annual vegetable crops, hay, green-manure crops, short-term perennial crops, a plant nursery, etc.

OVERVIEW OF THE DESIGN PROCESS

- Determine your aims, requirements, time and resources
- Collect information and map the site
- Decide on the speed of planting and succession stages
- Design windbreak/hedges and edges
- Design the canopy layer
- Design the shrub layer
- Design the perennial/ground-cover layer
- Design the annuals, biennials and climbers
- Design the nitrogen fixers
- Design clearings, living spaces and paths

Leaf of New Zealand flax (*Phormium tenax*).

Chapter 10

Designing wind protection

Shelter is beneficial in almost every kind of productive land use. Not only is the productivity of virtually any crop increased by shelter, but there are many other advantages to creating a beneficial microclimate.

You may be very lucky and already have a wonderfully sheltered site, in which case you won't need to do much in the way of extra wind protection. More likely, though, you will have one or more exposed edges to your site, and in this case it is essential that you create shelter. This will nearly always be by growing suitable plants to form a windbreak hedge.

Windbreak hedges are one type of edge and, like other edges, can be sites of high productivity, despite their exposure to wind. The plants used there are often pioneers, found naturally at woodland edges, and they frequently improve soil conditions for other trees.

For rural field sites, it is likely that all the boundaries will require windbreaks if these are not already present. In suburban gardens, the main problem areas are gaps between buildings, which act as wind tunnels.

The microclimate resulting from good wind protection means that, compared with an exposed site:

- there is a reduction in wind speed in the garden and thus less damage to flowers, fruits and leafy plants

- increases in daytime air temperatures of 2°C (3.6°F) or more are common

- there is an increase in the surface temperature of leaves, making photosynthesis more productive

- there is an increase in soil temperature of up to 3°C (5.4°F)

- evaporation of water from soil is reduced

- crop yields are raised by 10-30 per cent, depending on the crop. A windbreak hedge usually takes much less than 10 per cent of the available area, so a hedge is never wasting productive space – overall yields are increased even without taking into account any yields from the hedge itself.

Although primarily there to create a good microclimate, windbreak hedges can have other secondary uses.

- They can help accumulate minerals in leaf litter and nearby soil, especially nitrogen if nitrogen-fixing trees or shrubs are used.

- They may be a source of bee fodder. There are lots of flowering plants suitable for hedges. Early flowers such as those on willow and some *Elaeagnus* species can be particularly valuable for wild bees. However, the exposure, particularly on the outer edge, may be a problem for bees at times.

- They may be a source of edible products, usually fruits. Fruiting on the outside (exposed) edge of the windbreak may be erratic because of the exposure to wind and frost, but the inner edge should be more productive. Examples include cherry plum (*Prunus cerasifera*) and autumn olive (*Elaeagnus umbellata).*

- They can be a source of wildlife food and shelter – small birds in particular love to live in hedges, although some may prove to be a problem if they compete for fruits!

- They can provide logs and poles from coppicing or thinning. You won't want to cut too much out of your windbreaks, but they can be designed to include some coppiced trees, or fast-growing trees that are cut and removed after a while once slower-growing shrubs have grown.

- They can provide fibres for tying, e.g. New Zealand flax (*Phormium tenax*).

Principles of hedges and windbreaks

The diagram below shows the significant effect that a windbreak can have on the wind flow in a forest garden.

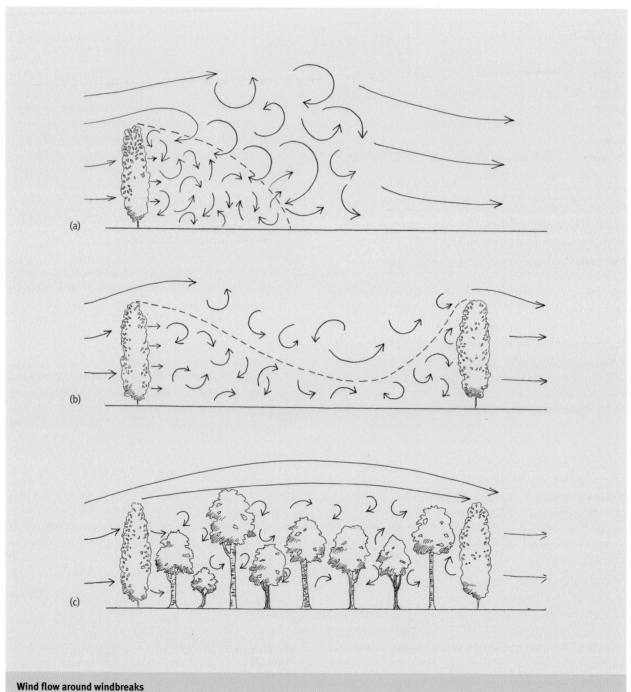

Wind flow around windbreaks
(a) The quiet zone of protection where wind hits a simple windbreak. (b) Where a second windbreak exists, the zone of protection extends. (c) In a mature forest garden most of the wind goes over the top.

Zones of protection

When wind meets a windbreak hedge, some wind filters through the hedge and the rest is deflected over the top. With low-growing plants, the area of maximum wind protection – called the quiet zone, with about a 50-per-cent wind-speed reduction – extends for seven or eight times the height of the windbreak, so if you have a 4m (13')-high windbreak, the quiet zone will be about 30m (100') long. Beyond this, up to fifteen or even twenty times the height of the windbreak, there is still some protection, but there is also turbulence – this is called the wake zone. This is likely to be the situation in the early stages of a forest garden when trees and shrubs are still small.

A second windbreak, say at the other side of the forest garden, will also lengthen the quiet zone and create its own quiet zone in front of it.

As trees in a forest garden grow, the length of the quiet zone will increase, as wind sweeps over the top surface of the canopy trees. Eventually, the whole forest garden will lie in a quiet zone, with wind protection on each side.

The main winds to worry about are the strongest prevailing winds – usually from the south-west or west in most of Britain – which are the ones that do most damage. West-facing windbreaks should be chosen to hold their leaves late into autumn to give maximum protection for fruit crops. East-facing windbreaks are most useful to protect from cold winds in spring and should be chosen to come into leaf early in spring.

Detrimental effects on other plants

Plants in a hedge are spaced close and form a dense mat of roots spreading through the soil on either side of the hedge. This results in severe root competition on the inside of the hedge (within the forest garden) for a distance of between half the height and the full height of the hedge. You may find it hard to grow other shrubs or trees here because of the root competition. One option is to use this strip for a permanent path (see page 303, Chapter 20).

There is obviously significant shading inside a windbreak placed on the southern side of a garden. There can also be a rain shadow effect, particularly if evergreens are used in the hedge, resulting in a dry, shady and root-filled area next to the hedge.

How high?

Trees or shrubs chosen for windbreaks grow fast – much faster than most crop trees within the forest garden. So a quiet zone will quickly form and aid the growth of young trees. Ideally, choose plants for the windbreaks that will grow to a height that means most of the forest garden is in a quiet zone as quickly as possible. To do this, work backwards from the dimensions of the garden, dividing by eight to arrive at a windbreak height (see examples in box).

> **EXAMPLE WINDBREAK HEIGHT CALCULATIONS**
>
> For a garden 15m (50') wide, windbreaks of 2m (6'6") high at either side would suffice. However, if most of your crop trees are larger then slightly larger windbreaks may be desirable.
>
> For a garden 80m (260') wide, windbreaks of 10m (33') high would be good, or alternatively windbreaks of 5m (16') high, with a third, intermediate, windbreak near the centre of the area.

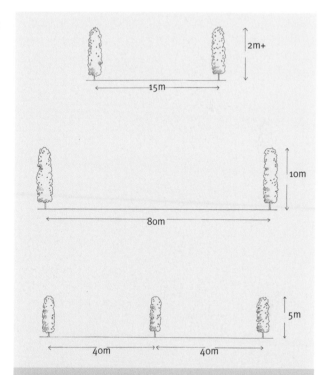

Optimum windbreak height
(a) To protect an area of 15m, a windbreak of 2m or a little more is fine. (b) For a larger area of 80m, one option is to have windbreaks 10m high; another option (c) is to have a third windbreak and all three windbreaks at 5m high – this produces less shading.

These examples assume you are on level ground. If you are not, everything gets skewed: if your land slopes towards the prevailing wind (south to west in Britain) then all the distances will be compressed and you'll need higher windbreaks to protect the same area. If your land slopes away from the prevailing wind then you'll need less-high windbreaks to protect the same area.

You can include pioneer trees in your windbreak with the explicit aim of removing them after 5 to 10 years. These trees should be fast-growing deciduous or coniferous trees (alders, pines, etc.). Their function is to create shelter fast, while lower shrubs grow beneath or beside them to form the permanent windbreak. Some may try to regrow after cutting but will probably be shaded out by the established shrubs.

How long?

Ideally, protect every side of the garden. Obviously, the entire side of a forest garden exposed to the prevailing winds should be protected as the highest priority. In Britain it is also worth protecting against cold easterly winds, which can damage early-flowering plants in spring. If you protect only the edge exposed to prevailing winds, watch out for wind barrelling into the garden from the sides as it whips around the edges of the windbreak.

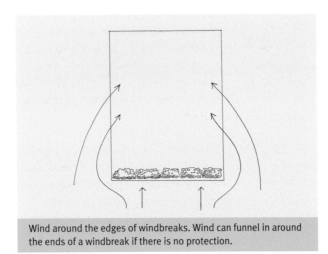

Wind around the edges of windbreaks. Wind can funnel in around the ends of a windbreak if there is no protection.

Frost pockets

A frost pocket is created when cold airflow is stopped on a slope. On a cold frosty night, cold air flows downhill, just like a liquid. When it comes to a barrier such as a hedge, it pools upslope of the hedge and a frost pocket is formed, where the frost will be more severe and lie longer in the day.

If you are creating hedges on a slope then you may also be creating frost pockets. Try to avoid this if possible by planting hedges slightly off the contour, so that the cold air, when it meets the hedge, flows alongside it; you then allow it to escape through a deliberate small gap at the end (but be careful not to create a wind tunnel effect – see below). If you have a hedge at the bottom of your site then there may be nothing you can do but to adapt to the frost pocket there.

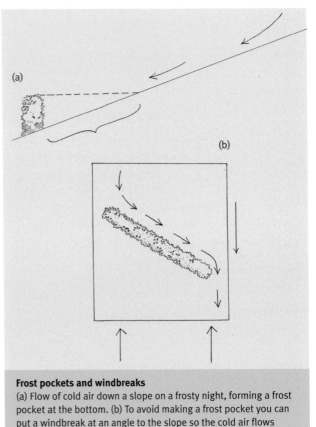

Frost pockets and windbreaks
(a) Flow of cold air down a slope on a frosty night, forming a frost pocket at the bottom. (b) To avoid making a frost pocket you can put a windbreak at an angle to the slope so the cold air flows along it and then down to the bottom of the site.

Gaps

Try to avoid gaps in windbreaks if possible, as they cause a wind tunnelling effect – the wind speed increases by 15 per cent or so through the gap and batters whatever it encounters on the inside.

Some gaps are unavoidable, for instance access gateways, etc. If you must have a gap, then try to design the windbreak to minimise the problems. An offset gap works well but is not well-suited to a boundary edge because of its shape. A windbreak baffle can be added inside the forest garden to take the brunt of the wind. Or a diagonal gap can be designed in a windbreak that is thick enough. These are illustrated in the diagram below.

(a)

(b)

(c)

Access gaps through windbreaks
(a) A baffle is used to break the wind impact. (b) A diagonal gap.
(c) An offset gap.

How dense?

The denser the windbreak, the greater the protection in the quiet zone – porous windbreaks are less effective. The old advice that porous windbreaks are best was based on 1950s research that has been superseded. But very dense windbreaks lead to more turbulence in the wake zone, so if you can design your windbreaks to ensure that the whole area needing protection is inside

a quiet zone, then dense windbreaks are fine. If for some reason you have to have windbreaks further apart, then moderately dense windbreaks are best.

Deciduous windbreaks in leaf can be just as dense as evergreens. Most crops in a forest garden need protection from spring to autumn, so deciduous plants can do the job pretty well. Ideally they should leaf out early and drop their leaves late. For example, autumn olive (*Elaeagnus umbellata*) does both and is good in all windbreaks; willows (*Salix* spp.) leaf out early but do not hold on to the leaves late, so are better in east-facing windbreaks; whereas Italian alder (*Alnus cordata*) leafs out only moderately early, but holds on to its leaves late in autumn, so is better in west-facing windbreaks.

Make sure that the hedge is dense down to the ground. A gap of up to 60cm (2') is OK, as not much wind gets through this low, but a gap higher than that leads to a wind-tunnel effect. If you are planting trees that will not stay dense down low after several years, then you can interplant with smaller shrubs when you plant the hedge or possibly at a later date – though establishment is more difficult later when the tree roots will be quite competitive.

What form?

I strongly advise you to plant windbreaks using trees or shrubs that grow to the size you want and will not require regular trimming or cutting. There is absolutely no need to trim hedges or windbreaks to keep them thick or functional if the right plants are used from the start. (The one possible exception is when you also want the windbreak hedge to be animal proof.)

The best wind protection occurs with windbreaks forming a vertical face to the wind – rounded cross-sections lead to an aerofoil effect, reducing the length of the quiet zone. A vertical face is not always possible, as most plants do not grow to form a vertical face, though some do. As the forest garden matures, the shape of the exposed windbreak is not so important, because wind will flow right over the top of the garden.

How thick?

Windbreak hedges can consist of a single row of trees or shrubs, or several rows. Which is best partly depends on how large your site is: for a smaller site, a single row is preferable to allow you the maximum area for forest garden plants. For a larger site, a multi-row hedge will give better protection.

If you do plan multi-row hedges, you'll often have a row of larger trees or shrubs, and row(s) of smaller shrubs too, to make a thick windbreak dense to the ground. In mimicking a forest edge, the smaller shrubs are often placed on the outside (exposed) edge of the windbreak and the larger trees/shrubs on the inside. In fact you get better shelter planting the smaller shrubs on the inside edge of the trees in a windbreak because this gives a more vertical profile to the wind.

Planting

In the UK and other regions with plentiful rainfall, large shrubs and small trees should be planted at 1-1.5m (3-5') apart and smaller shrubs at 0.6-1m (2-3') apart. In areas with very dry summers, spacing may need to be greater. You want the plants to grow into each other to make a dense mass.

Plant in late autumn or winter. Small plants are fine, in fact they are preferable in the exposed position a hedge is likely to be in: 0.5-1m (20-36") is ideal. They can be bare-rooted plants or container-grown, ideally in a deep-cell container that will give good stability; no staking is required. Shrubs grown in round pots may well need to be staked with bamboo canes or hazel sticks for a year or two.

It is very important to mulch the new hedge immediately. You want your plants to grow as fast as possible to give you the quickest protection, and weeds must be eliminated to achieve this. If you are planting into bare, weed-free soil, then any kind of organic mulch free of weed seeds can be used – chipped bark, etc.

You can plant windbreak plants straight into grass/pasture and use a mulch to kill off the grass at the same time as the plants establish. In this case, use an impermeable mulch: either something biodegradable such as card or thick newspapers (weighed down with branches), or a black plastic or ground-cover woven mulch. Plant through holes specifically cut for your trees or shrubs, with the aim of removing the mulch after 3-4 years. The mulch should be 1m (3') wide for each row of the new windbreak hedge. Occasional weeding should be undertaken in the first couple of years to keep the hedge reasonably weed free.

Windbreak species

An extensive list of possible windbreak species is given in Appendix 2, but my favourites are listed in the table opposite.

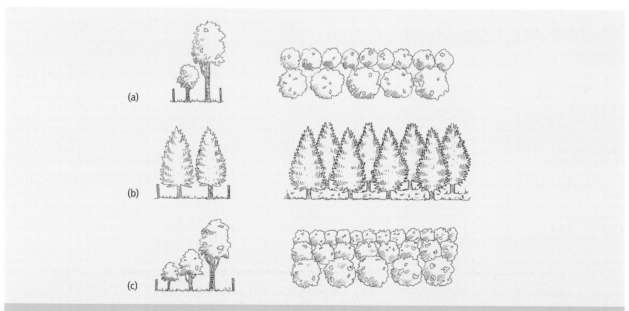

Multi-row hedge designs
(a) Using a tree and shrub together, with tree outermost. (b) Two rows of coniferous trees. (c) A three-row windbreak, with the largest tree outermost.

Making use of existing fences

Solid fences can still be used to train trees or shrubs against, although this won't affect their sheltering effect as they are already solid – but they present a beneficial micro-climate with their flat vertical face. They usually need wires attaching so that plants can be trained in a flat form.

Existing wire fences can be utilised as trellises, but they are usually too low to be of much value as a windbreak. Wire fences some 90cm (3') high can have plants such as black-berries and grape vines trained along them. Because there is a small area low down in front of a windbreak hedge (i.e. to the exposed side) that benefits from some wind protection as the wind is deflected over the windbreak, a wire fence with a windbreak planted behind can be a productive site.

WINDBREAK SPECIES			
Species		**Maximum height**	**Comments**
Alnus cordata	Italian alder	15m (50')	Very fast. Nitrogen fixer. Tolerant of drier soil than other alders.
Alnus rubra	Red alder	20m (66')	Very fast. Nitrogen fixer. Moist soil.
Alnus viridis	Green alder	4m (13')	Fast. Nitrogen fixer. Moist soil.
Berberis spp.	Barberries	2-4m (6'6"-13')	Some evergreen. Moderately fast. Fruits edible but small and liked by birds. Spiny.
Elaeagnus x *ebbingei*		3.5m (12')	Moderately fast. Evergreen. Nitrogen fixer. Edible fruits in spring; low yield.
Elaeagnus umbellata	Autumn olive	5m (16')	Fast. Nitrogen fixer. Excellent edible fruits in autumn; bears well in exposed locations.
Hippophae rhamnoides	Sea buckthorn	3m (10')	Fast. Nitrogen fixer. Very spiny; suckers can be a problem. Excellent edible fruits.
Phormium tenax	New Zealand flax	2.5m (8')	Evergreen. Good bee and fibre plant. Hardiness an issue in some places.
Pinus nigra var. *maritima*	Corsican pine	25m (80')	Evergreen. Fast.
Pinus radiata	Monterey pine	20m (66')	Evergreen. Fast.
Prunus cerasifera	Cherry plum	12m (40')	Moderately fast. Good edible fruits; low yield.
Rosa rugosa	Apple rose	1.8m (6')	Fast, suckers slowly. Good edible large hips.
Rubus tricolor	Chinese bramble	2m (6'6") – scrambles	Evergreen. Non-prickly, bears nice edible fruits. Infills under trees/shrubs well.
Salix 'Bowles Hybrid'	Willow	12m (40')	Very fast. Vertical form. Moist soil.

WIND PROTECTION IN MY GARDEN

With my forest garden in Dartington, I was lucky enough to start with great wind protection from the prevailing storm winds to the south-west and west, so I didn't need to do too much on this side of the garden. The east was very exposed, though, so I planted mainly autumn olive (*Elaeagnus umbellata*) and beefed up a section of it a few years later with 'Bowles Hybrid' willow underplanted with the vigorous Chinese bramble (*Rubus tricolor*). Within 5-6 years the new windbreak hedges were creating a significant beneficial microclimate in the forest garden and everything in the garden started growing faster.

New leaves and flowers of Californian bayberry (*Myrica californica*).

Chapter 11

Canopy species

By 'canopy species' I don't necessarily mean large trees. In a wild forest, the canopy *does* tend to be large trees, but in a forest garden the canopy may be 3m (10') high in some places, and consist of shrubs and not trees, so in this chapter I include both trees and large shrubs. Some of the same species may appear in the understorey shrub / small-tree layer, beneath larger trees.

Quince (*Cydonia oblonga*) 'Krymsk'.

Cydonia oblonga, QUINCE

Deciduous/Evergreen: D   **Zone:** 4
Sun/shade preference: ◐
Shade tolerance: ◖
Performance rating: ✓✓
Fertility: SF   **Flowers:** White

> **WILD FOODS**
>
> When I'm talking of unusual food plants there is a crossover with wild foods, of which there are many, both in the UK and elsewhere. Many wild food plants can be introduced into forest gardens and become one of the semi-wild cultivated crops there.
>
> A word about edibility and toxicity. There is no easy dividing line between 'safe edible' and 'toxic'. Many foods require processing in some way to make them safe (or even palatable) to eat. Most dried legume seeds, for example, are toxic and require soaking and/or cooking to make them safe to eat. My choice of species to include in this book has been determined by the condition that the plants used must be suitable for eating with no, or just a little, preparation. If you want to go the whole hog and use more specialised wild foods then do so – there are some great books around to help you – but be aware that the food preparation time for some wild foods is enormous.

This is not to be confused with *Chaenomeles* quinces, which are described in Chapter 13 (page 167). Long grown for its usually pear-shaped fruits, which are acid and aromatic, quince is used cooked on its own or with other fruits and sometimes made into preserves. Many older varieties are susceptible to quince leaf blight, which is worse in humid forest garden conditions and can cause defoliation and fruiting failure. Resistant varieties do well.

Rootstocks: Quince A (semi-vigorous), Quince C (semi-dwarfing). Quince C will need staking for several years.
Size: Quince A: 3-5m (10-16') high and wide. Quince C: 2.5-4m (8-13') high and 4m (13') wide.
Cultivation: Plant pot-grown or bare-rooted trees in winter. Quince A tolerates most soils, Quince C prefers

Common fruiting trees

Most people will want some of the more common fruiting trees in their forest gardens. These fruits are well known, and the trees are reliable croppers and easily available.

fertile soils. A little shade is tolerated but mostly good sun is required.

Flowering: May/June in the UK – not susceptible to spring frosts.

Fruiting: Time until fruiting begins, and maximum yields when full grown:

Quince A: 4-5 years. Annual yield 15kg (33lb).

Quince C: 3-4 years. Annual yield 15kg (33lb).

Uses: Fruits are usually eaten cooked.

Harvest and storage: Harvest in October or as fruits start to soften. They will store in a cool place for a month or two.

Cooking/processing: Best cooked with other fruits.

Secondary uses: Bee plants.

Propagation: Usually grafted. Quinces often take from cuttings too.

Maintenance: Not much pruning needed. If cropping regularly then some feeding will be required.

Cultivars: The blight-resistant varieties that I recommend are:

Krymsk

Serbian Gold

In dry regions, such as the east of the UK, some of the older varieties may succeed, for example:

Meeches Prolific

Vranja

Ficus carica, FIG

Deciduous/Evergreen: D   **Zone:** 6
Sun/shade preference: ◯
Shade tolerance: ◯
Performance rating: ✓✓
Fertility: SF   **Flowers:** n/a

Figs are likely to do increasingly well in the UK as the climate warms up, and there are numerous fantastic French varieties that may be suitable in the next few decades. Figs need warmth to harden off new growth.

Rootstocks: Grown on own roots.

Size: 3-6m (10-20') high by 2-4m (6'6"-13') wide.

Cultivation: Likes well-drained soil and sun. In the UK, unrestricted trees usually grow lush and don't fruit well; try to restrict the roots by lining a large planting hole or growing the fig in a large container, perhaps sunk into the ground. Plant bare-rooted trees in winter; pot-grown trees in winter or spring. Figs are traditionally grown as a fan against a wall.

Flowering: Late – misses late frosts.

Fruiting: Starts in 3-4 years. Annual yield 5-15kg (11-33lb).

Uses: Fruits are eaten raw or cooked.

Harvest and storage: Pick as the fruits soften and droop – sometimes spits appear in the skin or a drop of nectar is exuded from the eye. They don't store for long.

Cooking/processing: Use fresh!

Propagation: Hardwood cuttings of 1-2cm (0.4-0.8")-diameter shoots.

Maintenance: Summer pruning to restrict new shoot growth to 4-5 leaves. Remove any fruits in autumn that are larger than pea size, as they won't overwinter.

Cultivars:

Brown Turkey

Brunswick

White Marseilles

Apple (*Malus domestica*) in flower.

Malus domestica, APPLE

Deciduous/Evergreen: D   **Zone:** 3
Sun/shade preference: ◯
Shade tolerance: ◑
Performance rating: ✓✓✓
Fertility: SF–SS   **Flowers:** White, pink

Most folk will want to grow apples in their forest garden, and they are pretty easy and straightforward. Apples are usually grafted on to specific rootstocks, both to control their size and to give resistance against pests and diseases of the roots. The dwarf rootstocks make bushy shrubs instead of trees and are discussed in Chapter 13, Shrub species.

One option for heavily cropping large fruiting trees, such as large apples or plums on vigorous rootstocks, is to graft several varieties on to a single vigorous rootstock. This gives you the advantages of a larger tree but you can spread the cropping season by using varieties that ripen at different times. If you think that dealing with 100kg (220lb) of fruit all at once might be too much for you, then this is worth considering. You'll probably have to graft such a tree yourself (see 'grafting' in Chapter 8, page 83), as they are not often grown by nurseries.

Malus domestica is a hybrid of several other apple species, selected over thousands of years.

Rootstocks: In the UK, M25 (vigorous), MM111 (vigorous), MM106 (semi-vigorous) and M26 (semi-dwarf – this requires staking for several years). Many others are used in other parts of the world. Occasionally trees are grown on their own roots. Most people don't want to be up high ladders picking apples, so MM106 and M26 are the most popular rootstocks. However, for juice and cider apples, which can be collected from the ground, the larger rootstocks may be entirely appropriate.

Size: Own root, M25 and MM111: 6-8m (20-26') high by 6m (20') wide.

MM106: 4-5m (13-16') high and wide.

M26: 2.5-4m (8-13') high by 3.5m (12') wide.

Cultivation: The main rootstocks have been bred to be tolerant of most garden conditions. MM111 and MM106 are particularly tolerant of heavy clay soils, which become quite wet in winter. M26 has fairly shallow roots and doesn't like as much competition as the other rootstocks described. Plant pot-grown or bare-rooted trees in winter.

Late-ripening dessert varieties need the best locations, with maximum sun. Early-ripening desserts still need plenty of sun (the sugars in dessert apples require lots of energy to manufacture). Cooking apples don't need so much sun and can tolerate partial shade quite happily.

Flowering: Between early April and mid-May in the UK. Not too frost-susceptible.

Fertility: Most varieties are not self-fertile, so at least two varieties that flower at a similar time are usually required. Apples are usually divided into flowering groups to make this easier.

Fruiting: Time until fruiting begins, and maximum yields when full grown:

Own root, M25, MM111: 7-10 years (can be reduced by intensive tying down of branches). Annual yield 45-180kg (100-400lb).

MM106: 3-4 years. Annual yield 35-70kg (77-155lb).

M26: 2-4 years. Annual yield: 25-55kg (55-120lb).

Uses: Fruits are eaten raw or cooked.

Harvest and storage: Harvest when ripe. Store in a cool place.

Cooking/processing: Apples are good in chutneys and dried as apple rings.

Secondary uses: Good bee plants.

Propagation: Usually by grafting.

Diseases: In a humid climate like the UK's, diseases such as apple scab and canker can be very damaging. Mildew and fireblight are also serious diseases. This makes variety choice really important, as there are plenty available that have disease resistance.

Maintenance: With most varieties, pruning is normally undertaken every year (or at least every 2-3 years) to maintain a supply of new wood and thus fruiting. Tip bearers (which bear their fruit at the tips of branches rather than on short spurs along recent growth) do not require annual pruning but will often yield less. If you don't prune (apart from taking out dead or diseased branches), then the overall yield will stay about the same but the fruit size will decrease over time.

Apples are heavy-cropping trees and require feeding to sustain cropping. Pay attention to nitrogen and potassium in particular and try to grow nitrogen fixers and potassium accumulators (e.g. comfreys, *Symphytum* spp.) nearby (see Chapter 6).

Try to encourage moth predators such as bats (by putting up bat boxes) to reduce damage from codling moth.

Cultivars: There are thousands of apple varieties, and sometimes the choice can seem overwhelming. Try to narrow the choice down for yourself by thinking of:
- when you want the apples to ripen
- compatible flowering times
- disease-resistant varieties
- local varieties, as well as varieties from regions up to 200km south, and knowledge of varieties that do well nearby. Bear in mind that climate change may make traditional local varieties less suitable within a couple of decades (see Chapter 3).

Nursery catalogues give some information; if you need more, refer to the *Directory of Apple Cultivars* (see Resources section).

Recommended apple varieties

Of the many possible varieties, I have grown most of the following, which are of good quality and disease-resistant.

Late-summer apples – ripening July/ August
Beauty of Bath
Devonshire Quarrenden
Discovery
Gladstone
Laxton's Epicure

Early-autumn apples – ripening September
Ellison's Orange
James Grieve
Katy
Peasgood Nonsuch
Pinova
Saturn
Scrumptious
Worcester Pearmain

Late-autumn apples – ripening October, keeping until November/ December
American Mother
Charles Ross
Egremont Russet
Jupiter
Pineapple Russet of Devon
Ross Nonpareil
Sunset
Taunton Cross
Woolbrook Pippin

Midwinter apples – ripening November, keeping until January/ February
Blenheim Orange
Cheddar Cross
Chivers Delight
Cornish Aromatic
Fiesta

Lucombe's Pine
Pitmaston Pineapple

New Year apples – ripening December/ January, keeping until February/March
Ashmead's Kernel
London Pippin
Rosemary Russet

Spring apples – keeping until March–June
Brownlees Russet
Red Belle de Boskoop
Sanspareil
Winston

Summer and autumn cooking apples
Emneth Early
Grenadier
Keswick Codlin
Lord Derby
Rev W Wilks

Late-keeping cooking apples
Annie Elizabeth
Bramley's Seedling
Crawley Beauty
Howgate Wonder
Lane's Prince Albert
Newton Wonder
Ponsford

Cider apples
Brown's Apple (sharp)
Chisel Jersey (bittersweet)
Dabinette (bittersweet)
Tommy Knight (sweet)
Tremlett's Bitter (bittersweet)
Yarlington Mill (bittersweet)

Juice apples
Sweet:
Halstow Natural
Johnny Andrews
Worcester Pearmain

Medium sharp:
Ashmead's Kernel
Charles Ross
Court of Wick
Crimson King
Devonshire Quarrenden
Egremont Russet
Ellison's Orange
Fiesta
Forge
Golden Harvey
Golden Pippin
Greensleeves
Isle of Wight Pippin
James Grieve
Katy
Lord Lambourne
Lucombe's Pine
Red Belle de Boskoop
Red Falstaff
Rosemary Russet
Sidney Strake

Full sharp:
Bramley's Seedling
Brown's Apple
Golden Noble
Howgate Wonder
Lane's Prince Albert
Lord of the Isles
Newton Wonder
Ponsford
Tom Putt

Medlar (*Mespilus germanica*) 'Royal'.

Mespilus germanica, MEDLAR

Deciduous/Evergreen: D Zone: 6
Sun/shade preference: ◐
Shade tolerance: ◑
Performance rating: ✓✓✓
Fertility: SF Flowers: White

Medlars are wonderful fruits. They were much grown in medieval times in Britain but are fairly rare these days. Perhaps they fell out of favour because you need to spit out the seeds when eating the fresh fruits – no longer considered 'polite' behaviour! I like them fresh – spitting and all – and make a nice jam out of them. The flavour is somewhere between date and baked apple.

Rootstocks: Hawthorn (*Crataegus monogyna*) (semi-vigorous), Quince A (semi-vigorous), Quince C (semi-vigorous).
Size: Hawthorn rootstock: 4-6m (13-20') high and 3-5m (10-16') wide. Smaller on Quince (see pears, *Pyrus* spp., page 115).
Cultivation: Plant bare-rooted trees in winter. I prefer trees on hawthorn rootstock, because hawthorn will grow anywhere – wet, dry, acid or alkaline soils. Medlar tolerates a lot of shade and needs only a little sun to fruit, though full sun gives bigger yields.
Flowering: May – late enough to miss frost damage.
Fruiting: Starts in 2-3 years. Annual yield 10-20kg (22-44lb).
Uses: The fruits are eaten raw or processed.
Harvest and storage: In hot summers, medlars can now soften and ripen on the tree – check for softness and a darkening of the skin colour. Otherwise pick at the first frosts and store inside in a cool place; they will ripen in a week or two. Once ripe they need using in a few days.
Cooking/processing: They are lovely fresh (the pips need

spitting out); otherwise they make a great jam or can be mixed with other fruits to make a leather (see page 324, Chapter 22).
Secondary uses: Bee plants.
Propagation: Grafted.
Maintenance: Very little to do. Does not need regular pruning. No pests or diseases.
Cultivars: I have found little difference in flavour between varieties, but the fruit size does vary, as does the tree shape. The following are the most common cultivars in the UK.
Large Russian: weeping tree. Fruit 4cm (1.6") across.
Nottingham: bushy, weeping tree. Fruit 3cm (1.2") across.
Royal: open tree. Fruit 4cm (1.6") across.

Prunus armeniaca, APRICOT

Deciduous/Evergreen: D Zone: 5
Sun/shade preference: ○
Shade tolerance: ○
Performance rating: ✓✓
Fertility: SF Flowers: White

Apricots have a reputation for being tricky to grow in the UK; this was largely true until new varieties started being introduced a few years ago. These newer types are more resistant to bacterial canker, which can be a serious disease in humid climates. As the climate warms up, apricots will become easier still to grow. Late frosts can wipe out a crop, so they are more reliable against walls.

Rootstocks: In the UK, St Julien A and Torinel (both semi-vigorous). Others are used in other parts of the world.
Size: 4m (13') high and wide.
Cultivation: Plant bare-rooted trees in winter. Give shelter, full sun and a site as free of frosts in spring as possible. Good air circulation reduces disease risks.
Flowering: Early – February/March. Susceptible to frost damage, though the newer varieties are less so.
Fruiting: Starts in 4-5 years. Annual yield: fans 5-14kg (11-31lb), trees 14-55kg (31-120lb).
Uses: Fruits are usually eaten raw.
Harvest and storage: Harvest when they soften. They won't store for long.
Cooking/processing: Ideally use fresh. Otherwise make jam or dry them after halving and de-stoning.
Secondary uses: Bee plants. In a few varieties the kernels are sweet and edible (like sweet almonds), but most are poisonous.

Propagation: Grafting.

Maintenance: Does not require regular pruning. Cut out any diseased or dying wood between May and September to reduce the risk of introducing disease.

Cultivars: The newer varieties I recommend are:

Flavorcot
Goldcot
Hargrand
Harogem
Tomcot

'Early Moorpark' and 'Moorpark' are not recommended for forest gardens unless they are grown against a wall.

Prunus avium, SWEET CHERRY

Deciduous/Evergreen: D **Zone:** 3
Sun/shade preference: ○
Shade tolerance: ◐
Performance rating: ✓✓✓
Fertility: SF–SS **Flowers:** White

Sweet cherries have long been grown in the UK but have been on the decline for decades because the large trees traditionally grown require slow hand picking, and because of bird predation problems. They are not difficult trees to grow, but you are unlikely to get much fruit unless you net them, which is fairly impractical for trees on Colt rootstock. Luckily, a recent dwarf rootstock gives much smaller trees (almost too small to be considered canopy trees), which can be netted more easily.

Rootstocks: Colt (semi-vigorous), Gisela (dwarf). Gisela requires good staking.
Size: Colt: 8-10m (26-33') high by 6m (20') wide.
Gisela: 2.5-3m (8-10') high by 2m (6'6") wide.
Cultivation: Plant bare-rooted trees in winter away from frost pockets. Prefers a well-drained soil. Tolerates some shade. Gisela needs a fertile soil.
Flowering: April – somewhat susceptible to late-spring frosts.
Fertility: Many varieties are not self-fertile, but some of the recent ones are.
Fruiting: Colt: 3-4 years. Annual yield: fans 5-14kg (11-31lb), standards/bushes 15-55kg (33-120lb).
Gisela: 2-3 years. Annual yield 10-20kg (22-44lb).
Uses: Fruits are usually eaten raw.
Harvest and storage: Harvest when the fruits colour and soften. They don't store for long.

Cooking/processing: Use fresh!

Secondary uses: Bee plant. The same species, *Prunus avium*, is used as a fast-growing forestry tree, but forestry selections do not fruit well.

Propagation: Grafting.

Maintenance: Does not require regular pruning. Cut out any diseased or dying wood between May and September to reduce the risk of introducing disease.

Cultivars: To reduce bird predation, one option is to use cherries that do not ripen red – there are some that ripen almost white, some yellow and some black, and these are less likely to be attacked. Choose varieties that are resistant to canker and fruit splitting, which is more likely in the humid conditions of a forest garden. Many of the recent varieties – mostly from Canada – have been bred with this in mind.

Sweet cherry cultivars I recommend are:

Black Oliver   Summer Sun
Celeste   Sunburst
Lapins   Sylvia
Penny   Vega
Stella

Prunus cerasus, SOUR CHERRY

Deciduous/Evergreen: D **Zone:** 3
Sun/shade preference: ○
Shade tolerance: ◐
Performance rating: ✓✓✓
Fertility: SF **Flowers:** White

Sour cherries, like sweet ones, need protection from birds, but they are hardier trees and can tolerate more demanding conditions than sweet cherries, in particular more shade.

Rootstocks: Colt (semi-vigorous), Gisela (dwarf). Gisela requires good staking.
Size: Colt: 3.5m (12') high and wide.
Gisela: 2m (6'6") high by 1.5m (5') wide.
Cultivation: Plant bare-rooted trees in winter in any reasonable soil. Tolerates a lot of shade – can even be grown on north walls with no sun at all.
Flowering: Later than sweet cherry – less susceptible to late spring frosts.
Fruiting: Colt: 3-4 years. Annual yield: fans 5-9kg (11-20lb), standards/bushes 13-18kg (29-40lb).
Gisela: 2-3 years. Annual yield 3-8kg (7-18lb).

Uses: Fruits are usually eaten cooked.

Harvest and storage: Pick fruits when they colour and soften – can be picked just as they are starting to ripen if you need to beat the birds to the fruit. They are hardier and easier to grow than sweet cherry, but don't store for long.

Cooking/processing: Use cooked.

Secondary uses: Bee plant.

Propagation: Grafting.

Maintenance: Does not require regular pruning. Cut out any diseased or dying wood between May and September to reduce the risk of introducing disease.

Cultivars:

Morello

Prunus domestica & *P. insititia*,
PLUMS (INCLUDING **GAGES**,
BULLACES AND **DAMSONS**)

....

Deciduous/Evergreen: D   Zone: 5
Sun/shade preference: ◐
Shade tolerance: ◖
Performance rating: ✓✓✓✓
Fertility: SF–SS   Flowers: White

Plums are often on the list of desirable forest-garden trees. Like apples, they are grown on specific rootstocks, although there aren't currently any really dwarfing stocks for plums. Also like apples, several varieties of plum can be grown on a single rootstock, which can make sense if large crops of fruits that won't store fresh for long are going to be a problem for you.

Whereas true plums and gages are placed in *Prunus domestica*, bullaces and damsons are placed in *Prunus insititia* (sometimes as a subspecies of *P. domestica*). Whatever the genetics, these plum-like fruits grow on trees that tend to be shrubbier than plums: sometimes thorny, and more tolerant of wetter climates, they are hardier and thriftier than plums. Bullaces and damsons have long been naturalised in British hedgerows. Bullaces tend to have quite small fruits, about half the length of a plum, and are not always very sweet, though they sweeten after a frost. Damson fruits are between bullaces and plums in size.

Rootstocks: In the UK, Myrobalan (vigorous), St Julien A

(semi-vigorous), Pixy (semi-dwarf). Pixy requires staking for several years. Others are used in other parts of the world.

Size: Myrobalan: 6-7m (20-23') high and wide.
St Julien A: 3.5-4.5m (12-15') high and wide.
Pixy: 2.7-3.5m (9-12') high and wide.

Cultivation: The main rootstocks have been bred to be tolerant of most garden conditions. Myrobalan is tolerant of wet and alkaline soils; St Julien is tolerant of dry soils. Late-ripening dessert varieties need the best locations, with maximum sun. Early-ripening desserts still need plenty of sun. Cooking plums do not need so much sun and can tolerate partial shade. Plant bare-rooted trees in winter away from frost pockets.

Flowering: April in the UK. Susceptible to late-frost damage.

Fertility: Many varieties are not self-fertile, so at least two varieties that flower at a similar time are usually required. Plums are usually divided into flowering groups to make this easier.

Fruiting: Time until fruiting begins, and maximum yields when full grown:
Myrobalan: 5-6 years. Annual yield about 65kg (143lb).
St Julien: 3-5 years. Annual yield 40-50kg (88-110lb).
Pixy: 2-3 years. Annual yield 15-30kg (33-66lb).

Uses: Fruits are eaten raw, cooked or processed.

Harvest and storage: Harvest when soft and ripe. Process quickly, as they will not store for long.

Cooking/processing: Plums dry well after halving and de-stoning. They can also be bottled. If you can't process them all at once you can freeze them and use later.

Secondary uses: Good bee plants.

Propagation: Usually grafted.

Maintenance: Plums are tip bearers, bearing their fruit at the tips of branches, and as such do not require annual pruning to sustain cropping. Of course, dead or diseased branches should be cut out. Any pruning should be undertaken between May and October to minimise the risk of silverleaf infection.

Plums are heavy-cropping trees and require feeding to sustain cropping. Pay attention to nitrogen and potassium in particular and try to grow nitrogen fixers and potassium accumulators nearby (see Chapter 6). Try to encourage moth predators such as bats to reduce damage from moths.

Cultivars: It is important to choose varieties that are resistant to bacterial canker, which can be a debilitating disease in humid climates like the UK's.
As for apples, try to narrow the choice down for yourself by thinking of:
• when you want the plums to ripen
• compatible flowering times

- disease-resistant varieties
- local varieties and knowledge of varieties that do well nearby.

Recommended plum varieties

The following are good-quality, disease-resistant plums for UK conditions. Most bullaces, damsons and mirabelles are also disease-resistant.

Early-summer plums – ripening July/August
Czar (also cooked)
Denniston's Superb
Jubilee
Mirabelle de Nancy
Opal
Oullins Golden Gage
Purple Pershore (also cooked)
Warwickshire Drooper
Yellow Egg (also cooked)

Late-summer plums – ripening August/September
Farleigh Damson
Jefferson
Manaccan
Shropshire Prune (used cooked)

Autumn plums – ripening September/October
Langley Bullace
Marjorie's Seedling
Merryweather Damson (also cooked)
Shepherd's Bullace (used cooked)

Prunus persica, PEACH & NECTARINE

Deciduous/Evergreen: D   Zone: 4
Sun/shade preference: ◯
Shade tolerance: ◯
Performance rating: ✓✓
Fertility: SF   Flowers: Pink

In the UK, peaches and nectarines have a reputation of being difficult to grow unless you fan-train them against a wall and protect them from rain in the spring. This is because peach leaf curl can be a devastating disease in humid climates, causing defoliation and poor fruiting.

As the climate warms up, peaches should become easier to grow in time. Nectarines, which are even more susceptible to leaf curl than peaches, should be attempted only against walls in the UK. Having said that, there are some good peach varieties that are fairly resistant to leaf curl and I think it is worth growing these even if you get poor yields in a wet season. With these varieties, management and coexistence with the disease is possible.

Rootstocks: St Julien A is the most-often used in the UK.
Size: 3-5m (10-16') high and wide.
Cultivation: Plant bare-rooted trees in winter. Needs a warm, sunny, sheltered position.
Flowering: Early – susceptible to late-frost damage.
Uses: Fruits are eaten, usually raw.
Harvest and storage: Pick fruits when they soften. They don't store for long.
Cooking/processing: Use fresh.
Fruiting: Starts in 2-3 years. Annually, trees yield 13-36kg (29-79lb); fans 9-14kg (20-31lb).
Secondary uses: Bee plants.
Propagation: Grafting.
Maintenance: Fan-trained trees obviously need regular summer pruning. Diseased or dying wood should be cut out in summer.
Cultivars: Choose only those with fair resistance to peach leaf curl:

Avalon Pride	Redwing
Dixired	Robin Redbreast
Hylands	Rochester
Redhaven	

Prunus salicina, JAPANESE PLUM

Deciduous/Evergreen: D   Zone: 3
Sun/shade preference: ◐
Shade tolerance: ◑
Performance rating: ✓✓✓
Fertility: SS–SF   Flowers: White

Japanese plums are more compact trees and more resistant to diseases than the European plum (*P. domestica*), but they flower early and this is their main drawback in the UK. They also need plenty of summer heat to ripen their wood. However, as the climate warms they are likely to do increasingly well in UK conditions.

Japanese plum fruits are usually larger than European plums, 3-5cm (1.2-2") across and heart-shaped. The flavour of fully tree-ripened fruits is excellent; far superior to the imported fruit, which is picked unripe.

Rootstocks: St Julien A is the most often used in the UK.
Size: 3-5m (10-16") high and wide.
Cultivation: Plant bare-rooted trees in winter. Needs a warm, sunny, sheltered position away from frost pockets.
Flowering: Early – susceptible to late-frost damage. Most cultivars must be cross-pollinated by another Japanese plum.
Uses: Fruits are eaten, usually raw.
Harvest and storage: Pick fruits when they soften. They don't store for long.
Cooking/processing: Use fresh.
Fruiting: Starts in 3-4 years. Annually, trees yield 15-40kg (33-88lb).
Secondary uses: Bee plant.
Propagation: Grafting.
Maintenance: Diseased or dying wood should be cut out in summer.
Cultivars:
Beauty: Early August. Bright red fruit with amber-streaked flesh, richly flavoured.
Methley: July. Reddish-purple fruit that ripen over a period of about two weeks; good flavour. Self-fertile.
Satsuma: Mid-August. Fruit small-to-medium, with dark red skin and red flesh; sweet and juicy. Partially self-fertile.
Shiro: Mid-August. Fruit large and yellow, with translucent juicy flesh of excellent sweet flavour. Self-fertile.

European pear (*Pyrus communis*) 'Nouveau Poiteau'.

Pyrus communis, P. pyrifolia & *P. ussuriensis,* PEARS

Deciduous/Evergreen: D   Zone: 4
Sun/shade preference: ○
Shade tolerance: ◑
Performance rating: ✓✓✓
Fertility: SS–SF   Flowers: White

Pears are slightly more fussy than apples or plums in their requirements; they really do need lots of sun and will sulk if they don't get it. However, there are lots of good varieties that do well in UK conditions, and with the warming climate their productivity in the UK should increase over the next few decades.

Asian pears derive from two Asiatic *Pyrus* species, *P. pyrifolia* and *P. ussuriensis*, and bear fruit of a completely different character from European *P. communis* pears. Asian pear fruits are usually round (apple-shaped) and are eaten fresh, when they have a crunchy texture and perfumed aroma.

Perry pears are normally grown on pear rootstock so become huge trees in time, though they can be grown on quince rootstocks too. The fruits of perry pears are astringent so they are not nice to eat raw! Perry is the pear version of apple cider, and the pears are harvested from the ground in the same way as most cider apples.

Rootstocks: Pear (*Pyrus communis*) (very vigorous), Pyrodwarf (semi-vigorous), Quince A (semi-vigorous), Quince C (semi-dwarf). Quince C will need staking for several years. Other rootstocks are used in other parts of the world.
Size: Pear: 8-20m (26-66') high and 8m (26') wide.
Pyrodwarf: 4-6m (13-20') high and wide.

Quince A: 3-5m (10-16') high and 4.5m (15') wide.
Quince C: 2.5-4m (8-13') high and 4m (13') wide.
Cultivation: Plant bare-rooted trees in winter. The main rootstocks have been bred to be tolerant of most garden conditions, and pear rootstock tolerates poor infertile soils. Quince C rootstock prefers fertile soils.

All pear trees need as much sun as possible, so take special care designing the canopy to their south and west in a forest garden.
Flowering: Usually April in the UK – susceptible to late-frost damage.
Fertility: Most varieties are not self-fertile, so at least two varieties that flower at a similar time are usually required. Pears are usually divided into flowering groups to make this easier.
Fruiting: Time until fruiting begins, and maximum yields when full grown:
Pear: 10+ years. Annual yield 35-100kg (77-220lb).
Quince A: 4-5 years. Annual yield 15-45kg (33-100lb).
Quince C: 3-4 years. Annual yield 15-45kg (33-100lb).
Uses: The fruits are eaten raw or cooked.
Harvest and storage: Harvest summer pears as they soften and change colour. Harvest late pears in October. Store in a cool place and check frequently for ripening.

Cooking/processing: Pears dry well (quarter and de-core), and this is the best way of using up a glut.
Secondary uses: Good bee plants.
Propagation: Usually grafted.
Maintenance: With most varieties, pruning is normally undertaken every year (or at least every 2-3 years) to maintain a supply of new wood and thus fruiting. Pears are not as heavy cropping as apples and plums; nevertheless if they are cropping well they will require feeding to sustain cropping. Pay attention to nitrogen and potassium in particular and try to grow nitrogen-fixers and potassium accumulators nearby (see Chapter 6).
Cultivars: It is preferable to choose varieties that are resistant to canker and pear scab. Fireblight is likely to become a bigger problem in the UK as the climate warms up, so resistance to this disease will become more important.
As for apples, try to narrow the choice down by thinking of:
* when you want the pears to ripen
* compatible flowering times
* disease-resistant varieties
* local varieties / varieties from up to 200km south
* knowledge of varieties that do well nearby.

Recommended pear varieties

Diseases are not so prevalent on pears, but many varieties have tender flowers that are easily frost-damaged. The following varieties are good in UK conditions.

Summer pears – ripening July/August
Beurre Giffard
Jargonelle

Early-autumn pears – ripening September/October
Dr Jules Guyot
Hessle
Improved Fertility
Invincible
Merton Pride
Onward
Williams

Late-autumn pears – ripening October/November
Beurre Hardy
Conference

Cromwell
Louise Bonne of Jersey
Nouveau Poiteau

Winter pears – ripening November/February
Beurre Dumont
Glou Morceau
Winter Nelis

Cooking pears
Catillac
Kieffer

Asian pears
Chojuro
Shinko

Perry pears
Gin
Thorn

Less common fruiting trees

There are some fantastic lesser-known trees with great edible fruits. Some you may well have seen in ornamental gardens, where their fruits are admired but never eaten!

Juneberry (*Amelanchier lamarckii*) 'Ballerina'.

Amelanchier spp., JUNEBERRIES / SERVICEBERRIES

Deciduous/Evergreen: D   **Zone:** 4
Sun/shade preference: ◯
Shade tolerance: ◗
Performance rating: ✓✓✓
Fertility: SF   **Flowers:** White

Species include *Amelanchier canadensis*, *A. lamarckii*, *A. laevis* and *A. lamarckii* 'Ballerina'. The larger juneberries are perhaps not as useful as the shrubby saskatoon (*A. alnifolia*, described in Chapter 13, page 165) but may still deserve a place in the forest garden. They are members of the Rosaceae from North America, where they grow in woods and thickets.

Size: 5-6m (16-20') high by 3-4m (10-13') wide.
Cultivation: Plant pot-grown trees in winter or spring. Unfussy as to soil; tolerate part shade.
Flowering: Late April and early May in the UK.
Fruiting: Starts in 2-3 years. Fruits ripen early July in the UK and are currant-sized, purplish-black and sweet, with a flavour like a sweet blackcurrant.
Uses: Fruits are edible, usually eaten raw.
Harvest and storage: Harvest when the fruits soften. A harvesting comb (berry picker) is good. The fruits are much loved by birds.

Cooking/processing: Make into a jam or fruit leather.
Secondary uses: Bee plants; flowers are ornamental in spring. Good in hedges.
Propagation: By seed (stratify for 3 months) or grafting.
Maintenance: Little required.
Cultivars: 'Ballerina' is a known good flowering and fruiting large shrub.

Arbutus unedo, STRAWBERRY TREE

Deciduous/Evergreen: E   **Zone:** 7
Sun/shade preference: ◯
Shade tolerance: ◗
Performance rating: ✓✓
Fertility: SF   **Flowers:** White

This is a large, dense, evergreen shrub from the Mediterranean region, where the fruits are often eaten raw and used to make a wine and liqueur.

Size: 6-8m (20-26') high and wide in time, though slow-growing.
Cultivation: Plant pot-grown trees in winter or spring in acid or neutral soil. Tolerates part shade.
Flowering: Flowering takes place in October and November, at the same time as the fruits from the previous flowering ripen.
Fruiting: Starts after 2-4 years. Fruits are round, 2cm (0.8"), red, and have a nice delicate taste when fully ripe; they have stone cells like pears, which are not edible before ripeness. They can be made into wine.
Uses: Fruits are eaten fresh or processed.
Harvest and storage: Pick fruits when they soften and turn reddish. Birds may take some fruits. They don't store for long.
Cooking/processing: Can be made into wine and liqueurs.
Secondary uses: Very good bumble-bee plant. Bark used for tanning.
Propagation: Seed or hardwood cuttings.
Maintenance: Little needed. The dense bushy growth can make underplanting difficult, but the canopy can be raised by pruning off lower branches.
Cultivars: 'Rubra' is a good fruiting form but with slightly smaller fruits than the species.

Asimina triloba, PAWPAW

Deciduous/Evergreen: D   Zone: 5
Sun/shade preference: ◐
Shade tolerance: ◖
Performance rating: ✓✓✓
Fertility: SS   Flowers: Maroon

Not to be confused with the tropical pawpaw, the American pawpaw is a hardy deciduous large shrub valued in North America for its large flavourful fruit. In its native habitat in south-eastern USA it is an understorey shrub, but in the UK it needs good light. It is pollinated by flies, and should become more reliable in the UK as the climate warms.

Size: 6m (20') high and wide, though slow-growing.
Cultivation: Plant pot-grown trees with care in winter or spring – dislikes being transplanted. Likes similar conditions to grapes – sun, shelter and acid-to-neutral soil. Tolerates shade but needs sun in the UK.
Flowering: May/June in the UK.
Fruiting: Named varieties start after a few years.
Uses: Fruits are eaten, usually raw.
Harvest and storage: Pick when fruits soften. They don't store well.
Cooking/processing: Eat fresh, or scoop out the pulp and freeze.
Secondary uses: The seeds, leaves and bark are insecticidal and their extracts are being investigated as anti-cancer medicines.
Propagation: By seed (stratify for 3 months, slow to germinate) or grafting on to seedling rootstock. Seedlings from known mothers are likely to have good potential as there has been no real breeding of this species.
Maintenance: Little required.
Cultivars: American varieties that are early ripening include:
Davis
NC-1
Pennsylvania Golden
Prolific
Sunflower
Taylor

Bentham's cornel (*Cornus capitata*).

Cornus spp., DOGWOODS

Deciduous/Evergreen: D   Zone: 5/7
Sun/shade preference: ○
Shade tolerance: ◖
Performance rating: ✓✓✓
Fertility: SF   Flowers: [*C. mas*] Yellow
[*C. capitata* /*C. kousa*] Cream

Dogwood species include *Cornus capitata* (Bentham's cornel), *C. kousa* (Chinese dogwood) and *C. mas* (Cornelian cherry). Their native habitat is woodland and scrub.

Some of the larger dogwoods have excellent edible fruits. These include the fairly well-known Cornelian cherry, and the Chinese dogwood often seen in ornamental gardens on account of its huge showy flowers. *C. capitata* is semi-evergreen and hardy to zone 7. *C. mas* crops better with cross-pollination.

Size: 4-6m (13-20') high by 3-5m (10-16') wide.
Cultivation: Plant in winter (bare-rooted) or spring (pot-grown). Unfussy as to soil; tolerate some shade. *C. mas* fruits better in a sheltered site.
Flowering: *C. mas* flowers very early, in February; the others flower in early summer.
Fruiting: Starts after a few years.
C. capitata: Ripens late autumn. Fruit is round, knobbly, red and 3-4.5cm (1.2-1.8") across. The pulp has a banana-like flavour; the skin is rather bitter.
C. kousa: Ripens fairly late autumn. Fruit is round, knobbly and red, 2-3cm (about 1") across. The fruit has an excellent tropical flavour; the skins are rather bitter.

C. mas: Ripens mid-to-late summer. Fruits are like small cherries, red and astringent before fully ripe, with good flavour.

Uses: Fruits are eaten raw or cooked.

Harvest and storage: Pick *C. mas* fruits when they start to soften and are still astringent – the astringency goes when cooked or dried. *C. kousa* and *C. capitata* fruits should be left as long as possible so the fruits are really soft. Neither store for long.

Cooking/processing: *C. mas* makes a nice jam or fruit leather – lightly cook the fruits and put through a Moulinex sieve to get a pulp first. *C. kousa* and *C. capitata* fruits are best eaten fresh.

Secondary uses: Ornamentals.

Propagation: Mostly by seed – needs stratification. Propagate *C. mas* varieties by grafting.

Maintenance: Little required.

Cultivars: *C. kousa* var. *chinensis* has larger fruits and crops more heavily than the species. 'Big Apple' is a variety with very large fruits selected in North America. Good fruiting varieties of *C. mas* include 'Elegant', 'Gourmet' and 'Jolico'. *C.* 'Norman Hadden' is a hybrid that bears heavily.

Hawthorn (*Crataegus ellwangeriana*) in full flower.

Crataegus spp., HAWTHORNS

Deciduous/Evergreen: D   **Zone:** 5
Sun/shade preference: ○
Shade tolerance: ◗
Performance rating: ✓✓✓
Fertility: SF   **Flowers:** White

Species include *Crataegus arnoldiana*, *C. durobrivensis*, *C. ellwangeriana*, *C. pinnatifida major*, *C. schraderiana* and *C. tanacetifolia*. Their native habitat is woodland and hedges.

There are hundreds of hawthorn species worldwide and most, if not all, of them have edible fruits. These vary widely, from the dry, thin-pulped and poor-flavoured fruits of the British native hawthorn (*C. monogyna*) to excellent juicy fruits, 2-3cm (0.8-1.2") across with a fine 'appley' flavour, like *C. ellwangeriana* and others. Some of these fruiting species deserve a place in almost every forest garden!

Size: 4-6m (13-20') high by 3-4m (10-13') wide.
Cultivation: Plant bare-rooted trees in winter. Trees are usually grafted on to *C. monogyna* rootstock, which will grow in almost any kind of soil. Hawthorns are tolerant of shade, but fruit better with some sun.
Flowering: In spring; flowers fairly frost-tolerant.
Fruiting: Starts in 2-4 years. Fruits are usually red, ripening in September and October.
Uses: Fruits are eaten raw, cooked or processed.
Harvest and storage: Best harvested, when fruits soften, by putting down a sheet or tarp and shaking the

Chinese dogwood (*Cornus kousa* var. *chinensis*).

branches. The fruits will store for a few weeks.

Cooking/processing: Lightly cook the fruits and put through a Moulinex sieve to get a pulp first. Then this makes a great jam or dried leather.

Secondary uses: Bee plants.

Propagation: By seed (requires stratification) or grafting.

Maintenance: Little required. Some species are very thorny. Canopies can be raised in time by pruning off lower branches.

Cultivars:

All the following bear fruits of good quality and size. Most have not had named varieties selected.

C. arnoldiana: Fruits 1.5-2cm (0.6-0.8"); excellent flavour raw. Thorny tree.

C. durobrivensis: Fruits 1.5-2cm (0.6-0.8"); excellent flavour raw. Thorny tree.

C. ellwangeriana: Fruits 1.5-2cm (0.6-0.8"); excellent flavour raw. Thorny tree.

C. gemosa: Fruits 1.2-2cm (0.5-0.8"). Thorny tree.

C. orientalis: Fruits 1.5-2cm (0.6-0.8"), yellow/red. Similar tree to *C. tanacetifolia*.

C. pedicellata: Fruits 1.5cm (0.6"), fair flavour raw; ripens very late autumn. Few thorns.

C. pinnatifida major 'Big Golden Star': Fruits 3-3.5cm (1.2-1.4"), best cooked and sweetened. Thornless tree.

C. schraderiana: Fruits 1.5-2cm (0.6-0.8"); excellent flavour raw. Thorny tree.

C. tanacetifolia: Fruits 1.5-2cm (0.6-0.8"); excellent flavour raw. Thornless tree of low vigour, smaller than most of the other trees here.

TREES TOLERATING WINTER WATERLOGGING

Alders (*Alnus* spp.)
Downy birch (*Betula pubescens*)
English oak (*Quercus robur*)
Hawthorns (*Crataegus* spp.)
Sessile oak (*Quercus petraea*)

Decaisnea fargesii, BLUE BEAN

Deciduous/Evergreen: D   **Zone:** 5
Sun/shade preference: ◯
Shade tolerance: ◖
Performance rating: ✓✓
Fertility: SF   **Flowers:** Greenish-yellow

An unusual edible plant originating in moist woods in China, this is grown in ornamental gardens for its amazing bright-blue pods. It is the pulp in these pods that is edible, with a fine, delicate, melony flavour.

Size: 4-6m (13-20') high and 2-4m (6'6"-13') wide.

Cultivation: Plant bare-rooted trees in winter. Unfussy as to soil, tolerates partial shade.

Flowering: Early summer.

Fruiting: Starts in 3-4 years. Pick pods when they are bright blue and soft.

Uses: The pulp in the pods is eaten raw.

Hawthorn (*Crataegus ellwangeriana*) fruits.

Harvest and storage: Pick the pods when blue and soft. They don't store for long.

Cooking/processing: Use fresh – open the pods along the suture line and scoop out the pulp with a spoon. The small black seeds can be removed or eaten. The skin of the pods is not edible.

Secondary uses: The pod skins contain latex and have been used as a rubber source.

Propagation: By seed – needs 4 months' stratification.

Maintenance: None required.

Diospyros spp., PERSIMMONS

Deciduous/Evergreen: D   Zone: 5/6
Sun/shade preference: ◯
Shade tolerance: ◯
Performance rating: ✓✓
Fertility: SS   Flowers: White

Species include *Diospyros kaki* (Japanese, kaki or oriental persimmon), *D. lotus* (date plum) and *D. virginiana* (American persimmon). These originate from dry woodland habitats.

This family is not very well known in the UK and Europe. In the UK the Japanese persimmon is sometimes called Sharon fruit after the Israeli-grown fruits for sale here; it is less hardy than the other two species mentioned here, to zone 6. All the family have very nice edible fruits that are astringent before properly ripe.

Japanese persimmons fruit erratically in the UK at present, as they need a long hot summer to ripen the fruits; fruiting should improve as the climate warms. Date plum and American persimmons fruit well here. The fruits hang on to the tree after the leaves have fallen and sometimes ripen as late as November or December.

Size: *D. kaki*: 4-6m (13-20') high and wide. *D. lotus*: 10m (33') high by 6m (20') wide. *D. virginiana*: 15m (50') high by 8m (26') wide.

Cultivation: Plant bare-rooted trees with care in winter – dislikes transplanting. Unfussy as to soil conditions. Sun is preferred – essential for *D. kaki*.

Flowering: In summer.

Fertility: Some *D. kaki* varieties do not need pollination; others do. *D. lotus* and *D. virginiana* are not self-fertile, and male and female trees are needed for fruiting.

Fruiting: Starts after 3-6 years. *D. kaki* fruits are 5-7cm (2-2.7") across, *D. lotus* about 1.5cm (0.6") across, and *D. virginiana* about 2.5-3.5cm (1-1.4") across.

Uses: The fruits are eaten, usually raw.

Harvest and storage: Harvest as late as possible, usually after the leaves have dropped. Store in a cool place for up to a month or two. Bring into the warm to ripen.

Cooking/processing: Best used fresh.

Secondary uses: Bee plants. Unripe fruits are high in tannins and can be used for tanning and dyeing.

Propagation: By seed (needs 2-3 months' stratification) or grafting on to seedling rootstock of the same species.

Maintenance: Little required.

Cultivars:

D. kaki has numerous varieties, mostly from China and Japan. For UK conditions the varieties grown in southern France are recommended, namely:

Fuyu
Kostata
Mazelli

D. lotus has no varieties available.

D. virginiana has several good fruiting varieties selected in the USA, and seedlings of these varieties have good potential. Varieties best suited to British conditions include:

Early Golden
Garretson
John Rick
Meader
Miller
Runkwitz
Szukis

The Russians have hybridised Japanese and American persimmons to produce hardier plants than *D. kaki*, but with fruit size similar to *D. kaki*. Two such varieties are:

Nikita's Gift
Russian Beauty

TANNINS

Several fruits contain tannins while they are unripe, which make them taste astringent and unpleasant (they will pucker your mouth up!). These include persimmons and *Elaeagnus* fruits. As the fruits reach full ripeness the tannins fade and the fruits become delicious. So if you happen to try an unripe *Elaeagnus* fruit and find it unpleasant, don't write them off! Many fruits are unpleasant before they are ripe (pears, for example).

Fruits of *Elaeagnus* x *ebbingei* ripen in spring.

Autumn olive (*Elaeagnus umbellata*) in flower.

Elaeagnus x *ebbingei*

Deciduous/Evergreen: E   Zone: 6
Sun/shade preference: ○
Shade tolerance: ●
Performance rating: ✓✓
Fertility: SS   Flowers: White

Elaeagnus umbellata, **AUTUMN OLIVE**

Deciduous/Evergreen: D   Zone: 3
Sun/shade preference: ○
Shade tolerance: ◐
Performance rating: ✓✓✓
Fertility: SS   Flowers: White

One of the evergreen *Elaeagnus*, this garden hybrid is useful for dense, all-year protection in hedges, and bears edible fruit in spring: a nice early nibble, though it never fruits really heavily.

Size: 4m (13') high and wide.
Cultivation: Plant pot-grown trees in winter or spring; stake well. Unfussy as to soil, tolerates deep shade and exposure. Drought-tolerant.
Flowering: October/November, very fragrant. Not self-fertile: two genetically different plants are required for fruiting.
Fruiting: March to May. Fruits are red, oval, 1.5-2cm (0.6-0.8") long, and astringent before ripe.
Uses: Fruits in spring are eaten, usually raw.
Harvest and storage: Pick fruits when they colour and soften. They store for a week or two.
Cooking/processing: Lightly cook the fruits and put through a Moulinex sieve to get a pulp. This can be used to make a jam or leather, or simply eaten as a cooked fruit.
Secondary uses: Bee plant. Nitrogen fixer.
Propagation: Semi-ripe cuttings in summer.
Maintenance: Little needed. Tolerant of trimming if necessary.
Cultivars: 'Limelight' is a good pollinator for the species.

This deciduous *Elaeagnus* would certainly get on to my top ten list of plants for a forest garden. It is a great multi-purpose plant originating from thickets and woods in eastern Asia, and the fruits make fine jams and leathers. Good in hedges and windbreaks – in the UK it comes into leaf in February and loses leaves in December, so is not out of leaf for long. In some warmer regions of the world it is considered a weedy nuisance.

Size: 5m (16') high and wide in the UK; larger in warmer climes.
Cultivation: Plant bare-rooted trees in early-to-mid winter (comes early into growth in late winter). Unfussy as to soil, tolerates some shade and exposure – good in hedges.
Flowering: Early spring.
Fruiting: Starts in 2-3 years. Fruits 7-10mm (0.3-0.4") across; they are speckled red and astringent until really ripe. Fruit ripens in September/October.
Uses: The fruits are eaten raw, cooked or processed.
Harvest and storage: Pick fruits when dark red, even if still astringent – the astringency goes with cooking or drying. It is easiest to lay a tarp or sheet on the ground and hand-pick, dropping fruits as you go. They store for a few weeks.
Cooking/processing: Lightly cook fruits and put through a Moulinex sieve to get a pulp. This can then be used to make a great jam or fruit leather.

Secondary uses: Great plant for wild /bumble bees. Very good nitrogen fixer.
Propagation: By seed (needs 3 months' stratification) or hardwood cuttings.
Maintenance: Little needed.
Cultivars: Good fruiting varieties from the USA and the UK include:
Big Red
Brilliant Rose
Hidden Springs
Jewel
Newgate
Red Cascade
Sweet 'n' Tart

Autumn olive (*Elaeagnus umbellata*) fruits.

AUTUMN OLIVE JAM

One of my favourite jams, this preserves the wonderful flavour of autumn olive fruits.

2.5kg (5lb 8oz) autumn olive fruits
2.5kg (5lb 8oz) sugar

- Place the fresh autumn olive fruits in a pan with just enough water to cover the bottom. Bring to the boil and simmer for 5-10 minutes, stirring frequently.

- The fruits are now soft enough to easily go through a Moulinex sieve (food mill). Put them through in batches, throwing away the seeds that are left.

- Place the pulp back into the pan and bring to the boil. Add the sugar, bring to a rolling boil and check for setting. Once set, bottle into hot jars and seal.

Snowbell tree (*Halesia carolina*) showing the young fruits.

Halesia carolina, SNOWBELL TREE / SILVERBELL TREE

Deciduous/Evergreen: D **Zone:** 5
Sun/shade preference: ◐
Shade tolerance: ◐
Performance rating: ✓✓✓
Fertility: SF **Flowers:** White

An almost-unknown tree in Europe, this tree of American moist woods produces a really good crop of young crunchy fruits with a cucumber/pea-like flavour; great in salads or pickles.

Size: In the UK, 3-4m (10-13') high and wide in time, but slow-growing and bushy.
Cultivation: Plant bare-rooted trees in winter. Unfussy as to soil, but prefers sun.
Flowering: Mid-spring, with white flowers in profusion – very ornamental.
Fruiting: Starts after 3-4 years. The fruits are four-winged, green and 2-3cm (0.8-1.2") long. They are ready to eat from late June for 3 weeks or so.
Harvest and storage: Pick green fruits as soon as they are large enough – 1cm (0.4")+. Use quickly.
Cooking/processing: They need only light cooking for a few minutes.
Secondary uses: Good bee plant. Flowers are edible in salads too.
Propagation: By seed – needs 3 months' stratification.
Maintenance: None needed.

Sea buckthorn (*Hippophae rhamnoides*) 'Leikora'.

Hippophae spp., SEA BUCKTHORNS

Deciduous/Evergreen: D **Zone:** 3/7
Sun/shade preference: ◯
Shade tolerance: ◑
Performance rating: ✓✓✓✓
Fertility: M/F **Flowers:** Yellowish-brown

Species include *Hippophae rhamnoides* (sea buckthorn) and *H. salicifolia* (Himalayan or willow-leaved sea buckthorn). They originate from well-drained open sites. *H. salicifolia* is less hardy, to zone 6-7.

Size: *H. rhamnoides* – 3-4m (10-13') high by 5m+ (16'+) wide, sometimes lower.
H. salicifolia – 10m (33') high by 6-8m (20-26') wide.
Cultivation: Plant bare-rooted trees in early-to-mid winter (they come early into growth). Give well-drained soil and full sun; they tolerate exposure.
Flowering: Spring, tolerant of frosts.
Fruiting: Starts in 2-3 years. Fruits are round or oval, 8-15mm (0.3-0.6") long, orange, juicy and borne in clusters close to stems.
Uses: Fruits are eaten, usually cooked or processed. They are acid when raw.
Harvest and storage: Pick when fruits colour and soften in late summer. They are borne close to the branches and usually have to be hand-picked – a messy business as some fruits burst and cover your hands in juice. Alternatively, cut off heavily fruiting branches (a kind of coppicing), cut them into sections and freeze in a freezer; once frozen, the fruits knock off easily. They don't keep for long.
Cooking/processing: Lightly cook the fruits and put

through a Moulinex sieve to get a pulp. This can then be used to make a fine jam or mixed with other fruit pulps to make leathers.
Secondary uses: Good bee plant and nitrogen fixer. Good for hedging.
Propagation: Hardwood cuttings for named selections.
Maintenance: The main disadvantage with *H. rhamnoides* is that it suckers vigorously and will require management to stop it going where you don't want it. *H. salicifolia* suckers less but the fruits are not so easy to harvest.
Cultivars: Good fruiting selections (and males) have been made from *H. rhamnoides*:

Females:	**Males:**
Frugna	Polmix
Hergo	Romeo
Leikora	
Orange Energy	

Morus spp., MULBERRIES

Deciduous/Evergreen: D **Zone:** 5
Sun/shade preference: ◕
Shade tolerance: ◑
Performance rating: ✓✓✓
Fertility: SF **Flowers:** Pinkish-green

Mulberry species include *Morus nigra* (black mulberry), *M. alba* (white mulberry), *M. rubra* (red mulberry) and their hybrids. They are great fruiting trees, reliable and with wonderful fruits: no forest garden should be without one (at least)! In addition, the leaves can be cooked and eaten – in parts of the Mediterranean they are used like vine leaves to wrap parcels of food. In the UK, you need to protect very young trees from snails and slugs, which like to graze on the bark. Mulberry is one of the latest trees to leaf out. Fruits ripen over several weeks in August and September; birds make take some.

Size: 5-10m (16-33') high and wide, but can be kept smaller by pruning.
Cultivation: Plant pot-grown/bare-rooted trees in winter or early spring (comes late into growth). Unfussy as to soil; needs some sun and shelter (branches are brittle).
Flowering: Late spring – misses any frosts.
Fruiting: Starts in about 2 years for good fruiting selections. Seedling trees may take 15 years!
Uses: The fruits are eaten, usually fresh.
Harvest and storage: Pick over a long period as fruits

ripen. It is easiest to lay down a sheet or tarp and lightly shake or tap the branches. The fruits do not store.

Cooking/processing: Treat fruits as for raspberries. Leaves can be steamed, used to wrap food before cooking, layered in lasagnes, etc.

Secondary uses: Edible leaves – cooked. Russian mulberry (*M. alba* var. *tatarica*) is used in windbreaks.

Propagation: Grafting or semi-ripe cuttings.

Maintenance: Little needed. If pruning to keep low, prune in early summer. It is possible to coppice mulberries for leaf production on a 1-4-year cycle; in this system it is advisable to plant some fertility-enhancing plants nearby to sustain leaf production.

Cultivars:

M. alba:	*M. nigra*:
Pakistan	Black Tabor
	Chelsea

Hybrids (*M. alba* x *M. rubra*):
Capsrum
Carman
Illinois Everbearing
Italian
Ivory
Wellington

Prunus cerasifera, CHERRY PLUM & MIRABELLE

Deciduous/Evergreen: D   **Zone:** 4
Sun/shade preference: ◐
Shade tolerance: ◖
Performance rating: ✓✓✓
Fertility: SS   **Flowers:** White

Cherry plums and mirabelles are hardy trees and bear delicious fruits that ripen in July, before most plums. Cropping tends to be quite erratic because of the early flowering, though the recent varieties 'Golden Sphere' and 'Gypsy' are more reliable. Despite their erratic fruiting, cherry plums are worth a place if you have space, as they pretty much look after themselves.

Rootstocks: Myrobalan (vigorous), St Julien (semi-vigorous). Also on own roots.

Size: Own root and Myrobalan: 6-7m (20-23') high and wide. St Julien A: 3.5-4.5m (12-15') high and wide.

Cultivation: Plant bare-rooted trees in winter. Unfussy as

to soil. Tolerate exposure but fruiting will be poor there.

Flowering: Early spring – susceptible to frost damage.

Fruiting: Starts in 3-4 years. Fruits are like small plums, with excellent flavour.

Uses: Fruits are eaten, usually fresh.

Harvest and storage: Pick fruits as they colour and soften. They won't store for long.

Cooking/processing: Eat fresh! If you have a glut then halve, de-stone and dry.

Secondary uses: Bee plant; also hedges and windbreaks.

Propagation: Grafting or seed (needs 3 months' stratification).

Maintenance: Little required.

Cultivars:
First
Golden Sphere
Gypsy
Magda Jensen
Ruby

Prunus spinosa, BLACKTHORN / SLOE

Deciduous/Evergreen: D   **Zone:** 4
Sun/shade preference: ◐
Shade tolerance: ◖
Performance rating: ✓✓✓
Fertility: SS   **Flowers:** White

Blackthorn is a suckering spiny shrub or small tree that flowers in early spring and bears bluish-purple fruits, 1-1.5cm (0.4-0.6") across; often in large quantities. It is well known in Britain as a fruiting wild plant; I would probably not suggest that you plant it in your forest garden, but if you already have it growing (perhaps in one of the hedges) then it is certainly worth utilising.

Size: Usually 2-4m (6'6"-13') high, sometimes more, suckering to form shrubby colonies.

Cultivation: Plant bare-rooted trees in winter. Unfussy as to soil. Tolerates exposure and some shade but fruiting will be poor there.

Flowering: Early spring – fairly frost-tolerant.

Fruiting: Starts in 3-4 years. Fruits are like small plums or bullaces – sour and astringent when raw.

Uses: The fruits are eaten after processing.

Harvest and storage: Fruits are best harvested by beating branches, with a basket or sheet beneath.

Cooking/processing: Remove astringency by crushing or bruising fruits; heating has a sweetening effect.

Secondary uses: Bee plant. Flowers can also be cooked and eaten (e.g. battered and fried). Useful in hedges and windbreaks. Hollow branches make good peashooters!
Propagation: By seed – needs 3 months' stratification.
Maintenance: Little required. If it needs cutting back, beware of the spines.

Sambucus nigra, EUROPEAN ELDER

Deciduous/Evergreen: D   Zone: 5
Sun/shade preference: ◐
Shade tolerance: ◖
Performance rating: ✓✓✓
Fertility: SF   Flowers: White

Elder is well known as a wild food plant in European hedgerows and woods, so you may not need to plant it if you have plenty around anyway. There are, however, some good flowering/fruiting varieties that are worth growing if you do plant it in your forest garden. I actually value elder more for the flower crop than the fruit crop. The red elder (*S. racemosa*) and American elder (*S. canadensis*) are included in Chapter 13 (pages 174 and 185).

Size: 4-6m (13-20') high and wide.
Cultivation: Plant bare-rooted trees in early-to-mid winter (comes early into growth). Likes a moist, rich soil but is not too fussy. Tolerates exposure and shade, but flowers and fruits best in sun.
Flowering: May-June over a period of 4-5 weeks.
Fruiting: Starts in 2 years. Fruits ripen August/September.
Uses: The flowers are used to make drinks or can be cooked. The fruits are eaten, usually cooked with other fruits.
Harvest and storage: Flowers are picked on sunny days when they are shedding pollen. Fruits are best harvested by using a harvesting comb (berry picker) – if necessary picking whole heads of fruits first. Neither flowers nor fruits store for long.
Cooking/processing: The flowers are used to make cordials, wine, etc., and can also be fried. The fruits are best cooked – even better made into wine, which needs to be aged for 2-3 years.
Secondary uses: Hedging.
Propagation: Hardwood cuttings – very easy.
Maintenance: Little needed. If you want to keep it bushy and lower for access to flowers or fruits, it can be coppiced or trimmed to head height every few years.

Cultivars: Good flowering and fruiting selections are:
Bradet
Cae Rhos Lligwy (green fruits, less likely to be taken by birds)

Donau	Samdal
Franzi	Samidan
Godshill	Samnor
Haschberg	Sampo
Ina	Samyl
Sambu	Viridis (green fruits, less likely to be taken by birds)

Devon sorb apple (*Sorbus devoniensis*).

Sorbus spp., ROWANS, WHITEBEAMS & SERVICE TREES

Deciduous/Evergreen: D   Zone: 6
Sun/shade preference: ○
Shade tolerance: ◖
Performance rating: ✓✓✓
Fertility: SF   Flowers: Cream

Species include *Sorbus devoniensis* (Devon sorb apple), *S. domestica* (service tree) and *S. thibetica* (Tibetan whitebeam).

Many species in the *Sorbus* family have edible fruits, though I include only a few of the better ones here. The British natives *S. aria* (whitebeam) and *S. torminalis* (wild service tree) bear quite acceptable fruits. The rowans (*S. aucuparia*, etc.) tend to bear quite bitter fruits that really are not very nice – there are better trees to plant in your forest garden!

Size: *S. devoniensis*: 6m (20') high by 4m (13') wide.
S. domestica: 10m (33') high by 6m (20') wide, though slow-growing.
S. thibetica: 10-15m (33-50') high and wide.

Cultivation: Plant in winter (bare-rooted) or spring (pot-grown). Unfussy as to soil; all tolerate some shade.
Flowering: Spring – tolerant of frosts.
Fruiting: Starts in 3-5 years. Fruits ripen in autumn. *S. devoniensis* fruits are borne in large bunches: each fruit is 1.5cm (0.6") across, mealy, with an almond flavour. *S. thibetica* fruits are similar but slightly larger. Service tree (*Sorbus domestica*) fruits are like small apples or pears, 3-4cm (1.2-1.6") long, juicy and aromatic, and astringent until really ripe.
Uses: Fruits are eaten raw, cooked or processed.
Harvest and storage: Pick fruits as they soften in autumn. They will store for a few weeks.
Cooking/processing: *S. devoniensis* and *S .thibetica* can be treated like medlars (*Mespilus germanica*, see page 111). *S. domestica* is best cooked to remove any astringency.
Secondary uses: Juice from service tree fruit (*Sorbus domestica*) is used in cider-making in Europe.
Propagation: By seed (needs 3 months' stratification) and grafting.
Maintenance: Little required.
Cultivars:
S. devoniensis:
Devon Belle
S. domestica:
Rosie
S. thibetica:
John Mitchell

Trees for nuts and seeds

There are a couple of very important things to think about if you want to include nut trees in your forest garden.

Harvesting

Most nuts have to be harvested from beneath the tree as they either fall naturally or are shaken down. If they are to be allowed to land on the ground and collected from there, it is no good having a thick perennial layer of plants actively growing – you'll be forever peering amongst the foliage to search for nuts. Commercial growers use either grass or bare soil beneath nut trees for this reason. But there are other possibilities in a forest garden – for example, you could have a dense patch of comfrey (*Symphytum* spp.) beneath the tree canopy, which is cut to the ground in autumn just before the nuts start to fall. You'll then, in effect, have bare soil to harvest from. The

comfrey plants will regrow strongly the next spring, though you'll have mostly bare soil there over the winter.

Another option for harvesting is to use nets. This allows for a wider range of plants to be grown under the nut trees, but preferably nothing over about one metre high. An open-weave net is placed on top of the herbaceous perennial / ground-cover layer just before nut harvest and kept there for the 2-3 weeks of the harvest, and then removed. Nuts are hand-harvested off the net. The perennial / ground-cover plants still get light and are not growing strongly at harvest time, so will not get tangled in the net. For more on harvesting nuts see Chapter 22.

Squirrels

The second important factor to consider is squirrels – grey (American) squirrels in Britain, red squirrels in mainland Europe, and both in North America. Squirrels love nuts. They will take hazelnuts from trees well before they are ripe, and will take most other nuts before they fall from trees. One exception is sweet chestnuts, where the prickly burrs do seem to deter squirrels, so they don't become a nuisance until the chestnuts drop. In Britain, grey squirrels will also strip bark from walnut and hickory trees, half killing them in the process.

If you want to grow nuts then you have to do something about squirrels. By 'something' I mean you have to control their numbers. Squirrel deterrents do not work well, unless you can station a friend or relative (preferably with a shotgun) beneath your nut trees for several weeks. To be perfectly clear: if you don't want to control squirrel numbers, then don't waste space in your forest garden by planting nut trees (with the exception of sweet chestnut) – you won't get any nuts. I talk more about squirrels in Chapter 23.

Araucaria araucana, MONKEY PUZZLE

Deciduous/Evergreen: E **Zone:** 6
Sun/shade preference: ○
Shade tolerance: ○
Performance rating: ✓✓
Fertility: M/F **Flowers:** Pale yellow

Most people know this amazing-looking tree – and either love it or hate it. Originating from open mountain slopes in South America, it has distinctive sharp leaves. I love it, because it bears delicious nuts with a chestnut/plantain flavour, in huge heads 20cm (8") across, each with 200-300 nuts inside. Trees become tall with fairly small crowns after a long time – they are slow-growing when young. The main disadvantages are that you need male and female trees for fruiting, and you can't tell which is which when they are young. Also, fruiting doesn't start for a long time! So, this is one for the larger forest garden, perhaps, where you can put a few in. Treat as a long-term overstorey tree with crops for your children!

Size: Eventually 20m (66') high. 5m (16') high after 10 years.
Cultivation: Plant pot-grown trees in winter or spring. Likes a moist soil, humid climate and sun.
Flowering: Summer.
Fruiting: Starts after about 25 years! Ripe cone 'heads' disintegrate in autumn, dropping the nuts.
Uses: The nuts are eaten boiled or roasted.
Harvest and storage: Pick nuts off the ground /nets, etc. Harvest is mid-September in southern England; later in September further north. They will store in the cool for 6-12 months.
Cooking/processing: Best lightly cooked in the shell: boil or roast for 10 minutes, then cut the shell lengthways with a sharp knife to release the kernel halves.
Propagation: By seed – slow to germinate.
Maintenance: None needed.

Siberian pea tree (*Caragana arborescens*).

Caragana arborescens, SIBERIAN PEA TREE

Deciduous/Evergreen: D **Zone:** 2
Sun/shade preference: ○
Shade tolerance: ○
Performance rating: ✓✓
Fertility: SF **Flowers:** Yellow

A legume from eastern Asia, where it occurs on well-drained open sites, this is more a seed producer than a nut tree, and one that can be grown with squirrels around. It is one of the few hardy woody legumes. It is slow growing in the UK, preferring a more continental climate, and so may often be in the shrub rather than canopy layer.

Size: In the UK often 2-3m (6'6"-10') high by 2m (6'6") wide; twice that in warmer climes.
Cultivation: Plant bare-rooted or pot-grown trees in winter. Give full sun and well-drained soil. Tolerates exposure.
Flowering: Mid-spring. Bee-pollinated.
Fruiting: Starts after 3-5 years. Pods develop (5cm (2") long by 0.6cm (0.25") wide) with small pea-like seeds inside.
Uses: The young pods are eaten fresh; the young seeds are also eaten fresh or cooked. The dry seeds can be soaked and cooked like dried peas.
Harvest and storage: Very young pods are picked when about 3cm (1.2") long. Larger pods can be picked when still green for the seeds. Ripe pods turn brown and are picked before they split for dry seed, which stores for years.
Cooking/processing: Young pods and green seeds make

a lovely raw nibble. Ripe seed needs soaking overnight and boiling for 15-20 minutes.

Secondary uses: Very good bee plant. A nitrogen fixer and good in windbreaks. Sometimes grown for chicken fodder.

Propagation: By seed – not dormant.

Maintenance: Little needed.

Carya spp., HICKORIES / PECAN

Deciduous/Evergreen: D **Zone:** 5
Sun/shade preference: ◐
Shade tolerance: ◑
Performance rating: ✓✓
Fertility: SS **Flowers:** Greenish-yellow

Species include *Carya illinoinensis* (pecan), *C. laciniosa* (shellbark hickory) and *C. ovata* (shagbark hickory). Most trees in this North American family bear lovely edible nuts, with a flavour quite similar to walnut, although apart from pecan most need a heavy-duty nut cracker to crack the nuts. They are all very slow-growing for their first few years while they put down a big taproot. Not all do well in temperate climes – the ones listed top right are the best. Most need summer heat to ripen the new wood. They are currently best in the southern half of Britain but, with climate change, may be possible further north.

Size: Pecans 6m (20') high; others eventually 15-20m (50-66') high and wide in the UK.

Cultivation: Plant pot-grown trees with care in winter – dislikes transplanting. Give a sunny, sheltered site.

Flowering: Late spring and early summer. Wind-pollinated.

Fruiting: Grafted varieties start in 5-7 years; seedlings from them in about 10 years. Northern pecan nuts are about the size of acorns. Shellbark nuts are up to 6cm (2.5") long – larger than walnuts – and shagbarks up to 4cm (1.6") long.

Uses: The nuts are eaten raw or cooked.

Harvest and storage: Harvest from the ground or use nets. Dry nuts if necessary. Dried nuts will store for 1-2 years.

Cooking/processing: Use like walnuts (*Juglans regia*, see page 133). See above regarding cracking.

Secondary uses: Edible sap, tapped like maple sap. Hard timber.

Propagation: By seed (needs 3 months' stratification) or grafting on to seedling rootstock.

Maintenance: Little needed.

Cultivars:

C. illinoinensis:

So-called northern pecan varieties (below) are most suited to British conditions – the larger southern varieties need too much heat (at least for a few more decades).
Carlson No.3
Cornfield
Lucas

C. laciniosa:
Henry

C. ovata:
Grainger
Weschke
Wilcox
Yoder No.1

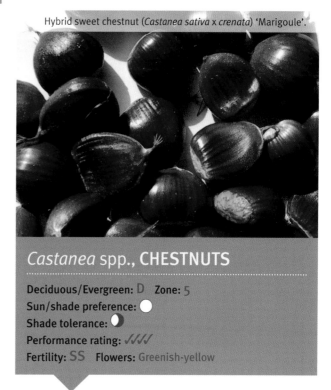
Hybrid sweet chestnut (*Castanea sativa* x *crenata*) 'Marigoule'.

Castanea spp., CHESTNUTS

Deciduous/Evergreen: D **Zone:** 5
Sun/shade preference: ○
Shade tolerance: ◑
Performance rating: ✓✓✓
Fertility: SS **Flowers:** Greenish-yellow

Species of use in the UK are *Castanea sativa* (sweet chestnut) and *C. sativa* x *crenata* (hybrid sweet chestnut). This is one of the most promising nut crops for the UK, especially in the wetter west where some of the other nuts are less at home. There are some fantastic varieties that I've been trialling for over 10 years, which give huge crops of large nuts for very little work. If you can't use them all fresh, try drying them – they will store for years and are much easier to shell when dry. There are no dwarf rootstocks as yet for sweet chestnut, but one option to keep trees a little smaller is to coppice them, say every 10 years (when they will be about 8m/26' high and wide), and accept that for a year or two after coppicing there will be little or no fruiting. Grow a good-pollinating variety to ensure cross-pollination.

Size: Eventually 15-20m (50-66') high by 10-15m (33-50') wide.

Cultivation: Plant bare-rooted trees in winter. Likes sun and a well-drained acid-to-neutral soil.

Flowering: Midsummer – misses any frosts. Wind- and insect-pollinated.

Fertility: Most trees are not self-fertile. It is best to grow at least one known good-pollinating variety along with other varieties.

Fruiting: Starts in 3-4 years. Nuts fall from late September to early November in the UK. Ten-year-old trees can yield 25-50kg (55-110lb) a year.

Uses: The nuts are eaten boiled, roasted and ground into flour.

Harvest and storage: Pick nuts from the ground or nets daily. Use heavy-duty gloves to twist off any burrs remaining. Store fresh nuts in a cool, humid place, where they will store for a few weeks.

Cooking/processing: Cook by roasting, or cutting in half and boiling for 5-10 minutes, when the kernel halves should come free easily. Dry whole nuts in a dehydrator. Dried nuts store for years; after shelling, the kernels can be ground for flour.

Secondary uses: Bee plant. Useful timber.

Propagation: Named varieties are propagated by grafting on to seedling rootstock or one of the hybrid varieties. Some of the hybrids can be propagated from softwood cuttings.

Maintenance: Little required. Canopy can be raised in time by pruning off lower branches. Heavily cropping trees will need feeding.

Cultivars: For a single tree, choose the partly self-fertile cultivar Marigoule.

Good fruiters:
Bouche de Betizac (hybrid)
Bournette (hybrid, also a partial pollinator)
Maridonne (hybrid)
Marigoule (hybrid, also a partial pollinator, and partly self-fertile)
Marlhac (hybrid)
Marron de Lyon

Best pollinators:
Belle Epine (also a good fruiter)
Marron de Goujounac

DROUGHT-TOLERANT TREES

Black locust (*Robinia pseudoacacia*)
Judas tree (*Cercis siliquastrum*)
Eucalyptus (*Eucalyptus* spp.)
European pear (*Pyrus communis*)
Fig (*Ficus carica*)
Maidenhair tree (*Ginkgo biloba*)
Hawthorns (*Crataegus* spp.)
Pines (*Pinus* spp.)
Sweet chestnut (*Castanea sativa*)

Hazel (*Corylus avellana*).

Corylus spp., HAZELS

Deciduous/Evergreen: D **Zone:** 4-5
Sun/shade preference: ○
Shade tolerance: ●
Performance rating: ✓✓✓
Fertility: SF **Flowers:** Greenish-yellow, red

Species are *Corylus avellana* (hazel) and *C. maxima* (filbert). In fact these two have hybridised for a long time and most varieties are a mixture. The term 'cobnuts' can refer to either!

Easy to grow and not too large, these deserve a place in all squirrel-free forest gardens. Your own hazelnuts will taste so much better than the imported nuts so often grown in Turkey. They are self-fertile but cross-pollination improves yield.

Size: 5-6m (16-20') high and wide.
Cultivation: Plant bare-rooted trees in winter in a well-drained soil. Shade is tolerated but fruiting is best in sun.
Flowering: Late winter and early spring, over about 6 weeks. Wind-pollinated.
Fruiting: Starts after 2-3 years. Nuts ripen in September. Average annual yield is 5kg (11lb) per tree.
Uses: Nuts are eaten raw or cooked.
Harvest and storage: Harvest from the ground or nets. A Nut Wizard harvester (see page 324, Chapter 22) is great for hazels. Dry if necessary. Dried nuts will store for years.
Cooking/processing: Shelling is the main hassle. I have built a nut-cracking machine, which works extremely well (see *Agroforestry News*, Vol 13 No 3 for plans). The kernels are great raw or roasted.
Secondary uses: Poles from coppicing are useful but you won't get fruiting for a year or two after coppicing.
Propagation: By stool layering – usually grown on own roots. Seed requires 16 weeks' stratification.
Maintenance: Little needed if growing as a large bush. If growing as a single-stemmed tree, then suckers will need to be cut out every year, preferably during the summer. Hazels are not heavy feeders.
Cultivars:

Butler	Hall's Giant
Corabel	Kent Cob
Cosford	Pearson's Prolific
Emoa 1	Tonda di Giffoni
Ennis	Webb's Prize Cob
Gunslebert	

Size: 15-25m (50-80') high and 4-6m (13-20') wide – tall and narrow.
Cultivation: Plant pot-grown or bare-rooted trees in winter. Unfussy as to soil, but likes sun.
Flowering: Summer.
Fruiting: May take 20 years before it starts!
Uses: The nuts are eaten, usually cooked.
Harvest and storage: Harvest fruits when they fall. The flesh needs removing – ideally put them in a concrete mixer with 2cm (0.8") stones and water, and allow the stones to scrub the flesh away: the clean nuts will be left. Allow to surface dry. They will store for several months in the cool.
Cooking/processing: Cook by roasting or boiling for 10 minutes. Easy to shell.
Secondary uses: The leaves and leaf extract are used medicinally on a large scale: the active compounds are a vasodilator – they improve blood flow, especially in the brain.
Propagation: By seed (not dormant) or grafting.
Maintenance: None needed.
Cultivars:

Females:	**Male:**	**Self-fertile:**
King of Dongting	Saratoga	Dr Causton
McFarland		
Ohasuki		

Ginkgo biloba, MAIDENHAIR TREE

Deciduous/Evergreen: D   Zone: 4
Sun/shade preference: ◐
Shade tolerance: ◐
Performance rating: ✓
Fertility: M/F   Flowers: Cream-yellow

The maidenhair tree is a widely grown ornamental, but not many people seem to know that it bears edible nuts, probably because both male and female trees are required to get fruit. The fruit flesh itself is not edible – worse, it smells like rancid butter – but the nuts inside, about 1.5cm (0.6") long, are a very nice cooked food, and they have long been used in China. The main disadvantage is the long time before fruiting begins.

Heartnut (*Juglans ailantifolia* var. *cordiformis*) fruits hang in bunches.

Juglans ailantifolia var. *cordiformis*, HEARTNUT

Deciduous/Evergreen: D **Zone:** 4
Sun/shade preference: ○
Shade tolerance: ◑
Performance rating: ✓✓✓
Fertility: SS **Flowers:** Greenish-yellow

Probably the best of the 'unknown' nuts in this section, the heartnut, which originates in Japan, has fantastic potential in the UK and elsewhere. Heartnut trees are faster-growing and less frost-prone than true walnuts, yet they readily bear nuts of similar quality. The huge foliage makes them look quite tropical. The nuts themselves are heart-shaped, just a little smaller than walnuts, with a fine flavour.

Size: 15m (50') high and wide in time.
Cultivation: Plant bare-rooted trees in winter – dislikes transplanting. Give a sunny site; otherwise unfussy.
Flowering: Spring, moderately frost-tolerant.
Fruiting: Grafted varieties start in 4-5 years; seedlings of the varieties in 6-8 years. Nuts are borne on long strings of 10-25 nuts within green husks. The nuts fall in-husk, and husks must be removed. Yields are not as high as walnut yields.
Uses: The nuts are eaten raw or cooked.
Harvest and storage: Harvest fruits when they fall on the ground within the blackened burr. Ideally put them in a concrete mixer with 2-4cm (0.8-1.6") stones and water, and allow the stones to scrub the burr away – the clean nuts will be left. Alternatively, you can soak the nuts for a few hours and scrub by hand. Dry and they will store for 1-2 years.

Cooking/processing: As for walnut (*Juglans regia*, see right). Shelling is a hassle – see note on my nut-cracking machine in hazels entry (*Corylus* spp., page 131).
Secondary uses: The hulls can be used for dyeing a range of brown and tan colours. The sap can be tapped and used like maple sap (see page 139).
Propagation: Grafting or seed (needs 3 months' stratification).
Maintenance: Little required. See note on allelopathy in walnut entry (*Juglans regia*), opposite.
Cultivars:
Brock
Campbell CW3
Fodermaier
Imshu
Locket
Rhodes
Simcoe
Stealth

TREES FROM SEED

Growing fruiting trees from seed is worth it only if the parent has not been highly bred. With something like heartnut (*Juglans ailantifolia* var. *cordiformis*) you have a very good chance of getting trees that fruit at least as well as the parent trees. However, with something like apple, which has been bred for thousands of years, you are very unlikely to get a tree with fruits as nice as the parents.

Juglans nigra, BLACK WALNUT

Deciduous/Evergreen: D **Zone:** 4
Sun/shade preference: ○
Shade tolerance: ◑
Performance rating: ✓✓
Fertility: SS **Flowers:** Greenish-yellow

This is another nut tree that is relatively unknown in the UK; native to North America, it is better known there. Black walnuts are fast-growing large trees that bear roundish nuts of walnut size. The nuts need a heavy-duty nut cracker to open them, and the kernels have a very good flavour. Seedling trees of named varieties have good potential because little breeding work has been done. Not described in detail here but of similar character, and also with good potential, are the butternut (*Juglans cinerea*) and buartnut (*Juglans* x *bixbyi*, a hybrid of butternut and heartnut).

Size: 20m+ (66'+) high and wide in time.
Cultivation: Plant bare-rooted trees in winter – dislikes transplanting. Give a sunny site; otherwise unfussy.
Flowering: Spring. Moderately frost-tolerant.
Fruiting: Grafted varieties start in 4-5 years; seedlings of the varieties in 6-8 years. Nuts are borne in twos and threes within round green husks. The nuts fall in-husk, and husks must be removed. Yields are not as high as for walnuts.
Uses: The nuts are eaten raw or cooked.
Harvest and storage: Harvest fruits when they fall on the ground within the blackened burr. Process as for heartnuts (*Juglans ailantifolia* var. *cordiformis*, see left). Dry and they will store for up to a year.
Cooking/processing: As for walnut. Shelling is a hassle – see note on my nut-cracking machine in hazels entry (*Corylus* spp.), page 131.
Secondary uses: The hulls can be used for dyeing brown. Sap can be tapped and used like maple sap.
Propagation: Grafting or seed (needs 3 months' stratification).
Maintenance: Little required. See note on allelopathy in walnut entry (*Juglans regia*), right.
Cultivars:
Bicentennial
Emma K
Thomas
Weschcke

Flowering: Late spring – choose later-flowering varieties for the UK to avoid frost damage.
Fruiting: Grafted varieties start in 4-5 years. Nuts are borne in clusters of 2-3 nuts, falling out from green husks when ripe.
Uses: The nuts are eaten raw or cooked.
Harvest and storage: Pick nuts from the ground or nets. They fall free of burrs and a Nut Wizard harvester (see page 324, Chapter 22) picks them up well. Dry to store. Dried nuts will store for 2-3 years. Walnuts take 10-15 years to build up to large crops.
Cooking/processing: Superb raw or roasted. Again, shelling is a hassle – see note on my nut-cracking machine in hazels entry (*Corylus* spp.), page 131.
Secondary uses: The hulls can be used for dyeing brown. Sap can be tapped and used like maple sap.
Propagation: Grafting.
Maintenance: Walnut blight and leaf spot can be serious diseases in Britain – try to grow resistant varieties. The walnut family has an allelopathic effect on many other species: this means that the chemicals in leaves and roots have a growth-suppressing effect, for example on apples, and on members of the bean and tomato families. So be careful what you underplant walnuts with. Cropping walnuts need feeding.
Cultivars: The following are late-flowering and fairly resistant to the two main diseases in Britain.

Corne du Perigord	Franquette
Ferjean	Mayette
Fernette	Meylanaise
Fernor	Ronde de Montignac

Not so disease-resistant, but still recommended, are:
Chandler
Hartley

Juglans regia, WALNUT

Deciduous/Evergreen: D **Zone:** 4
Sun/shade preference: ○
Shade tolerance: ◐
Performance rating: ✓✓
Fertility: SS **Flowers:** Greenish-yellow

Walnuts are some of the tastiest nuts to grow, though they are not quite as trouble-free as many other nuts.
Size: 20m (66') high and 15m (50') wide in time, but slow-growing.
Cultivation: Plant bare-rooted trees in winter – dislikes transplanting. Give a sunny site; otherwise unfussy.

Walnut (*Juglans regia*) – spot the snake (see page 332).

Cones of stone pine (*Pinus pinea*).

Pinus spp., PINES

Deciduous/Evergreen: E   **Zone:** 5/7
Sun/shade preference: ◐
Shade tolerance: ◐
Performance rating: ✓✓
Fertility: SF   **Flowers:** Greenish-yellow

Species include *Pinus armandii* (Chinese white pine), *P. cembra* (arolla pine), *P. cembroides* (piñon pine), *P. edulis* (Rocky Mountain piñon), *P. monophylla* (singleleaf piñon), *P. koraiensis* (Korean nut pine), *P. gerardiana* (Nepal nut pine), *P. sibirica* (Siberian nut pine) and *P. pinea* (stone pine). *Pinus radiata* (Monterey pine) and *P. nigra* var. *maritima* (Corsican pine) are useful windbreak trees.

Although all pine species bear edible pine nuts, only a few, such as those listed above, are large enough to be worth eating – many are so small that only rodents will find it profitable. The Mexican piñons prefer a dry hot climate, and do better in the east of the UK, while stone pine does very well in the west. The cones need to be picked when ripe before they open, which can be tricky when trees are large – commercial harvesters sometimes use long bamboo poles to knock them down; otherwise someone (the piñero) has to shin up and cut them off. *P. pinea* is less hardy, to zone 7. All crop better with cross-pollination.

Size: Varies: the piñons tend to be large shrubs in the UK, up to 3-5m (10-16') high and wide. Stone pine can reach 20m (66') high and 10m (33') wide, with a high umbrella-like canopy.
Cultivation: Plant pot-grown trees in winter or spring. Give sun and a well-drained soil. They tolerate exposure.

Flowering: Summer.
Fruiting: Starts after 8-10 years. Cones may take one or two years to ripen, depending on the species.
Uses: The seeds are eaten raw or cooked.
Harvest and storage: Harvest cones when you see them start to open or when they are old enough in autumn. They need to be twisted off or cut off branches with a long-handled pruner or saw if necessary. Most cones open in the warmth and the nuts fall out. Dry pine nuts store for several years. Pines are never really heavy croppers – 10kg (22lb) is a good crop from a full-sized tree, which is why pine nuts are so expensive to buy.
Cooking/processing: Best eaten raw. Shelling is a hassle – see note on my nut-cracking machine in hazels entry (*Corylus* spp.), page 131.
Secondary uses: Herb teas may be made from the pine needles.
Propagation: Easy from seed (needs 1-3 months' stratification).
Maintenance: Little required.

Prunus dulcis, ALMOND

Deciduous/Evergreen: D   **Zone:** 6
Sun/shade preference: ◐
Shade tolerance: ◐
Performance rating: ✓✓
Fertility: SF–SS   **Flowers:** White, pink

It is possible to grow your own almonds in the UK! I have had good crops of almonds for several years now, and as the risk of late-spring frosts decreases with climate warming, they will become more reliable. New growth is susceptible to spring frost damage. Even the self-fertile varieties crop better with cross-pollination.

Rootstocks: Seedling almond, St Julien A, Myran.
Size: 5-6m (16-20') high and wide in time.
Cultivation: Plant bare-rooted trees in winter. Plant in a sheltered site, in full sun, not in a frost pocket.
Flowering: Early spring – susceptible to frost damage. Choose late-flowering varieties for the UK.
Fruiting: Starts in 3-4 years. Fruits ripen in October, when the green husks split and the nuts fall out.
Uses: The nuts are eaten raw or cooked.
Harvest and storage: Nuts fall free of the burrs and are collected from the ground or nets. Dry them to store. Dried in-shell almonds will store for 1-2 years.
Cooking/processing: Use raw or roasted. Shelling is a

hassle – see note on my nut-cracking machine in hazels entry (*Corylus* spp.), page 131.
Propagation: Grafting.
Maintenance: Cut out dead or diseased wood in summer. Almonds are not heavy feeders.
Cultivars: The following are late-flowering varieties that are disease-resistant.
Ferraduel
Ferragnes
Ingrid *
Lauranne
Mandaline
Robijn *
* These are peach–almond crosses. The trees are hardier than true almonds but can sometimes suffer from peach leaf curl, and also cross-pollinate with peaches to make the kernels bitter.

Quercus spp., OAKS

Deciduous/Evergreen: D/E   **Zone:** 3-7
Sun/shade preference: ◯
Shade tolerance: ◗
Performance rating: ✓✓
Fertility: SF   **Flowers:** Greenish-yellow

The native English oaks, *Quercus robur* and *Q. petraea* (hardy to zone 5), can both be used in a forest garden – they crop heavily once every few years. *Q. ilex* (holm oak) and *Q. macrolepis* (vallonea oak) are two European low-tannin species. *Q. ilex* is slow-growing and bushy for many years. *Q. douglasii* (blue oak) and *Q. kelloggii* (Californian black oak) are two American low-tannin species. All these are hardy to zone 7.

Most American oaks need hot summers to ripen their new wood and don't currently do so well in the UK, where the new fruiting wood often dies back in winter.

The acorns of all oaks can be eaten, but most are full of tannins that are poisonous to humans, so they must be processed to remove the tannins first (see box). There are also a few oak species that have 'sweet' acorns (i.e. very low or no tannins), which need little or no processing. One of the best of the 'sweet' acorns is *Q. ilex*. It is a form of this, called the ballota oak (*Q. ilex* subsp. *ballota*), that has long been grown in Spain and Portugal for sweet acorns.

Size: Large trees, to 20-30m (66-100') high when fully grown.
Cultivation: Plant potted or bare-rooted trees in winter. Unfussy as to soil. Give sun or part shade.
Flowering: Late spring and early summer.
Fruiting: Varies with species. *Q. ilex* starts in 3-5 years. Many oaks bear a heavy crop only every few years.
Uses: Acorns are edible after processing.

ACORN MEAL

Luckily, it is really quite easy to remove the tannins from acorns. The tannins are water-soluble, and if you look into acorn preparation where acorns have been widely used, often as a staple (e.g. in North America), you'll find that they are usually shelled and crushed, and the meal placed in fine net bags in a stream of running water for a few days.

Most of us do not have a handy stream in our back gardens, so follow these steps.

- After collecting, leave the acorns to ripen in a dry place for a week or so – the kernels will shrink away from the shells. Then cut the shells in half lengthways and pop out the two kernel halves with the point of a knife.

- Roughly grind the kernels to a 'chopped nut' consistency in a blender or coffee grinder.

- Half fill a jar with the chopped acorn meal. Fill the jar up to the top with water and put it somewhere cool – a fridge is good.

- Twice a day, pour off as much water as you can and top up with fresh water. Do this for 3-4 days, and you'll find the water, having started off brown as the tannins leach into it, gets progressively clearer.

- After 3-4 days the tannins are gone and you can drain the meal to use. We sometimes make rather good acorn flapjacks, but you can use the meal in many savoury or sweet dishes. For more recipes consult the excellent book *Acorns and eat 'em* (see Resources section).

Harvest and storage: Harvest acorns from the ground: the easiest method is with a Nut Wizard harvester (see page 324, Chapter 22). Store in a cool place for several months.

Cooking/processing: To remove kernels, cut acorns in half lengthways and use the point of a knife to prise out halves. If low in tannin, use these straight in breads, cakes, etc. See box on page 135 for the processing of tannins and reference for acorn recipes.

Secondary uses: Good timber.

Propagation: By seed – not dormant.

Maintenance: Little required.

Trees with edible leaves

A few species of tree have excellent edible leaves. Lime trees (*Tilia* spp.) in particular can supply the base ingredient for many salads, and I would always include these in my forest garden.

Small-leaved lime (*Tilia cordata*).

Tilia spp., LIMES / LINDENS

Deciduous/Evergreen: D   **Zone:** 2-5
Sun/shade preference: ○
Shade tolerance: ●
Performance rating: ✓✓✓
Fertility: SF   **Flowers:** Pale yellow

See also page 178 (Chapter 13, Shrub species).

Species include *Tilia americana* (basswood), *T. cordata* (small-leaved lime – this has the nicest leaves), *T. platyphyllos* (large-leaved lime) and *T. tomentosa* (silver lime). All are woodland trees.

Lime trees are one of my most-used salad plants in my forest garden. It is the young leaves which are eaten, used as the base ingredient in a salad (instead of something like lettuce). Their flavour is very mild (as indeed is that of a lettuce), so more flavourful herbs and leaves are added to the salad to make it more interesting.

As this is a leaf crop you don't want to grow huge lime trees with the leaves out of reach, so aim to coppice regularly, with the first coppice after 6-8 years, and then every 1-5 years after that (or every 4-5 years if being used as a support for a fruiting climber – see page 292, Chapter 18), to keep a rounded bush shape. I coppice high (i.e. in fact pollarding), cutting off all growth at a height of about 1.5m (5'), which safeguards the new shoots from deer browsing. The only disadvantage with coppicing is that coppiced trees do not seem to want to flower – lime-flower tea being delicious and quite popular. If you want lime flowers you'll have to grow a full-sized tree 20m (66') high and 12m (40') wide – you need a large forest garden to justify it. *T. americana* and *T. cordata* are hardy to zone 2-3; others to zone 5.

Size: 4m (13') high and wide if coppiced as above.

Cultivation: Plant bare-rooted trees in winter. Unfussy as to soil. Tolerate deep shade, but are slower-growing there.

Uses: The young leaves at the ends of the shoot tips are eaten, usually raw in salads.

Harvest and storage: Pick young leaves and very shaded leaves all through the growing season. Use quickly.

Cooking/processing: Lime leaves can be used to make a nice pesto.

Secondary uses: Bee plant. Coppiced branches can be used for firewood or growing fungi. The leaves are rich in minerals – it acts like a green manure tree, with the leaf litter rapidly improving soil conditions.

Propagation: By seed – needs long stratification.

Maintenance: Just coppicing.

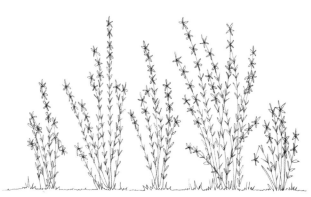

FOREST GARDEN SALADS

When I make a forest garden salad I tend to try to put in some base-ingredient leaves – leaves such as lime tree (*Tilia* spp.) or mallow (*Malva* spp.), which do not have a strong flavour but add bulk. Then I add in more flavourful leaves of other perennials, herbs, etc. Rarely are two salads the same – as I wander around harvesting I'll put in a little of this and a little of that. I usually add some flowers and sometimes fruits too. The result, once chopped with a nice dressing applied, is a really interesting and flavourful salad. A few of the salads I made last year for the forest gardening courses I run are listed below.

23 May 2009
Alexanders (*Smyrnium olusatrum*) leaves
Apple rose (*Rosa rugosa*) flowers
Fennel (*Foeniculum vulgare*) leaves
Green celery (*Apium graveolens*) leaves
Greenwax golden bamboo (*Phyllostachys viridiglaucescens*) shoots
Lemon balm (*Melissa officinalis*) leaves
Musk mallow (*Malva moschata*) leaves
Ramsons (*Allium ursinum*) leaves and flowers
Red valerian (*Centranthus ruber*) leaves
Small-leaved lime (*Tilia cordata*) leaves
Sorrel (*Rumex acetosa* 'Schavel') leaves
Sweet cicely (*Myrrhis odorata*) leaves and young seeds
Turkish rocket (*Bunias orientalis*) flowers
Violet (*Viola labradorica*) leaves

24 May 2009
Apple mint (*Mentha suaveolens*) leaves
Garlic mustard (*Alliaria petiolata*) leaves
Golden garlic (*Allium moly*) leaves
Large-leaved lime (*Tilia platyphyllos*) leaves
Lovage (*Levisticum officinale*) leaves
Mountain sorrel (*Oxyria digyna*) leaves
Oregano (*Origanum vulgare*) leaves
Orpine (*Sedum telephium*) leaves
Sea kale (*Crambe maritima*) flowers
Siberian purslane (*Claytonia sibirica*) leaves and flowers
Silver lime (*Tilia tomentosa*) leaves
Sweet cicely (*Myrrhis odorata*) leaves and young seeds
Szechuan pepper (*Zanthoxylum schinifolium*) young leaves

5 September 2009
Apple mint (*Mentha suaveolens*) leaves
Chicory (*Cichorium intybus* 'Rosso Treviso'/'Witloof') leaves
French scorzonera (*Reichardia picroides*) leaves
Lovage (*Levisticum officinale*) leaves
Mountain sorrel (*Oxyria digyna*) leaves
Oregano (*Origanum vulgare*) leaves
Parsley (*Petroselinum crispum*) leaves
Pot marigold (*Calendula officinalis*) leaves and flowers
Salad burnet (*Sanguisorba minor*) leaves
Salal (*Gaultheria shallon*) fruits
Sweet cicely (*Myrrhis odorata*) leaves
Welsh onion (*Allium fistulosum*) leaves
Wild angelica (*Angelica sylvestris*) leaves
Wood mallow (*Malva sylvestris*) flowers

6 September 2009
Autumn olive (*Elaeagnus umbellata*) fruits
Fennel (*Foeniculum vulgare*) leaves
Green celery (*Apium graveolens*) leaves
Large-leaved lime (*Tilia platyphyllos*) leaves
Lemon balm (*Melissa officinalis*) leaves
Nasturtium (*Tropaeolum majus*) leaves and flowers
Red valerian (*Centranthus ruber*) leaves
Saltbush (*Atriplex halimus*) leaves
Siberian purslane (*Claytonia sibirica*) leaves
Silver lime (*Tilia tomentosa*) leaves
Small-leaved lime (*Tilia cordata*) leaves
Sorrel (*Rumex acetosa* 'Schavel') leaves
Turkish rocket (*Bunias orientalis*) flowering shoots

Toona sinensis, CHINESE CEDAR

Deciduous/Evergreen: D **Zone:** 5
Sun/shade preference: ○
Shade tolerance: ◐
Performance rating: ✓✓
Fertility: SF **Flowers:** Pale green

The common name is a misnomer – this is not a conifer and certainly not a cedar! It is a Chinese woodland tree that bears delicious young foliage with a strong onion/garlic-like flavour. The Chinese use it as a vegetable – it is very strong raw – and by picking the new shoots you will be pruning the tree naturally to keep it shrubby.

Size: A full-grown tree is 15m (50') high and 10m (33') wide, but it can be kept shrubby – say, no more than 3-4m (10-13') high and wide – by picking the shoots and coppicing from time to time.
Cultivation: Plant bare-rooted or pot-grown trees in winter. Likes sun and hot summers, tolerates most soils.
Uses: The young shoots are eaten, usually lightly cooked.
Harvest and storage: Pick young shoots before the leaves fully emerge and use quickly.
Cooking/processing: Steam for 5-10 minutes.
Propagation: By seed – needs 2 months' stratification.
Maintenance: Little apart from occasional coppicing if required.

Trees for herbs and spices

A few trees are spice plants. Bay is well known but the temperate pepper trees less so.

Laurus nobilis, BAY

Deciduous/Evergreen: E **Zone:** 6
Sun/shade preference: ○
Shade tolerance: ●
Performance rating: ✓✓✓
Fertility: SF **Flowers:** Pale yellow

Most people use bay leaves but few realise how easy it is to grow a bay tree. It fits very well into a forest garden environment too. It is easy to include in the shrub layer too, being shade-tolerant.

Size: Can grow to 6m (20') high and wide in time, but is easy to keep shrubby if required.
Cultivation: Plant pot-grown trees in winter or spring in most soils. Sun or part shade.
Uses: The leaves (and sometimes the fruits) are used as a spice.
Harvest and storage: Pick leaves at any time of year. They will dry in the warmth in a few days and then store for many months. The fruits are very strongly flavoured too, but in Britain are produced only in the south.
Cooking/processing: Use fresh or dry as a seasoning.
Secondary uses: Oil from the seed is used in soaps and as an insect repellent. Bay can be included in hedges – it's tolerant of trimming.
Propagation: By seed (not dormant) or cuttings.
Maintenance: Little required.

Szechuan pepper (*Zanthoxylum schinifolium*).

Zanthoxylum spp., PEPPER TREES

Deciduous/Evergreen: D **Zone:** 6
Sun/shade preference: ○
Shade tolerance: ◐
Performance rating: ✓✓✓
Fertility: SF **Flowers:** Pale green

Unrelated to tropical black pepper, these hardy Asian shrubs are my favourite spice plants in my own forest garden. Easy to grow and highly productive, they produce aromatic (often citrusy) and peppery fruits, which you can just air-dry and use in a pepper mill instead of black pepper.

All *Zanthoxylum* produce peppery fruit, though the aroma varies between species. My favourites of the larger shrubs are *Zanthoxylum armatum* (Nepalese pepper), *Z. schinifolium* (Szechuan pepper) and *Z. simulans* (Szechuan pepper).

The flowers are small, green and unshowy, though loved by bees. They are followed by heads of reddish fruits. Each fruit consists of a single black seed, the size of a peppercorn, surrounded by a red papery shell. It is the papery shell that is the peppery part – the seeds are tasteless – but the whole fruit, seed plus papery shell, is usually harvested and dried.

Size: 3-4m (10-13') high and wide.
Cultivation: Plant pot-grown plants in winter. Give sun; otherwise unfussy.
Flowering: Late spring / early summer.
Fruiting: Starts after 3-4 years. 10-year-old bushes yield 1.5kg (3lb 5oz) dried fruit annually.
Uses: The young leaves can be used as a spice, and the papery fruit 'shells' are also a peppery spice.
Harvest and storage: Pick fruits when the papery shells begin to split, showing the black seeds inside. Pick a whole head of fruits at a time, stems and all. Dry in the warmth and sieve out most of the stalks. They will then store for a year, but in ambient air temperatures the aroma is lost within a few months – storing in the freezer retains the aroma for much longer.
Cooking/processing: Use dried fruits (i.e. the fruit shell plus seed) directly in a pepper mill.
Secondary uses: Bee plants. The young leaves are used for flavouring and in pickles – the leaves have the same aroma as the fruits.
Propagation: By seed – needs 3 months' stratification.
Maintenance: You may want to prune out crossing branches to make harvesting easier – branches are spiny.

Trees with other edible parts

Various trees, including the maples and birches, can be tapped for sap. The fruit heads of several sumach species can be used to make a drink.

Acer spp., **MAPLES** & *Betula* spp., **BIRCHES**

Deciduous/Evergreen: D **Zone:** 3-5
Sun/shade preference: ◯
Shade tolerance: ◖
Performance rating: ✓✓
Fertility: SF **Flowers:** Greenish-yellow

These are worth mentioning as sources of edible sap. Maple syrup, of course, is concentrated sap from the sugar maple, *Acer saccharum* (hardy to zone 3). This doesn't grow so well in the UK, where the sycamore (*Acer pseudoplatanus*, hardy to zone 5) is a better candidate for tapping. Any of the birches (e.g. *Betula pubescens*, downy birch, and *B. pendula*, silver birch) can be tapped too. Birches are hardy to zone 3.

Edible tree sap, whether from maples, birches, alders or the walnut family, has a very dilute solution of sugars, often about 1 per cent. This will start to ferment quite quickly, so it must be used or processed within a day or two. Of course, fermented tree sap wines can be delicious, and are fairly easy to make. Concentrating the sap into a syrup uses a lot of heat energy to evaporate all the water off – you need 60-65-per-cent sugars for a stable syrup. The raw sap on its own can be a nice drink too, however, and in many parts of the world is used as a spring tonic.

Size: Mostly large trees: 15-25m (50-80') high.
Cultivation: Plant pot-grown or bare-rooted trees in winter. Unfussy as to soil, but they will need to be in some sun.
Uses: Trees are tapped for sap.
Harvest and storage: Tap as described in box overleaf. The sap must be used quickly or it will start to ferment.
Cooking/processing: See above.
Secondary uses: Useful timber. However, growth is slowed by tapping and there is a risk of introducing infections, which would affect timber value.
Propagation: By seed – needs long stratification.
Maintenance: None needed.

TAPPING A TREE FOR SAP

Trees are tapped for sap in late winter / early spring, as the sap starts to rise. You can tap a tree as follows.

Drill a hole through the outer bark with a brace and bit, going about 3cm (1.2") deep. Use a drill bit the same diameter as the spile or plastic pipe you are going to insert.

Insert a tight-fitting plastic tube into the hole (in North America they have purpose-made metal spiles to insert in the hole, to which a tube is fitted).

The sap flows down the tube into a container, which is emptied daily.

When the sap starts to turn cloudy, it is time to finish the tapping. Remove the tube and plug the hole with a cork or other tight-fitting plug of wood.

Fruit head of stag's horn sumach (*Rhus typhina*).

Rhus spp., SUMACHS

Deciduous/Evergreen: D   Zone: 2
Sun/shade preference: ○
Shade tolerance: ◐
Performance rating: ✓✓✓
Fertility: SF   Flowers: Greenish-yellow

The amount of sap obtained is roughly proportional to the crown size of the tree, so large-crowned trees yield the most. If you just want a little sap for fresh drinks, though, any tree of these species over about 15cm (6") diameter can be used. In a forest garden, trees on the boundary may be suitable.

Species of use are *Rhus glabra* (smooth sumach) and *R. typhina* (stag's horn sumach), both from North America. Many of the sumach family bear large flower spikes, which are followed by heads of tiny red fruits. These fruits have a distinctly lemony flavour – though you wouldn't want to bother eating them as a fruit. Note: do not use species not listed here unless you are sure of edibility, nor those of the poison ivy species (sometimes included in *Rhus*).

Size: *R. glabra*: 3m (10') high and wide. *R. typhina*: 3-4m (10-13') high and wide.
Cultivation: Plant pot-grown trees in winter. Give sun; otherwise unfussy as to soil.
Flowering: Summer.
Fruiting: Fruit heads ripen in late summer and autumn.
Uses: The fruit heads are used to make a lemony drink.
Harvest and storage: Pick fruit heads as they turn red. Make drinks (see box, top right) straight away.
Cooking/processing: See box, top right.
Secondary uses: The leaves are high in tannins and good for dyeing (yellow to brown) and mordanting.
Propagation: By seed (needs 2-3 months' stratification) or digging up a sucker.
Maintenance: *R. typhina* in particular suckers widely – hence many gardeners' dislike of it! You'll have to regularly cut the suckers off at ground level if you don't want it to spread.

SUMACH LEMONADE

An old traditional use for sumach flowerheads is to make a still-lemonade-like drink.

- Pick ripe fruit heads and soak in water overnight, then strain. To extract more flavour, the small fruit can be stripped from the stalks and whizzed with water in a blender, then strained.

Firewood from coppice

If you have a need for fuel then some of the forest garden can be devoted to coppice firewood production. These trees will be coppiced, usually on a fairly short rotation of up to 10 years, and will usually need to be treated as part of the canopy layer so they grow fast in good light conditions. Many different species can be used; some of the possibilities are given below. The larger coppiced branches of most species can also be used for growing fungi.

TREE SPECIES FOR FIREWOOD COPPICING		
Species		**Comments**
Alnus glutinosa	Common alder	One of the few alders to coppice well – Italian and red alders do not. Nitrogen-fixing.
Castanea sativa	Sweet chestnut	Coppiced wood is also good for fence posts, etc. You won't get nuts for a while after each coppicing.
Corylus avellana	Hazel	A good use of hazel if nut production is impractical owing to squirrels.
Eucalyptus spp.	Eucalyptus	If growing for medicinal leaves, coppice is the best management. Makes good fuel.
Fraxinus excelsior	Ash	Can coppice every 3-5 years. Ash roots are hungry and very competitive, but coppiced tree roots are kept under control.
Robinia pseudoacacia	Black locust	Fast-growing, and good, dense wood. Watch out for suckering, which is stimulated by coppicing. Nitrogen-fixing.
Tilia spp.	Limes	If growing for leaves, then coppicing is best method of controlling tree size.

Medicinal trees

There aren't many trees that most folk want in their forest gardens primarily for medicinal use, but eucalypts often make it in there. Many people use eucalyptus oils already, and it is only a short step to growing and using your own.

> ## *Eucalyptus* spp., EUCALYPTUS
>
> **Deciduous/Evergreen:** E   **Zone:** 7/8
> **Sun/shade preference:** ◯
> **Shade tolerance:** ◯
> **Performance rating:** ✓✓
> **Fertility:** SF   **Flowers:** White, yellow, red

The main constituent of the essential oil found in eucalyptus trees is eucalyptol which, like menthol from mint, is used in many cold and cough medicines. It is also widely used in cosmetics and flavourings.

Species include *Eucalyptus johnstonii* (Johnston's gum), *E. delegatensis* (Tasmanian oak) and *E. urnigera.*

Eucalypts are sometimes tarnished with a bad reputation because of the plantations of them grown in dry Mediterranean-type climates, where they can have detrimental effects on the groundwater table, amongst other things. It does NOT, however, follow that all eucalypts are bad trees! In fact as medicinal trees they are very valuable, and the occasional tree in a forest garden will enhance the diversity.

Commercially, eucalyptus oils are distilled from the leaves, branches and wood of various *Eucalyptus* species, many of which are barely frost hardy. A few of the hardier types do contain good amounts of essential oils, though, and I recommend these are treated as coppiced trees to keep the leaves within easy reach. On a home scale it is not worth distilling oils. Instead, for a bad cold, cut a few leafy shoots and place them in a bowl; pour boiling water on top and inhale the vapour. Or leave some leafy shoots half under your pillow at night. *E. johnstonii* is hardy to zone 8; *E. delegatensis* and *E. urnigera* to zone 7.

Size: 4m (13') high and 1.5m (5') wide (coppiced every 5 years).
Cultivation: Plant pot-grown trees in winter or spring. Fine in most soils with reasonable drainage; give sun.
Propagation: By seed (not dormant) – they are very small but quite easy to germinate.

Maintenance: Coppicing keeps the shoots within easy reach. Coppice in late spring to avoid silverleaf disease. Eucalypts can have growth-suppressing allelopathic effects on some other species under their canopy, including apples, pines, beans and potatoes.

Nitrogen-fixing trees

The canopy layer is where nitrogen-fixing plants can work most efficiently, in almost full sun conditions, and most forest gardens will contain some nitrogen-fixing trees and shrubs here. Some of the taller trees can almost be a nitrogen-fixing upper canopy: in my forest garden, Italian alders (*Alnus cordata*) comprise most of the very tall trees. Falling leaves from tall species spread further, and thus the nitrogen from them is spread more widely into the forest garden than from low species.

> ## *Acacia* spp., WATTLES
>
> **Deciduous/Evergreen:** E   **Zone:** 8
> **Sun/shade preference:** ◯
> **Shade tolerance:** ◯
> **Performance rating:** ✓✓
> **Fertility:** SF   **Flowers:** Yellow

Species include *Acacia dealbata* (mimosa / silver wattle) and *A. decurrens* (black wattle), both from Australia. Acacias are leguminous.

Some readers may be surprised to find a largely tropical genus of trees mentioned here, but in fact some of the wattles are fast-growing and hardy enough for consideration in milder areas. In my forest garden in south-west England I have started putting in mimosa to take advantage of the mild winter conditions that we are increasingly getting.

Size: 10m (33') high by 5m (16') wide; can be coppiced to keep shrubby.
Cultivation: Plant pot-grown trees in spring to avoid frosts. Give full sun and a reasonably well-drained soil.
Secondary uses: Good bee plant in late winter / early spring.
Propagation: By seed – not dormant.
Maintenance: Coppice or raise canopy if necessary by pruning off lower branches.

Alnus spp., ALDERS

Deciduous/Evergreen: D   Zone: 3/6
Sun/shade preference: ◯
Shade tolerance: ◐
Performance rating: ✓✓✓
Fertility: SF   Flowers: Pale green

Species include *Alnus cordata* (Italian alder), *A. glutinosa* (common alder / European alder), *A. rubra* (red alder) and *A. sinuata* (Sitka alder). Alders are actinorhizal.

These are some of my favourite nitrogen-fixing trees, tolerating exposure and damp soils. I use Italian alder most because it tolerates drier summer soils, and because it is a nice conical shape that doesn't cast too much shade. Italian and red alders coppice poorly. *A. cordata* and *A. rubra* are hardy to zone 6; *A. glutinosa* and *A. sinuata* to zone 3.

Size: *A. cordata*: 20m (66') high by 6m (20') wide.
A. glutinosa: 20m (66') high by 15m (50') wide. Can be coppiced.
A. rubra: 30m (100') high by 6m (20') wide.
A. sinuata: 10m (33') high by 4m (13') wide. Can be coppiced.
Cultivation: Plant bare-rooted trees in winter. They prefer a moist soil (*A. cordata* tolerates drier soils in summer than the others); wet soil is tolerated for long periods.
Secondary uses: Edible sap. Coppiced *A. glutinosa* branches can be used for firewood and mushroom growing.
Propagation: By seed (easy; needs 1-2 months' stratification).
Maintenance: The canopy can be raised by pruning off lower branches up to halfway up the tree. Some lower branches may want to be retained for climbers (see page 292, Chapter 18).

Caragana arborescens, SIBERIAN PEA TREE

For full details see page 128, in 'Trees for nuts and seeds'. The Siberian pea tree is one of the few hardy leguminous trees and is a good fixer of nitrogen.

Cercis spp., REDBUDS & JUDAS TREE

Deciduous/Evergreen: D   Zone: 6-7
Sun/shade preference: ◯
Shade tolerance: ◯
Performance rating: ✓✓
Fertility: SF   Flowers: Pink

Species include *Cercis occidentalis* (western redbud) and *C. siliquastrum* (Judas tree). *Cercis* species are leguminous.

Cercis are small trees or large shrubs from warm temperate areas, very ornamental in flower (the flowers come out before the leaves). The Judas tree is so named because it is reputed to be the tree that Judas Iscariot hanged himself from after betraying Christ.

Size: About 5m (16') high and wide – slow-growing.
Cultivation: Plant pot-grown or bare-rooted plants in winter or spring. Give sun or light shade, and soil with reasonable drainage.
Secondary uses: Bee plants; edible flowers.
Propagation: By seed – scarify and stratify for 8 weeks.
Maintenance: Little required.

Elaeagnus spp. (deciduous), ELAEAGNUS

Deciduous/Evergreen: D   Zone: 3
Sun/shade preference: ◯
Shade tolerance: ◐
Performance rating: ✓✓✓
Fertility: SS   Flowers: White

Species include *Elaeagnus angustifolia* (oleaster), *E. commutata* (silverberry) and *E. umbellata* (autumn olive).

Elaeagnus spp. (evergreen), ELAEAGNUS

Deciduous/Evergreen: E   Zone: 6
Sun/shade preference: ◯
Shade tolerance: ●
Performance rating: ✓✓✓✓
Fertility: SS   Flowers: White

Species include *E. glabra, E. pungens* and *E.* x *ebbingei*.

Elaeagnus is a versatile genus whose species are excellent nitrogen fixers (actinorhizal) in temperate climates. The evergreen types are smaller, less hardy and more shade-tolerant. Full descriptions of *E. umbellata* and *E.* x *ebbingei* are given in the 'Less common fruiting trees' section, pages 122-123.

Size: *E. angustifolia*: 7m (23') high by 3m (10') wide.
E. commutata: 4-5m (13-16') high by 3-4m (10-13') wide.
E. glabra (evergreen): 3-4m (10-13') high and wide.
E. pungens (evergreen): 3-4m (10-13') high by 2-3m (6'6"-10') wide.
E. umbellata (autumn olive): 4-6m (13-20') high and wide.
E. x *ebbingei* (evergreen): 3-4m (10-13') high and wide.
Cultivation: Plant bare-rooted plants in winter; pot-grown in winter or spring. Stake evergreens. Unfussy as to soil.
Secondary uses: Edible fruits: evergreens in spring; deciduous in autumn.
Propagation: By seed (needs 2-3 months' stratification) or hardwood cuttings.
Maintenance: Little needed. All are very tolerant of trimming if required.

Hippophae spp., SEA BUCKTHORNS

For full details see page 124, in 'Less common fruiting trees'. Sea buckthorns are actinorhizal nitrogen fixers that also produce useful edible fruits.

Maackia amurensis, AMUR MAACKIA

Deciduous/Evergreen: D   Zone: 4
Sun/shade preference: ◯
Shade tolerance: ◯
Performance rating: ✓✓
Fertility: SF   Flowers: Cream

This is an uncommon hardy leguminous tree.

Size: 10-15m (33-50') high by 7-10m (23-33') wide.
Cultivation: Plant bare-rooted trees in winter. Tolerates most well-drained soils; needs sun.
Secondary uses: Good timber. The bark is being investigated for anti-cancer chemicals.
Propagation: By seed – not dormant.
Maintenance: Raise canopy over time by pruning off lower branches.

Californian bayberry (*Myrica californica*).

Myrica spp., BAYBERRIES / WAX MYRTLES

Deciduous/Evergreen: D/E   Zone: 6/8
Sun/shade preference: ◯
Shade tolerance: ◖
Performance rating: ✓✓✓✓
Fertility: SF   Flowers: Greenish-yellow

Species included here are *Myrica californica* (Californian bayberry), *M. cerifera* (wax myrtle) and *M. rubra* (red bayberry). *Myrica* species are actinorhizal.

This is an interesting family that includes the UK native bog myrtle, *Myrica gale* (see page 179, Chapter 13). The three species listed above are all evergreen, the first two of which are unusual in being wax-producing plants. *M. rubra* is hardy to zone 8.

Size: 4-8m (13-26') high by 2-3m (6'6"-10') wide.
Cultivation: Plant pot-grown or bare-rooted plants in winter. Most prefer acid soil. Sun or shade.
Harvest and storage: Pick leaves from late spring to autumn (and winter for evergreens). Dry like bay leaves to store.
Cooking/processing: Use leaves as a seasoning as you would bay leaves.
Secondary uses: Bee plant. The fruits and leaves can be used for flavouring. Wax on the outside of fruits is used to make candles, etc. (see box). The fruits of *M. rubra* are larger and edible.
Propagation: Usually by seed – de-wax them first, then give them 2-3 months' stratification.
Maintenance: Very little required.

WAX MYRTLE CANDLES

A very fertile *Myrica cerifera* shrub will yield 3kg (nearly 7lb) of waxy berries a year, which can be used to make wax candles.

- Place the berries in a pan with water to cover them to a depth of 15cm (6"). Bring the pan to the boil, stirring the fruits about and rubbing them against the sides of the pan to rub off the wax.

- In a short time the wax floats on the water. Scoop this off with a spoon and strain it through a coarse cloth to filter out any solids.

- Melt the wax a second time and form it into candles, either by dipping a wick repeatedly in the wax or by using a mould.

- 4kg (9lb) of berries yields 1kg (2lb 3oz) wax. The candles are slightly aromatic and smokeless after snuffing – early American settlers often preferred them to paraffin or tallow candles.

Robinia pseudoacacia, BLACK LOCUST / FALSE ACACIA

Deciduous/Evergreen: D **Zone:** 3
Sun/shade preference: ○
Shade tolerance: ◐
Performance rating: ✓✓
Fertility: SF **Flowers:** White

This tree will be familiar to American readers, but few folk seem to know that it is one of the most widely grown timber trees in the world, with quality timber like oak. One of the few hardy leguminous trees, it bears flowers that bees love, and a lot of *Robinia* honey is made in Eastern Europe, where good timber forms have been bred. The leaves are small and the canopy lets plenty of light through. The tree's main disadvantages are thorniness (less so in the selected forms) and its propensity to sucker, especially when coppiced.

Size: Up to 25m (80') high and 15m (50') wide.
Cultivation: Plant bare-rooted trees in winter. Give sun and a reasonably well-drained soil.
Secondary uses: Bee plant. The leaves are insecticidal. Valuable timber.
Propagation: By seed (not dormant); named selections by root cuttings.
Maintenance: Raise canopy over time by pruning off lower branches. Look out for suckers.

Shepherdia argentea, BUFFALO BERRY

Deciduous/Evergreen: D **Zone:** 2
Sun/shade preference: ○
Shade tolerance: ◑
Performance rating: ✓
Fertility: SS **Flowers:** Yellow

This North American shrub is closely related to *Elaeagnus*.

Size: 4-6m (13-20') high and wide.
Cultivation: Plant pot-grown plants in winter (comes early into growth). Unfussy as to soil; prefers sun.
Secondary uses: Bee plant. Edible fruit (not self-fertile). Good for hedging.
Propagation: By seed – requires 3 months' stratification.
Maintenance: Little required.

Italian alders (*Alnus cordata*) in winter.

Chapter 12

Designing the canopy layer

I regard the canopy layer design as the single most important part of the design of a forest garden. Tree density is critical when you are trying to grow other crops beneath the tree canopy. It is easy to mistakenly plant too densely – as Robert Hart found – because tiny trees look insignificant and there appears to be loads of space between them.

Having said that, don't be worried about making a few mistakes in the canopy design. Nothing is set in stone – if you find in time that you have planted too densely in one area, you can always remove a few trees to rectify the situation.

I would advise you *always* to do the planning of the canopy layer on paper, using a scale plan of your garden site. Use the map you made as described in Chapter 9, page 94, at a scale of 1:100 or 1:200.

You need to have come up with a list of trees you want for the canopy layer. This will depend on your preferences for types of crop, etc., and a wide range of trees is possible, as described in Chapter 11. However, you probably won't know whether you have too many, too few or about the right number of trees for this layer until you start the design process described below. As a rough rule of thumb, you'll have room for about one tree per 20-40m² of garden – the lesser area in smaller gardens and the greater in larger gardens, where some of the trees you are likely to use will be larger. But in the design process you can always add or take away trees as appropriate.

Canopy tree spacing and canopy profile

In general, don't plant canopy trees closer than their maximum potential width allows. You don't want many canopies touching each other or intermingling, because they will cause deep shade beneath and any rubbing

branches can aid the spread of diseases. However, because the forest garden is growing in three dimensions, it is possible on a plan view to have canopies overlapping, while in reality they are at different heights. So, for example, in my forest garden I quite often have tall Italian alders (*Alnus cordata*), high-pruned so they have a clean trunk of 7-8m (23-26'), with a fruiting tree to the south and partially beneath the alder canopy. Because of the orientation, the fruit tree loses almost no light as a result of the alder, yet it gains from extra frost and wind protection and benefits from the extra nitrogen in the alder leaves and roots.

Italian alder with a fruit tree. The tree can be tucked under the alder canopy on the southern side.

Try to fit in the canopy cross section with the surrounding landscape. This will not only give benefits in terms of wind flow over the forest garden (most wind eventually going right over the top of the garden instead of through it), but it also looks 'right' in the landscape. So if you have open fields on either side, aim for a dome-shaped cross section; if you have forest on one side, aim for a half dome, curving up to the forest, and so on. This gives you an indication of where to place the higher and lower canopy trees within the garden. Of course you might well have windbreak plants on an exposed edge that affect the canopy cross-section shape too.

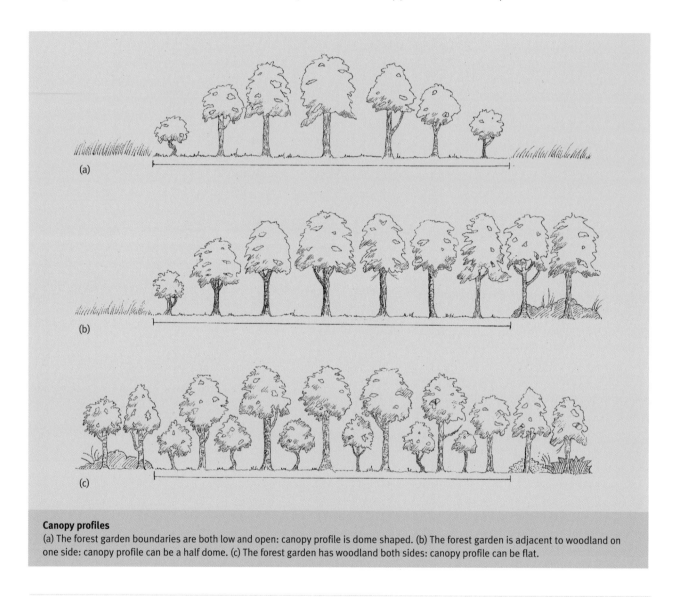

Canopy profiles
(a) The forest garden boundaries are both low and open: canopy profile is dome shaped. (b) The forest garden is adjacent to woodland on one side: canopy profile can be a half dome. (c) The forest garden has woodland both sides: canopy profile can be flat.

As well as following the cross-section guidance above, try to place lower-canopy trees to the southern end of the forest garden and higher trees to the northern end. This just minimises the amount of shade cast by the trees on to whatever is growing to their north. This may conflict with the cross-section 'rule', however – for example, if there is an open field to the north and you want the canopy layer to reduce in height down to the northern edge. In this instance, compromise and move the peak of the cross-section dome further to the north.

In a northern temperate climate such as the UK's, for fruiting trees it is best to aim for a gap between trees (when fully grown) of a quarter to a half of the tree-canopy

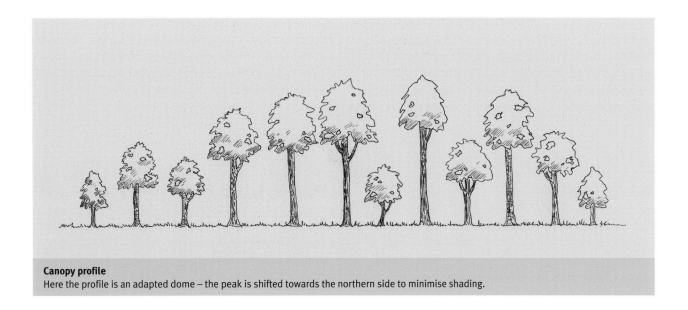

Canopy profile
Here the profile is an adapted dome – the peak is shifted towards the northern side to minimise shading.

width, to give a broken canopy that will allow significant light through to lower layers. In large forest gardens you can squeeze up tree canopies closer in places if you want (but never closer than to allow a full canopy to grow), and expect and allow for a less-productive area below, because there is usually an excess of space in the herbaceous perennial layer for crops. Most fruiting plants get 70-90 per cent of their energy from direct sunlight. Just one or two hours of direct sun filtering through to shrubs or other plants in the lower layers can double the amount of energy they receive and make a huge difference to productivity.

When trees are spaced further apart than recommended above, the garden feels less forest-like and even less orchard-like. Very close spacing leads to tall, leggy and unproductive trees which (if they are fruit trees) fruit only high up, on the top of the canopy.

Example 1: For two trees of diameter 5m (16'), leave a gap between fully grown canopies of 1.25-2.5m (4-8'). A gap of 2m (6'6") would require that the trees are planted 7m (23') apart.

Example 2: For trees of different sizes, use the average of the tree diameters to work out the gap. So for trees of 3m and 5m (10' and 16') diameters respectively (average 4m/13'), leave a gap between full canopies of 1-2m (3'-6'6"). In practice, a gap towards the lower end of the range is most suitable when the smaller tree is to the south of the larger one, and a gap towards the higher end

of the range when the smaller tree is to the north. If the trees are east–west of each other, a mid-range gap is fine.

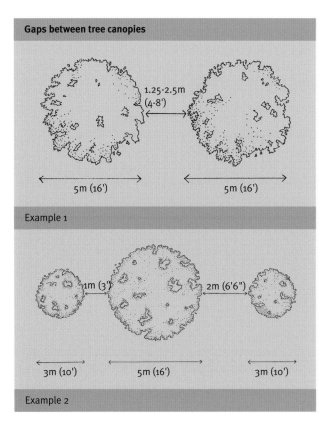

Gaps between tree canopies

1.25-2.5m (4-8')

5m (16')   5m (16')

Example 1

1m (3')   2m (6'6")

3m (10')   5m (16')   3m (10')

Example 2

In warmer and more southerly climes, these gaps between canopies can be reduced a little because the energy from the sun is greater.

Try not to always use the maximum or minimum gaps between tree canopies. Patchiness is good in many ways – it leads to varied niches below the trees, and it makes the forest garden feel more natural and wild. Try to encourage variations in vertical and horizontal density as well as variations in the timing or seasonality of growth patterns.

For a forest garden to be self-sufficient in nitrogen, aim for a total area of nitrogen-fixing trees (in the canopy layer) and shrubs (in the canopy or shrub layer) of 10-30 per cent of the total canopy area. If you have mostly heavily fruiting fruit trees as your other canopy trees, then aim towards the higher end of this range. Less-heavily cropping trees won't need quite so much. See page 53, Chapter 6, for more on nitrogen fixers.

Putting the canopy design together

I describe the canopy design as a juggling act, both in your head and physically on the map you are working with. There is a whole host of factors to think about at the same time, which at first can seem a bit daunting. Make a start and you'll soon see how it works.

For your list of trees, find out the size and shape of each one (width x height): you can find this information in Chapter 11, as well as in some garden directories of plants, and on the excellent Plants for a Future database at www.pfaf.org. You also need to note down the trees' preferences for sun, soil, shelter and pollination. Cut out a card circle to scale for each tree to fit on to your map (you can get circle cutters for paper and card, which save a lot of time), and, if there is space, jot down the plant's preferences for light, soil, etc. on the circle so they are to hand. Use blu-tac to temporarily stick the tree circles to your map.

Some trees may be managed in a way that makes their maximum size different from that of a mature tree. Coppiced trees, for example, will be shrub-sized: for example, I have several coppiced lime trees (*Tilia* spp.) for edible leaves, coppiced on a 5-year rotation, which gives them a maximum diameter of about 5m (16'). A mature lime tree will be much larger than this. Many fruiting trees can also be coppiced to keep them smaller, though there will be a delay before new shoots fruit – of 1 year for fast-fruiting

species (e.g. hazels, hawthorns and mulberries) and 2-3 years for slower-fruiting species (e.g. hickories, pecan, sweet chestnuts and persimmons). Other trees may be pruned to keep them smaller than their maximum size; where this is suitable it is noted in Chapter 11.

Give the design process plenty of time. Unless you have a tiny garden, you can't do it very well in a few hours! Stick your map with the tree circles on a board or have it on a desk where it can be for months if necessary. Spend perhaps an hour or two at a time on the design and then give yourself a break. Come back a day or a week later and you'll find you have some new ideas about tree placement. Moving one tree will usually force a daisy chain of tree moving, leading to some expected and some unexpected results.

If there are large gaps then you'll have space to add in more trees – you might need to think about what others you want. Remember the nitrogen-fixing trees too. If the trees seem too squashed together you might have to remove some.

You might need to go out into the proposed garden from time to time to help visualise the design you currently have. Where you have existing trees on the site, it can be very useful to use a sun compass (a compass mounted on a base marked with the angles of sunrise, sunset and sun angle at different times of year). With this you can stand at a given point and work out just how much sun will actually fall just there over the year. This might help you decide on whether it really is a good spot for a sun-demanding fruit tree or whether a less-demanding tree would be more suitable.

Diagram 1 (opposite) shows the direction of sunrise and sunset at different months of the year in the UK (mid-month and with north = true north. If the deviation of magnetic north from true north is more than a few degrees for your region then you need to skew the plan when you align it with the compass.) This is fairly accurate for most temperate regions. Copy the plan on to card and mount a simple compass in the centre so you can line up north on the card with north on the compass.

Diagram 2 shows the maximum angle of sun throughout the year at latitude 50° (London UK). In temperate latitudes, for every 100 miles north of this latitude, reduce the angles by 1°; for every 100 miles south increase the angles by 1°. Take the card copy of your plan and hold it

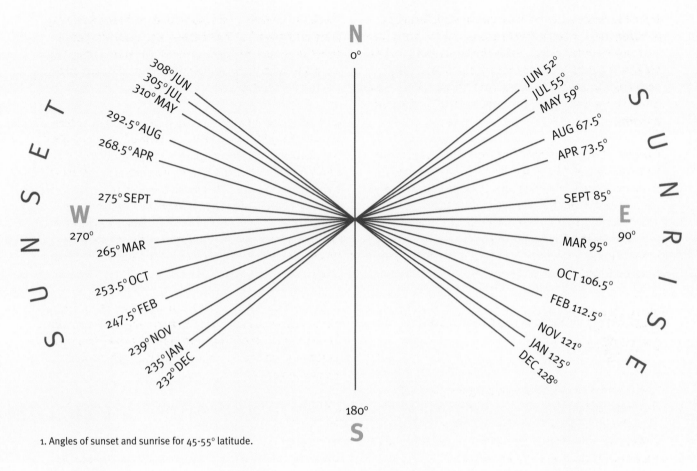

1. Angles of sunset and sunrise for 45-55° latitude.

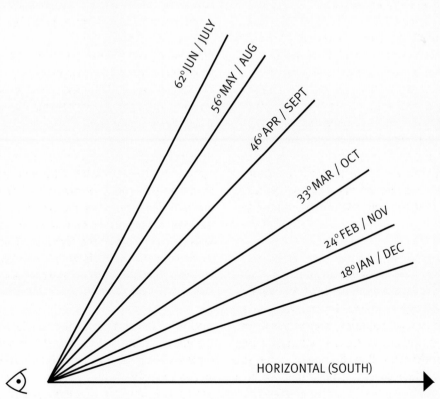

HORIZONTAL (SOUTH)

2. Maximum angle of sun for 50° latitude.

to your eye where marked, keeping the horizontal flat, to see how high the sun will get.

Try to think about all the following during this canopy design process.

- The overall height profile you want for the garden.

- Gaps between canopies.

- Aspect and site features, e.g. steep slopes – these may present both opportunities and problems.

- Soil differences across the site.

- Microclimates in the garden. Tender trees will usually do better to the leeward side of other trees.

- Each tree's individual requirements for light/shade, moisture and nutrients.

- Pollination requirements. Trees needing cross-pollination with another need to be sited fairly near (say within a tree or two), otherwise bees may not fly easily from tree to tree, and wind-blown pollen will not travel so far in a forest.

- Allelopathy and competition – a few trees can have detrimental effects on other plants (see box).

- Beneficial effects of other trees – shelter, nitrogen fixation, etc.

- Canopy height – canopies can be raised in time by pruning off lower branches; this is best for non-fruiting trees.

- Placement of nitrogen-fixing trees. They are best placed near to heavy-cropping fruit trees and heavily cropped plants such as bamboos; often north of the plants that are to benefit from the fertilisation, to minimise shading.

- Species mixing – try to mix species so that trees of the same family or species are generally not adjacent (unless pollination requires it), for pest and disease prevention.

- Any aesthetic objectives you might have.

- Finally, although you are working with a plan view, try to think in three dimensions.

TREES WITH DETRIMENTAL EFFECTS ON OTHERS

Most trees are not especially competitive with other plants or detrimental to them in other ways, but a few trees are well known for such effects.

- The walnut (*Juglans* spp.) and eucalyptus (*Eucalyptus* spp.) families are renowned for having growth-suppressing (allelopathic) effects on various plants beneath their canopies. Not all plants are affected, however. With walnuts, the apple and legume families are affected, so you should avoid planting these beneath trees of the walnut family. I have not noticed any effects beneath isolated coppiced eucalyptus trees, so it would seem that their effects occur when grown in large numbers.

- Some trees, e.g. ash (*Fraxinus excelsior*), poplars (*Populus* spp.) and tree willows (*Salix* spp.) have very competitive roots (shrub willows less so), and it may be difficult to grow other trees or shrubs very near them.

Continue your design process until you are happy with the plan, then stick the circles on to the plan. There is never an 'ideal' finished plan – you could go on forever playing with your tree circles – but you do have to stop planning and go and plant trees at some point! Ask yourself, have you achieved your aims? Usually you'll be planning prior to intended planting in autumn or winter, so you'll have a self-imposed deadline to work to. I would say allow a minimum of 2 months for the canopy design process. I spent 6 months on mine; about 2 hours per week.

Once you have your design, you need to physically mark out the tree-planting positions in your garden. Rather than measuring all the distances, measure accurately your normal pace length (measure 20 paces and divide by 20) and then pace out the distances, converting the measurements on your map into paces. Start by pacing out a small number of fairly accurate markers throughout the garden, then using these as intermediate starting points for further measuring (taking measurements from successive points leads to much inaccuracy). Mark the tree positions with bamboo canes or straight sticks. You are now ready to plant.

Finally, bear in mind that a forest garden is a complex system and can never be completely described, predicted or controlled. Although you'll come up with a final plan for the trees, allow for ongoing development in response to circumstances. Trees die sometimes, or it becomes obvious that they are in the wrong place. You might need to move a few before they are too big, or remove a tree entirely. This is all perfectly natural – you aren't trying to create a formal garden preserved in aspic.

Example canopy designs

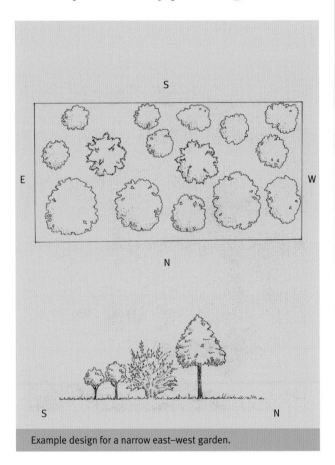

Example design for a narrow east–west garden.

This garden is long and thin; the long dimension running east–west. Wind exposure is not an issue so hedges are not required.

The canopy profile is designed to rise from south to north to minimise shading. The north edge allows for four large trees and a coppiced lime tree, which is smaller and doesn't mind shade. The southern side of the garden consists mostly of fruit trees on semi-dwarfing rootstocks – plums, pears and apples. The pears are located in the centre of the planting,

where they get more shelter. There are also a couple of autumn olives (*Elaeagnus umbellata*), which are large shrubs rather than trees. The autumn olive and the larger Italian alder (*Alnus cordata*) are nitrogen fixers and should effectively provide most or all of the nitrogen that the fruit trees require.

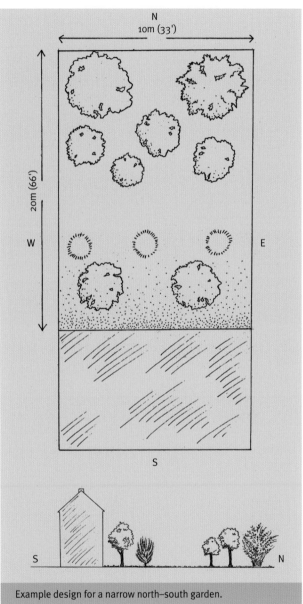

Example design for a narrow north–south garden.

This is another long thin garden, this time aligned north–south, with a house located on the south side – a common-enough arrangement in towns. Again, wind exposure is not an issue.

The occupants want an open sunny area for sitting and recreation, but this can't be located right next to the house as it is shady for most of the year there. Instead, shade-tolerant trees and shrubs are grown near the house (cooking apples require much less sun than eating apples, as they don't need the energy to develop so many sugars), reducing in height to the open area. To the north of the open area are a Siberian pea tree (*Caragana arborescens* – a nitrogen fixer) and fruit trees rising in height to the north end of the garden. The profile shows the canopy height reducing in both directions to the open area, to maximise the light and minimise shading there.

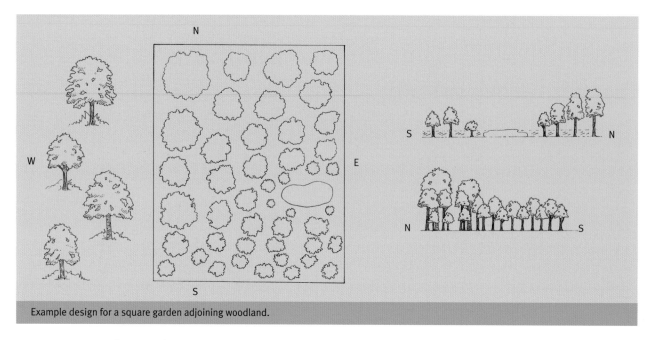

Example design for a square garden adjoining woodland.

A more square garden site, this has woodland adjoining to the west. Again, wind exposure is not an issue.

The tree size rises from east to west and from south to north. The western edge of the forest garden can be used for large trees, as the woodland abutting the garden there makes for a smooth canopy profile for the westerly winds to sweep over the garden. Note the pond site within the garden: ponds are best located in quite good light conditions to allow for a diverse and healthy pond ecosystem, so here there is a decrease in canopy height to the south and west of the pond, to allow plenty of sunlight to get through. To the north of the pond, the canopy again increases in height towards the north.

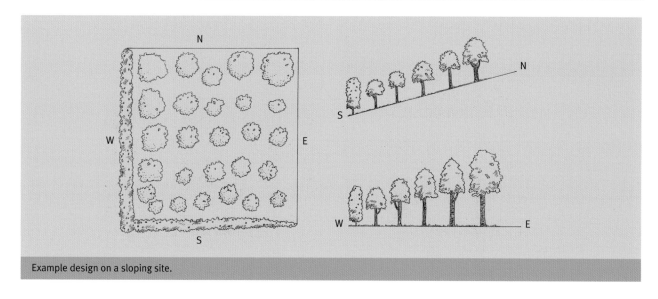

Example design on a sloping site.

The garden pictured bottom left is another squarish site, but this time on a southerly slope. Wind exposure from the south-west is an issue, so windbreak hedges are planted along the southern and western edges.

The canopy profiles show that the canopy height increases from west to east. It also rises from south to north, but there is not quite such a strong requirement to do this in order to minimise shading, because of the slope of the land. A small slope (say up to 10°) south can be more-or-less ignored at the planning stage – it won't make much difference. More than 10° can make a difference, which becomes very significant on steep slopes of 25° or more.

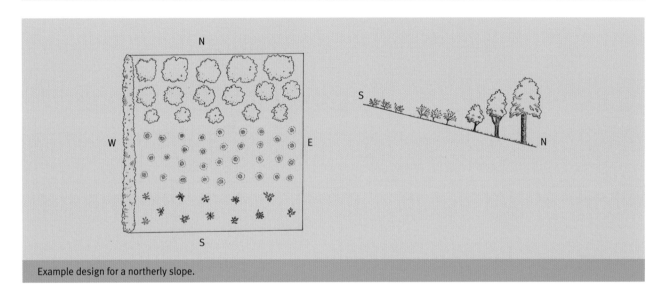

Example design for a northerly slope.

A square site, this one slopes to the north. Wind exposure to the west is an issue, so a windbreak hedge is planned along the west edge.

This example illustrates quite well how northerly slopes are not ideal for forest gardens in high latitudes. Any trees planted towards the southern edge of the site will significantly shade almost everything to their north. In this example, luckily(!) the owners want to grow a reasonable area of annual vegetables, so a whole patch of the southernmost side of the garden is allocated to vegetables. A second swathe is allocated to low bush fruit (currants, etc.), which grow only a metre or so high. The northernmost half of the garden then becomes the forest garden proper, with tree canopies increasing steeply towards the north side. The bush fruit can be underplanted – and the fruit bushes treated as a low 'canopy' – you don't always have to have trees!

Ripening fruits of saskatoon (*Amelanchier alnifolia*).

Chapter 13

Shrub species

The shrubs described here vary from small upright species to those growing 3m (10') high or so. Some of these latter larger shrubs may of course serve as the canopy species in some forest gardens. Also, some trees may in fact be treated as shrubs, if they are heavily pruned or coppiced – for example, lime trees (*Tilia* spp.) and Chinese cedar trees (*Toona sinensis*), and so may appear in the shrub layer rather than the tree layer in a garden.

Note that although many fruiting shrubs may tolerate shade, fruiting itself is usually reduced in shade. However, it does not follow that 'sun is always best', for if the shaded shrubs' yield is in addition to that of the trees causing the shading, then the overall forest garden yield may still be greater. Redcurrants, for example, fruit pretty well in deciduous shade, and can be placed beneath shade-bearing trees such as ash (*Fraxinus excelsior*), where few other fruiting plants will thrive. Their fruit yield, while not so great as in a lighter situation (probably 50-70 per cent), is still a good utilisation of the space.

Common fruiting shrubs

Most folk will know some or all of these plants, and perhaps have some in their gardens already. It is worth noting that productive and disease-resistant varieties should be chosen at the outset, rather than risking unknown free materials from friends!

DWARF FRUIT TREES

For details of fruit trees see Chapter 11, Canopy species. I don't generally recommend really dwarf fruit trees (in fact shrubs) for forest gardens because they are more prone to diseases and suffer easily from competition. However, on occasion apples on rootstocks, such as M27 and M9 (growing 1.5m and 2m (5' and 6'6") high respectively) might be suitable.

Jostaberry (*Ribes* x *culverwellii*).

Ribes x *culverwellii*, JOSTABERRY

Deciduous/Evergreen: D   **Zone:** 5
Sun/shade preference: ○
Shade tolerance: ◑
Performance rating: ✓✓✓✓
Fertility: SF   **Flowers:** Pinkish-white

This is a hybrid of blackcurrant and gooseberry (*Ribes nigrum* and *Ribes uva-crispa*, see pages 158 and 160), which has the advantages of no thorns, larger fruit than currants and no disease problems. Jostaberry is a single-trunked, multistemmed shrub.

Size: 1.5-3m (5-10') high by 1-2m (3'-6'6") wide.
Cultivation: Plant bare-rooted bushes or cuttings in winter. Tolerates most soil conditions and a little shade.
Flowering: Spring; pollinated by bees. Frost-tolerant.
Fruiting: July/August; good cropper. Fruits sweet and gooseberry-like.
Uses: Treat like gooseberry (*Ribes uva-crispa*, see page 160).
Harvest and storage: Treat like gooseberry.

Cooking/processing: As for gooseberry.
Secondary uses: Bee plant.
Propagation: Hardwood cuttings in late autumn.
Maintenance: Little required apart from occasional pruning to sustain a supply of new wood.
Cultivars: Some available in Germany, but jostaberry is usually unnamed elsewhere.

Ribes divaricatum, WORCESTERBERRY

Deciduous/Evergreen: D **Zone:** 4
Sun/shade preference: ○
Shade tolerance: ◑ ○
Performance rating: ✓✓✓✓
Fertility: SF **Flowers:** Greenish-purple

With its large thorns, this is a useful bush in hedges and other places to deter animals and humans! Worcesterberry has fruits like small gooseberries and makes a single-trunked multistemmed shrub.

Size: 2-3m (6'6"-10') high by 1.5m (5') wide.
Cultivation: Plant bare-rooted bushes or cuttings in winter. Tolerates most soil conditions and some shade.
Flowering: Spring; frost tolerant. Pollination by bees.
Fruiting: July/August. Fruits abundantly; fruits 1-1.5cm (0.4-0.6") across.
Uses: Treat like gooseberry (*Ribes uva-crispa*, see page 160).
Harvest and storage: Treat like gooseberry.
Cooking/processing: As for gooseberry.
Secondary uses: Bee plant; hedging.
Propagation: Hardwood cuttings in late autumn.
Maintenance: Pruning to keep within bounds.

Blackcurrant (*Ribes nigrum*).

Ribes nigrum, BLACKCURRANT

Deciduous/Evergreen: D **Zone:** 5
Sun/shade preference: ○
Shade tolerance: ◑
Performance rating: ✓✓✓
Fertility: SF **Flowers:** Reddish-brown

Most British gardeners know and love this plant and the strong-flavoured black fruits it bears. Reliable and easy to grow, blackcurrant gets planted in most forest gardens, where it forms a stooling multistemmed shrub.

Size: Up to 2m (6'6") high by 1m (3') wide.
Cultivation: Plant bare-rooted bushes or cuttings in winter. Tolerates most soils and light shade. Fruiting falls off in more shade.
Flowering: Mid-spring. Moderately frost-resistant; pollinated by bees.
Fruiting: Between mid-June and mid-September, depending on variety. Bushes crop for 15-20 years.
Uses: Fresh fruit, jams, fruit leathers, sauces (e.g. great with yoghurt, cooked pies, etc.).
Harvest and storage: Crops well, up to 4kg (9lb) per bush. Easy to use for making preserves. Fresh fruits store for a week or two.
Cooking/processing: Too juicy on their own to make a fruit leather, but they are great mixed in with a firmer pulp – for example plum.
Secondary uses: Bee plant. Leaves used in teas. Fruits used for dyeing purple.
Propagation: Hardwood cuttings in late autumn – you can plant cuttings straight out into the garden in most soils.

Maintenance: Prune occasionally, removing a few of the older branches close to the ground, to stimulate new growth. In shady conditions blackcurrant becomes leggy, fruiting higher up – which can be an advantage. Big bud mite, linked with reversion virus, can reduce productivity: a few varieties are resistant; otherwise maintain some distance from hazel trees, which is the alternate host.

Cultivars:

Ben Alder: Mid-season. Late flowering, producing high yields of large fruits of good quality.

Ben Connan: Mid-late season. Late flowering; heavy yields of large fruits on compact bushes.

Ben Gairn: Early season. New disease- and reversion-resistant variety giving high yields of large fruits with excellent flavour.

Ben Hope: Mid-season. New variety with good resistance to disease and big bud mite (and thus avoiding reversion). Very vigorous upright bush, heavy cropper with fruits of excellent flavour.

Ben Lomond: Mid-late season. Late flowering; large fruits with excellent flavour. Bushes moderately vigorous.

Ben More: Mid-late ripening. Very late flowering; heavy yields of very large fruits on vigorous bushes.

Ben Nevis: Mid-late season. Late flowering; fruit large and slightly sweet. Very heavy yields on bushes of moderate vigour.

Ben Sarek: Mid-late season. Late flowering; heavy yields of large fruit on small spreading bushes.

Ben Tirren: Very late season. Late flowering; heavy yields of large fruit of very good flavour.

Black Reward: Mid-late season. Late flowering; fruit medium-large with good flavour, in long clusters. Very vigorous bushes give good yields.

Byelorussian Sweet: Early season. Very hardy; large fruits; high yielding. A hardy Russian selection with frost-resistant flowers.

Hystawneznaya: Very early season (mid-June). Fruit medium-sized. A hardy Russian selection with frost-resistant flowers.

Jet: Very late season. Very late flowering; fruits medium-sized and easily picked; bushes very vigorous.

Redcurrant (*Ribes rubrum*).

Ribes rubrum,
REDCURRANT / WHITECURRANT

Deciduous/Evergreen: D   Zone: 6
Sun/shade preference: ○
Shade tolerance: ●
Performance rating: ✓✓✓
Fertility: SF   Flowers: Greenish-yellow

Another versatile *Ribes* species that is more shade-tolerant than other species, redcurrant is a useful fruiting shrub for shady sites. It makes a single-trunked, multistemmed shrub. Whitecurrant is the same species as redcurrant and exactly the same apart from the fruit colour.

Size: 2m (6'6") high by 1m (3') wide; less if heavily pruned.

Cultivation: Plant bare-rooted bushes or cuttings in winter. Tolerates most soil conditions and quite deep deciduous shade, fruiting well in shade.

Flowering: Early to mid-spring; resistant to frosts. Bee-pollinated.

Fruiting: Mid-June to early September, depending on variety. Bushes crop for 10-15 years.

Uses: Fresh fruit (moderately acid), jelly (seeds in jam are too large for most people), fruit leathers, sauces, and cooked in pies, etc.

Harvest and storage: Yields up to 4kg (9lb) per bush annually. Fresh fruits store for a week or two.

Cooking/processing: Cook lightly and put through a Moulinex sieve to remove seeds. The pulp can then easily be processed. Mix with a firmer pulp (or nuts, etc.) to make leathers.

Secondary uses: Bee plant.

Propagation: Hardwood cuttings in late autumn – you can plant cuttings straight out into the garden in most soils.

Maintenance: In shady conditions redcurrant becomes leggy, fruiting higher up – this can be an advantage and save your back. Birds love the fruit – whitecurrants (see below) and later-ripening varieties of redcurrants are taken less. Little pruning is required unless there is a lack of new wood.

Cultivars:

Redcurrant:

Cherry: Early season. Fruits very large and deep red; good cropper. Vigorous bushes.

Jonkheer van Tets: Early season. Fruits large and dark red; heavy cropping. Aphid-resistant; vigorous bushes.

Junifer: Very early season. Very early flowering; heavy cropping.

Laxton's Number One: Early-mid season. Heavy crops of medium-large fruits, easily picked. Flowers late. Vigorous bush.

Red Lake: Mid-season. Bears heavy crops of very large, dark red fruits of good flavour on long trusses. Late flowering.

Redstart: Late season. Heavy cropper, bearing medium-sized fruits of good flavour. Small bush.

Rondom: Late season. Late flowering; fruits medium-sized on moderate-length trusses, easily picked. Very productive.

Rovada: Late season. Large fruits borne in long trusses; heavy cropper.

Stanza: Mid-late season. Medium-large, deep red fruits; heavy cropper. Vigorous bush; late flowering.

Whitecurrant:

Blanka: Late season – ripens in August. Very heavy cropper.

White Versailles: Mid-season. Moderate cropper of good-flavoured fruits.

Ribes uva-crispa, GOOSEBERRY

Deciduous/Evergreen: D   Zone: 5
Sun/shade preference: ○
Shade tolerance: ◑
Performance rating: ✓✓✓
Fertility: SF   Flowers: Greenish-white

A thorny relative of the currants, gooseberry bears larger and sweeter fruits and is fairly shade-tolerant. It makes a single-trunked multistemmed shrub.

Size: 1-1.5m (3-5') high and wide.

Cultivation: Plant bare-rooted or potted bushes in winter. Tolerates most soil conditions and quite a lot of shade.

Flowering: Spring; fairly frost-resistant. Pollinated by bees.

Fruiting: Mid-June to late August, depending on variety. Green acid gooseberries can be harvested in May for cooking. Bushes crop for 25 years or so.

Uses: Fresh ripe fruit is sweet and may be used in jams, fruit leathers, sauces, cooked pies, etc. Unripe fruits are sometimes cooked and sweetened.

Harvest and storage: Annual yield is about 4kg (9lb) per bush in good light; less in shade. Fresh fruits store for a week or two.

Cooking/processing: Makes a nice fruit leather but the pulp needs a little thickening.

Secondary uses: Bee plant.

Propagation: Hardwood cuttings in late autumn – best placed in an outside nursery bed.

Maintenance: In shady conditions gooseberry becomes leggy, fruiting higher up – which can be an advantage. American gooseberry mildew can be damaging: choose mildew-resistant varieties if possible. Occasional pruning may be needed to sustain cropping.

Cultivars: All the following are resistant to American gooseberry mildew.

Annelli: Late season. Fruit red and of good flavour. Bushes vigorous.

Black Velvet: Mid-season. Fruit dark, reddish-black and oval, with very good flavour.

Gold Ball: Late season. Fruit yellowish-green with good flavour.

Hamamekii: Mid-season. Fruit red with good flavour. Bushes vigorous.

Hino Red: Mid-season. Fruit medium-sized, dark red with very good flavour.

Hino Yellow: Mid-season. Fruit yellowish-green, medium-large with good flavour. Bushes compact.

Invicta: Mid-season. Heavy crops of medium-sized green fruits of good flavour. Bushes vigorous and spreading.
Pax: Early season. Fruits dark red and round, with excellent flavour. Bushes bear only a few thorns.

Rubus fruticosus, BLACKBERRY

Deciduous/Evergreen: D   **Zone:** 6
Sun/shade preference: ○
Shade tolerance: ●
Performance rating: ✓✓✓
Fertility: SF   **Flowers:** White

In a natural environment, blackberry moves by tip layering (i.e. its arching shoots touch the ground and root where they touch). In a 'normal' garden environment these and similar berries are usually not allowed to layer and move. But, like raspberry (*Rubus idaeus,* see right), these plants stay healthier and more productive if you can allow them to move – at least sometimes.

In a forest garden it is easy to allow blackberries to move. I encourage them to clamber into the low branches on the south or west sides of shrubs and trees, to keep the fruits off the ground and better hidden from birds.

Size: 2-4m (6'6"-13') – long, scrambling shrubs.
Cultivation: Plant potted or bare-rooted bushes in winter. Tolerates most soils and deep shade, although fruiting reduces in shade.
Flowering: Spring. Frost-tolerant; pollinated by bees.
Fruiting: August to October.
Uses: Fresh fruit; also cooked. Jams, cooked in pies, etc. Not flavourful enough to dry well.
Harvest and storage: Most varieties ripen over several weeks. Fresh fruits don't store for long.
Secondary uses: Bee plant. The crisp young shoot tips are edible, very nice cooked (use only when any spines are still soft). Leaves used for teas. Purplish dyes can be made from shoots and fruit. Stems used for basketry (can be de-spined by pulling through a hole).
Propagation: Hardwood cuttings in winter take reasonably well. Tips will root where they touch the soil and become new plants.
Maintenance: Little needed. It is advisable to use thornless varieties in a forest garden so you can readily distinguish and remove weed brambles.

Cultivars:
Adrienne: Early season. Bears long fruits of excellent flavour; easily picked. Spineless; good cropper.
Ashton Cross: Mid-season. Thin, thorny, very vigorous canes. Fruits are small-medium-sized with good flavour. Heavy cropper.
Bedford Giant: Early season. Thorny, vigorous canes. Large fruit with average flavour. Heavy cropper.
Black Satin: Mid-late season. Vigorous canes, resistant to cane spot. Fruits are large, firm and keep well. Productive.
Helen: Very early season. Spineless canes; compact bush. Fruits are large with a very good flavour.
Himalaya: Mid-late season. Canes long, stout, thorny and extremely vigorous. Fruit medium-sized with average flavour. Moderate cropping. Good in barriers and windbreaks.
Loch Ness: Mid-late season. Canes thornless. Fruits large and firm; very heavy cropper.
Oregon Thornless: Mid-late season. Thornless, evergreen or semi-evergreen canes of moderate vigour. Fruits medium-sized, roundish-oval, firm and sweet with good flavour. Bears good crops in fertile soils.
Thornfree: Late season. Vigorous, thornless canes. Fruit medium-large, firm, with good sweet-acid flavour. Very heavy cropping.
Waldo: Mid-season. Canes spineless and moderately vigorous. Fruit large, firm, with good flavour and keep well. Heavy cropper.

Rubus idaeus, RASPBERRY

Deciduous/Evergreen: D   **Zone:** 3
Sun/shade preference: ○
Shade tolerance: ◐
Performance rating: ✓✓✓
Fertility: SF   **Flowers:** White

This is one fruit almost everyone will want in their forest garden. Raspberry is a forest-edge plant, and its normal behaviour is to move by suckering with an expanding forest edge as part of the succession to forest.

In a 'normal' garden environment a raspberry bed is usually surrounded by mown paths or otherwise not allowed to expand and take over the garden. The result is that the raspberry plants fairly quickly exhaust the soil of particular micro-nutrients; they get stressed and then diseased, often with virus diseases. Ten years is the expected productive life of such a bed.

In a forest garden I strongly recommend that you allow your raspberries to move! As a result they will stay healthy and productive for much longer. This doesn't mean you have to let them go anywhere, however – you can still control where they move if you want.

Also in a 'normal' garden, raspberries are usually tied up vertically and netted against birds. This is something you should not need to do in a forest garden. Instead, allow the fruiting raspberry canes to arch over and rest on other shrubs or perennials; the fruits are better hidden from birds on arching canes. To harvest, pick each cane up and look underneath for the fruits. Of course the birds will get a few fruits, but there should be plenty for you too.

Size: About 2m (6'6") high, spreading by suckers, each cane biennial.

Cultivation: Plant bare-rooted or pot-grown canes in winter. Tolerates most soils and quite a lot of shade. Try to plant where the canes can arch over and rest on smaller sturdy plants so they can support the fruiting canes.

Flowering: Spring; fairly frost-tolerant. Pollinated by bees.

Fruiting: Late June to November (to December in mild areas).

Uses: Fresh fruit; also cooked. Jams, etc.

Harvest and storage: Most varieties ripen over several weeks. Fresh fruits don't store for long.

Cooking/processing: The pulp needs mixing with something thicker (for example, plum pulp) before drying into a leather.

Secondary uses: Bee plant. Leaves used for teas.

Propagation: Dig up suckers.

Maintenance: Little required. Dead canes can be broken off or cut down. It is advisable to use thornless varieties in a forest garden so you easily distinguish and remove weed brambles.

Cultivars:

Summer-fruiting raspberries:

Glen Ample: Mid-season. Canes vigorous, upright and spineless. Fruits medium-large, bright red, round-conical and firm, with excellent flavour but crumbly in cool climates; easily picked. Crops heavily.

Glen Clova: Early-mid season. Canes erect and strong. Fruits of good flavour, medium-large, round, bright red, ripening over a long period. Heavy cropper.

Glen Garry: Early-mid season. Canes heavy yielding, spineless and moderately vigorous. Fruits very large, conical, firm and pale red, with excellent flavour.

Glen Lyon: Early-mid season. Canes establish quickly; are spineless and moderately vigorous. Fruits medium-large, bright red, firm and easily picked, with acid flavour. Keeps well.

Glen Magna: Late season. Canes erect, vigorous, moderately numerous with few spines. Fruits very large, deep red, long and conical; moderately firm with excellent flavour. Crops very heavily.

Glen Moy: Early season. Canes erect, vigorous, spine-free. Fruits large and firm with good flavour. Crops well. Occasionally produces autumn fruits on the young canes.

Glen Prosen: Mid-season. Canes moderately vigorous. Fruits firm; medium-sized with good flavour. Crops well.

Glen Rosa: Mid-season. Canes moderately vigorous and upright; spineless. Fruits medium-sized, red and firm with fairly good flavour; good quality and easily picked. Moderate cropper; good in cool climates.

Glen Shee: Canes vigorous, quite upright and spineless. Fruits slightly pale, firm and fleshy, with soft skin and fair flavour.

Glen Yarra: Mid-season. Canes strong, erect and spineless. Fruits medium-large, firm and red. Adapted to warm winter regions.

Leo: Very late season – until late August. Canes upright and very vigorous but slow to multiply in early years; long laterals. Fruits large, round, pubescent and bright orange-red; firm and slightly acid with good flavour. Moderate cropper; tolerant of poor soils.

Malling Admiral: Mid-late season. Canes vigorous and fairly erect. Fruits large, red and firm with good flavour. Pulls easily off plug. Crops very well.

Malling Jewel: Mid-season. Canes sturdy. Fruits large and red with good flavour. Pulls easily off plug and hangs well on canes. Heavy cropper; frost-resistant. Late flowering; easily picked.

Malling Joy: mid- and late season. Canes tall and spreading; produce a large number of laterals and should be spaced wider than normal. Fruits large, blunt and conical; very firm, slightly pubescent with good, slightly acid flavour. Pulls easily off plug. Very heavy cropper.

Malling Promise: Early season – June. Canes vigorous, but slow to multiply at first. Fruits good flavour, large, bright red, soft and crumbly. Pulls easily off plug. Heavy yielding and frost-resistant.

Octavia: Late season. Useful variety with large fruits ripening in August and September.

Tulameen: Mid- and late season. Canes vigorous, fairly upright and spine-free except at base. Fruits very large, red, firm and of good flavour; easily picked. Ripens over a very long period. Very productive.

Autumn-fruiting raspberries:

All Gold: Yellow fruited sport of Autumn Bliss.

Autumn Bliss: Ripens mid-August onwards. Canes very prolific, fairly erect and of moderate height – doesn't need much support. Fruits large, red and firm with mild flavour; easily picked. A good reliable cropper.

Fallgold: Canes moderately vigorous and productive. Fruits large, round, yellow, sweet and freeze well. Very hardy.

Zeva: Ripens from mid-August. Canes vigorous though slow to establish; medium height. Fruits very large, conical, dark red, soft and crumbly with very good flavour. Very heavy cropper.

Rubus x *loganobaccus*, **LOGANBERRY** & *Rubus* spp., **RUBUS HYBRIDS**

Loganberries and *Rubus* hybrid berries have fruits that are like larger, longer versions of blackberries. See *Rubus fruticosus* (blackberry), page 161, for cultivation details. The flowers, like blackberry's, are white.

Cultivars:

Boysenberry: Mid-season. Canes vigorous, slender and spiny. Fruits dark reddish-purple; very large with excellent flavour. Heavy yielding.

Loganberry: Mid-season. Moderate vigour. Fruit large, claret-red and juicy with excellent flavour. Heavy cropper. Thornless clone available.

Sunberry: Early season. Canes stout, thorny and extremely vigorous. Fruit medium-large, purplish-black with pleasant flavour. Heavy cropping.

Tayberry: Very early season. Canes moderately vigorous; branching. Fruits very large, dark purplish-red with very good sweet-acid flavour; easily picked. High yielding. A thornless variety ('Buckingham Tayberry') is available.

Rubus phoenicolasius, **JAPANESE WINEBERRY**

Deciduous/Evergreen: D   Zone: 5
Sun/shade preference: ◯
Shade tolerance: ◑
Performance rating: ✓✓✓
Fertility: SF   Flowers: Whitish-pink

This unusual *Rubus* species is quite common in Britain. The name perhaps comes from the wine-red colour of the fruits, which are of good flavour and don't have to be made into wine!

Size: 1.5-2m (5'-6'6") high by 2m (6'6") wide, with arching biennial stems.

Cultivation: Plant pot-grown canes in early-mid winter (comes early into growth). Tolerates most soils; needs some sun for good fruiting but tolerates shade.

Flowering: Spring; fairly frost-tolerant.

Fruiting: Late July to early September; fruits abundantly. Fruits are protected from pests by leafy calyces until ripe.

Uses: As for raspberry (*Rubus idaeus*; see page 161).

Harvest and storage: Fresh fruits do not store for long, but ripen over a long period.

Cooking/processing: As for raspberry.

Secondary uses: Bee plant.

Propagation: Layering via rooting stem tips, or by seed.

Maintenance: Cut out dead old prickly stems to ease access. Don't let shoot tips root unless you want the bush to spread. Stems are very prickly, so care is needed when attending.

Cultivars: None available.

Vaccinium australe & V. corymbosum, NORTHERN BLUEBERRIES

Deciduous/Evergreen: D/E **Zone:** 2-6
Sun/shade preference: ●
Shade tolerance: ◐
Performance rating: ✓✓✓✓
Fertility: SF **Flowers:** White

Northern blueberries are very hardy; these are what we normally think of when referring to blueberries. Most northern blueberries are highbush (i.e. at least 1m/3' high) although some are 'half high', making lower bushes.

Vaccinium ashei & V. darrowii, SOUTHERN BLUEBERRIES

Deciduous/Evergreen: E **Zone:** 6-9
Sun/shade preference: ●
Shade tolerance: ◐
Performance rating: ✓✓✓
Fertility: SF **Flowers:** White

Southern blueberries are less hardy than the northern types. They are often evergreen and require less winter chilling. Some varieties are highbush and others half high.

Blueberries are self-fertile but cross-pollination with a second variety improves yields. They are acid-loving shrubs with delicious fruits.

Size: 1-1.5m (3-5') high and wide.
Cultivation: Plant pot-grown bushes in winter. Acid soil (under pH 5.5) is essential for most varieties, though a few of the southern types will tolerate pH 6.0. They require sun – tolerate only light shade.
Flowering: Spring; bee-pollinated.
Fruiting: Summer. Crops for 50 years.
Uses: Fresh fruits may be eaten raw or cooked.
Harvest and storage: Bushes can yield 5kg (11lb) annually. Fresh fruits store for a week or two. Whole fruits can be dried.
Secondary uses: Very good bumble-bee plant. Purple dyes can be made from fruits and leaves.

Propagation: By softwood cuttings in summer.
Maintenance: If bushes start losing productivity, prune out some of the oldest unproductive wood in March. Birds often go for the fruits.
Cultivars:
Berkeley: Northern highbush. Mid-season. Bush vigorous, upright, open-spreading and very productive. Fruits medium-large, light blue and firm with mild sweet flavour; fair quality. Resistant to cracking. Fruits fall if harvest is delayed; yields better on heavy soils.
Bluecrop: Northern highbush. Early season. Bush upright and moderately vigorous, with good autumn colour. Fruits large, very light blue, firm and moderate quality; a good cropper. Resistant to drought and fruit cracking. Still the leading cultivar in the world despite its age.
Bluetta: Northern highbush. Early season. Bush compact/spreading, moderately vigorous and productive. Fruit small-medium-sized, light blue and firm; softens rapidly after ripening. Difficult to prune.
Chandler: Northern highbush. Mid-late season. Bush vigorous, upright, well branched and high yielding. Fruits large and light blue; firm with good flavour. Ripens over a long period.
Darrow: Northern highbush. Very late season. Bush upright and vigorous. Fruits very large, firm and light blue; very good quality. Resistant to cracking.
Duke: Northern highbush. Early-mid season. Bush vigorous and upright with numerous canes; fairly late flowering. Fruits medium-sized, light blue and firm with mild flavour.
Earliblue: Northern highbush. Early season. Bush with strong upright growth and good autumn colour; productive but erratic. Fruits large, aromatic, light blue and good quality. Resistant to cracking and premature drop.
Herbert: Northern highbush. Mid-season. Bush many-branched, fairly open and spreading; moderately vigorous. Fruits very large, medium blue, in very heavy compact clusters with excellent flavour. Resistant to cracking.
Jersey: Northern highbush. Late season. Bush upright and spreading. Fruits small-medium; excellent flavour. Suited to mechanical harvesting and widely grown for processing.
Misty: Southern highbush. Bush tall, upright and vigorous with small crown. Fruits large, light blue and firm.
Patriot: Northern highbush. Early season. Bush small (1.2m, 4'), open-spreading and very hardy. Fruits large, light blue and very good quality.
Reka: Northern highbush. Early season. Bush very high yielding. Fruits medium-sized.
Sunshine Blue: Southern highbush. Bush small (1.2m, 4'),

wide. Fruits small; firm with good flavour. Stores well. Tolerates soil up to pH 6 and drought.

Less common fruiting shrubs

Most of these shrubs are cultivated in different parts of the world for their fruits, and some have been bred for good fruiting selections. They can add a lot of diversity to the shrub layer and provide wonderful extra flavours.

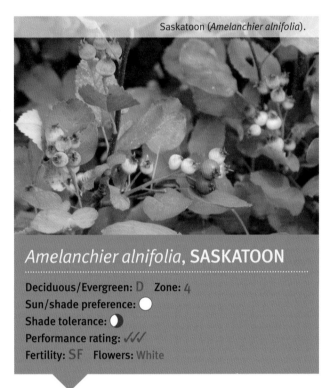

Saskatoon (*Amelanchier alnifolia*).

Amelanchier alnifolia, SASKATOON

Deciduous/Evergreen: D Zone: 4
Sun/shade preference: ◑
Shade tolerance: ◑
Performance rating: ✓✓✓
Fertility: SF   Flowers: White

A hardy North American large shrub with excellent blueberry-like fruits, the saskatoon is one of the juneberries or serviceberries. The fruits of other *Amelanchier* species can also be eaten – see page 117, Chapter 11.

Size: 2-3m (6-10') high by 2m (6'6") wide – slowly suckering.
Cultivation: Plant pot-grown seedlings or divided plants in winter. Tolerates most soils and light shade.
Flowering: Spring. Quite ornamental; moderately frost-tolerant.
Fruiting: Starts in 2-3 years. Fruits dark blue-purple, usually ripening in July in the UK.
Uses: Use fresh or cooked.
Harvest and storage: Picking is fast with a harvesting comb (berry picker). Average annual yield 4kg (9lb) per plant. Fresh fruits store for a week or two.
Cooking/processing: Makes a nice jam. Cook lightly and use a Moulinex sieve to remove seeds.
Secondary uses: Bee plant; hedging.
Propagation: By seed – requires 5 months' stratification.
Maintenance: Little required. Birds love to eat this fruit! So you may need to net bushes.
Cultivars: Cultivars have been selected in Canada, including:
Martin: Early-flowering variety with large fruits of excellent flavour.
Northline: Upright shrub to 2m (6'6") high; freely suckering. Fruits slightly pear-shaped, large and sweet, with good flavour.
Regent: Hardy, bushy shrub 1.2-2m (4'-6'6") high; suckering and very productive with very sweet fruit; fair flavour (somewhat seedy). Bears fruit after 2 years.
Smoky: Spreading bush, 2-2.5m (6'6"-8') high, bearing large, red-purple, round fruit (to 1.8cm, 0.7") 2-3 years after planting. Fruit is sweet with fair flavour; ripens July. Very cold- and drought-resistant.
Thiessen: Small roundish tree or open bush to 5m (16') high; moderately suckering. Large fruits with fair flavour; productive.

Strawberry tree (*Arbutus unedo* f. *rubra*).

Arbutus unedo, STRAWBERRY TREE

For full details see page 117, Chapter 11 (Canopy species). Dwarf varieties, which are shrubs, are listed here.

Cultivars:
Compacta: Dwarf to 2m (6'6") high.
Elfin King: Dwarf to 2m (6'6") high; flowers and fruits prolifically.
A. unedo f. *rubra*: flowers and fruits prolifically; fruits are a little smaller than average.

Purple chokeberry (*Aronia prunifolia*) 'Nero'.

Aronia arbutifolia, *A. melanocarpa* & *A. prunifolia*, CHOKEBERRIES / ARONIA BERRIES

Deciduous/Evergreen: D **Zone:** 4
Sun/shade preference: ○
Shade tolerance: ◑
Performance rating: ✓✓✓✓
Fertility: SF **Flowers:** White

I always think that 'chokeberry' is such an unfair name for this American woodland shrub, which is pleasant to eat when ripe. The fruits are very high in nutritional compounds and the juice is often added to fruit juice mixes; the berries are grown commercially for juice in mainland Europe.

Size: *A. arbutifolia* (red chokeberry): 3m (10') high by 1.5m (5') wide.
A. melanocarpa (black chokeberry): 2m (6'6") high by 3m (10') wide.
A. prunifolia (purple chokeberry): 3m (10') high by 2.5m (8') wide.
Cultivation: Plant pot-grown or bare-rooted plants in winter. Tolerate most soils. Tolerate shade but fruiting is reduced out of sun.
Flowering: Late spring; fairly frost-tolerant.
Fruiting: August/September. Fruiting starts in 2-3 years.
Uses: Fruits currant-sized; eaten raw, cooked, or made into juice or preserves.
Harvest and storage: Picking is easiest with a harvesting comb (berry picker). Bushes in sun fruit heavily. Fresh fruits will store for a week or two.
Cooking/processing: The fruits make a nice jam and can

be mixed in with other pulps to make leathers. Cook lightly and use a Moulinex sieve to remove seeds.
Secondary uses: Bee plants. Hedging.
Propagation: By seed – requires 3 months' stratification. Cultivars are propagated by cuttings.
Maintenance: Little required.
Cultivars: These have been selected for large fruits and heavy cropping:
A. melanocarpa:
Hugin
A. prunifolia:
Nero
Viking

Berberis spp., BARBERRIES

Deciduous/Evergreen: D/E **Zone:** 6
Sun/shade preference: ○
Shade tolerance: ◑
Performance rating: ✓✓✓
Fertility: SF **Flowers:** Yellow

This is a large group of deciduous and evergreen shrubs found in the wild in scrub and woodland situations. Most folk know of ornamental *Berberis* growing in gardens, often as prickly hedges. Barberries do make good animal (and human)-proof hedges, but they also all have edible fruits. The fruits are small, acidic and loved by birds, and in a forest garden they may be useful as a sacrificial crop, to tempt birds away from something more valuable. I occasionally nibble on the fruits in season, and more often on the dried fruits of *B. lycium*, which dry on the bush and remain over winter.

Size: Variable, but most are about 3m (10') high by 2m (6'6") wide. Some are deciduous (e.g. *B. aristata*, *B. 'Georgei'*, *B. koreana* and *B. vulgaris*); others evergreen (e.g. *B. asiatica*, *B. buxifolia*, *B. darwinii* and *B. lycium*).
Cultivation: Plant pot-grown or bare-rooted plants in winter. Exposed evergreens may need staking. They tolerate most soils and shade. Evergreen species tolerate deep deciduous shade.
Flowering: Spring and summer.
Fruiting: Late summer and autumn. Fruits usually 1-1.6cm (0.4-0.7") long; acid.
Uses: Can be eaten raw or cooked, or made into preserves.
Harvest and storage: Best treated as an occasional nibble. Fresh fruits don't store for long.

Cooking/processing: Using a harvesting comb (berry picker) works on many barberry species and is the only sensible way to harvest a lot of barberry fruits.
Secondary uses: Bee plants. Hedging. Yellow dye from bark and roots. Medicinal roots (source of berberine, which has anti-cancer and other properties).
Propagation: By seed (requires 2-3 months' stratification) or semi-ripe cuttings.
Maintenance: Little required. They tolerate cutting and pruning. Birds like the fruits.
Cultivars:
Heavily fruiting hybrids including *B.* x *carminea* 'Buccaneer' and *B.* x *lologensis* 'Mystery Fire' are recommended. Scientists in the USSR-bred 'Rubin' from *B. koreana* as a good fruiting variety high in vitamins.

Japanese plum yew (*Cephalotaxus harringtonii* var. *drupacea*).

Cephalotaxus spp., PLUM YEWS

Deciduous/Evergreen: E   Zone: 6
Sun/shade preference: ◐
Shade tolerance: ●
Performance rating: ✓✓✓✓
Fertility: M/F   Flowers: Pale green

See also page 176, in 'Shrubs for nuts and seeds'.

Originating from Chinese and Japanese forests, these make a good understorey crop in very shaded locations. When I take people round my forest garden, the plum yews usually elicit a 'what are *they*?' response. They look like small yew trees, yet bear greenish cherry-sized fruits (they don't really look like plums!). This is one of my favourites of the unusual fruits: the flavour when ripe is sweet butterscotch / pine nut – very distinctive. The Chinese

plum yew is *C. fortunei*; the Japanese plum yew is *C. harringtonii*.

Size: 3-5m (10-16') high and wide, but slow-growing and take 15-20 years to reach full size.
Cultivation: Plant pot-grown plants in winter or spring. They tolerate most soils, prefer some shade and tolerate deep shade, fruiting well there. Slow-growing for a few years – protect from weeds.
Flowering: In May in the UK. Flowers fairly inconspicuous. Wind-pollinated.
Fruiting: Starts after 4-5 years. Fruits ripen late October and November in the UK. The green fruits darken and soften when ripe.
Uses: Fresh fruit – I eat them raw off the bush.
Harvest and storage: Pick fruits when they darken in colour and soften in November. Fresh fruits store for a week or two.
Cooking/processing: I have never processed the fruits. They are quite juicy and would need to be mixed with a firmer pulp to make a leather.
Secondary uses: The oily peanut-sized kernel in the seed is also edible, with a resinous flavour. Leaves and shoots are strongly medicinal (they contain anti-cancer compounds).
Propagation: by seed – requires 3 months' stratification (slow germination). Cuttings.
Maintenance: Little required.

Chaenomeles spp., FLOWERING QUINCES

Deciduous/Evergreen: D   Zone: 5
Sun/shade preference: ○
Shade tolerance: ◖
Performance rating: ✓✓✓
Fertility: SF   Flowers: Pink, red, white

I regard these as more versatile crops than true quince (*Cydonia oblonga*) in a forest garden. The flowers are much hardier so they are reliable croppers, they are shade-tolerant, and the fruits, while acid, have a wonderful range of lemon and orange citrus flavours. My favourite use of the fruits is to make drinks from them (see box overleaf). They are too acid to eat raw for most folk, though I know people who love them raw, which goes to show how different people's palates are.

Size: *C. x californica*: 1.8m (6') high and wide.
C. cathayensis: 3m (10') high and wide.
C. japonica: 1m (3') high by 2m (6'6") wide.
C. speciosa: 3m (10') high by 5m (16') wide.
C. x superba: 1.5m (5') high by 2m (6'6") wide.
Cultivation: Plant bare-rooted or pot-grown plants in winter (they come early into growth). Tolerate most soils and a lot of shade.
Flowering: Spring; frost-tolerant.
Fruiting: Starts at a young age. Fruits are generally 3-4cm (1.2-1.6") across, although *C. cathayensis* bears fruits 10-12cm (4-5") across.
Uses: Cooked, made into preserves, or made into drinks.
Harvest and storage: Fruits ripen in September and October, often turning yellowish. They will store in a cool place for several weeks. I often chuck some straight in the freezer, after which they liquidise much more easily.
Cooking/processing: See 'Quince lemonade' box, opposite. You can also make jelly and cook the fruits, especially with other fruit, to add a lemony flavour.
Secondary uses: Bee plants; hedges.
Propagation: By seed – requires 3-5 months' stratification. Cuttings.
Maintenance: Little or none required. These are fantastic low-maintenance fruiting plants.
Cultivars: All can be used; the following are known heavy croppers with larger fruits.
C. x californica:
Enchantress: Compact shrub; flowers dark rose-pink; fruits large and yellow.
Masterpiece: Flowers pink-red, early; fruits large and ovate.
C. cathayensis: bears fruits 7-10cm (2.7-4") diameter.
C. japonica:
Cido: bred in the Baltic region of the former USSR. Heavy cropping with larger fruits.
C. speciosa:
Aurora: Tall-growing; flowers pink with yellow overtones. Fruits large and orange.
Falconnet Charlet: Vigorous; flowers light and dark pink; fruits large and apple-shaped.
Grandiflora: Strong sprawling grower. Flowers white, pink and yellowish; fruits ovate and large.
C. x superba:
Boule de Fer: To 2m (6'6") high; very thorny. Flowers early; fruits are carmine-red. A heavy cropper.
Crimson and Gold: Bears masses of apple-sized fruits.
Fusion: Fruits very young, with large fruits.
Nicoline: To 1.8m (6') high with abundant scarlet flowers, followed by large, rounded fruits, deep yellow.
Ruby Glow: Vigorous and upright with few thorns; flowers red, fruits large, ovate.

Goumi (*Elaeagnus multiflora*).

Elaeagnus multiflora, GOUMI

Deciduous/Evergreen: D **Zone:** 6
Sun/shade preference: ◐
Shade tolerance: ◑
Performance rating: ✓✓✓
Fertility: SF–SS   **Flowers:** White

This Japanese woodland shrub looks like a smaller version of autumn olive (*Elaeagnus umbellata*), with cherry-sized fruits. It is usually self-sterile, so it's probably wise to grow two selections for cross-pollination.

Size: 2-3m (6'6"-10') high and wide.
Cultivation: Plant bare-rooted or pot-grown plants in winter (comes early into growth). Tolerates most soils and some shade.
Flowering: Spring.
Fruiting: Starts in 3-4 years. Fruits 2-2.5cm (0.8-1") long; oval.
Uses: Fresh fruit, jams and other preserves.
Harvest and storage: Fruits ripen in early August in the UK, turning reddish. They are astringent before fully ripe.

Harvest as they darken from orange to red. They don't store for long.

Cooking/processing: Fruits contain one seed, which needs removing when processing; cook lightly and use a Moulinex sieve. The pulp makes great jams and leathers.

Secondary uses: Bee plants; hedging; nitrogen-fixing.

Propagation: By seed – requires 2-3 months' stratification.

Maintenance: Little required. If birds are interested in the fruits then harvest and process them.

Cultivars: 'Sweet Scarlet': Selected in the USA, self-fertile, it fruits heavily with large, sweeter fruits than the species.

Fuchsia spp., FUCHSIAS

Deciduous/Evergreen: E **Zone:** 8
Sun/shade preference: ◐
Shade tolerance: ◐
Performance rating: ✓✓✓
Fertility: SF **Flowers:** White, red, purple

Many people are surprised to learn that all fuchsia fruits are edible. However, outside of their native South America, only a small number of *Fuchsia* varieties seem to bear fruit, because most have been bred for flowers – which do not get pollinated by hummingbirds as they would in the wild. Bees like the flowers but this rarely results in pollination. The fruits are cherry-sized, dark blue or black, with a flavour reminiscent of plum with a peppery after-tone – very nice. Top growth is hardy to about -5°C to -10°C (23-14°F). Root hardiness is greater and the plants will become herbaceous perennials in colder climes.

Fuchsia magellanica is the hardiest species and the one detailed here.

Size: 1-3m (3-10') high and wide.

Cultivation: Plant pot-grown plants in spring to avoid frost damage to young plants. Prefers a well-drained soil and sun or light shade. Avoid frost pockets.

Flowering: Summer.

Fruiting: Autumn. Fruits 1.5-2.5cm (0.6-1") long.

Uses: The fruits are cherry-sized and excellent to eat, with an unusual peppery plum flavour.

Harvest and storage: Pick fruits as they darken and soften. Use quickly. They ripen in late summer and autumn over a long period.

Cooking/processing: I just eat them raw. No doubt you could make a jam out of them, but they are probably too juicy to dry as a leather on their own.

Secondary uses: Bee plant. Hedging in mild areas. The wood is used as a black dye.

Propagation: By semi-ripe cuttings in summer.

Maintenance: Mulch in winter in colder areas to protect roots. Cut out any dead wood in spring.

Cultivars:

Globosa: Bushy, 0.6-1m (2-3') high. Bears numerous fruits.

var. *gracilis*: Graceful shrub, 1-2m (3'-6'6") high. Flowers dainty, slender and scarlet-purple.

Phyllis: Very hardy, bushy, upright; 30-45cm (1-1'6") high. Flowers rosy-cerise and numerous.

Riccartonii: Very hardy, upright, 2-3m (6'6"-10') high. Flowers scarlet-purple.

Salal (*Gaultheria shallon*).

Gaultheria shallon, SALAL / SHALLON

Deciduous/Evergreen: E **Zone:** 6
Sun/shade preference: ○
Shade tolerance: ●
Performance rating: ✓✓✓
Fertility: SF **Flowers:** White

Another very nice fruiting shrub for a shady location, salal is native to the understorey of forests in western North America. It bears currant-sized fruits with a blueberry-like flavour.

Size: 1.2m (4') high by 1.5m (5') wide, spreading by suckers.

Cultivation: Plant pot-grown plants in winter. Requires acid soil. Tolerates deep shade and fruits well in shade.

Flowering: Late spring and summer.

Fruiting: August and September. Fruiting starts in 2-3

years. Fruits are dark blue, 1cm (0.4") across, sweet and very nice; borne abundantly.

Uses: Fresh fruit, jams, cooked, etc. The flavour is like blueberry.

Harvest and storage: Hand-pick when fruits darken and soften. The fresh fruits keep for a week or so.

Cooking/processing: The seeds are tiny, so you can use the entire fruit in jams, leathers, etc.

Secondary uses: Very good bumble-bee plant. Hedging.

Propagation: By seed – requires 4 months' stratification. You can also dig up suckers.

Maintenance: Little required. Salal is slow-growing when young, but will sucker about 30cm (1') a year, so trim back shoots that come up where you don't want them. This is an excellent crop for shady areas.

Cultivars: None selected for better fruiting.

Juniperus communis, JUNIPER

Deciduous/Evergreen: E   **Zone:** 3
Sun/shade preference: ◯
Shade tolerance: ◑
Performance rating: ✓✓
Fertility: M/F   **Flowers:** Yellow

Juniper is an evergreen native shrub of open ground, best known for its fruits, used in gin. It is best to grow a few plants from seed or buy several seedling plants, so you get male and female bushes to ensure fruiting.

Size: Very variable – 1-5m (3-16') high and wide.

Cultivation: Plant bare-rooted or pot-grown bushes in winter. Likes a well-drained soil and sun or light shade.

Flowering: Summer.

Fruiting: Fruits take 2-3 years to ripen, ripening in autumn.

Uses: Usually used cooked as a flavouring or to make gin!

Harvest and storage: Pick when fruits darken. Dry to store.

Cooking/processing: Great as a seasoning.

Secondary uses: Shoots used for teas. Hedging.

Propagation: By seed – requires 6 months' stratification. Germination is slow.

Maintenance: Little required.

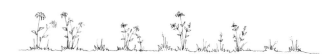

DROUGHT-TOLERANT SHRUBS

Broom (*Cytisus scoparius*)
Buffalo berries (*Shepherdia* spp.)
Chilean guava (*Myrtus ugni*)
Chinkapin (*Castanea pumila*)
Elaeagnus (*Elaeagnus* spp.)
Fever bush (*Garrya elliptica*)
Four-wing saltbush (*Atriplex canescens*)
Hawthorns (*Crataegus* spp.)
Highbush cranberry (*Viburnum opulus* var. *americanum*)
Honeysuckle (*Lonicera periclymenum*) (climber – see Chapter 17)
Juniper (*Juniperus communis*)
Lavenders (*Lavandula* spp.)
Lemonade bush (*Rhus aromatica*)
Rosemary (*Rosmarinus officinalis*)
Sage (*Salvia officinalis*)
Salal (*Gaultheria shallon*)
Saltbush (*Atriplex halimus*)
Sea buckthorn (*Hippophae rhamnoides*)
Siberian pea tree (*Caragana arborescens*)
Tree lupin (*Lupinus arboreus*)
Wattles (*Acacia* spp.)

Lonicera caerulea, BLUE HONEYSUCKLE / HONEYBERRY

Deciduous/Evergreen: D   **Zone:** 2
Sun/shade preference: ◯
Shade tolerance: ◑
Performance rating: ✓✓
Fertility: SS   **Flowers:** Pale yellow

This is an unusual fruiting bush from Siberia and nearby regions, which prefers a continental climate.

Size: 1.5m (5') high and wide.

Cultivation: Plant potted or bare-rooted plants in winter (comes early into growth). Tolerates most soils. Prefers sun for good fruiting, but tolerates some shade.

Flowering: Spring (March/April in the UK). Frost-tolerant.

Fruiting: Summer. Fruits are small, 0.8-1cm (0.3-0.4") long and dark blue.

Uses: Fresh fruit, cooked, made into preserves, etc. Flavour is like a blueberry with more acidity.

Harvest and storage: Pick when they darken and soften, and use quickly.

Cooking/processing: The seeds are tiny so the whole fruit can be used in jams, leathers, etc.

Secondary uses: Bee plant.

Propagation: Semi-ripe cuttings in late summer or hardwood cuttings in winter.

Maintenance: Little required.

Cultivars: 'Blue Velvet', 'Maistar' and 'Mailon' are all varieties with larger fruits.

Lycium barbarum, GOJI BERRY

Deciduous/Evergreen: D **Zone:** 6
Sun/shade preference: ◐
Shade tolerance: ◖
Performance rating: ✓✓
Fertility: SF **Flowers:** Light purple

See also page 184, in 'Shrubs with other edible parts'.

This has become popular in the last few years as a 'superfruit' – well, frankly, I think all fruits are superfruits and contain loads of good things. Nevertheless, goji is easy to grow and the fruits are nicest eaten dried – they have a mild liquorice flavour. It has naturalised in many parts of the UK.

Size: 2-3m (6'6"-10') high and wide – a straggly, untidy, thorny shrub.

Cultivation: Plant bare-rooted or pot-grown plants in winter. Tolerates most soils and shade. Prefers some sun for good fruiting.

Flowering: Summer; flowers similar to nightshade flowers.

Fruiting: Autumn. Fruiting starts at a young age. Fruits are red and oval, 1.5-2cm (0.6-0.8") long.

Uses: Fresh fruit – nice enough, but nicer dried.

Harvest and storage: Pick when ripe and dry to store.

Cooking/processing: The fruits are best dried; they can be dried whole in a dehydrator.

Secondary uses: Bee plant. The shoots and leaves make good cooked greens, with a slightly minty flavour.

Propagation: By seed – not dormant. Arching shoots can root at the tips where touching the ground.

Maintenance: Little required. You may want to stop the shrub layering itself too much and spreading.

Cultivar: 'Crimson Star' is an improved fruiting variety.

Oregon grape (*Mahonia aquifolium*).

Mahonia aquifolium, M. nervosa & *M. repens*, OREGON GRAPES

Deciduous/Evergreen: E **Zone:** 5
Sun/shade preference: ○
Shade tolerance: ●
Performance rating: ✓✓✓
Fertility: SF **Flowers:** Yellow

The fruits of all *Mahonia* species are edible. They are all purple, currant-sized and acidic in flavour, and make good preserves. The shrubs are tough evergreens that need little looking after. The species listed here all originate from woods in western North America.

Size: *M. aquifolium* (Oregon grape) is 1.5m (5') high by 1m (3') wide. *M. nervosa* (dwarf Oregon grape) and *M. repens* (creeping Oregon grape) are 1m (3') high.

Cultivation: Plant bare-rooted or pot-grown plants in winter. They tolerate most soils, drought and deep shade, though they fruit better with some sun.

Flowering: Late winter and spring.

Fruiting: Summer.

Uses: Cooked or used in jams or preserves.

Harvest and storage: Pick and process quickly.

Cooking/processing: The fruits are too acidic for most people to eat raw but make a nice jam.

Secondary uses: Bee plants; hedging. Edible flowers; blue/violet dyes from the fruits. *M. nervosa* and *M. repens* make a good ground cover.

Propagation: By seed – requires 4 months' stratification. Dig up and replant suckers of lower-growing species.

Maintenance: Little required. *M. nervosa* and *M. repens*

sucker slowly. All three species are very tough and low-maintenance shrubs, useful for shady areas.

Cultivars: 'Apollo' is a good fruiting variety of *M. aquifolium*.

Myrtus ugni (syn. *Ugni molinae*), CHILEAN GUAVA

Deciduous/Evergreen: E   **Zone:** 8
Sun/shade preference: ○
Shade tolerance: ◐
Performance rating: ✓✓
Fertility: SF   **Flowers:** White

This was grown commercially in the UK in Victorian times, and is one of the nicest of the uncommon fruits for fresh eating. It does originate from Chile – but the fruits bear no resemblance to tropical guavas!

Size: 1-2.5m (3-8') high and wide.
Cultivation: Plant pot-grown bushes in spring to avoid frost damage to young plants. Give well-drained soil, sun or part shade; also needs shelter from cold winter winds.
Flowering: Late spring.
Fruiting: Fruits ripen in early winter, November/December. They are 1cm (0.4") across, dark red, sweet and aromatic with a strawberry flavour.
Uses: Fresh fruit – very good.
Harvest and storage: Fruits ripen slowly in early winter and need not be harvested too frequently. They store well for a few weeks.
Cooking/processing: Best eaten raw.
Secondary uses: The leaves are used in teas.
Propagation: By seed – not dormant.
Maintenance: Little required.
Cultivars: None selected for fruiting. 'Flambeau' has variegated leaves.

Poncirus trifoliata, TRIFOLIATE ORANGE

Deciduous/Evergreen: D   **Zone:** 5
Sun/shade preference: ○
Shade tolerance: ◐
Performance rating: ✓✓
Fertility: SF   **Flowers:** White

Most *Citrus* species cannot be grown outside in temperate regions, but their close Asian relative *Poncirus* can. It bears golfball-sized fruits that can be used as a lemon substitute.

Size: 2-3m (6'6"-10') high and wide; slow-growing.
Cultivation: Plant bare-rooted or pot-grown plants in winter. Give a well-drained soil and sun or light shade.
Flowering: Late spring and summer.
Fruiting: Takes several years to start. Fruits are 3-4cm (1.2-1.6") across and orange; mostly peel.
Uses: Squeeze for lemon-like juice or use the peel for preserves, etc.
Harvest and storage: Autumn. Stores for a few weeks in a cool place.
Cooking/processing: The fruits have a thick rind and only a small fleshy part. The rind can be grated and used to make a marmalade-style preserve.
Secondary uses: Bee plant; hedging. Also used as *Citrus* rootstock.
Propagation: By seed – not dormant.
Maintenance: Little needed.
Cultivars: None selected for fruiting.

Prunus tomentosa, NANKING CHERRY

Deciduous/Evergreen: D   **Zone:** 2
Sun/shade preference: ○
Shade tolerance: ◐
Performance rating: ✓✓
Fertility: PSF   **Flowers:** White

This is an interesting Chinese bush cherry, producing round fruits with a good cherry flavour, and much easier to protect from birds than true cherries because of their small size.

Size: 1.5-2.5m (5-8') high and wide.
Cultivation: Plant pot-grown plants in winter. Tolerates most soils; prefers some sun.
Flowering: Spring, susceptible to late-spring frosts.
Fruiting: Fruits ripen in late summer. About 1-1.2cm (0.4-0.5") across, they contain a single seed.
Uses: Best eaten fresh, or cooked like pie cherries.
Harvest and storage: Pick when fruits colour and the birds get interested. Process quickly.
Cooking/processing: As for ordinary tree cherries.
Secondary uses: Bee plant.
Propagation: By seed – requires 3 months' stratification.
Maintenance: Little required. Net from birds if necessary.
Cultivars: None selected for fruiting.

Apple rose (*Rosa rugosa*).

Ribes odoratum, **BUFFALO CURRANT**

Deciduous/Evergreen: D   Zone: 3
Sun/shade preference: ◯
Shade tolerance: ◑
Performance rating: ✓✓✓
Fertility: SF   Flowers: Yellow

Rosa spp., **ROSES**

Deciduous/Evergreen: D   Zone: 2
Sun/shade preference: ◯
Shade tolerance: ◑
Performance rating: ✓✓✓✓
Fertility: SF   Flowers: Pinkish-purple

A rare North American species of currant, this has aromatic yellow flowers and distinctive fruits.

Size: 1-1.5m (3-5') high and wide.
Cultivation: Plant pot-grown plants in winter. Tolerates most soils and sun or part shade.
Flowering: Spring. Flowers yellow and ornamental, with a clove-like aroma.
Fruiting: July/August.
Uses: Fresh fruit, etc. – similar to blackcurrants.
Harvest and storage: Fruits 1.2cm (0.5") across with a nice flavour, like a spicy blackcurrant. Use within a week or two. Yields are not as high as with blackcurrants.
Cooking/processing: As for blackcurrants.
Secondary uses: Bee plant. The leaves are used in teas.
Propagation: Hardwood cuttings in autumn.
Maintenance: Little required.
Cultivars: 'Crandall' fruits reliably and pretty well.

Rosehips from all species of rose are edible, and are rich in nutrients such as vitamin C. In all hips there is a thin layer of edible flesh surrounding the seeds and hairs, which are not edible. The larger hips can easily be nibbled fresh and have a sweet flavour. The easiest way of processing rose hips is to cut them in half and extract the juice using a steam juice extractor – this avoids fiddling about removing the seeds. The juice can then be made into cordial, syrup, jelly, etc. Alternatively, mince the whole hips and immediately place them in boiling water for 15 minutes, then strain and use the liquid. Flowers of all roses can also be added to salads to make a pretty and aromatic addition.

Rosa rugosa, the apple rose or rugosa rose, is my favourite, for its huge, round rose hips – it is also very hardy and disease-free. You can cut these hips in half, scoop out the seeds/hairs with a teaspoon, and dry the flesh easily to store for using to make great herb teas. The details that follow are for this species.

Size: 1.5-2m (5'-6'6") high – suckering and spreading slowly.
Cultivation: Plant pot-grown or bare-rooted plants in winter. They tolerate most soils and part shade.
Flowering: Late spring to late summer / early autumn. Bee-pollinated.
Fruiting: The hips are large, 2.5-3cm (1-1.2") across, and borne abundantly from late summer onwards.

Uses: Eaten fresh, and in preserves, herb teas, etc.

Harvest and storage: Harvest over a long period from late summer into autumn. Fresh fruits store for a week or so.

Cooking/processing: Rosehips can be dried for a supply of rosehip tea: halve and scoop out seeds and hairs, then liquidise the fruits and dry. The dried pulp can be powdered by hand. You can also make rosehip syrup or jam – see box below.

Secondary uses: Bee plant; hedging. The flowers are edible and can be used in salads and for perfuming baths, etc.

Propagation: By seed – requires 4 months' stratification. Dig and replant suckers.

Maintenance: Little required.

Cultivars: None selected for fruiting.

ROSEHIP JAM

- Halve the hips and scoop out seeds and hairs with a teaspoon.
- Put the fruits through a Moulinex sieve or liquidise.
- Cook for 5-10 minutes with a little water, then add sugar as per a normal jam recipe.

ROSEHIP SYRUP

- Liquidise or sieve whole hips.
- Put the pulp into boiling water.
- Allow to stand for 15 minutes, then strain.
- Add sugar to the liquid, boil and bottle.

Sambucus racemosa, RED ELDER

Deciduous/Evergreen: D   **Zone:** 4
Sun/shade preference: ◯
Shade tolerance: ◑
Performance rating: ✓✓✓
Fertility: SF   **Flowers:** Creamy white

This is a smaller European species of elder than the European elder, *Sambucus nigra* (see page 126), with red fruits. It has identical uses to that of *S. nigra* but, being smaller, is more suited to the understorey of a forest garden. Note that the American elder (*Sambucus canadensis*) is listed later (page 185) as a flower crop.

Size: 3m (10') high and wide.

Cultivation: Plant pot-grown or bare-rooted plants in winter. Tolerates most soils and considerable shade.

Flowering: Mid-spring.

Fruiting: Summer. Fruits red, 4mm (0.2") across, in large heads.

Uses: Used cooked or for wine, etc., like *S. nigra*.

Harvest and storage: As for *S. nigra*.

Cooking/processing: As for *S. nigra*.

Secondary uses: Edible flowers – used in the same way as those from *S. nigra* or *S. canadensis* (e.g. dip in batter and fry). Hedging.

Propagation: By seed – requires 9 months' stratification. Hardwood cuttings.

Maintenance: Little required. This is another maintenance-free shrub bearing reliable crops.

Vaccinium arctostaphylos, CAUCASIAN WHORTLEBERRY

Deciduous/Evergreen: D   **Zone:** 6
Sun/shade preference: ◯
Shade tolerance: ◑
Performance rating: ✓✓✓
Fertility: SF   **Flowers:** Yellow

This is one of several larger *Vaccinium* species (the blueberry family), which fruit prolifically.

Size: 3m (10') high by 2m (6'6") wide.

Cultivation: Plant pot-grown shrubs in winter or spring. Requires acid soil. Fruits well in considerable shade.

Flowering: Spring.

Fruiting: Summer. Bears sweet, dark blue fruits, 8-10mm (0.3-0.4") across.

Uses: Fresh fruit, or dry like blueberries.

Harvest and storage: Bears masses of fruits over several weeks. Fresh fruits will store for a week or two.

Cooking/processing: Like blueberries, they are best eaten fresh.

Secondary uses: Very good bee plant.

Propagation: By seed – requires 3 months' stratification.

Maintenance: Little required.

Viburnum opulus var. *americanum* / *V. trilobum*, HIGHBUSH CRANBERRY

Deciduous/Evergreen: D   Zone: 2
Sun/shade preference: ◯
Shade tolerance: ◑   //
Performance rating: ✓✓✓
Fertility: SF   Flowers: White

See also page 186, in 'Medicinal shrubs'. The highbush cranberry is also known as cramp bark, with a long history of medicinal use.

Unrelated to the true cranberry (*Vaccinium macrocarpon* – see page 207, Chapter 15), the highbush cranberry is an American *Viburnum* that is closely related to the European guelder rose (*Viburnum opulus*). It is known as *V. trilobum* in North America. It bears bright red fruits with a bitterness that I'm not fond of; however, others like it and it is grown commercially in North America for the fruits, used to make preserves such as highbush cranberry jelly.

Size: 3m (10') high and wide.
Cultivation: Plant pot-grown or bare-rooted shrubs in winter. Good in most soils; tolerates wet soils and quite deep shade.
Flowering: Early summer. Pollinated by bees and other insects.
Fruiting: Autumn.
Uses: Usually cooked in pies, made into jelly, etc. Flavour improves after frosts. An acquired taste.
Harvest and storage: Fruits abundantly, bearing large heads of bright red juicy fruits, 1cm (0.4") across. Unpicked fruits will often dry on the bush – birds are not fond of them until midwinter. Fresh fruits will store for a week or so.
Cooking/processing: In North America commercial plantations are harvested to make into a bitter cranberry-like jelly. To make highbush cranberry jelly use 50 per cent fruit pulp and 50 per cent sugar, and follow a standard jelly recipe.
Secondary uses: Bee plant. Hedging. Bark used medicinally ('cramp bark') as an anti-spasmodic.
Propagation: By seed – requires 6 months' stratification. Hardwood cuttings.
Maintenance: Little required.
Cultivars: 'Phillips' and 'Wentworth' are selected good fruiting varieties.

Shrubs for nuts and seeds

A few shrubs can be useful sources of edible nuts and seeds. Most need reasonable sunlight to crop well (plum yews being an exception).

BAMBOOS

For full details see page 181, in 'Shrubs with other edible parts'.

All bamboos have edible seeds. Bamboo seed is highly valued in China and other parts of Asia as an edible grain. Bamboos are grasses, after all, and bamboo seed is like a sweet rice grain. Many bamboos flower rarely, so cannot be relied on for seed, though some of the smaller species, which are not so good for canes or edible shoots, flower quite often – *Pleioblastus simonii* (Simon bamboo) has flowered well for me. The ripe seeds can be beaten from the bamboo canes by using a tennis racquet or something similar while holding a basket to catch the grains. Like most grass seeds, the papery husk must be removed before eating.

Ripening bamboo grain from Simon bamboo (*Pleioblastus simonii*).

175

Castanea pumila, **CHINKAPIN**

Deciduous/Evergreen: D   **Zone:** 5
Sun/shade preference: ◯
Shade tolerance: ◑
Performance rating: ✓✓
Fertility: SS   **Flowers:** Greenish-yellow

These are dwarf sweet chestnuts, originating from North America, making bushy shrubs rather than trees, and bearing smaller but sweeter nuts in small, spiny burrs.

Size: 2-4m (6'6"-13') high, sometimes suckering.
Cultivation: Plant pot-grown shrubs in winter. Prefers a slightly acid, well-drained soil. Tolerates shade but fruits better with some sun. Prefers hot summers; may suffer some dieback in winters following cool summers.
Flowering: Summer. Pollinated by wind, insects and bees.
Fruiting: Autumn. Nuts are 1.2cm (0.5") across.
Uses: The nuts are very sweet, eaten raw or cooked just like sweet chestnuts. Cut them in half and use a knife point to prise out the halves of kernel from the soft brown shell.
Harvest and storage: Pick from the ground or off the tree as burrs split. Can be dried.
Cooking/processing: As for sweet chestnuts.
Secondary uses: Bee plant.
Propagation: By seed – sow in autumn.
Maintenance: Little required.
Cultivars: None.

Cephalotaxus spp., **PLUM YEWS**

For full details see page 167, in 'Less common fruiting shrubs'. Seeds are produced singly within the fruits. The seeds are peanut-sized and contain an edible kernel, oily and slightly resinous – not unlike pine nuts.

European bladdernut (*Staphylea pinnata*).

Staphylea pinnata, **EUROPEAN BLADDERNUT** & S. trifolia, **AMERICAN BLADDERNUT**

Deciduous/Evergreen: D   **Zone:** 5
Sun/shade preference: ◯
Shade tolerance: ◑
Performance rating: ✓✓
Fertility: SF   **Flowers:** White

These are two shrubby woodland shrubs that bear edible small nuts. As with other small nuts, shelling is an issue – I put them through my nut-cracking machine on a small setting, which works well. If you are serious about growing any hard-shelled nuts then you should also think about efficient methods for cracking them! The designs for my nut cracker are given in *Agroforestry News*, Vol 13 No 3.

Size: *S. pinnata*: 2-3m (6'6"-10') high and wide. *S. trifolia*: 3-5m (10-16') high and wide.
Cultivation: Plant bare-rooted or pot-grown shrubs in winter. They tolerate shade and most soils, though they like a moist soil.
Flowering: Late spring, missing late frosts. Pollinated by flies.
Fruiting: Autumn. Fruits are green air-filled bladders, 3-4cm (1.2-1.6") long, containing a few seeds. Those of *S. pinnata* are 1.2cm (0.5") across; those of *S. trifolia* are 0.6cm (0.25") across.
Uses: Fresh fruit – good.
Harvest and storage: Harvest when bladders turn light brown and dry, between September and November. Bladders will easily crush and seeds can be removed. Dry seeds to store.

Cooking/processing: The kernels are soft and tasty. I usually eat them raw but they would be great in cakes, biscuits, etc.
Secondary uses: Edible oil from seeds. Erosion control – the plants have a dense, fibrous, shallow root system.
Propagation: By seed – they require 13-22 weeks of warm stratification, followed by 13 weeks of cold stratification.
Maintenance: None required. Will regenerate well from pruning.

Xanthoceras sorbifolium,
YELLOWHORN

Deciduous/Evergreen: **D**   Zone: **4**
Sun/shade preference: ○
Shade tolerance: ◑
Performance rating: ✓✓
Fertility: **SF**   Flowers: White

This is a shrub from Northern China, bearing numerous angular seeds. The kernels have a fine Brazil-nut flavour and texture.

Size: 2-3m (6'6"-10') high and wide. May slowly sucker.
Cultivation: Plant pot-grown shrubs in winter, in any well-drained soil; likes plenty of sun and shelter from cold spring winds. Best in areas with hot dry summers. Slow-growing.
Flowering: Mid-spring (May in UK) – susceptible to late-spring frosts. Ornamental.
Fruiting: Fruits are leathery thick-walled capsules, top-shaped, 4-6cm (1.5-2.5") across at the top, which enclose 8-10 brown seeds.
Uses: Fresh fruit, roasted, ground into flour and cooked. Seeds must be shelled first.
Harvest and storage: Harvest as fruits dry out. Dry seeds to store.
Cooking/processing: Can be dried like sweet chestnuts. After shelling they can be ground into a flour.
Secondary uses: Bee plant. Edible oil from seeds.
Propagation: By seed – not dormant. Root cuttings, and dig and replant suckers.
Maintenance: Responds well to feeding.

Shrubs with edible leaves

I harvest a lot of leaves from shrubs (or trees treated as shrubs), mainly for salads. Picking leaves at normal standing height is a pleasure – not so onerous as harvesting from ground level all the time.

Saltbush (*Atriplex halimus*).

Atriplex canescens, **FOUR-WING SALTBUSH** & *A. halimus,* **SALTBUSH**

Deciduous/Evergreen: **E**   Zone: **7**
Sun/shade preference: ○
Shade tolerance: ○
Performance rating: ✓✓
Fertility: **SF**   Flowers: Pink

These are grey-leaved shrubs from sunny, exposed locations in the Mediterranean and American prairies.

Size: *A. canescens* 2m (6'6") high and wide. *A. halimus:* 1.5m (5') high and wide.
Cultivation: Plant pot-grown shrubs in spring. Give sun and a well-drained soil. Needs a favourable location in the UK. Protect in cold winters.
Uses: The leaves are edible raw or cooked, and have a slightly salty taste. Best used in salads.
Harvest and storage: Harvest all year round and use immediately.
Cooking/processing: None required.
Secondary uses: Hedging. Young shoots can also be lightly cooked and eaten.
Propagation: By seed – not dormant. Also semi-ripe cuttings.

Maintenance: None required. Shrub is kept smaller by regular picking of leaves/shoots. Good in seaside locations.

Beech trees (*Fagus sylvatica*) behind flowering stems of Babington's leek (*Allium ampeloprasum* var. *babingtonii*).

Fagus sylvatica, **BEECH**

Deciduous/Evergreen: D   Zone: 5
Sun/shade preference: ○
Shade tolerance: ●
Performance rating: ✓✓✓
Fertility: SF   Flowers: Greenish-yellow

Beech is another great salad leaf crop, but is best grown in a forest garden as trimmed shrubs, 2-3m high and wide, rather than as large trees, which take up a lot of space.

Size: Trimmed to 2-3m (6'6"-10') high and wide.
Cultivation: Plant bare-rooted trees in winter, in sun or shade and any soil.
Uses: Young leaves are used in salads – they have a lemony flavour.
Harvest and storage: Pick leaves within 3 weeks of leafing in May.
Cooking/processing: None required.
Secondary uses: None from trimmed trees. Edible oil from seeds on large trees.
Propagation: By seed – requires 16 weeks' stratification.
Maintenance: Annual trimming in winter.

Tilia spp., **LIMES / LINDENS**

For full details see page 136, Chapter 11 (Canopy species).

Limes produce excellent salad leaves. Coppiced lime trees are shrubs and are usually designed in this layer. Coppicing can take place on any time span, from annually (making a shrub about 2m/6'6" high and wide) to 5-yearly (3.6m/12') or 10-yearly (6m/20') or more.

Toona sinensis, **CHINESE CEDAR**

For full details see page 138, Chapter 11 (Canopy species). Chinese cedar has excellent shoots with a garlicky flavour, which can be used raw or cooked.

Shrubs for herbs and spices

Some of the shrubs listed below – rosemary and sage, for example – are well known, but there are some great lesser-known spice shrubs that are well worth introducing into your forest garden.

Calycanthus spp., **AMERICAN ALLSPICE**

Deciduous/Evergreen: D   Zone: 5/7
Sun/shade preference: ○
Shade tolerance: ◖
Performance rating: ✓✓✓
Fertility: SF   Flowers: Red

These American shrubs include *C. floridus* (Carolina allspice), hardy to zone 5, and *C. occidentalis* (California allspice), hardy to zone 7.

Size: 2.5-3m (8-10') high and wide.
Cultivation: Plant pot-grown shrubs in winter. Tolerates most soils; give sun or light shade.
Uses: The dried bark is a good cinnamon substitute.
Harvest and storage: Harvest branches of 2-3 years old in July/August and peel off bark. Dry to store.
Cooking/processing: Use like cinnamon sticks.
Secondary uses: The leaves contain camphor – used medicinally as a disinfectant and an insect repellent.
Propagation: By seed – requires 3 months' stratification.
Maintenance: Little required.

Drimys lanceolata, MOUNTAIN PEPPER

Deciduous/Evergreen: E   **Zone:** 8
Sun/shade preference: ◐
Shade tolerance: ◖
Performance rating: ✓✓
Fertility: M/F   **Flowers:** White

This is an unusual Australian and Tasmanian spice shrub, with peppery seeds.

Size: 4m (13') high by 2.5m (8') wide.
Cultivation: Plant pot-grown shrubs in spring after frosts. Likes sun or part shade, and shelter from cold winds.
Flowering: Spring.
Fruiting: Autumn.
Uses: The seed is used as a pepper substitute; the leaves as flavouring.
Harvest and storage: Pick ripe seeds in October. Dry to store.
Cooking/processing: Use the dried seeds directly in a pepper mill.
Propagation: Usually by seed – not dormant.
Maintenance: Little required.

Laurus nobilis, BAY

For full details see page 138, Chapter 11 (Canopy species). Bay can easily be kept in the shrub layer by trimming.

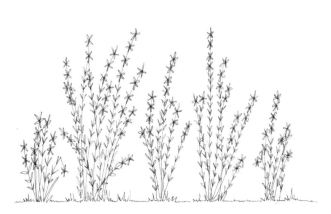

Northern bayberry (*Myrica pensylvanica*).

Myrica gale, BOG MYRTLE & *M. pensylvanica,* NORTHERN BAYBERRY

Deciduous/Evergreen: D   **Zone:** 2
Sun/shade preference: ○
Shade tolerance: ◖
Performance rating: ✓✓✓✓
Fertility: SF   **Flowers:** Greenish-yellow

This is an interesting and useful family of deciduous and evergreen plants. As well as all parts being aromatic and usable as flavourings, the fruits are covered in wax, which is still used commercially in Canada to make candles. All the *Myrica* species are also excellent nitrogen-fixing plants (see page 144, Chapter 11, for details of the larger species as canopy trees).

Size: *M. gale:* 1-2m (3'-6'6") high and wide.
M. pensylvanica: 2m (6'6") high and wide.
Cultivation: Plant bare-rooted or pot-grown plants in winter. Likes acid soil and sun or light shade. Bog myrtle will grow in wet soil.
Flowering: Spring.
Fruiting: Autumn.
Uses: The leaves and fruits are used for flavouring. The flavour of both species is somewhat bay-like.
Harvest and storage: The leaves can be used fresh in season, and can also be dried in summer. The fruits are small but can be harvested quickly by running your hand along the branches.
Cooking/processing: Use the leaves like bay leaves in cooking. Fruits used in cooking should be placed in a muslin bag so they can be removed after use.

Secondary uses: Nitrogen-fixing. Wax from the fruits used to make candles (see page 145).
Propagation: By seed – requires 2-3 months' stratification.
Maintenance: Little required.

Myrtus communis, MYRTLE

Deciduous/Evergreen: E   Zone: 8
Sun/shade preference: ○
Shade tolerance: ○
Performance rating: ✓
Fertility: SF   Flowers: White

This is the true Mediterranean myrtle – unrelated to the bayberries / wax myrtles, *Myrica* spp.

Size: 0.6-2m (2'-6'6") high and wide in the UK.
Cultivation: Plant pot-grown shrubs in spring after last frosts. Give sun and shelter from cold winds.
Uses: Leaves used as flavouring. In warm climes the fruits can be used too.
Harvest and storage: Pick leaves from spring to autumn; fruits in the autumn. Dry both to store.
Cooking/processing: Use leaves and fruits in cooked dishes.
Secondary uses: Bee plant.
Propagation: By seed – not dormant.
Maintenance: Little required. Really needs a nice warm site.

Rosmarinus officinalis, ROSEMARY

Deciduous/Evergreen: E   Zone: 7
Sun/shade preference: ○
Shade tolerance: ○
Performance rating: ✓✓
Fertility: SF   Flowers: Blue

Most folk are familiar with this evergreen shrub, at least in the kitchen. Given good drainage and sun it is easy to grow.

Size: 1.2m (4') high and wide.
Cultivation: Plant pot-grown shrubs in spring. Give sun, shelter from cold winds and a well-drained soil.
Uses: Leaves used for flavouring; flowers in salads.
Harvest and storage: Pick leaves all year round. Dry to store.
Cooking/processing: Use leaves in cooked dishes.

Secondary uses: Bee plant.
Propagation: By seed – not dormant. Semi-ripe cuttings may be taken in summer.
Maintenance: Little required.

Salvia officinalis, SAGE

Deciduous/Evergreen: E   Zone: 5
Sun/shade preference: ○
Shade tolerance: ◑
Performance rating: ✓✓✓
Fertility: SF   Flowers: Lavender

Sage is another very well-known herb. It thrives in a well-drained soil and sun.

Size: 60cm (2') high by 1m (3') wide.
Cultivation: Plant pot-grown shrubs in winter or spring. Prefers sun and a well-drained soil. Tolerates light shade.
Uses: Leaves used for flavouring; also flowers in salads.
Harvest and storage: Pick leaves all year round. Dry to store.
Cooking/processing: Use leaves in cooked dishes.
Secondary uses: Bee plant.
Propagation: By seed – not dormant.
Maintenance: Little required.

Vitex agnus-castus, CHASTE TREE

Deciduous/Evergreen: D   Zone: 7
Sun/shade preference: ○
Shade tolerance: ○
Performance rating: ✓
Fertility: SF   Flowers: Violet

This is a pretty shrub from southern Europe, with aromatic leaves and flowers.

Size: 3m (10') high and wide.
Cultivation: Plant pot-grown shrubs in spring after frosts and protect young plants in winter. Give sun and shelter from cold winds.
Uses: Leaves used as a spice flavouring.
Harvest and storage: Pick the leaves from May to October. Dry to store.
Cooking/processing: Use leaves in cooked dishes.

Secondary uses: Bee plant. The fruits are used as a pepper substitute, but the plants need to be in a warm climate to fruit. Young branches are used for basketry.

Propagation: Seed – not dormant.

Maintenance: Little required. Plants are especially tender when very young and should be given extra protection in regions with cold winters.

Zanthoxylum piperitum, JAPANESE PEPPER / SANSHO

Deciduous/Evergreen: D   **Zone:** 6
Sun/shade preference: ◗
Shade tolerance: ◗
Performance rating: ✓✓✓
Fertility: SF   **Flowers:** Greenish-yellow

Originating from scrub and hedges in Japan, Japanese pepper bears large crops of aromatic and peppery fruits. It is grown commercially as a spice crop in Japan. See also *Zanthoxylum armatum* (Nepalese pepper), *Z. schinifolium* (Szechuan pepper) and *Z. simulans* (Szechuan pepper), described on page 138, Chapter 11, which may also be in the shrub layer.

Size: 2m (6'6") high and wide.
Cultivation: Plant pot-grown plants in winter. Tolerates most soils and sun or part shade. Slow-growing for several years.
Flowering: Early summer.
Fruiting: Autumn.
Uses: The fruits are used as a peppery spice.
Harvest and storage: Fruits are picked and dried in autumn. Each fruit consists of a single black seed surrounded by a thin papery (when ripe) fruit skin. It is this papery skin that is the peppery part – the seeds are tasteless – but usually the whole fruits are picked, dried, then used in a pepper mill. Young leaves are picked in spring and sometimes pickled.
Cooking/processing: The dried fruits are used in a pepper mill.
Secondary uses: Bee plants. Young leaves are used for flavouring.
Propagation: By seed – requires 4 months' stratification.
Maintenance: Little required.

Shrubs with other edible parts

Some shrubs have edible parts that don't fit into any of the categories above, including two of my favourite forest garden plants – bamboos (for edible shoots) and American elder (for flowers).

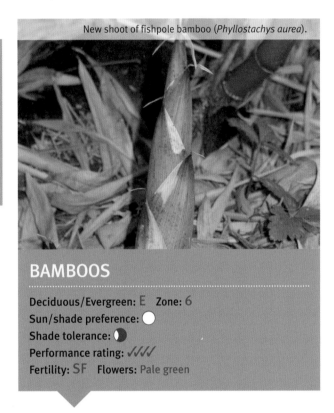
New shoot of fishpole bamboo (*Phyllostachys aurea*).

BAMBOOS

Deciduous/Evergreen: E   **Zone:** 6
Sun/shade preference: ○
Shade tolerance: ◗
Performance rating: ✓✓✓
Fertility: SF   **Flowers:** Pale green

See also page 175, in 'Shrubs for nuts and seeds'.

All bamboos have edible shoots. Species include: *Phyllostachys* spp., *Pleioblastus* spp., *Pseudosasa japonica*, *Semiarundinaria* spp. and *Yushania* spp.

Few people in most of Asia would be without multipurpose bamboo plants to provide food and canes for numerous uses, and I feel much the same way. They are a fantastic source of mineral-rich food at a time when there is often a shortage from other plants.

Bamboo species are often divided into clumping and running types. Clumping types form neat roundish clumps and expand only very slowly. Running types can put up new shoots a couple of metres from the existing edge of an established bamboo grove. Bamboos sometimes have a reputation for being uncontrollable and invasive and, certainly, the running types try to expand, but the answer is management – simply cut the shoots coming up where they are not wanted (preferably when small enough to eat too), and those shoots will not regrow. Alternatively, you can put in rhizome barriers to stop the spread. Although running types obviously need more management to stop them expanding where you don't want them, they are also more productive and put up many more shoots.

The young shoots of all bamboos are edible. *Phyllostachys* spp. (most of which are running) are the best in the UK. New shoots emerge from the ground in spring and/or summer at the same diameter as the cane would be when fully grown. After a new plant is planted out, the canes will steadily get taller and thicker year by year until they get to the maximum for that species and climate (the same species will produce bigger canes in warmer climates). In the UK for the larger species, average shoot diameter can be from 2.5cm (1") (e.g. *Phyllostachys viridiglaucescens*) to 6-8cm / 2.5-3" (e.g. *P. vivax*). The amount of edible material is related to the square of the diameter, so size really matters for yield.

For edible shoots, a minimum cane diameter of 1.2cm (0.5") is sensible – there is not enough edible material in smaller shoots to make it worthwhile harvesting them.

Size: Varies with species and climate. In the UK, 3-8m (10-26') high.

Cultivation: Plant pot-grown plants in winter. Most soils are tolerated as long as they stay reasonably moist in summer. Bamboo tolerates deep shade but gives best performance in partial to moderate shade.

Uses: The shoots are rich in minerals and eaten cooked, and sometimes raw (see box, right).

Harvest and storage: The new shoots can be cut from when they begin to show through the soil until they are about 1m (3') high, but only the top 30cm (1') is edible. It is easiest to cut the new shoot at soil level, but you can also dig the soil away and cut it where it joins the rhizome, to maximise the edible material. Shoots emerge over a period of 2-3 months for most species.

Secondary uses: Canes for garden use, etc. (see page 186). The seeds are edible as a grain like rice (see page 175, in 'Shrubs for nuts and seeds').

Propagation: Division of clumps. By seed (not dormant), but this is not often produced.

Maintenance: Regularly harvested bamboos will require plentiful nitrogen, so it's best to plant some nitrogen fixers nearby. If you want to be extra sure that the bamboo cannot expand past a certain point, then you can enclose the area with a rhizome barrier. This is usually made of thick flexible plastic and must be dug in at least 45cm (1.6') deep.

Cultivars: The table opposite gives information by species on shoot quality and the start of shoot emergence (early spring = April/May; late spring = late May/June; summer = late June/July/early August; early autumn = late August/ September. These dates are for southern England – add on a week for central Britain and two weeks for the north).

EATING BAMBOO SHOOTS

Bamboo shoots are prepared by making a slit lengthwise through the middle, then removing the outer tough leafy sheaths in layers to expose the white and pale green flesh.

The flesh of some species is free of bitterness and can be eaten raw in salads. Most are bitter when raw and require steaming for 10 minutes, which removes the bitterness completely. Cooked shoots have a mild courgette-like flavour with hints of celery and peas.

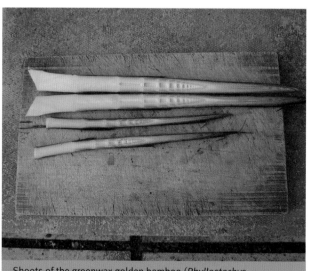

Shoots of the greenwax golden bamboo (*Phyllostachys viridiglaucescens*) cut in half.

BAMBOO SHOOTS			
Species		**Emergence**	**Comments**
Phyllostachys angusta	Stone bamboo	Late spring	Free of bitterness
Phyllostachys aurea	Fishpole bamboo	Early autumn	Free of bitterness – good
Phyllostachys aureosulcata	Yellow grove bamboo	Late spring	Free of bitterness
Phyllostachys bambusoides	Giant timber bamboo	Summer	Bitter when raw
Phyllostachys dulcis	Sweetshoot bamboo	Early spring	Prized, major Chinese edible shoot
Phyllostachys edulis	Moso bamboo	Late spring	Prized, major Japanese edible shoot
Phyllostachys flexuosa	Chinese weeping bamboo	Late spring	Very bitter raw
Phyllostachys glauca	Yunzhu bamboo	Late spring	Slight bitterness
Phyllostachys nidularia	Big node bamboo	Early spring	Slight bitterness
Phyllostachys nigra	Black bamboo	Summer	Bitter when raw
Phyllostachys nuda	Nuda bamboo	Spring	Very slight bitterness – good
Phyllostachys rubromarginata	Red margin bamboo	Summer	Good quality
Phyllostachys sulphurea f. *viridis*	Green sulphur bamboo	Late spring	Slight bitterness – fair
Phyllostachys violascens	Violet bamboo	Late spring	Slight bitterness
Phyllostachys viridiglaucescens	Greenwax golden bamboo	Early summer	Free of bitterness – good
Phyllostachys vivax	Smooth-sheathed bamboo	Early autumn	Slightly bitter
Pleioblastus simonii	Simon bamboo	Summer–early autumn	Fair quality
Pseudosasa japonica	Arrow bamboo	Summer–early autumn	Free of bitterness – good
Semiarundinaria fastuosa	Narihira bamboo	Early autumn	Slightly bitter
Yushania anceps	Anceps bamboo	Summer–early autumn	Free of bitterness – good
Yushania anceps 'Pitt White'	Pitt White bamboo	Midsummer	Free of bitterness – good
Yushania maculata	Maculata bamboo	Summer–early autumn	Free of bitterness – good

Ceanothus americanus, NEW JERSEY TEA

Deciduous/Evergreen: D **Zone:** 5
Sun/shade preference: ◯
Shade tolerance: ◑
Performance rating: ✓✓✓✓
Fertility: SF **Flowers:** White

This is a versatile and ornamental shrub, with a long history of use as a beverage plant in North America.

Size: 1.2m (4') high and wide.
Cultivation: Plant pot-grown shrubs in winter or spring. Likes any reasonably well-drained soil, and sun or light shade.
Flowering: Summer, over a long period.
Uses: The leaves are dried and used to make a pleasant tea.
Harvest and storage: Harvest leaves just before flowering and dry quickly.
Cooking/processing: Dry leaves in warm ambient air temperatures.
Secondary uses: Nitrogen fixing. The flowers are rich in saponins and used as a soap source. The roots are a source of red dye.
Propagation: By seed – not dormant.
Maintenance: Little required.

Lycium barbarum, GOJI BERRY

For full details see page 171, in 'Less common fruiting shrubs'.

As well as being grown for its fruit, goji is also used as a perennial vegetable plant. The young shoots and leaves are harvested in the spring and summer and cooked (just steam) like a spinach; they have a cress-like, sometimes almost minty flavour. Eat in small quantities to begin with if you are unused to this plant, as some people have reactions to members of this family (the Solanaceae: potato/tomato family).

Rhus aromatica, LEMONADE BUSH

Deciduous/Evergreen: D **Zone:** 2
Sun/shade preference: ◯
Shade tolerance: ◑
Performance rating: ✓✓✓
Fertility: SF **Flowers:** Yellow

This is a low-growing American shrub, long-used traditionally to make drinks. See also *Rhus glabra* and *Rhus typhina*, described in Chapter 11 (page 140) – although these are classified as canopy species they might sometimes be in the shrub layer, and they have the same uses as lemonade bush.

Size: 1-1.5m (3-5') high and wide.
Cultivation: Plant pot-grown or divided shrubs in winter. Tolerates most soils. Prefers a sunny spot.
Flowering: Late spring. Bee-pollinated.
Fruiting: Late summer and autumn. Produces large spikes of tiny red furry fruits.
Uses: Fruits used to make drinks.
Harvest and storage: The ripe fruit spikes hold well on the bushes and can be harvested over a long period. Simply cut off with secateurs.
Cooking/processing: Soak the ripe fruiting spikes in cold water overnight to make a lemonade-type drink.
Secondary uses: Bee plant. Hedging. Leaves and fruits are rich in tannins for dyeing (yellow/brown) and tanning.
Propagation: By seed – requires 6 months' stratification. Dig and replant suckers.
Maintenance: Little needed.

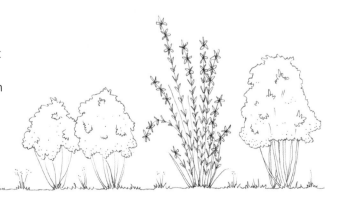

American elder (*Sambucus canadensis*) 'York'.

Sambucus canadensis, AMERICAN ELDER

Deciduous/Evergreen: D   Zone: 3
Sun/shade preference: ○
Shade tolerance: ◑
Performance rating: ✓✓✓
Fertility: SS   Flowers: White

Almost certain to get on my top ten list of forest garden plants, this is a wonderful flowering shrub, and if elder-flowers are a crop you value then you should seriously consider having this. Whereas European elder (*Sambucus nigra* – see page 126, Chapter 11) flowers for about 4 weeks from mid-May to mid-June, American elder flowers in the UK from July to November (especially if unpollinated), so you can get fresh flowers all through summer and autumn. It dies down to the ground in winter in very cold climates. Grow only one clone if you are growing for a flower crop.

American elder is a slowly suckering shrub. Each stem lives 4-6 years then dies back to be replaced by new ones.

Size: 2.5-3m (8-10') high and wide.
Cultivation: Plant bare-rooted plants or cuttings in winter. Tolerates most soils and substantial shade.
Flowering: Large heads (20cm, 8") produced from July onwards until November.
Fruiting: If two different selections are grown then fruits will be produced in autumn.
Uses: The fruits are very similar to European elder fruits and with the same edible uses. The flowers are used like other elders – for teas, soaked in water to make a drink, to make cordials or wine, or cooked by dipping in batter and frying, etc.
Harvest and storage: Pick flowers when fully open and the pollen is freely falling. Pick a head at a time, minimising the amount of green stalk picked. Use very quickly.
Cooking/processing: As for European elder. Soak 6-10 heads for 24 hours in 5 litres of water with 2-4 chopped lemons (and sugar if required) to make a great summer drink.
Secondary uses: Hedging. If pollinated, fruits are edible like native elders.
Propagation: Hardwood cuttings in autumn.
Maintenance: Little required. Remove dead old stems to make access easier if necessary.
Cultivars: Grow one plant, or several of one clone (e.g. 'Johns' or 'York', both bred for flower and fruit production) for maximum flowering.

Medicinal shrubs

I am not a herbalist, but the plants I mention below are well known in terms of their medicinal properties and efficacy. Make sure you know what you are doing or consult a qualified herbalist before you use plants medicinally.

Garrya elliptica & *G. fremontii,* FEVER BUSH / QUININE BUSH

Deciduous/Evergreen: E   Zone: 7
Sun/shade preference: ○
Shade tolerance: ◑
Performance rating: ✓✓
Fertility: SF   Flowers: Grey-green

The fever bushes are handsome evergreen shrubs, often grown ornamentally in mild areas for their beautiful catkins.
Size: Up to 4m (13') high and wide.
Cultivation: Plant pot-grown shrubs in spring to avoid frosts. Give sun or part shade and a well-drained soil.
Uses: Long used medicinally in North America. The leaves (and sometimes the bark) are used as a febrifuge (to reduce fevers).
Secondary uses: Bee plants.

Propagation: By seed – requires 3 months' stratification.
Maintenance: Little required.

Lavandula spp., LAVENDER

Deciduous/Evergreen: D **Zone:** 5
Sun/shade preference: ◯
Shade tolerance: ◯
Performance rating: ✓✓
Fertility: SF **Flowers:** Lavender, blue, violet

Lavandula angustifolia (English lavender), *L.* x *intermedia* (lavandin), *L. latifolia* (broad-leaved lavender) and *L. stoechas* (French lavender) are all aromatic grey-leaved evergreen shrubs well known for their ornamental and medicinal values.

Size: 60-90cm (2-3') high by 75cm (2'6") wide.
Cultivation: Plant pot-grown shrubs in spring after frosts. Give sun or light shade and a well-drained soil.
Uses: The leaves and the oil distilled from them are widely used in perfumery, cosmetics, and as an external antiseptic. The oil is being investigated for its anti-cancer properties.
Secondary uses: Bee plant. The leaves and flowers are used for flavouring.
Propagation: By seed – not dormant.
Maintenance: The top growth is often trimmed off annually for use.

Viburnum opulus var. americanum / V. trilobum, CRAMP BARK

For full details see page 175, in 'Less common fruiting shrubs'. *Viburnum opulus* var. *americanum* is known as *V. trilobum* in North America, where it is called highbush cranberry. The dried bark is widely used in herbal medicine as an antispasmodic. The fruits are edible but an acquired taste.

Shrubs for poles and canes

Most people need poles or canes to use in the garden – for temporary structures to support climbers, to make cages for fruit protection, and so on. The plants listed here are easy to grow in shadier parts of the garden.

BAMBOOS

For full details see page 181, in 'Shrubs with other edible parts'. Species include *Phyllostachys* spp., *Pleioblastus* spp., *Pseudosasa japonica*, *Semiarundinaria* spp. and *Yushania* spp.

The culms (canes) of most bamboo species can be cut and dried for use, especially those from the erect species. For production of canes, vigorous species that send up lots of new shoots each year are preferable. Running species are much more productive than clumping bamboos.

For most garden uses, canes of diameter 1-2.5cm (0.4-1") are desirable. The box below gives a number of recommended species for producing canes in that range, and one species for larger canes.

BAMBOOS FOR CANE PRODUCTION

For canes of 1-2.5cm (0.4-1") diameter:

Phyllostachys bissetii	Bisset bamboo
Phyllostachys violascens	Violet bamboo
Phyllostachys viridiglaucescens	Greenwax golden bamboo
Pleioblastus simonii	Simon bamboo
Pseudosasa japonica	Arrow bamboo
Semiarundinaria fastuosa	Narihira bamboo
Yushania anceps	Anceps bamboo
Yushania anceps 'Pitt White'	Pitt White bamboo
Yushania maculata	Maculata bamboo
Yushania maling	Maling bamboo

For larger canes, 5-7cm (2-2.7") in diameter:

Phyllostachys vivax	Smooth-sheathed bamboo

All canes will need side shoots trimming off after cutting (this takes more time than cutting the cane). *Pseudosasa japonica* and the *Yushania* species have less leafy side shoots, so are quicker to trim up.

You can cut fresh canes when they are only a year or less old, but they will not have lignified (hardened), so will last only a few months outdoors before rotting. Culms take 3 years to mature and lignify, so if you want durable canes then you must cut only these older ones and then dry them. You need to be systematic and paint a dot of colour on each year's canes, so you can easily identify the 3-year-old ones. I've seen it documented that you should cut a cane though a node (one of the ridges that appear on the canes at intervals), where it is solid, so that rainwater doesn't collect to rot the culm and possibly damage the rhizome; however, I cut at ground level and have never had any problems, so this is what I recommend. Be careful not to leave cane stubs to trip over, as this can be quite dangerous. Cut the canes with loppers or with a pruning saw.

Once the cane is cut, all branches should be cut off close to the stem with secateurs, and the fine whippy top cut off. These can be used for small plant stakes, fine basketry or a mulch (they are quite good on a muddy path). The canes then need to dry slowly, and should be laid flat under cover but in good ventilation, turning occasionally – I hang them up underneath a dense coniferous tree canopy. Each 4mm (0.2") of cane diameter requires about 1 month of drying, thus 1.2cm (0.5") canes need 3 months of drying, and 2.5cm (1") canes need 6 months' drying.

Corylus avellana, HAZEL

For full details see page 130, Chapter 11 (Canopy species).

If coppiced every 2 to 4 years, hazel plants are kept in the shrub layer. Two-year-old shoots will be 1.5-2.5cm (0.6-1") diameter and 2-3m (6'6"-10') long and ideal for many garden uses. Hazel is shade-tolerant and coppiced plants can be positioned in deciduous shade.

Shrubs for tying materials

There are a number of shrubs with long, tough, sword-shaped leaves that are excellent for using as garden twine and for tying jobs.

Cabbage palm (*Cordyline australis*).

Cordyline australis, CABBAGE PALM

Deciduous/Evergreen: E **Zone:** 8
Sun/shade preference: ◐
Shade tolerance: ◐
Performance rating: ✓✓
Fertility: SF **Flowers:** White

Suited to mild areas near the coast, this New Zealand palm is a good understorey plant.

Size: 3-5m (10-16') high by 1m (3') wide.
Cultivation: Plant pot-grown shrubs in spring after frosts. Tolerates substantial shade. Shelter from cold winds.
Uses: Long leaves (60cm, 2' long) are cut and split, then used as twine.
Secondary uses: As with most palms, the starchy trunk can be used for food, but you'll kill the plant in doing so!
Propagation: By seed – not dormant.
Maintenance: Little required.

New Zealand flax (*Phormium tenax*).

Phormium tenax,
NEW ZEALAND FLAX

Deciduous/Evergreen: E **Zone:** 7
Sun/shade preference: ○
Shade tolerance: ●
Performance rating: ✓✓✓
Fertility: SF **Flowers:** Orange-red

This New Zealand plant is the best shrub for tying materials I have come across. I plant it scattered throughout my forest garden so there is always some handy. I also have a windbreak of it, which is highly effective, though noisy in windy conditions when the leaves clatter together. *P. colensoi* (mountain flax) is a smaller version, growing to half the size but with the same uses.

Size: 2.5m (8') high by 3m (10') wide. The flower spikes can reach 4m (13') high.
Cultivation: Plant pot-grown shrubs in winter or spring – the latter in colder areas to miss frosts. Tolerates substantial shade and dry or wet soil.
Flowering: July. Rich in nectar; bee-pollinated.
Uses: Long leaves (1-1.5m, 3-5' long) are cut and split, then used as twine.
Harvest and storage: Leaves need to be used fresh for twine.
Secondary uses: Bee plant. Leaves are used for basketry, paper and fibre. Brown dye is made from the flowers. Nectar and seeds are edible (the latter good in cakes and bread mixes).
Propagation: By seed – not dormant.
Maintenance: Little required.

Cultivars: There are numerous ornamental cultivars, but the leaves from those with stripy or coloured leaves are often not as strong.

Flowers of New Zealand flax (*Phormium tenax*) are loved by bees.

Shrubs for basketry materials

Commercial plantings of shrubs such as willow for basketry materials need field conditions with full light. However, if you just want enough material for making one or two baskets a year it is very easy to fit these into a forest garden. Willows still need good light – positioning is important – but there are other shrubs that tolerate more shade. Not included here, but in Chapter 15 (Ground-cover and herbaceous perennial species), page 253, is periwinkle, which is very shade-tolerant and has long pliable stems suitable for fine basketry.

Cornus stolonifera, RED OSIER

Deciduous/Evergreen: D   **Zone:** 2
Sun/shade preference: ◔
Shade tolerance: ◑
Performance rating: ✓✓✓
Fertility: SF   **Flowers:** White

The shoots of this American species are bright red or yellow – very ornamental.

Size: 2m (6'6") high and 4m (13') wide – suckering.
Cultivation: Plant bare-rooted plants or cuttings in winter. Tolerates part shade and wet soils.
Uses: Branches used for basketry – can be coppiced annually.
Secondary uses: Red dye from the roots. Hedging.
Propagation: Hardwood cuttings in autumn.
Maintenance: Little required apart from coppicing.

Salix spp., WILLOWS

Deciduous/Evergreen: D   **Zone:** 4
Sun/shade preference: ◔
Shade tolerance: ◔
Performance rating: ✓✓✓✓
Fertility: SF   **Flowers:** Whitish-yellow

Willows are very easy to grow, with a long tradition of basketry use. If coppicing annually, keep them well mulched to avoid severe weed competition in spring, which can kill stools. Almost all species can be used, but the main basketry ones are *Salix purpurea* (purple willow), *S. triandra* (almond-leaved willow) and *S. viminalis* (osier). *S.* 'Bowles Hybrid' is a useful windbreak tree.

Size: Annual coppice growth: *S. purpurea* 2m (6'6"); *S. triandra* 2.5m (8'); *S. viminalis* 4m (13').
Cultivation: Plant rooted plants in winter or cuttings at any time of year. Give sun or light shade. They tolerate wet soils.
Uses: Branches are used for basketry, fencing etc. – usually coppiced annually.
Harvest and storage: Best to use within a few months of cutting. If dried with bark on, soak for a few days before working.
Secondary uses: The bark has been used medicinally as an anti-inflammatory.

Propagation: Cuttings, taken any time.
Maintenance: Little apart from coppicing. Deer like to nibble young shoots, so protect if necessary.
Cultivars: Many have been selected. Better-known varieties include:
S. purpurea:
Dicky Meadows
Goldstones
Green Dicks

S. triandra:	*S. viminalis:*
Black Hollander	Brown Merrin
Black Maul	Reader's Red

SHRUBS TOLERATING WINTER WATERLOGGING

Bog myrtle (*Myrica gale*)
Green alder (*Alnus viridis*)
Highbush cranberry (*Viburnum opulus* var. *americanum*)
Willows (*Salix* spp.)

Symphoricarpos spp., SNOWBERRIES

Deciduous/Evergreen: D   **Zone:** 3
Sun/shade preference: ◔
Shade tolerance: ●
Performance rating: ✓✓✓
Fertility: SF   **Flowers:** White, pink

Species include *Symphoricarpos albus* (snowberry), *S.* x *chenaultii* (Chenault coralberry) and *S. orbiculatus* (coralberry). These are suckering woodland shrubs from North America, with distinctive white fruits.

Size: 2m (6'6") high and wide.
Cultivation: Plant pot-grown shrubs in winter in any soil. They tolerate quite deep shade. Excellent basketry crops for shadier areas.
Uses: Young branches used for basketry.
Secondary uses: Bee plants. Fruits are 'edible' but not nice.
Propagation: By seed – requires 9 months' stratification.
Maintenance: Little required. Can spread widely and are sometimes regarded as a nuisance.

Shrubs for dye parts

There are hundreds of shrubs that can be used for dyeing. The following are just a couple of the more well-known ones, which also happen to be nitrogen fixers.

Cytisus scoparius, BROOM

Deciduous/Evergreen: D **Zone:** 5
Sun/shade preference: ○
Shade tolerance: ◐
Performance rating: ✓✓✓
Fertility: SF **Flowers:** Yellow

Broom is easy to grow and a good pioneer for the first years of a forest garden, and is one of the few native nitrogen-fixing shrubs in Britain. It tends to be relatively short-lived – 15 years or so – so you can plan for it to be replaced in time. It is a legume, so needs sun.

Size: 2.5m (8') high by 1m (3') wide.
Cultivation: Plant pot-grown shrubs in winter. Give sun or light shade and a well-drained soil.
Flowering: Summer.
Uses: Leaves and bark used for dyeing yellow and green.
Secondary uses: Bee plant; nitrogen fixing; stems for basketry; hedging.
Propagation: Usually by seed – not dormant (needs scarification).
Maintenance: None needed.

Genista tinctoria, DYER'S GREENWEED

Deciduous/Evergreen: D **Zone:** 2
Sun/shade preference: ○
Shade tolerance: ◑
Performance rating: ✓✓
Fertility: SF **Flowers:** Yellow

Dyer's greenweed is another leguminous pioneer with a long history of dye use. It forms a small straggly shrub that rarely looks impressive but persists well, in sun or light shade.

Size: 90cm (3') high and wide.
Cultivation: Plant pot-grown shrubs in winter. Give sun or light shade and a well-drained soil.
Flowering: Summer.
Uses: Leaves, flowers and shoots are used for dyeing yellow and green.
Secondary uses: Bee plant. Nitrogen-fixing.
Propagation: By seed – not dormant (needs scarification).
Maintenance: None needed.

Dyer's greenweed (*Genista tinctoria*) in winter.

Shrubs for soap sources

Whenever I tell people that some plants can be used directly as sources of soap (saponins) there is usually a mixture of interest and scepticism. Rubbing oneself with leaves does admittedly have associations with hunter-gatherers of the past! It doesn't have to be like that, though. Most plants that contain saponins can be used to make a soapy lather by tearing or chopping leaves and soaking/agitating them in water for a few hours. The lather can then be used for washing hands, clothes or whatever.

Ceanothus americanus, NEW JERSEY TEA

For full details see page 184, in 'Shrubs with other edible parts'. The flowers of this plant are rich in saponins and used as a soap source – they lather when crushed in water and leave a pleasant scent after use.

Lewis's mock orange (*Philadelphus lewisii*).

Philadelphus spp., MOCK ORANGE

Deciduous/Evergreen: D   **Zone:** 5
Sun/shade preference: ◐
Shade tolerance: ◑
Performance rating: ✓✓
Fertility: SF   **Flowers:** White

These shrubs are well known for their ornamental and fragrant flowers in summer.

Size: 3m (10') high and wide.
Cultivation: Plant pot-grown shrubs in winter, in sun or part shade and any soil.
Flowering: Summer.
Uses: The leaves, flowers and bark are all high in saponins – they lather in water and are used for washing.
Propagation: By seed – requires 4 months' stratification.
Maintenance: None needed.
Cultivars: Numerous cultivars are available; all can be used.

Catkins of green alder (*Alnus viridis*).

Alnus viridis, GREEN ALDER

Deciduous/Evergreen: D   **Zone:** 4
Sun/shade preference: ◐
Shade tolerance: ◑
Performance rating: ✓✓✓
Fertility: SF   **Flowers:** Greenish-yellow

This mainland European shrub is also found in North America. This one didn't quite make it to Britain after the last ice age but is quite at home here.

Size: 2.5-3m (8-10') high and wide.
Cultivation: Plant pot-grown or bare-rooted shrubs in winter, in sun or part shade. Likes a moist soil.
Uses: Excellent actinorhizal nitrogen fixer for temperate climates.
Secondary uses: Red dye from bark. Hedging.
Propagation: By seed – requires 2 months' stratification.
Maintenance: Can be coppiced or pollarded from time to time if required.

Nitrogen-fixing shrubs

The following shrubs can be used to provide a good proportion of the nitrogen requirement in a forest garden.

Amorpha fruticosa, FALSE INDIGO

Deciduous/Evergreen: D   Zone: 4
Sun/shade preference: ◯
Shade tolerance: ◑
Performance rating: ✓✓✓✓
Fertility: SF   Flowers: Purple & yellow

False indigo is a lax, open shrub of variable size that is sometimes considered a weed in warmer parts of the world. It is a legume.

Size: 2.5-5m (8-16') high and wide.
Cultivation: Plant pot-grown shrubs in winter. Needs sun or light shade and shelter – the branches are brittle and can break in exposed locations. Coppices well.
Uses: A useful nitrogen-fixing shrub, which is open and offers lots of underplanting opportunities.
Secondary uses: Bee plant.
Propagation: By seed – requires scarification.
Maintenance: Wind-damaged branches should be cut back. The whole shrub can be cut back or coppiced if desired.

Cytisus scoparius, BROOM

For full details see page 190, in 'Shrubs for dye parts'. Broom is a very good nitrogen-fixing shrub, although its small size limits the amount of nitrogen fixed overall.

Elaeagnus multiflora, GOUMI

For full details see page 168, in 'Less common fruiting shrubs'. Goumi is an excellent actinorhizal nitrogen fixer for temperate climates.

Genista tinctoria, DYER'S GREENWEED

For full details see page 190, in 'Shrubs for dye parts'. This is a moderate nitrogen fixer, because of its sparse leaf cover and small size. It is leguminous.

Bush clover (*Lespedeza bicolor*).

Lespedeza bicolor, BUSH CLOVER

Deciduous/Evergreen: D   Zone: 5
Sun/shade preference: ◯
Shade tolerance: ◑
Performance rating: ✓✓✓
Fertility: SF   Flowers: Pinkish-purple

Bush clover is a lax, shrubby legume from Eastern Asia that is sometimes planted for its ornamental purplish-rose-coloured flowers.

Size: 2.5m (8') high and wide.
Cultivation: Plant pot-grown shrubs in winter, in sun or light shade and a well-drained soil.
Uses: A very good shrub legume for fixing nitrogen. Several other *Lespedeza* species can be used similarly, including *L. maximowiczii* and *L. thunbergii* (both also called bush clover).
Secondary uses: Bee plant. Animal fodder.
Propagation: By seed – not dormant.
Maintenance: None required.

Lupinus arboreus, TREE LUPIN

Deciduous/Evergreen: E Zone: 8
Sun/shade preference: ◯
Shade tolerance: ◖
Performance rating: ✓✓
Fertility: SF Flowers: Yellow

An American shrubby legume, the tree lupin is found on well-drained soils.

Size: 2m (6'6") high and wide.
Cultivation: Plant pot-grown shrubs in spring after frosts. Give sun or light shade and a well-drained neutral-to-acid soil. Can self-seed in mild locations in the UK.
Uses: Very good nitrogen-fixing legume.
Secondary uses: Bee plant.
Propagation: By seed – not dormant. Soft basal cuttings in spring.
Maintenance: None needed.

Myrica gale, BOG MYRTLE & *M. pensylvanica,* NORTHERN BAYBERRY

For full details see page 179, in 'Shrubs for herbs and spices'. These are excellent nitrogen fixers for temperate climates. *Myrica* species are actinorhizal.

Shepherdia canadensis, RUSSET BUFFALO BERRY

Deciduous/Evergreen: D   Zone: 2
Sun/shade preference: ◖
Shade tolerance: ◖
Performance rating: ✓
Fertility: SS Flowers: Yellow

An American actinorhizal plant, the russet buffalo berry prefers hot summer regions.

Size: 2.5m (8') high and wide.
Cultivation: Plant pot-grown shrubs in winter. Likes most soils and sun or very light shade.
Uses: Excellent nitrogen fixer in temperate climates.
Secondary uses: Edible fruits. Hedging.
Propagation: By seed – requires 3 months' stratification.
Maintenance: None required.

Barberry (*Berberis* x *lologensis*) 'Mystery Fire' in flower.

Chapter 14

Designing the shrub layer

In many ways, fitting shrubs into the design is much easier than designing the tree layers. Shrubs are nearly always considered after the trees and their positions have been decided upon, and it is easier to find a position that should be fairly optimal for each of the shrubs considered.

Whereas the design of the canopy tree layer should always be done meticulously and usually on a paper map, you can be a bit more liberal with the shrub design. The larger shrubs probably do need to be marked on your design map, but the smaller ones probably don't. Plants that are only a metre high and wide – many of the common bush fruits, for example – can be fitted into the garden in many places.

You do not have to choose all the shrubs at the outset either, especially if you are taking several years to plant up and develop the garden. In this case you can approach the design of the shrub and lower layer on a year-by-year basis until the planting is complete. This will also give you time to raise some of the less common plants by seed, cuttings, etc. if you want to.

Some of the factors to think about in the design of the shrub layer are the same as when considering placement of canopy trees, as follows.

- Aspect and site features, such as steep slopes. These present opportunities and problems.

- Soil differences across the site.

- Microclimates in the garden. Tender shrubs will usually do better to the leeward side of other trees.

- Each shrub's individual requirements for light/shade, moisture and nutrients.

- Pollination requirements. Shrubs needing cross-pollination with another need to be sited in fairly close proximity, otherwise bees may not fly easily from shrub to shrub; also, wind-blown pollen will not travel so far in a forest.

- Allelopathy and competition (see box on page 152) – the negative effects of any canopy trees.

- The beneficial effects of nearby canopy trees – shelter, nitrogen fixation, etc.

- Placement of nitrogen-fixing shrubs. These are best placed near to heavily fruiting fruit trees or shrubs, and heavily cropped plants such as bamboos. They may need to be placed to the south of the plants they are to fertilise so they get reasonable light.

- Placement of shrubs of the same family/species. In general, try to mix species so that are not adjacent (unless pollination requires it), for pest and disease prevention.

- Space. For fruiting shrubs especially, try to allow them enough space to reach their full potential size, which will maximise the crop they can bear.

Pawpaw (*Asimina triloba*).

GUILDS

The design of the tree, shrub, herbaceous perennial and climbing layers of a forest garden have been separated in this book to make the design process clearer. However, the layers are intimately connected and the design for a particular patch of ground should take into account the relations between the different layers.

'Guilds' in a forest garden are groups of species that support each other in beneficial ways, aiding self-maintenance and reducing the work required to maintain the system. So in an ideal guild you'll have plants of various types performing the following functions.

- Nitrogen-fixing plants to supply nitrogen.
- Mineral-accumulator plants to help supply other nutrients.
- Beneficial-insect plants to minimise pest problems.
- Bee plants, both for wild and honey bees.
- Plants with differing root systems, to exploit the soil space and soil layers efficiently.
- Aromatic plants to confuse pests and increase system health.
- Ground-cover plants to densely cover the soil surface.

If you are utilising plants that grow together in a natural situation (e.g. they are both native) you may well have a good idea of how they will complement or antagonise each other. It is more likely, though, that you will be creating mixtures of plants that are not found in nature. This is fine, but make sure you think about design strategies to minimise competitive problems.

There is no fixed minimum size for an area to be considered as a guild. I like to have plenty of plants performing most of the above functions – which, although it might mean less space for directly cropped plants, means that the ecosystem is highly resilient and low-maintenance. In a very small garden you might want to compromise and have fewer of these system-maintenance plants and more harvestable crops, but you will lose some resilience and increase the maintenance level as a result.

During the design process, from time to time, look at areas of your forest garden – are there types of plant from the above list that are missing? Can you fit them in one of the layers?

There are also some extra factors to consider about placement of shrubs.

- Vertical access is needed to harvest or tend some canopy trees (especially most fruiting trees). You need to physically stand below the drip line of the tree to pick fruit either by hand or with a long-handled picker. This is NOT a good place to put shrubs, which will interfere with the access and cause extra work.

- The best position for most shrubs is between canopy trees, outside the drip lines, where light levels are highest. Allow enough space so that at maximum size the shrub won't impinge much, if at all, beneath the drip line of cropped fruit trees. If you don't know the maximum size, look it up in a plant dictionary or at Plants for a Future (www.pfaf.org).

Vertical access for harvesting. Below the drip line is an inconvenient place for shrubs.

- Under a continuous canopy (i.e. where the tree canopies touch) or beneath large trees in shady locations, shrubs will grow taller and thinner than usual. This is usually thought of as bad, but in fact it can be quite useful sometimes – so, for instance, redcurrants can be grown in quite shady spots where they will reach 1.5-1.8m (5-6') tall and bear their fruit at a height that is kinder on backs and knees for harvesting.

- When designing groups or clumps of shrubs adjacent to each other, try to place smaller shrubs to the south, to minimise shading.

- Frequently coppiced trees for firewood, etc. can be placed in the shrub layer too. If they are not fruiting trees then they will generally tolerate much more shade and still be productive.

As with canopy design, this part of the design is a juggling act. But if the trees are already planted then at least you can walk around the young garden and spot likely good places for different plants. Do this in summer when the trees are in leaf, because in winter when leaves have dropped there is an illusion of more space than there really is.

Examples of good and bad shrub positioning

The diagrams below and overleaf illustrate the above points, showing examples of poor positioning and good positioning of shrubs.

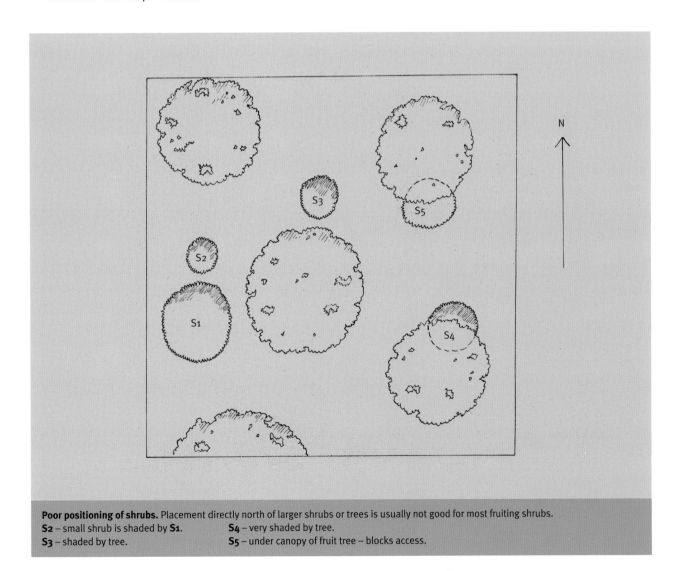

Poor positioning of shrubs. Placement directly north of larger shrubs or trees is usually not good for most fruiting shrubs.
S2 – small shrub is shaded by **S1**.
S3 – shaded by tree.
S4 – very shaded by tree.
S5 – under canopy of fruit tree – blocks access.

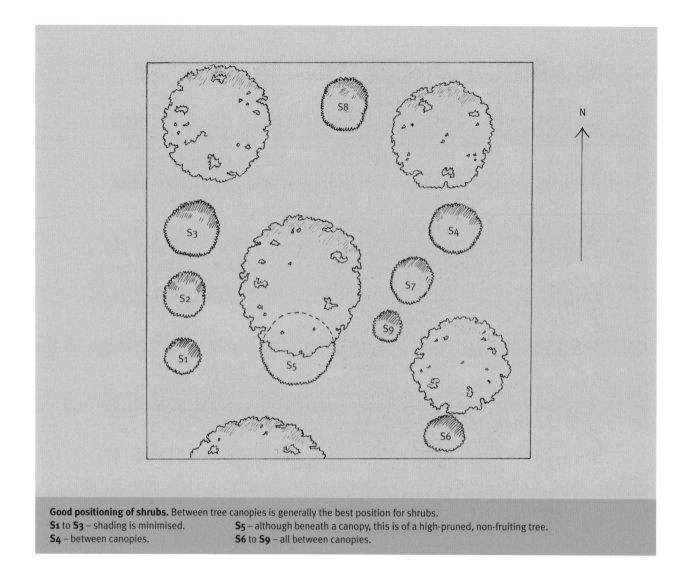

Good positioning of shrubs. Between tree canopies is generally the best position for shrubs.
S1 to **S3** – shading is minimised.
S4 – between canopies.
S5 – although beneath a canopy, this is of a high-pruned, non-fruiting tree.
S6 to **S9** – all between canopies.

The form in which many shrubs grow varies with the amount of light available: in less light they are often taller, thinner and leggier, while in full sun they are bushier, denser and smaller – as shown in the diagrams opposite.

These differences can be exploited in a forest garden, where a leggy shrub is nor bad per se, because it allows more space for underplanting with smaller plants.

ONGOING USE OF SPACE

As your trees mature you will find that there are places where there is unexpected space and others where the space seems less than expected. Where there seems to be more space you can continue planting shrubs or even just cuttings: indeed, I often go around in autumn and just stick in cuttings where there seems to be room – they get no care and attention and many don't make it, but it takes very little effort.

Shrubs are easy to cut and remove too, if you decide that particular plants are not working as you want. Don't shy away from cutting and removing shrubs, and replacing them with something you prefer – forest gardens are dynamic places!

Typical shrub growth in good light conditions.

The same shrubs in semi-shade: taller and thinner.

Chilean strawberry (*Fragaria chiloensis*).

Chapter 15

Herbaceous perennial and ground-cover species

There are many books, some very large, entirely focused on ground-cover plants, many of which can be grown in shady situations in a forest garden. In this chapter I concentrate on some that I have found most suitable, and which are known to have multiple benefits in terms of edible or medicinal uses, mineral accumulation, nitrogen fixation, beneficial-insect attraction, etc. But bear in mind that *any* plant that covers the ground well for much or all of the year is beneficial to the whole system in terms of keeping the soil protected. Not all of the plants I describe in this layer are edible; some are used for system functions such as soil protection, and may have other uses too.

Perennial/ground-cover layers

Although in my introduction to vertical layers in Chapter 2 I refer to the herbaceous perennial layer and the ground-cover layer as two separate layers, this is not always the case. Sometimes there is only one layer beneath shrubs. And that one layer might not necessarily be low – it might be a strong-growing perennial reaching 1m (3') high. In one location in your forest garden such a plant might be the only low layer beneath shrubs, but in another it may be underplanted with lower species. Because it is not easy to separate ground-cover layer species from perennial-layer species in a listing – lots of plants could be in either layer – they are grouped together in this chapter.

Very often, however, there will be two, and sometimes three distinct heights in this layer. In particular, to ensure a good ground cover, it is usually good practice to have a 'base' layer of desirable plants – with foliage not usually taller than about 30cm (1') – growing very low beneath other perennials. This allows for 'island' planting and other techniques for polycultures that I describe in the next chapter (see page 266). In other places the 'base' layer may be taller – say 60cm (2') high – which allows for tall vigorous perennials (for

example, the taller comfreys or poke root, *Phytolacca americana*) to grow through.

Base-layer plants are likely to get walked over from time to time. Different species have different tolerances to foot traffic, and few like constant traffic. Try to remember to take a different route each time so the same plants don't get trampled again and again. As well as being low, base-layer plants must be shade-tolerant and preferably still produce any crop in the shade.

In the tables overleaf I have given an indication of the root structure of recommended base-layer plants. Bear this in mind when planting other things amongst them, and try to mix shallow- and deep-rooted plants where possible, to utilise the soil space more effectively.

The ground-cover species described in this chapter are, in the main, also herbaceous perennials. Those that are not are low-growing shrubs and are identified as such. Climbing herbaceous perennials are listed in Chapter 17.

Some *Rubus* species make good ground cover, such as groundcover raspberry (*Rubus* 'Betty Ashburner').

RECOMMENDED LOW BASE-LAYER PLANTS

Species		Root structure
Aegopodium podagraria	Ground elder	Shallow
Ajuga reptans	Bugle	Shallow
Alchemilla mollis	Lady's mantle	Shallow
Allium tricoccum	Ramps	Shallow, bulbs
Allium ursinum	Ramsons	Shallow, bulbs
Asarum canadense	Wild ginger	Shallow
Asarum europaeum	Asarabacca	Shallow
Chrysosplenium oppositifolium / C. alternifolium	Golden saxifrage	Shallow
Claytonia sibirica	Siberian purslane	Shallow, tuberous
Cornus canadensis	Creeping dogwood	Shallow
Duchesnea indica	False strawberry	Shallow
Fragaria spp.	Strawberries	Shallow
Galax urceolata	Wand flower	Moderately deep
Galium odoratum	Sweet woodruff	Shallow
Gaultheria procumbens	Wintergreen	Shallow
Glechoma hederacea	Ground ivy	Shallow
Heuchera americana	Alum root	Moderately deep
Lotus corniculatus 'Plenus'	Bird's foot trefoil	Moderately deep
Lysimachia nummularia	Creeping jenny	Shallow
Mitchella repens	Partridge berry	Shallow
Oxalis acetosella	Wood sorrel	Deep
Oxalis oregana	Redwood sorrel	Moderately deep
Potentilla anserina	Silverweed	Deep, taprooted
Pulmonaria officinalis	Lungwort	Very deep, taprooted
Rubus nepalensis	Nepalese raspberry	Shallow
Rubus pentalobus	Creeping bramble	Shallow
Sanguinaria canadensis	Bloodroot	Deep
Symphytum ibericum	Dwarf comfrey	Deep
Tiarella cordifolia	Foam flower	Shallow
Vinca minor	Lesser periwinkle	Shallow
Viola spp.	Violets	Shallow
Waldsteinia fragarioides	Barren strawberry	Shallow
Waldsteinia ternata	Barren strawberry	Shallow

RECOMMENDED MEDIUM-HEIGHT BASE-LAYER PLANTS

Species		Root structure
Geranium macrorrhizum	Rock cranesbill	Moderately deep
Mentha longifolia	Horse mint	Shallow
Mentha suaveolens	Apple mint	Shallow
Rubus 'Betty Ashburner'	Groundcover raspberry	Shallow
Rubus tricolor	Chinese bramble	Shallow
Saponaria officinalis	Soapwort	Moderately deep
Symphytum officinale	Comfrey	Very deep
Symphytum x uplandicum	Russian comfrey	Very deep
Vinca major	Greater periwinkle	Shallow

A plant that is given a poor ground-cover rating in this chapter needs to be grown in conjunction with a lower-growing plant that covers the ground well if you want to minimise weeding.

Perennials/covers for edible fruits

These plants can be grown primarily as a fruit crop, though of course they may also have other functions.

Berberis spp., BARBERRIES

These are clumping shrubs – for full details and larger species see page 166, Chapter 13 (Shrub species). Some of the smaller species are useful in this layer. Plant at 60cm (2') spacing to form a good cover. *B. candidula* (deciduous) grows 45cm (1'6") high and 1.2m (4') wide. *B.* x *frikartii* 'Amstelveen' (evergreen) grows to 1m (3') high and wide. *B. wilsoniae* (deciduous) grows to 1m (3') high and wide. Good fruiting requires fairly good light conditions.

Cornus canadensis, CREEPING DOGWOOD

Deciduous/Evergreen: D   **Zone:** 2
Sun/shade preference: ◑
Shade tolerance: ●
Performance rating: ✓✓
Fertility: SF
Cover: ✓✓   **Flowers:** White

This is a low, creeping, North American perennial. Plant at 35cm (14") spacing to form a good cover. It tolerates some foot traffic.

Size: 15-20cm (6-8") high, spreading widely.
Cultivation: Plant pot-grown plants in winter. Likes a moist, acid soil.
Flowering: June; insect-pollinated.
Fruiting: August.
Uses: Edible fruit – about 6mm (0.25") across; rather lacking in flavour.

Harvest and storage: The fruits are harvested in autumn and should be used immediately.
Cooking/processing: Fruits are best cooked with other fruits or in a mixed jam or preserve. You might want to use a Moulinex sieve to remove the seeds.
Propagation: By seed or division.
Maintenance: None required.

Wild strawberry (*Fragaria vesca*).

Fragaria spp., STRAWBERRIES

Deciduous/Evergreen: D/E   **Zone:** 3-6
Sun/shade preference: ○
Shade tolerance: ◗
Performance rating: ✓✓✓
Fertility: SF
Cover: ✓-✓✓   **Flowers:** White

Species include *Fragaria chiloensis* (Chilean or beach strawberry), *F. moschata* (musk strawberry), *F. vesca* (wild or woodland strawberry), *F. vesca* 'Semperflorens' (alpine strawberry), *F. virginiana* (American or scarlet strawberry), *F. viridis* (Green strawberry) and *F.* x *ananassa* (cultivated strawberry).

Strawberries are low-growing perennials mostly spreading via runners (apart from selected runnerless forms) to form a carpet. *F. vesca* and *F. viridis* are often evergreen in mild winter regions. Hardiness varies, from zone 3 (*F. virginiana*) to zone 6 (*F. moschata*). They provide fair (*F.* x *ananassa*, *F. virginiana*) to good (*F. vesca*, *F. viridis*, *F. chiloensis*) ground cover. They tolerate some foot traffic.

Size: 15-25cm (6-10") high, spreading widely.
Cultivation: Plant out pot-grown plants or transplant rooted runners in winter (they come early into growth). Most soils are fine.

Flowering: April onwards; varies with species. Bee-pollinated.

Fruiting: June onwards.

Uses: Edible fruits, all very good. The species fruits have a more concentrated flavour than cultivated types but are smaller. Leaves can be used in salads or made into herb teas.

Harvest and storage: Harvest fruits in summer and autumn; leaves through the season.

Cooking/processing: Preserve fruits by making jam, or by drying after slicing (or cutting in two if small).

Secondary uses: Bee plants.

Propagation: Usually via runners.

Maintenance: None required unless you need to detach runners to stop it spreading.

Fuchsia spp., FUCHSIAS

For full details see page 169, Chapter 13 (Shrub species).

Fuchsias are included in this layer because in many cold-winter areas they grow like clump-forming herbaceous perennials rather than shrubs, often reaching half or two-thirds their shrub height each season.

Gaultheria procumbens, WINTERGREEN

Deciduous/Evergreen: E **Zone:** 4
Sun/shade preference: ◑
Shade tolerance: ●
Performance rating: ✓✓
Fertility: SF
Cover: ✓ **Flowers:** White

This is a low, spreading North American evergreen wood-land shrub. All other *Gaultheria* species can also be used similarly, though most are larger (see *Gaultheria shallon*, page 169, Chapter 13). Wintergreen tolerates some foot traffic.

Size: 20cm (8") high; spreading.

Cultivation: Pot-grown plants in acid compost should be planted out in winter. A moist, acid soil is essential.

Flowering: July/August; bee-pollinated.

Fruiting: October–December.

Uses: The fruits and leaves of wintergreen are strongly aromatic – both reminiscent of disinfectant – though the fruit of some of the other species is much nicer (see *G. shallon*, page 169, for example).

Harvest and storage: Fruit are harvested in autumn; leaves at any time.

Secondary uses: Great bee plants. The fruits are medicinal (antiseptic – they smell of disinfectant!).

Propagation: By seed or division of rooted suckers.

Maintenance: Good combined with another perennial – too low to be weed-suppressing on its own.

Rubus 'Betty Ashburner', GROUNDCOVER RASPBERRY

Deciduous/Evergreen: E **Zone:** 6
Sun/shade preference: ◑
Shade tolerance: ◐
Performance rating: ✓✓✓
Fertility: SS
Cover: ✓✓✓ **Flowers:** White

This is an evergreen spreading prostrate shrub with rooting shoot tips. It spreads 60-90cm (2-3') a year, covering large areas. The stems are slightly prickly. Plant at 60-100cm (2'-3'3") spacing to form a ground cover. As it appears not to be self-fertile, you need to have one of its parents (*R. pentalobus* or *R. tricolor*) nearby for cross-pollination. It tolerates foot traffic.

Size: 45cm (1'6") high, spreading widely.

Cultivation: Plant rooted layers or pot-grown plants in winter or spring in any reasonable soil and sun or shade.

Flowering: June/July; bee-pollinated.

Fruiting: Late July to early September.

Uses: Edible fruits, like small raspberries.

Harvest and storage: Harvest fruits in late summer and autumn. The fruits must be processed soon after harvesting.

Cooking/processing: You can make a jam from the fruits, similar to raspberry jam.

Secondary uses: Bee plant.

Propagation: By detaching rooting stems.

Maintenance: Little required, except stopping it going where you don't want it. A mown path will achieve this, or you can cut back arching growth a couple of times a year to stop it tip-layering.

Nepalese raspberry (*Rubus nepalensis*).

Rubus nepalensis, NEPALESE RASPBERRY / GROUNDCOVER RASPBERRY

Deciduous/Evergreen: E Zone: 7
Sun/shade preference: ◗
Shade tolerance: ●●
Performance rating: ✓✓✓
Fertility: SS
Cover: ✓✓✓ Flowers: White

A prostrate evergreen Himalayan shrub, Nepalese raspberry spreads up to 1m (3') a year, with shoot tips rooting. The stems are not prickly. Plant at 45-60cm (1'6"-2') spacing for a ground cover. It makes a fantastic cover beneath shrubs and in other shady places, and it fruits pretty well too. It tolerates foot traffic.

Size: 30cm (1') high, spreading widely.
Cultivation: Plant rooted layers or pot-grown plants in winter or spring in any reasonable soil and sun or shade.
Flowering: June/July.
Fruiting: August/September.
Uses: Edible fruits, like small raspberries.
Harvest and storage: Harvest fruits in late summer and autumn. The fruits must be processed soon after harvesting.
Cooking/processing: You can make a jam from the fruits, similar to raspberry jam.
Secondary uses: Bee plant.

Propagation: By detaching rooting stems.
Maintenance: Just stopping it going where you don't want it. A mown path will achieve this, or you can cut back arching growth a couple of times a year to stop it tip-layering.

Creeping bramble (*Rubus pentalobus*) 'Emerald Carpet' as a base-layer cover.

Rubus pentalobus (syn. *R. rolfei*; *R. calycinoides*), CREEPING BRAMBLE

Deciduous/Evergreen: E Zone: 7
Sun/shade preference: ○
Shade tolerance: ◗
Performance rating: ✓✓✓
Fertility: SF
Cover: ✓✓ Flowers: White

This is a very low-growing prostrate Taiwanese evergreen shrub, spreading to form a low carpet, with stems rooting as they go. The stems are slightly prickly. Plant at 60cm (2') spacing to form a ground cover. 'Emerald Carpet' is a particularly good carpeting variety. It forms an excellent cover beneath other perennials, and fruits well. As it's very low it can be prone to becoming weedy, so it's good to grow other, larger, perennials within it. It tolerates foot traffic.

Size: 10cm (4") high, spreading widely.
Cultivation: Plant rooted layers or pot-grown plants in winter or spring in any reasonable soil and sun or shade.
Flowering: June/July; bee-pollinated.
Fruiting: July/August.
Uses: Edible fruits, like small raspberries.
Harvest and storage: Harvest fruits in summer and autumn. The fruits must be processed soon after harvesting.

Cooking/processing: You can make a jam from the fruits, similar to raspberry jam.
Secondary uses: Bee plant.
Propagation: By detaching rooting stems.
Maintenance: Occasional weeding. Stopping it going where you don't want it. You can do this with a mown path, or just cut back arching growth a couple of times a year to stop it tip-layering.

Chinese bramble (*Rubus tricolor*).

Rubus tricolor, CHINESE BRAMBLE / GROUNDCOVER RASPBERRY

Deciduous/Evergreen: E **Zone:** 6
Sun/shade preference: ◐
Shade tolerance: ●●
Performance rating: ✓✓✓
Fertility: SS
Cover: ✓✓✓ **Flowers:** White

A fairly prostrate evergreen Asian shrub, the Chinese bramble grows at least 60cm (2') high and spreads up to 2m (6'6") per year. It can get higher as it arches over itself and/or other shrubs. The tips root as they go. The stems are not prickly. Plant at 1m (3') spacing or more to form a ground cover. It is too vigorous for small gardens but makes a great cover for larger areas. It is not self-fertile, so grow two or more different plants. It tolerates foot traffic.

Size: 60cm+ (2'+) high, spreading widely.
Cultivation: Plant rooted layers or pot-grown plants in winter or spring in any reasonable soil and sun or shade.
Uses: Edible fruits, like small raspberries.
Flowering: June/July; bee-pollinated.

Fruiting: mid-July to early September.
Harvest and storage: Harvest fruits in late summer and autumn. The fruits must be processed soon after harvesting.
Cooking/processing: You can make a jam from the fruits, similar to raspberry jam.
Secondary uses: Bee plant.
Propagation: By detaching rooting stems.
Maintenance: Consists of two jobs: 1) keeping the cover low enough to enable easy passage of foot traffic – I do this by walking over it from time to time; and 2) stopping it spreading further than you want. Use a mown path to achieve this, or cut back arching growth a couple of times a year to stop it tip-layering.

Chinese bramble (*Rubus tricolor*) fruit in August.

Cranberry (*Vaccinium macrocarpon*) 'Olson's Honkers'.

Vaccinium macrocarpon, AMERICAN CRANBERRY & *V. oxycoccos*, EUROPEAN CRANBERRY

Deciduous/Evergreen: E   Zone: 2
Sun/shade preference: ◐
Shade tolerance: ◐
Performance rating: ✓
Fertility: SF
Cover: ✗   Flowers: White

Vaccinium species include cranberries, blueberries and others. Cranberries are lower-growing than blueberries and have a different growth form, being creeping plants that root as they go. There are good fruiting varieties of American cranberry, including 'CN', 'Olson's Honkers' and 'Pilgrim', which have fruits up to 1.5cm (0.6") across. Fruits on European cranberry are smaller but have a similar flavour.

The cranberries have tiny leaves and bell-shaped flowers. They are prone to weed problems on fertile soils.

Size: 20cm (8") high; spreading.
Cultivation: Pot-grown plants in acid compost should be planted in winter or spring. Give a moist but well-drained soil, preferably sandy or peaty. Acid soil is essential.
Uses: The fruits are eaten or made into juice. They are quite acid – need sweetening for most people.
Flowering: June–August; bee-pollinated.
Fruiting: August–October.
Harvest and storage: Fruits are harvested in autumn – they contain natural preservatives and stay ripe on the plants for a long time.

Cooking/processing: The ripe fruits, once picked, store for a long time in cool temperatures. They can be dried or made into a jam (cranberry sauce).
Secondary uses: Great bee plants.
Propagation: By detaching rooted stems.
Maintenance: Weeding is often required.

Lingonberry (*Vaccinium vitis-idaea*) Koralle Group.

Vaccinium vitis-idaea, LINGONBERRY / COWBERRY

Deciduous/Evergreen: E   Zone: 5
Sun/shade preference: ○
Shade tolerance: ◐
Performance rating: ✓✓
Fertility: SF
Cover: ✓✓   Flowers: White

Lingonberry is a creeping evergreen shrub of northern temperate regions, spreading via rhizomes. It is found naturally on moors and mountains. Plant at 25cm (10") spacing for a ground cover. Good fruiting varieties with larger fruits include the Koralle Group.

Size: 25-50cm (10-20") high; spreading.
Cultivation: Pot-grown plants in acid compost should be planted in winter or spring. Give a moist but well-drained soil, preferably sandy or peaty. Acid soil is essential.
Uses: The fruits are edible, widely used in Scandinavia for making jams, preserves, etc.
Flowering: May/June; bee-pollinated.
Fruiting: August–October.
Harvest and storage: Fruits are harvested in autumn over a long period. They contain the same natural preservative – benzoic acid – as cranberries.

Cooking/processing: As for cranberries (see above).
Secondary uses: Great bee plant. The leaves are used for herb teas.
Propagation: Division in winter or spring. Can also be layered.
Maintenance: None required.

Perennials/covers for edible leaves & stems

Many herbaceous perennial or low shrubby plants have edible leaves (and sometimes stems), which can either be cooked as a vegetable or used raw in salads. Indeed, you may find that it is quite easy to provide all your salad requirements from this layer, even in shady or semi-shady conditions. Some of the plants in this section have other edible parts too.

Aegopodium podagraria, GROUND ELDER

Deciduous/Evergreen: D **Zone:** 5
Sun/shade preference: ○
Shade tolerance: ●
Performance rating: ✓✓
Fertility: SF
Cover: ✓✓ **Flowers:** Pale green

Spreading by rhizomes and usually considered a weed, ground elder is not something I would necessarily suggest planting, but if you have it already you can make use of it. It tastes better than it smells, and tolerates some foot traffic. The Romans introduced it to Britain as a pot-herb.

Size: 30-60cm (1-2') high when flowering.
Cultivation: Can be controlled by bordering with more competitive evergreens. Fine in any soil.
Uses: The leaves can be eaten raw in salads or cooked in soups, etc.
Harvest and storage: Leaves can be harvested throughout the season.
Cooking/processing: None required.
Secondary uses: Bee and beneficial-insect plant.
Propagation: By seed or rhizome cuttings.
Maintenance: Little required.

Agastache foeniculum, ANISE HYSSOP & *A. rugosa,* KOREAN MINT

Deciduous/Evergreen: D **Zone:** 8
Sun/shade preference: ○
Shade tolerance: ○
Performance rating: ✓✓
Fertility: SF
Cover: ✗ **Flowers:** Bluish-mauve

These perennials have beautiful flowers, much loved by bees.

Size: 30-60cm (1-2') high when flowering.
Cultivation: Plant young pot-grown plants in winter or spring. Requires a well-drained soil; *A. foeniculum* especially is likely to die out in wet conditions.
Uses: The leaves can be eaten raw in salads or cooked in soups, etc. They have a lovely anise flavour.
Harvest and storage: Leaves can be harvested throughout the season.
Cooking/processing: None required.
Secondary uses: Very good bee plant.
Propagation: By seed or division.
Maintenance: Little required.

Allium spp., THE ONION & GARLIC FAMILY

The onion and garlic family comprises a large number of perennials, mostly bulbous but some rhizomatous perennials. Nearly all alliums have edible leaves, flowers and bulbs, and here I just mention a few in a forest garden context. Many alliums require good sun conditions but there are a few well-known shade-tolerant species such as ramsons (*Allium ursinum*) and its American cousin, ramps (*Allium tricoccum*). Many form poor ground cover but are good grown through a low cover such as creeping bramble (*Rubus pentalobus*).

Babington's leek (*Allium ampeloprasum* var. *babingtonii*) in early spring.

Allium ampeloprasum var. *babingtonii*, BABINGTON'S LEEK / PERENNIAL LEEK

Deciduous/Evergreen: D   Zone: 6
Sun/shade preference: ◯
Shade tolerance: ◖
Performance rating: ✓✓✓✓
Fertility: SF
Cover: ✗   Flowers: Pinkish-purple

This is a bulbous perennial native to the British seashore. The leaves die down to the bulb in August. It comes into growth by October, grows through winter in the UK, and sends up a flowerhead in May. A head of bulbils (like small cloves of garlic) is produced at the top of the dried flower stalks in September.

Size: 45cm (1'6") high in spring; flowerhead to 1.5m (5') high.
Cultivation: Broadcast bulbils in late summer or plant out young plants in winter. Any reasonable soil.
Uses: Edible bulbs, stems, leaves and bulbils.
Harvest and storage: The bulb can be harvested in late summer and can be air-dried like onion bulbs and stored. The leek can be harvested over the winter – if cut at soil level it should regrow. Plants need to be 2-3 years old to attain a reasonable size.
Cooking/processing: The bulbs are garlic-sized but not subdivided into cloves, with a garlic/onion flavour – peel and crush to use. As a leek the plant is very similar to the annual leek, though the outer leaves are a little tough. The bulbils are also edible but fiddly to peel – better to use them whole before they form papery skins.
Secondary uses: Bee plant.

Propagation: By bulbils. Simply broadcast these in September where you want them to grow and where the existing vegetation cover is not thicker than 10-15cm (4-6").
Maintenance: None needed.

Babington's leek (*Allium ampeloprasum* var. *babingtonii*) bulbil heads in late summer.

Allium cepa Aggregatum Group, MULTIPLIER ONIONS & *A. fistulosum*, WELSH ONION

Deciduous/Evergreen: D   Zone: 5
Sun/shade preference: ◯
Shade tolerance: ◖
Performance rating: ✓✓✓
Fertility: SF
Cover: ✗   Flowers: Pinkish-purple

Multiplier onions include the shallot and the potato onion. All these species form a clump of bulbs, largest in shallots and potato onions (2-4cm, 0.8-1.6" diameter); Welsh onion bulbs are much smaller (1.2cm, 0.5").

Size: 30-50cm (1'-1'8") high.
Cultivation: Plant bulbs in winter or spring or sow seed in spring. Give any reasonably well-drained soil.
Uses: The bulbs are like small onions; the leaves like spring onions.
Harvest and storage: Late summer – some or all bulbs can be harvested, dried like onions and stored until spring. Leaves can be harvested for salads from spring to summer.
Cooking/processing: As for shallots or small onions.

Secondary uses: Bee plants.
Propagation: By replanting bulbs from autumn to spring, or by seed – not dormant.
Maintenance: Clumps should be replanted elsewhere from time to time to prevent a build-up of onion diseases.

Daffodil garlic (*Allium neapolitanum*).

Allium cepa Proliferum Group, **EGYPTIAN ONION / TREE ONION**

Deciduous/Evergreen: D   Zone: 4
Sun/shade preference: ◐
Shade tolerance: ◖
Performance rating: ✓✓✓
Fertility: SF
Cover: ✗   Flowers: Pinkish-purple

This species forms a clump of bulbs but also forms a head of bulbils at the top of the flowerhead.

Size: 50-100cm (1'8"-3'3") high.
Cultivation: Plant bulbils at any time of year. Likes sun and any reasonably well-drained soil.
Uses: The bulbils can be eaten – see Babington's leek, (*Allium ampeloprasum* var. *babingtonii*), page 209. The leaves can be eaten like spring onions.
Harvest and storage: Leaves are harvested in spring; bulbils in late summer. Dry bulbils to store.
Cooking/processing: The young bulbils can be used whole in soups, stews, etc. Mature bulbils must be peeled to remove the papery skin.
Secondary uses: Bee plant.
Propagation: By bulbils in autumn or spring.
Maintenance: Little needed. Watch out for slugs, even on established plants. Will move about by itself via the bulbil heads bending over, touching the ground, and bulbils rooting there.

Allium neapolitanum, **DAFFODIL GARLIC**

Deciduous/Evergreen: D   Zone: 7
Sun/shade preference: ○
Shade tolerance: ◖
Performance rating: ✓✓✓
Fertility: SF
Cover: ✗   Flowers: White

Clump-forming and bulbous, daffodil garlic dies down to the bulb in early summer, starts growing in October, grows through winter in suitable regions, and flowers in mid-spring. I like this especially for its garlic-flavoured leaves in late autumn and early winter.

Size: 30-50cm (1'-1'8") high,
Cultivation: Plant bulbs in autumn, or young plants in spring. Likes sun and any reasonably well-drained soil.
Uses: The leaves and flowers are excellent in salads or cooked.
Harvest and storage: The flattish leaves can be harvested through the winter in mild regions.
Cooking/processing: Treat like chives or spring onion leaves.
Secondary uses: Bee plants; edible bulbs.
Propagation: By seed or by replanting bulbs in summer/autumn.
Maintenance: Little required.

Allium tricoccum, RAMPS

See *Allium ursinum*, right.

Allium tuberosum, GARLIC CHIVES

Deciduous/Evergreen: D   Zone: 5
Sun/shade preference: ◐
Shade tolerance: ◑
Performance rating: ✓✓✓
Fertility: SF
Cover: ✗   Flowers: Pinkish-purple

This is a herb widely used in Asian cuisine, which deserves to be grown more in the UK.

Size: 30-50cm (1'-1'8") high.
Cultivation: Plant young plants in winter or spring. Give sun and any reasonably well-drained soil.
Uses: The leaves and flowers are great in salads or cooked.
Harvest and storage: The flattish leaves are used through the growing season.
Cooking/processing: Treat like chives or spring onion leaves.
Secondary uses: Bee plant.
Propagation: By seed or division of clumps.
Maintenance: Little required.

Ramsons (*Allium ursinum*).

Allium ursinum, RAMSONS / WILD GARLIC

Deciduous/Evergreen: D   Zone: 4
Sun/shade preference: ◑
Shade tolerance: ●
Performance rating: ✓✓✓✓
Fertility: SF
Cover: ✓✓   Flowers: White

Ramsons is a bulbous perennial, a well-known European woodland plant, in leaf for only a few months in late winter and spring. It self-seeds to form colonies. It provides good ground cover from February to June, though poor the rest of the year. Plant at 30cm (1') spacing to form a ground cover. The North American *Allium tricoccum*, ramps, is similar in most respects.

Size: 30cm (1') high and wide.
Cultivation: It is easiest to establish by sowing seed in summer – germinates the following late winter. Likes a moist, humus-rich soil. Tolerates acid soils.
Uses: The leaves and flowers are excellent in salads (garlic-flavoured) or cooked (briefly).
Harvest and storage: Harvest from February to May in the UK.
Cooking/processing: Add for the last few minutes in cooked dishes, as the flavour dissipates quickly in the cooking process.
Secondary uses: Bee plant. The bulbs are edible but small and not really worth it.
Propagation: By seed – ideally broadcast in June.
Maintenance: As ramsons dies down in June, it needs to be grown in a polyculture (see page 266, Chapter 16) with something else that will keep the soil covered from June

onwards, for the growing season at least. I have a patch that does very well with ground ivy (*Glechoma hederacea*).

Wild angelica (*Angelica sylvestris*).

Althaea officinalis, **MARSH MALLOW**

Deciduous/Evergreen: D   **Zone:** 3
Sun/shade preference: ○
Shade tolerance: ◐
Performance rating: ✓✓✓
Fertility: SF
Cover: ✓   **Flowers:** White-pink

Marsh mallow is a clump-forming perennial found in moist soil.

Size: Flowerheads grow to 1.5-2m (5'-6'6") high.
Cultivation: Plant out young plants in winter. Fine in any moist soil.
Uses: The leaves and flowers are edible raw; the roots raw or cooked.
Harvest and storage: The leaves and flowers are harvested in spring and summer. Harvest younger roots in winter from around the edge of the plant. They will store in sand for several months.
Cooking/processing: The leaves and flowers are edible in salads, but the hairy texture of the leaves is not altogether pleasant. The young roots are starch-rich, sweet and crunchy, and very nice raw or steamed.
Secondary uses: Bee and butterfly plant. Medicinal uses, particularly as an anti-inflammatory.
Propagation: By seed.
Maintenance: None required. Robust once established.

Angelica sylvestris, **WILD ANGELICA / WOOD ANGELICA**

Deciduous/Evergreen: D   **Zone:** 5
Sun/shade preference: ○
Shade tolerance: ◐
Performance rating: ✓✓✓
Fertility: SF
Cover: ✓✓✓   **Flowers:** Cream

Wild angelica is a vigorous clump-forming perennial, making an excellent tall ground cover. Plant at 90cm (3') spacing to form a good cover.

Size: 60-80cm (2'-2'8") high; flowerheads 2-3m (6'6"-10') high.
Cultivation: Sow seed in spring or plant out young plants in winter. Prefers a fertile, loamy soil.
Uses: The leaves are used in salads or cooked – they have an angelica flavour.
Harvest and storage: Leaves harvested in spring and summer.
Cooking/processing: Use the leaves for flavouring. You can also candy the stems, as with the normal biennial angelica. I use the leaves sparingly in salads.
Secondary uses: Attracts beneficial insects.
Propagation: By seed.
Maintenance: It can self-seed a little too freely, so you might want to cut off the seedheads before they ripen.

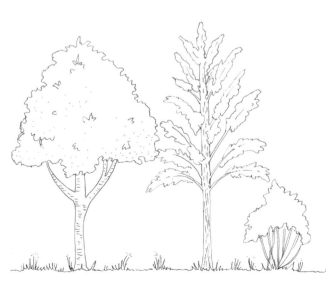

Aquilegia vulgaris, COLUMBINE

Deciduous/Evergreen: D Zone: 4
Sun/shade preference: ◐
Shade tolerance: ◑
Performance rating: ✓✓✓
Fertility: SF
Cover: ✗ Flowers: Blue

A short-lived, tall, branching perennial, columbine is often grown as selected forms in ornamental gardens, and frequently escapes into the wild.

Size: Grows to 1m (3') high when flowering.
Cultivation: Sow seed in autumn or plant out young plants in winter. At home in woods and damp places, it prefers neutral-to-alkaline soil.
Uses: Edible flowers and young leaves.
Harvest and storage: Young leaves are harvested all through the growing season. Do not pick any that show signs of mildew. Flowers are picked from April to July.
Cooking/processing: The young leaves make excellent eating, raw or cooked (steamed); they have a mild flavour. The flowers are great in salads, being sweet with nectar.
Propagation: Although short-lived it often self-seeds.
Maintenance: Little required.

Asparagus officinalis, ASPARAGUS

Deciduous/Evergreen: D Zone: 4
Sun/shade preference: ○
Shade tolerance: ○
Performance rating: ✓✓
Fertility: M/F
Cover: ✗ Flowers: Greenish-yellow

Asparagus is a tuberous perennial, which slowly expands.

Size: Flowerheads 1-1.5m (3-5') high.
Cultivation: Plant crowns in winter on a slight mound to improve drainage. Likes a well-drained soil.
Uses: The shoots are a well-known spring vegetable.
Harvest and storage: The shoots are harvested in spring.
Cooking/processing: Just steam for a few minutes and serve with melted butter.

Secondary uses: Bee plant.
Propagation: By seed or from crowns.
Maintenance: Very prone to weed problems, so grow through a low carpeting plant.

Asphodeline lutea, YELLOW ASPHODEL / KING'S SPEAR

Deciduous/Evergreen: D Zone: 6
Sun/shade preference: ○
Shade tolerance: ◑
Performance rating: ✓✓
Fertility: SF
Cover: ✗ Flowers: Yellow

Yellow asphodel is a clump-forming perennial from dry places in southern Europe.

Size: Flowerheads up to 1.5m (5') high, 30cm (1') wide.
Cultivation: Plant out young plants in winter. Fine in any well-drained soil.
Uses: Edible shoots, flowers and roots.
Harvest and storage: Young shoots are harvested in late summer, through winter to spring; flowers in spring; roots in winter. The roots can be stored in sand for several months.
Cooking/processing: The young shoots are cooked like asparagus – very good. The flowers are sweet and used in salads. The roots – child-finger-sized but abundant – are cooked and eaten and have a nutty flavour.
Propagation: By seed, or divide in late summer / early autumn.
Maintenance: Watch out for slugs, snails and rabbits eating the shoots.

Sea beet (*Beta vulgaris* subsp. *maritima*).

Beta vulgaris subsp. *maritima*, SEA BEET

Deciduous/Evergreen: E **Zone:** 6
Sun/shade preference: ◐
Shade tolerance: ◑
Performance rating: ✓✓
Fertility: SF
Cover: ✓ **Flowers:** Green

This clump-forming perennial (sometimes biennial) is often evergreen in mild areas. It is an ancestor of beetroot, perpetual spinach and Swiss chard.

Size: to 90cm (3') high and 30cm (1') wide when flowering.
Cultivation: Sow seed in spring or transplant young plants in winter or spring. Good in any well-drained soil.
Uses: The leaves are an excellent cooked vegetable.
Harvest and storage: The leaves can be harvested all year round, though mostly in spring and summer. The roots are harvested in winter and can be stored like beetroot.
Cooking/processing: Steam the leaves as a cooked vegetable or use in lasagne, stews, etc.
Secondary uses: The roots are good to eat, cooked, with a sweet-potato flavour. They are not usually much thicker than finger width.
Propagation: By seed.
Maintenance: Little required. Rabbits like to browse this!

Brassica oleracea, PERENNIAL BROCCOLI, COLLARDS & KALE

Deciduous/Evergreen: E **Zone:** 8
Sun/shade preference: ○
Shade tolerance: ◑
Performance rating: ✓
Fertility: SF
Cover: ✓ **Flowers:** Yellow

These clump-forming perennials include '9 Star Perennial Broccoli', 'Dorbenton Perennial Kale' and 'Tree Collards' (this latter can be over 4m/13' high). They are susceptible to all the usual brassica pests and diseases, including cabbage white caterpillars, pigeons, etc.

Size: Mostly 60-100cm (2'-3'3") high and wide.
Cultivation: Plant young plants in winter or spring. Give a fertile soil – they are hungry feeders.
Uses: The leaves and flowerheads are cooked and eaten as vegetables.
Harvest and storage: Leaves are usually harvested and cooked when young. '9 Star' has small cauliflower-type heads, which are harvested in summer.
Cooking/processing: Leaves are harvested at any time of year and steamed like cabbage.
Secondary uses: Bee plants.
Propagation: By seed or cuttings.
Maintenance: Flowering can reduce the life of the plants, so prevent flowering if possible. Watch out for pests and diseases from spring to autumn.

Perennial broccoli (*Brassica oleracea*) growing with Chinese bramble (*Rubus tricolor*).

Turkish rocket (*Bunias orientalis*).

Bunias orientalis, TURKISH ROCKET

Deciduous/Evergreen: D/E   Zone: 4
Sun/shade preference: ◯
Shade tolerance: ◑
Performance rating: ✓✓✓
Fertility: SF
Cover: ✓   Flowers: Yellow

Pig nut (*Bunium bulbocastanum*).

Bunium bulbocastanum, PIG NUT

Deciduous/Evergreen: D   Zone: 5
Sun/shade preference: ◯
Shade tolerance: ◑
Performance rating: ✓✓
Fertility: SF
Cover: ✓✓   Flowers: White

This is a clump-forming perennial that often keeps a rosette of leaves over the winter in the UK. Plant at 45cm (1'6") spacing to form a good cover.

Size: To 80cm (2'8") high and 30cm (1') wide when flowering.
Cultivation: Sow seed in spring or transplant young plants in winter. Any reasonable soil.
Uses: Edible leaves and flowerheads.
Harvest and storage: Young leaves are harvested in spring, larger leaves all year and flowerheads in summer.
Cooking/processing: The flowerheads are like a mustardy broccoli – excellent both raw in salads and steamed. The leaves too are mustardy – best cooked but the very young leaves can be used raw.
Secondary uses: Bee plant.
Propagation: By seed; also from pieces of root.
Maintenance: None required. Very sturdy once established.

Pig nut is a clump-forming perennial with finely cut leaves, native to Britain and Europe. It is sometimes called tuberous caraway because of its edible root, which in reality tastes more like chestnut.

Size: 60-80cm (2'-2'8") high and wide when flowering.
Cultivation: Transplant young plants in winter or spring. Fine in any soil.
Uses: Edible leaves, stems, seeds and roots.
Harvest and storage: Leaves are harvested through the growing season, seeds in autumn and tubers in winter.
Cooking/processing: The finely cut leaves are a great herb to use raw in salads or to season dishes – can be used in bulk. The seeds are used as a cumin-like spice. The tuberous root can be cooked and eaten, and has a sweet chestnut flavour.
Secondary uses: Attracts beneficial insects.
Propagation: By seed.
Maintenance: Little required, apart from a weed in spring.

Milky bellflower (*Campanula lactiflora*).

Campanula spp., BELLFLOWERS / HAREBELLS

Campanula spp. include both alpine and hardy perennial forms, listed separately below.

Deciduous/Evergreen: E   Zone: 3-5
Sun/shade preference: ○
Shade tolerance: ◑
Performance rating: ✓✓
Fertility: SF
Cover: ✓   Flowers: Blue, purple, pink, white

Alpine species include *Campanula cochleariifolia*, *C. portenschlagiana* and *C. poscharskyana*. This is a group of evergreen, clump-forming perennials. Plant at 30cm (1') spacing to form a good cover.

Size: up to 30cm (1') high and 20cm (8") wide.
Cultivation: Transplant young plants in spring. Alpine species grow in cracks in walls and rocky banks and need well-drained soil.
Uses: Edible flowers, eaten in salads. The leaves may also be used in salads, though are sometimes a little tough.
Harvest and storage: Harvest leaves all year round and flowers in spring and summer.
Cooking/processing: The leaves can also be added to stews, soups, etc.
Secondary uses: Great bee plants.
Propagation: By division or basal cuttings in spring, or by seed. They often self-seed.
Maintenance: Little required.

Deciduous/Evergreen: D/E   Zone: 2-8
Sun/shade preference: ○
Shade tolerance: ◑
Performance rating: ✓✓
Fertility: SF
Cover: ✓   Flowers: Blue, purple, pink, white

Hardy perennial bellflowers (deciduous unless noted) include *C. glomerata*, *C. lactiflora*, *C. latifolia*, *C. persicifolia* (evergreen) and *C. rapunculoides*. These are robust plants that can tolerate wetter conditions and more shade than the alpine species. Plant at 20-30cm (8-12") spacing to form a ground cover.

Size: 30-150cm (1-5') high and 20-30cm (8-12") wide.
Cultivation: Transplant young plants in winter in any ordinary soil.
Uses: Edible flowers, eaten in salads. The leaves may also be used in salads, though are sometimes a little tough.
Harvest and storage: Harvest leaves and flowers in spring and summer.
Cooking/processing: The leaves can also be added to stews, soups, etc.
Secondary uses: Great bee plants.
Propagation: By seed. They often self-seed.
Maintenance: Little required.

Cardamine pratensis, LADY'S SMOCK

Deciduous/Evergreen: E   Zone: 4
Sun/shade preference: ◑
Shade tolerance: ◑
Performance rating: ✓✓
Fertility: SF
Cover: ✗   Flowers: White

This well-known perennial wildflower likes moist shade, and retains a rosette of leaves over winter.

Size: 45cm (1'6") high and 30cm (1') wide.
Cultivation: Plant out pot-grown stock or divisions in winter or spring. Give any moist or wet soil.
Uses: The leaves and flowers can be eaten in salads – quite fiery and pungent. Later in spring the leaves have an unpleasant oily flavour.

Harvest and storage: Harvest leaves in winter; young leaves and flowers in spring.
Secondary uses: Bee plant.
Propagation: By seed or division.
Maintenance: Little required.

Red valerian (*Centranthus ruber*).

Centranthus ruber, RED VALERIAN

Deciduous/Evergreen: E Zone: 7
Sun/shade preference: ◐
Shade tolerance: ◐
Performance rating: ✓✓✓
Fertility: SF
Cover: ✓✓ Flowers: Pink

A clump-forming European perennial, red valerian self-seeds (especially into walls) to form larger colonies. It is evergreen in milder locations, and forms good ground cover on well-drained sites. Plant at 60cm (2') spacing to form a good cover.

Size: 60-100cm (2-3'3") high by 30-50cm wide (1'-1'8").
Cultivation: Transplant young plants in winter or sow seed into walls in spring. Likes a well-drained soil. Grows well in walls and rocky banks, etc. Very drought-tolerant.
Uses: The young leaves are great in salads, with a broad-bean-like flavour. They can get bitter in summer if the plants are in very dry locations.
Harvest and storage: Young leaves can be harvested any time of year.
Secondary uses: Very good butterfly plant. The roots are edible, having been used in soups in the past, though I haven't tried them yet.
Propagation: By seed or by division in spring.

Maintenance: Little required. The fleshy roots can grow into walls and, as they grow, expand and crack walls apart, so beware! It will self-seed freely where conditions are to its liking.

DROUGHT-TOLERANT PERENNIALS / COVERS

Bear's breech (*Acanthus mollis*)
Bugle (*Ajuga reptans*)
Cardoon (*Cynara cardunculus*)
Chinese bramble (*Rubus tricolor*)
Common Solomon's seal (*Polygonatum multiflorum*)
Coneflower (*Echinacea purpurea*)
Everlasting pea (*Lathyrus latifolius*) (climber – see Chapter 17)
Fennel (*Foeniculum vulgare*)
French sorrel (*Rumex scutatus*)
Garlic chives (*Allium tuberosum*)
Hop (*Humulus lupulus*) (climber – see Chapter 17)
Ice plant (*Sedum spectabile*)
Lemon balm (*Melissa officinalis*)
Lungwort (*Pulmonaria officinalis*)
Orpine (*Sedum telephium*)
Periwinkles (*Vinca* spp.)
Red valerian (*Centranthus ruber*)
Rock cranesbill (*Geranium macrorrhizum*)
Sea kale (*Crambe maritima*)
Wintergreen (*Gaultheria procumbens*)

Good King Henry (*Chenopodium bonus-henricus*).

Chenopodium bonus-henricus, GOOD KING HENRY

Deciduous/Evergreen: D Zone: 5
Sun/shade preference: ◐
Shade tolerance: ◑
Performance rating: ✓✓✓✓
Fertility: SF
Cover: ✓ Flowers: Pale green

Good King Henry is a clump-forming perennial native to Britain and Europe. Plant at 30cm (1') spacing to form a ground cover.

Size: 60cm (2') high by 40cm (1'4") wide.
Cultivation: Transplant young plants in winter. Fine in any soil.
Uses: Edible leaves and stems, cooked.
Harvest and storage: The leaves can be harvested throughout the growing season; the stems only when young.
Cooking/processing: This is a great spinach plant. The leaves and stems are just steamed for a few minutes before eating.
Secondary uses: The seeds can also be used in cooking – like poppy seeds. It is a good mineral accumulator.
Propagation: By seed.
Maintenance: None required.

Chrysosplenium alternifolium, GOLDEN SAXIFRAGE (ALTERNATE-LEAVED)

See *Chrysosplenium oppositifolium,* below.

Golden saxifrage (*Chrysosplenium oppositifolium*).

Chrysosplenium oppositifolium, GOLDEN SAXIFRAGE (OPPOSITE-LEAVED)

Deciduous/Evergreen: E Zone: 5
Sun/shade preference: ◐
Shade tolerance: ●
Performance rating: ✓✓✓
Fertility: SF
Cover: ✓✓ Flowers: Yellow

This European perennial grows prostrate on the ground. It can stay green most of the winter in mild areas. *C. alternifolium* is very similar and is used in the same ways. They form good ground cover in a damp shady spot, tolerating some foot traffic.

Size: 15cm (6") high, spreading low.
Cultivation: Transplant seedlings or divisions in winter or spring. Needs a damp site, and prefers acid soils.
Uses: A marvellous salad plant. The leaves and stems are crisp and mild.
Harvest and storage: The leaves and stems can be harvested throughout the growing season.

Propagation: By seed or division.
Maintenance: None required.

Cichorium intybus, **CHICORY**

Deciduous/Evergreen: D Zone: 3
Sun/shade preference: ◐
Shade tolerance: ◖
Performance rating: ✓✓✓
Fertility: SF
Cover: ✗ Flowers: Blue

Not all forms of this deep-rooted European plant are perennial; many cultivated forms are annual or biennial. Perennial varieties include 'Cerolio', 'Dentarella' ('Italian Dandelion'), 'Grumolo', 'Italo Rossico' ('Red Rib Dandelion'), 'Puntarella', 'Rossa di Treviso', 'Rossa di Verona' and 'Spadona'.

Size: This is a small, dandelion-like plant about 30cm (1') wide, but with a flower spike up to 1.2m (4') high.
Cultivation: Sow in spring or transplant young plants in winter/spring. Give any soil, though it grows most lushly in fertile soils.
Uses: The slightly bitter leaves are used in salads and added to cooked dishes.
Harvest and storage: Leaves are harvested through the growing season.
Cooking/processing: The leaves require just a few minutes' cooking.
Secondary uses: Chicory is a good mineral accumulator due to its deep roots. The roots can be harvested in autumn and winter and roasted to make a coffee-like drink. They store well in sand or a similar medium.
Propagation: By seed.
Maintenance: Little required once established.

Siberian purslane (*Claytonia sibirica*).

Claytonia sibirica (syn. *Montia sibirica*), **SIBERIAN PURSLANE**

Deciduous/Evergreen: D/E Zone: 3
Sun/shade preference: ◑
Shade tolerance: ●
Performance rating: ✓✓✓✓
Fertility: SF
Cover: ✓✓ Flowers: White

This clump-forming Asian perennial is evergreen in mild winter areas. It self-seeds in shade to form carpets, and dies down to an underground tuber in very cold or droughty weather. Plant at 30cm (1') spacing to form a good cover – it tolerates some foot traffic. A number of related species, including *C. caroliniana* and *C. virginiana* (spring beauty), are similar and can be used in the same ways.

Size: 20-30cm (8-12") high and wide.
Cultivation: Plant in winter or transplant profuse self-seedlings in spring. Fine in any reasonably moist soil.
Uses: A great salad plant – the leaves and stems are tender and crunchy with a beetroot-like flavour.
Harvest and storage: Leaves and stems can be harvested all year round.
Secondary uses: The tubers are eaten cooked, but are quite small.
Propagation: By seed or by division in spring.
Maintenance: None required.

Sea kale (*Crambe maritima*).

Crambe maritima, SEA KALE

Deciduous/Evergreen: D   Zone: 4
Sun/shade preference: ◐
Shade tolerance: ◐
Performance rating: ✓✓
Fertility: SF
Cover: ✓✓   Flowers: White

A well-known seashore plant, sea kale is part of the brassica family, and is clump forming. Plant at 60cm (2') spacing to form a good cover. Related larger species, which can be used similarly, include *C. cordifolia* (colewort: grows to 1.5m/5'; plant at 1.2m/4' spacing for a good cover) and *C. tatarica* (Tartar bread plant: grows to 90cm/3'; plant at 90cm/3' spacing for a good cover).

Size: 80cm (2'8") high; 50-60cm (1'8"-2') wide.
Cultivation: Plant root cuttings ('thongs') in winter or grow from seed and transplant in winter. Any well-drained soil.
Uses: Edible young leaves, flowerheads and roots.
Harvest and storage: Young leaves are harvested in spring (they are very tough when older); unopened flower-heads or open flowering heads in summer. Roots are dug up in winter – harvest the outer roots and leave the main taproot to regrow. Roots can be stored in damp sand for several months.
Cooking/processing: Young or blanched young leaves are best steamed, and have a cabbage-like flavour. The delicious flowerheads are eaten like (and taste like) broccoli, and can be eaten raw or cooked. The fleshy roots are starchy and best eaten cooked (roasted or boiled), when they are more digestible.
Secondary uses: Bee plant.

Propagation: By seed, division in spring or root cuttings in winter.
Maintenance: Watch out for brassica pests and diseases, but they are not usually too bad.

Cryptotaenia japonica, MITSUBA / JAPANESE PARSLEY

Deciduous/Evergreen: D   Zone: 8
Sun/shade preference: ○
Shade tolerance: ◐
Performance rating: ✓✓✓
Fertility: SF
Cover: ✗   Flowers: White

Mitsuba is a clump-forming Japanese perennial.

Size: 60cm (2') high and 20cm (8") wide.
Cultivation: Grow from seed, keeping young plants in part shade; plant in winter in any reasonable soil.
Uses: The leaves and stems are a lovely herb in both salads and cooked dishes.
Harvest and storage: Harvest leaves and stems throughout the growing season.
Cooking/processing: The leaves and stems need only a few minutes' cooking, and can be used in bulk quantities.
Secondary uses: Attracts beneficial insects.
Propagation: By seed.
Maintenance: Little required.

False strawberry (*Duchesnea indica*).

Duchesnea indica, FALSE STRAWBERRY / MOCK STRAWBERRY

Deciduous/Evergreen: SE   Zone: 6
Sun/shade preference: ◐
Shade tolerance: ●
Performance rating: ✓✓✓
Fertility: SF
Cover: ✓✓   Flowers: Yellow

This is an evergreen or semi-evergreen Asian perennial, spreading via runners. The foliage looks similar to that of strawberry plants. The fruits are almost spherical, red; 1-1.5cm (0.4-0.6") across. It is good as a lower ground-cover beneath other plants or interplanted with a taller perennial. It tolerates foot traffic.

Size: 15cm (6") high, spreading widely.
Cultivation: Transplant plants or rooted runners in winter into any reasonable soil.
Uses: The leaves can be added to salads – not a strong flavour, but quite pleasant. Fruits too can be added to salads, not for their flavour (which is like water), but for the crunchy seeds on their surface to add texture.
Harvest and storage: Harvest the leaves at any time; the fruits in summer and autumn.
Secondary uses: Bee plant.
Propagation: By seed or detaching runners.
Maintenance: None required unless you need to detach runners to stop it spreading.

Epilobium angustifolium (syn. *Chamerion angustifolium*), ROSEBAY WILLOWHERB / FIREWEED

Deciduous/Evergreen: D   Zone: 3
Sun/shade preference: ○
Shade tolerance: ◐
Performance rating: ✓✓
Fertility: SF
Cover: ✓✓   Flowers: Pinkish-purple

A robust herbaceous perennial, rosebay willowherb spreads via rhizomes to form large clumps. It is widespread on waste ground and after fires.

Size: 1-2m (3'-6'6") high; spreading.
Cultivation: Plant seedlings or divisions in winter, or just broadcast seed in spring. Fine in any soil.
Uses: The young shoots are best cooked as a vegetable. They are also excellent pickled.
Harvest and storage: Young shoots (20-30cm/8-12" high) are harvested from spring onwards.
Cooking/processing: Just steam for 10 minutes and serve with butter or a sauce.
Secondary uses: The stem pith is sweet and cucumber-flavoured, and makes a nice nibble.
Propagation: Seed or division. You may not need to sow it deliberately!
Maintenance: Little required. Will self-seed on any disturbed ground.

Fennel (*Foeniculum vulgare*).

Foeniculum vulgare, FENNEL

Deciduous/Evergreen: D **Zone:** 5
Sun/shade preference: ○
Shade tolerance: ◐
Performance rating: ✓✓✓
Fertility: SF
Cover: ✗ **Flowers:** Greenish-yellow

A clump-forming perennial, fennel has fine, feathery foliage that does not suppress weeds – grow it through a lower plant cover.

Size: 1-1.5m (3-5') high and 40cm (1'4") wide when flowering.
Cultivation: Grow young plants from seed and transplant in winter. Well-drained soil is essential.
Uses: All aerial parts are edible.
Harvest and storage: Leaves can be harvested through the growing season; seeds in autumn.
Cooking/processing: A well-known anise-flavoured herb, fennel leaves are good in salads or cooked. The seeds are used in cooked dishes, pickles, chutneys, etc.
Secondary uses: Very good for beneficial insects. Also a mineral accumulator.
Propagation: By seed or by division in spring.
Maintenance: Little required.

Galium odoratum (syn. *Asperula odorata*), SWEET WOODRUFF

Deciduous/Evergreen: D **Zone:** 4
Sun/shade preference: ○
Shade tolerance: ●
Performance rating: ✓✓
Fertility: SF
Cover: ✓✓ **Flowers:** White

Sweet woodruff is a low, spreading perennial, spreading via the roots. Plant at 25cm (10") spacing for a good cover. It tolerates a little foot traffic.

Size: 20cm (8") high; spreading.
Cultivation: Plant young plants out in winter. Give a moist but well-drained soil.
Uses: The fresh leaves are used as a garnish/flavouring in wines, liqueurs and other drinks.
Harvest and storage: Use leaves in season.
Secondary uses: Bee plant.
Propagation: By seed, division in spring, or softwood cuttings.
Maintenance: Little required. Good as a base-layer perennial.

Ground ivy (*Glechoma hederacea*).

Glechoma hederacea, GROUND IVY / ALEROOT

Deciduous/Evergreen: D   **Zone:** 6
Sun/shade preference: ◐
Shade tolerance: ◔
Performance rating: ✓✓✓
Fertility: SF
Cover: ✓✓   **Flowers:** Bluish-violet

Ground ivy is a lax, trailing, herbaceous perennial; evergreen in mild areas. Stems may root as they travel. It is sometimes regarded as a weed. It tolerates some foot traffic.

Size: 60cm (2') high; spreading.
Cultivation: Easiest to transplant a piece in spring if you don't already have it. Any moist soil.
Uses: The aromatic foliage is used for herb teas.
Harvest and storage: Leaves may be harvested at any time.
Secondary uses: Good bee plant. It was formerly used to clear beers.
Propagation: By seed, division of rooted stems, or softwood cuttings.
Maintenance: None required.

Hosta spp., HOSTAS

Deciduous/Evergreen: D   **Zone:** 4
Sun/shade preference: ◐
Shade tolerance: ●
Performance rating: ✓✓✓
Fertility: SF
Cover: ✓✓   **Flowers:** White, lavender, violet

Many hosta species are used as a vegetable, including *H. crispula*, *H. longipes*, *H. montana*, *H. plantaginea*, *H. sieboldii*, *H. sieboldiana*, *H. undulata* and *H. ventricosa*. Large-leaved cultivars of *H. sieboldiana* include 'Big Daddy', 'Blue Umbrella' and 'Elegans'.

Hostas are clump-forming Asian perennials. Plant at 40-60cm (1'4"-2') spacing for a good ground cover.

Size: most are 30-100cm (1'-3'3") high and wide.
Cultivation: Transplant young plants in winter – protect from slugs. Fine in any moist soil.
Uses: The curled leaf heads (rather like chicory chicons) are mostly eaten cooked, but can also be used raw in salads.
Harvest and storage: Leaf heads are harvested in spring. Plants will produce new ones to grow for the year.
Cooking/processing: The heads are usually steamed, fried or boiled – nice with a sauce or butter.
Propagation: By seed or by division in late summer or early spring.
Maintenance: Little required. Slugs and snails are fond of hostas so watch out, especially when plants are young.

Levisticum officinale, LOVAGE

Deciduous/Evergreen: D   **Zone:** 4
Sun/shade preference: ○
Shade tolerance: ◐
Performance rating: ✓✓✓
Fertility: SF
Cover: ✗   **Flowers:** Greenish-yellow

A clump-forming, deep-rooted perennial, lovage is best grown with a lower cover beneath.

Size: When flowering, 1.5-2m (5'-6'6") high and 40cm (1'4") wide.

Cultivation: Plant in winter in any reasonable soil.

Uses: This strong aromatic herb has a yeasty-celery flavour. The seeds are used as a spice.

Harvest and storage: Harvest leaves in spring and summer; seeds in autumn.

Cooking/processing: The leaves are used sparingly in salads or in soups, stews, etc. The seeds are best ground to use as a spice, with the same flavour as the leaves.

Secondary uses: Attracts beneficial insects.

Propagation: By seed.

Maintenance: None required.

Musk mallow (*Malva moschata*), showing different leaf forms.

Malva spp., MALLOWS

Deciduous/Evergreen: D   Zone: 4
Sun/shade preference: ◯
Shade tolerance: ◑
Performance rating: ✓✓✓
Fertility: SF
Cover: ✗   Flowers: Pinkish-violet

Many species can be used, including *Malva alcea* (hollyhock mallow), *M. moschata* (musk mallow), *M. sylvestris* (wood mallow) and *M. verticillata* (Chinese mallow). They are rosette-forming clumping perennials. *M. alcea* and *M. moschata* are evergreen in mild winter climates. The leaves of many species have varying forms, from entire to finely cut, making identification tricky.

Size: 60-100cm (2'-3'3") high and 20-30cm (8-12") wide.

Cultivation: Sow outside in spring or transplant young plants out in winter (they come early into growth). Give any soil that is not too acid. Best in not too fertile a soil, as this can cause an excess of nitrates in the leaves.

Uses: Edible leaves, flowers and young fruiting structures (known as 'cheeses', as that's what they look like).

Harvest and storage: Young leaves can be harvested at any time. Flowers are harvested in late spring and summer.

Cooking/processing: Mallows make an excellent muci-laginous salad leaf. The leaves also thicken stews and soups. The flowers are best used in salads. The 'cheeses' of most species are a nice nibble.

Secondary uses: Bee plants.

Propagation: By seed or by soft basal cuttings in spring.

Maintenance: Little required. These are often short-lived perennials, so expect them to die out after a few years.

Hollyhock mallow (*Malva alcea*).

Wood mallow (*Malva sylvestris*) 'Mystic Merlin'.

Ostrich fern (*Matteuccia struthiopteris*).

Matteuccia struthiopteris, OSTRICH FERN

Deciduous/Evergreen: D **Zone:** 2
Sun/shade preference: ◗
Shade tolerance: ●
Performance rating: ✓✓
Fertility: SF
Cover: ✓✓ **Flowers:** n/a

Lemon balm (*Melissa officinalis*).

Melissa officinalis, LEMON BALM

Deciduous/Evergreen: D **Zone:** 4
Sun/shade preference: ○
Shade tolerance: ◗
Performance rating: ✓✓✓
Fertility: SF
Cover: ✓✓ **Flowers:** Lilac

A fern from northern temperate regions, this spreads via rhizomes to form colonies. Plant at 60cm (2') spacing for a good cover. The curled young shoots uncurl as they grow, giving them the name 'fiddleheads'.

Size: To 1.5m (5') high or more; each plant 60cm (2') wide.
Cultivation: Plant young or divided plants in winter or early spring in any moist soil and in shade.
Uses: The young fiddleheads are cooked as a vegetable – they are still harvested commercially in the USA. This is one of the few ferns known to be safe to eat.
Harvest and storage: Pick fiddleheads when tightly curled in spring and up to 5-6cm (2-2.5") high.
Cooking/processing: The fiddleheads are cooked for 15 minutes (not less, as they can cause stomach upsets if undercooked). The flavour is like a cross between asparagus and broccoli.
Propagation: Division in early spring, or sow spores.
Maintenance: None needed.

Lemon balm is a clump-forming aromatic European perennial. It is herbaceous, but the centre may stay evergreen in mild winter climes. It can self-seed freely.

Size: 60-80cm (2'-2'8") high and 40cm (1'4") wide.
Cultivation: Plant young plants out in winter or early spring in a well-drained soil.
Uses: The leaves are good in salads in small quantities. The leaves and stems make great herb tea. Varieties with higher levels of essential oils are available.
Harvest and storage: Leaves for eating are mainly used in spring when tender, though for teas they can be used at any time in the season. They can be dried but lose a lot of flavour.
Cooking/processing: Not usually cooked, as the flavour is quickly lost.
Secondary uses: Bee plant and mineral accumulator. General protective aromatic plant.
Propagation: By seed or by division in spring. 'Citronella' has more essential oils.
Maintenance: I cut back the dead stems in late winter to allow the new growth as much light as possible.

Mentha spp., **MINTS**

The mints are eminently suitable for using in a forest garden, as long as you have a moist soil and don't mind them spreading. They are quite shade-tolerant, very aromatic (thus aiding the health of the whole system) and are great at attracting beneficial insects, as well as being nice edible plants. Some are evergreen in mild climes. Not all form good ground covers; those that do not should be interplanted with something more low-growing. They are all spreading perennials which move via shallow spreading rhizomes just beneath the soil.

Uses: The leaves and stems are used for flavouring, herb teas, etc. and can be dried.

Harvest and storage: Harvest leaves for fresh use at any time in the growing season. The essential oils peak just before flowering so pick leaves to dry then, and dry quickly.

Cooking/processing: Add to cooked dishes near the end of the cooking to retain flavour. Can be added to chutneys and pickles to give a minty edge.

Propagation: Propagate from seed (this has the advantage of genetic diversity) or from root or shoot cuttings.

Maintenance: This involves stopping them going where you don't want them, and I also go through in late winter cutting back or treading down the dead stems to allow new growth as much light as possible. Mint rust can be a serious disease where there is no genetic variability.

Bowles's mint (*Mentha* Bowles's mint).

Mentha Bowles's mint, **BOWLES'S MINT**

Deciduous/Evergreen: D   Zone: 5
Sun/shade preference: ◐
Shade tolerance: ●
Performance rating: ✓✓✓
Fertility: SF
Cover: ✗   Flowers: Pale mauve

Bowles's mint is also herbaceous, spreading sporadically, putting up shoots here and there.

Size: 90-120cm (3-4') high, spreading irregularly.
Cultivation: Plant root cuttings or young plants in winter into any moist soil.

Mentha aquatica, **WATER MINT**

Deciduous/Evergreen: D   Zone: 6
Sun/shade preference: ◐
Shade tolerance: ◑
Performance rating: ✓✓✓
Fertility: SF
Cover: ✗   Flowers: Mauve

Water mint is herbaceous, spreading sporadically, putting up shoots here and there.

Size: 60cm (2') high, spreading irregularly.
Cultivation: Sow seed on wet soil or compost. Young plants or root cuttings are best transplanted in winter into moist or wet soil. Tolerates marshy conditions.

Mentha longifolia, **HORSE MINT**

Deciduous/Evergreen: D   Zone: 6
Sun/shade preference: ◐
Shade tolerance: ◑
Performance rating: ✓✓✓✓
Fertility: SF
Cover: ✓✓✓   Flowers: Mauve

This is a vigorous spreading perennial. It is herbaceous but forms a good thick cover and the dead stems protect the soil well in winter. Plant 60-90cm (2-3') apart for a ground cover. It tolerates foot traffic.

Size: 1.5m (5') high, spreading thickly.
Cultivation: As for Bowles's mint.

Apple mint (*Mentha suaveolens*).

Mentha x *piperita*, PEPPERMINT

Deciduous/Evergreen: D   Zone: 3
Sun/shade preference: ○
Shade tolerance: ◑
Performance rating: ✓✓
Fertility: SF
Cover: ✗   **Flowers:** Pale mauve

Peppermint is a spreading herbaceous perennial, putting up shoots here and there. It has a nice aroma but comes late into growth and is prone to weed problems. Fine forms include subsp. *nigra*, 'Swiss' and 'Moroccan'.

Size: 60cm (2') high, spreading irregularly.
Cultivation: Plant root cuttings or young plants in winter into any moist soil.

Mentha *suaveolens*, APPLE MINT

Deciduous/Evergreen: D/E   Zone: 6
Sun/shade preference: ○
Shade tolerance: ◑
Performance rating: ✓✓✓
Fertility: SF
Cover: ✓✓✓   **Flowers:** Mauve

A spreading perennial, apple mint is evergreen in mild winter regions; otherwise herbaceous. Plant at 60cm (2') spacing for a ground cover. It tolerates foot traffic.

Size: 60-90cm (2-3') high, spreading thickly.
Cultivation: Plant root cuttings or young plants in winter into any moist soil.

Mentha *spicata*, SPEARMINT

Deciduous/Evergreen: D   Zone: 3
Sun/shade preference: ○
Shade tolerance: ◑
Performance rating: ✓✓✓
Fertility: SF
Cover: ✓   **Flowers:** Mauve

Another spreading herbaceous perennial, spearmint forms a better cover than peppermint. Plant at 45cm (1'6") spacing for a ground cover.

Size: 80-100cm (2'8"-3'3") high, spreading reasonably thickly.
Cultivation: Plant root cuttings or young plants in winter into any moist soil.

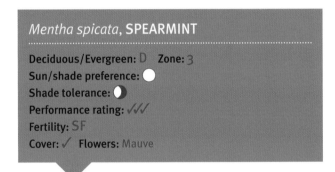

Sweet cicely (*Myrrhis odorata*), showing young fruits.

Myrrhis odorata, SWEET CICELY

Deciduous/Evergreen: D **Zone:** 5
Sun/shade preference: ◖
Shade tolerance: ◖
Performance rating: ✓✓✓
Fertility: SF
Cover: ✓ **Flowers:** White

Sweet cicely is a clump-forming, taprooted European perennial. Plant at 30-45cm (1'-1'6") spacing for a ground cover. It self-seeds where the winters are cold enough.

Size: 60-100cm (2'-3'3") high and 40cm (1'4") wide.
Cultivation: Plant young plants out in winter (comes early into growth). Good in any reasonably well-drained soil.
Uses: This is a fantastic anise-flavoured herb – all parts are edible.
Harvest and storage: Harvest leaves throughout the season, young seeds in summer, and roots in winter. The roots can be stored in sand for several months.
Cooking/processing: Use the leaves as a bulk ingredient in salads (or, traditionally, cook them to sweeten acid fruits). The young green seeds are a crunchy snack or can go in salads too. The roots are delicious raw or cooked (boiled or roasted like other root vegetables).
Secondary uses: Attracts beneficial insects and bees. It is a mineral accumulator.
Propagation: By seed (it shouldn't dry out, and requires 5 months' stratification) or division in spring or autumn.
Maintenance: Little required. Rabbits like to browse this.

Nasturtium officinale, WATERCRESS

Deciduous/Evergreen: E **Zone:** 2
Sun/shade preference: ○
Shade tolerance: ◖
Performance rating: ✓✓
Fertility: SF
Cover: ✓ **Flowers:** White

A lax perennial with rooting stems, watercress is evergreen in mild winter regions.

Size: 30cm (1') high; trailing and spreading.
Cultivation: Sow seed on a wet compost. Transplant outside in winter or spring. Prefers wet soil or shallow aquatic conditions but will grow in moist soil too.
Uses: A well-known vegetable.
Harvest and storage: Harvest leaves and stems throughout the season. Do not eat from streams that you suspect may be polluted.
Cooking/processing: Watercress makes a wonderful soup and can be used in salads, sandwiches and other cooked dishes.
Secondary uses: Bee plant. Water purifier.
Propagation: By seed or division of rooted stems.
Maintenance: None required.

Origanum vulgare, OREGANO / POT MARJORAM

Deciduous/Evergreen: D **Zone:** 5
Sun/shade preference: ○
Shade tolerance: ◖
Performance rating: ✓✓✓
Fertility: SF
Cover: ✓✓ **Flowers:** Pink

This familiar herb is a clump-forming European perennial. Space at 45cm (1'6") apart for a ground cover. It tolerates a little foot traffic.

Size: 45-60cm (1'6"-2') high and 30-40cm (12-16") wide.
Cultivation: Transplant young plants in winter or early spring in any well-drained soil that is not too acid.
Uses: Oregano is a well-known culinary herb. I use it a lot in salads.

Harvest and storage: Harvest leaves all through the season.

Cooking/processing: Best used fresh; it loses a lot of flavour when dried.

Secondary uses: Bee and butterfly plant. A useful under-storey aromatic for the health of the whole garden system.

Propagation: By seed, division in spring, or basal cuttings in late spring.

Maintenance: None required.

Oxalis acetosella, WOOD SORREL

Deciduous/Evergreen: D   **Zone:** 3
Sun/shade preference: ◑
Shade tolerance: ●
Performance rating: ✓✓✓
Fertility: SF
Cover: ✓   **Flowers:** Pinkish-white

A spreading European perennial, wood sorrel self-seeds where it is happy, creating carpets. Plant at 40cm (1'4") spacing to make a good cover.

Size: 20cm (8") high; spreading.

Cultivation: Plant out seed-grown plants in winter in a humus-rich soil, moist but well-drained.

Uses: The leaves are edible in salads or cooked, with a lovely lemony flavour. Like all sorrels, eat in moderation because of the oxalic acid they contain. Flowers are nice in salads.

Harvest and storage: Leaves can be harvested throughout the season; flowers in spring.

Cooking/processing: It can be cooked like other sorrels to make a soup, or used in other cooked dishes.

Secondary uses: Mineral accumulator. Wood sorrel has a network of small taproots, 15-20cm (6-8") deep, 5-6cm (2-2.5") long by 8-9mm (0.3") wide, which are sweet and delicious to eat raw in salads.

Propagation: By seed or division.

Maintenance: None required.

Oxalis oregana, REDWOOD SORREL

Deciduous/Evergreen: E   **Zone:** 7
Sun/shade preference: ◑
Shade tolerance: ●
Performance rating: ✓✓✓
Fertility: SF
Cover: ✓✓   **Flowers:** Pinkish-violet

A low, carpeting North American woodland perennial, evergreen in mild areas, redwood sorrel spreads via rooting stems. It tolerates a little foot traffic.

Size: 20cm (8") high, spreading widely.

Cultivation: Grow divided plants from spring, planting out in winter in a moist, acid soil.

Uses: Fresh leaves are used in salads, and have a lemony flavour. They can also be cooked. As with other sorrels, use in moderation.

Harvest and storage: Use leaves in season.

Cooking/processing: Can be cooked like other sorrels, to make a soup or used in other cooked dishes.

Secondary uses: A very good base-layer perennial plant.

Propagation: By division in spring.

Maintenance: Little required.

Mountain sorrel (*Oxyria digyna*).

Oxyria digyna, MOUNTAIN SORREL

Deciduous/Evergreen: D **Zone:** 2
Sun/shade preference: ◯
Shade tolerance: ◖
Performance rating: ✓✓✓
Fertility: SF
Cover: ✗ **Flowers:** Greenish-yellow

This is a clump-forming European perennial, which self-seeds willingly.

Size: 50cm (1'8") high and 40cm (1'4") wide.
Cultivation: Sow outside in spring or transplant young plants in winter in a well-drained but moist soil.
Uses: The leaves and stems are edible in salads or cooked; they have a melting texture and lovely lemony flavour. As with all sorrels, eat in moderation.
Harvest and storage: Harvest leaves throughout the season.
Cooking/processing: It can be cooked like other sorrels, to make a soup or used in other cooked dishes.
Propagation: By seed. Can self-seed readily.
Maintenance: None required.

Peltaria alliacea, GARLIC CRESS

Deciduous/Evergreen: D **Zone:** 6
Sun/shade preference: ◯
Shade tolerance: ◖
Performance rating: ✓✓
Fertility: SF
Cover: ✗ **Flowers:** White

A clump-forming European perennial, garlic cress is evergreen in mild winter regions. Plant at 30cm (1') spacing to form a good cover.

Size: 30cm (1') high and wide.
Cultivation: Broadcast seed outside in winter or spring. Fine in any soil.
Uses: The leaves have a garlic/mustard flavour – use raw in salads in small quantities, or cooked.
Harvest and storage: Harvest leaves at any time except in hot dry spells, when they become bitter.
Cooking/processing: The leaves get hotter as they develop, and from late spring onwards are best cooked; added to stews, soups, etc.
Secondary uses: The flowers also edible in salads.
Propagation: By seed, or division in spring or autumn.
Maintenance: None required.

Poke root (*Phytolacca americana*).

Phytolacca americana, POKE ROOT / POKEWEED / POKE

Deciduous/Evergreen: D   **Zone:** 4
Sun/shade preference: ◐
Shade tolerance: ◖
Performance rating: ✓✓✓
Fertility: SF
Cover: ✓✓   **Flowers:** White

POKE BERRY INK

Pokeweed berries yield a red ink or dye, which was once used by native Americans to decorate their horses. The United States Declaration of Independence was written in fermented poke berry juice (hence its other common name, 'inkberry'). Many letters written home during the American civil war were written in poke berry ink; the writing in these surviving letters appears brown.

Plantago spp., PLANTAINS

Deciduous/Evergreen: D   **Zone:** 5
Sun/shade preference: ◐
Shade tolerance: ◖
Performance rating: ✓✓✓
Fertility: SF
Cover: ✗   **Flowers:** Greenish-brown

This is a strong, vigorous American perennial. The plants slowly expand to form colonies. Note that the raw leaves and stems and the deep purple fruits are toxic and should never be eaten.

Size: 2-4m (6'6"-13') high and 60cm (2') wide.
Cultivation: Transplant young plants in winter or early spring (comes late into growth) in any reasonable soil.
Uses: Poke shoots are a well-known wild edible vegetable from North America.
Harvest and storage: The young shoots are harvested when up to 60cm (2') high and still green in spring.
Cooking/processing: The shoots are toxic when raw and must be prepared properly. Place in cold water, bring to the boil, then discard the water and replace with new boiling water and boil for 10 minutes. The cooked shoots are delicious – like a larger version of asparagus – great with butter or a sauce.
Secondary uses: Bee plant. The fruits are a source of purplish-black dyes and ink. Poke root is also a mineral accumulator.
Propagation: By seed (needs 3 months' stratification), or by division in spring.
Maintenance: None required.

All species can be used, the best being *P. lanceolata* (ribwort plantain) and *P. major* (greater plantain). They are European perennials, with narrow brown seedheads. Ribwort plantain has long narrow leaves while broad-leaved plantain leaves are much wider.

Size: 45cm (1'6") high and 35cm (1'2") wide when flowering.
Cultivation: Broadcast seed in spring or transplant young plants in winter. Fine in any soil.
Uses: The young leaves are eaten.
Harvest and storage: Harvest young leaves in spring or, if plants are cut back, the young regrowth in spring and summer.
Cooking/processing: The leaves are very gentle on the stomach, and are used chopped in salads or soups.
Secondary uses: Dye (yellow/brown) and medicinal plants. The leaves contain allantoin, which is useful for soothing sore skin and stings. The seeds are edible, harvested when the capsules are ripe, and used parched, ground and cooked.
Propagation: By seed. You may not need to introduce it deliberately!
Maintenance: None required.

Angular Solomon's seal (*Polygonatum odoratum*) shoots.

Polygonatum spp., SOLOMON'S SEALS

Deciduous/Evergreen: D   **Zone:** 3-6
Sun/shade preference: ◖
Shade tolerance: ●
Performance rating: ✓✓✓✓
Fertility: SF
Cover: ✓–✓✓   **Flowers:** Cream

All species can be used similarly, including *Polygonatum biflorum, P. commutatum, P. x hybridum, P. multiflorum, P. odoratum* and *P. verticillatum*. The larger species have thicker shoots, hence more edible material.

These are slowly spreading perennials. Plant at 30cm (1') spacing for a ground cover. *P. commutatum* (giant Solomon's seal) is the largest, and provides better ground cover; other species have a lower cover rating.

Size: 60-200cm (2'-6'6") high and 20-30cm (8-12") wide.
Cultivation: Plant out young plants in winter (they come early into growth) into a humus-rich soil.
Uses: The young shoots are cooked as a vegetable.
Harvest and storage: Young shoots are harvested in spring, cut at ground level when 20-30cm (8-12") high. The leaf cluster at the top is sometimes discarded as it can be bitter.
Cooking/processing: Cook briefly like asparagus – the shoots have a wonderful sweet flavour.
Secondary uses: Bee plants.
Propagation: By seed or by division in spring.
Maintenance: Little required. Slugs can damage young plants.

Reichardia picroides, FRENCH SCORZONERA

Deciduous/Evergreen: D   **Zone:** 8-9
Sun/shade preference: ○
Shade tolerance: ◖
Performance rating: ✓
Fertility: SF
Cover: ✗   **Flowers:** Yellow

A rosette-forming clumping plant from southern Europe, French scorzonera is evergreen in mild winter regions. I have trouble keeping it perennial owing to winter wet or our usual winter minimum temperatures of about -5°C (23°F).

Size: Up to 80cm (2'8") high when flowering, and 25cm (10") wide.
Cultivation: Raise plants from seed and transplant in spring after frosts. A well-drained soil is essential, otherwise it will die over winter.
Uses: The leaves are used in salads, and have a mild pleasant cucumber flavour.
Harvest and storage: Leaves can be harvested all year.
Cooking/processing: Can be added to stews, etc. – cooks in a few minutes.
Propagation: By seed.
Maintenance: Make sure you save seed every year from your plants in case they die off in the winter.

French sorrel (*Rumex scutatus*).

Rumex spp., SORRELS

Deciduous/Evergreen: D   Zone: 5
Sun/shade preference: ◐
Shade tolerance: ◑
Performance rating: ✓✓✓
Fertility: SF
Cover: ✗   Flowers: Green

Sorrel species include *Rumex acetosa* (sorrel), *R. acetosella* (sheep's sorrel), *R. alpinus* (monk's rhubarb), *R. patientia* (herb patience) and *R. scutatus* (French sorrel). These are clump-forming, deep-rooted perennials. They are mostly herbaceous, though some varieties of *R. acetosa* (e.g. 'Schavel') are evergreen.

Size: 40cm (1'4") high and 30cm (1') wide.
Cultivation: Transplant young plants in winter (they come early into growth). Fine in any soil.
Uses: Leaves are edible; raw in salads or cooked. Use in moderation, as the lemony acidity that you can taste is oxalic acid.
Harvest and storage: Leaves are mainly harvested in spring.
Cooking/processing: Cook in soups, stews and other dishes.
Secondary uses: Mineral accumulators.
Propagation: By seed or by division in spring.
Maintenance: Little required. Break off unripe seedheads if you don't want it self-seeding.

Sanguisorba minor (syn. *Poterium sanguisorba*), SALAD BURNET

Deciduous/Evergreen: D   Zone: 5
Sun/shade preference: ◐
Shade tolerance: ◑
Performance rating: ✓✓
Fertility: SF
Cover: ✗   Flowers: Magenta

This is a clump-forming European perennial. Leaf quality is best in damp habitats.

Size: 50cm (1'8") high and 30cm (1') wide.
Cultivation: Transplant young plants in winter into any moist soil.
Uses: The tender young leaves are used as a salad leaf. Coarser leaves can be eaten cooked.
Harvest and storage: Young leaves are harvested in spring before flowering.
Cooking/processing: Add older leaves to soups, stews, etc.
Secondary uses: Bee plant; mineral accumulator.
Propagation: By seed or by division in spring.
Maintenance: None required.

Scorzonera hispanica, SCORZONERA

Deciduous/Evergreen: D   Zone: 4
Sun/shade preference: ◐
Shade tolerance: ◑
Performance rating: ✓✓
Fertility: SF
Cover: ✗   Flowers: Yellow

This clump-forming European perennial Is best known as a root crop grown as an annual – but it is a perennial and is treated here as a leaf crop.

Size: 1.3m (4'3") high and 25cm (10") wide when flowering.
Cultivation: Sow outside in spring or transplant young plants in winter. Likes any well-drained soil.
Uses: The leaves are good in salads, and have a mild flavour. (They can be blanched to make them more tender.)

Harvest and storage: The leaves and young shoots are harvested in spring.

Cooking/processing: Leaves can be cooked in soups, stews, etc. but then lack much flavour. Roots (see 'Secondary uses') are boiled or roasted like other root crops.

Secondary uses: The roots are edible, cooked, and are tender even after several years of growth, but of course you'll kill the plant if you harvest it.

Propagation: By seed.

Maintenance: None required.

Ice plant (*Sedum spectabile*).

Sedum spectabile, ICE PLANT & *S. telephium*, ORPINE

Deciduous/Evergreen: D   Zone: 6
Sun/shade preference: ◯
Shade tolerance: ◖
Performance rating: ✓✓
Fertility: SF
Cover: ✓✓   Flowers: Pink, cream

Sedum spectabile is a clumping perennial with fleshy leaves and large purplish-pink flowers. *S. telephium* is a slowly spreading perennial with fleshy leaves. Many garden varieties are available. Plant at 30-40cm (1'-1'4") spacing for a ground cover.

Size: *S. spectabile*: 45cm (1'6") high and wide; *S. telephium* 60cm (2') high and 30cm (1') wide.

Cultivation: Transplant young plants in winter. They like any well-drained soil.

Uses: The leaves are great in salads, with a succulent texture and mild flavour.

Harvest and storage: Leaves can be harvested throughout the season, though they can get slightly bitter in very dry weather.

Cooking/processing: Best used raw.

Secondary uses: Fantastic bee plants.

Propagation: By seed, division in spring, or softwood cuttings in early summer.

Maintenance: None required.

Smilacina racemosa, FALSE SPIKENARD / FALSE SOLOMON'S SEAL

Deciduous/Evergreen: D   Zone: 4
Sun/shade preference: ◗
Shade tolerance: ●
Performance rating: ✓✓✓
Fertility: SF
Cover: ✓   Flowers: Cream

A clump-forming North American perennial, false spikenard spreads slowly via rhizomes. Plant at 45cm (1'6") spacing for a ground cover.

Size: 90cm (3') high and 60cm wide (2').

Cultivation: Transplant young plants in winter. Likes a humus-rich acid or neutral soil.

Uses: The young shoots are cooked like asparagus and are similar in flavour to Solomon's seals (*Polygonatum* spp.)

Harvest and storage: Young shoots are harvested in spring – cut at ground level when 20cm (8") high.

Cooking/processing: Cook briefly like asparagus.

Secondary uses: The small fruits can also be eaten.

Propagation: By seed in autumn or divide rhizomes in spring.

Maintenance: None required.

Stellaria graminea, LESSER STITCHWORT

Deciduous/Evergreen: D   Zone: 4
Sun/shade preference: ◑
Shade tolerance: ◑
Performance rating: ✓✓✓
Fertility: SF
Cover: ✓   Flowers: White

This European perennial is found in hedges and woodland, often over large areas.

Size: 50cm (1'8") high; sprawling.
Cultivation: Broadcast seed in spring or transplant young plants in winter. Happy in most soils.
Uses: The shoots are excellent in salads or lightly cooked as a vegetable.
Harvest and storage: Harvest young shoots from spring into summer.
Cooking/processing: Steam for a few minutes.
Secondary uses: Bee plant.
Propagation: By seed.
Maintenance: None required.

Taraxacum officinale, DANDELION

Deciduous/Evergreen: D   Zone: 5
Sun/shade preference: ○
Shade tolerance: ◑
Performance rating: ✓✓✓
Fertility: SF
Cover: ✓   Flowers: Yellow

You will probably have this growing already and may not feel disposed to deliberately plant it! It is a clump-forming, deep-rooted perennial, evergreen in mild winters.

Size: 40cm (1'4") high and wide.
Cultivation: You can raise improved leaf forms from seed and plant in winter in any moist soil.
Uses: A very good mineral accumulator. Leaves can be added to salads in moderation (wilt them over heat for a few seconds and they will lose a lot of the bitterness). The flowers make a lovely wine (see box, right).

Harvest and storage: The leaves are best harvested in spring, when they are less bitter. They can be blanched to remove the bitterness before harvest. Flowers are harvested mainly in spring when flowering is en masse, but potentially may be harvested at almost any time of year.
Cooking/processing: Normally used raw.
Secondary uses: The roots can be roasted, ground and infused in boiling water to make a coffee-like drink. Dandelion is a good attractant for beneficial insects.
Propagation: By seed.
Maintenance: None required. You might want to pick flowers or the young seedheads to prevent self-seeding.

DANDELION WINE

There are dozens of recipes for dandelion wine. This is just one of them, which gives great results.

- Pick enough dandelion heads to fill 2 litres (3.5 pints) by volume (use a measuring jug). Pick the flowers with no stalk and minimal green material attached to the head.

- Set 4.5 litres (1 gallon) of water to boil. When boiling, pour this over the flowers, cover with a cloth and leave to steep for 2 days.

- Bring the liquid back to the boil and add the peel from 4 oranges (no pith), and boil for 10 minutes.

- Strain into a plastic bucket and add 1.5kg (3lb 5oz) of sugar, stirring to dissolve.

- When cool, add the juice from the oranges and yeast. Pour into a fermenting vessel with an airlock.

- Rack off as usual and bottle once cleared. The wine is best drunk when aged for at least a year.

Urtica dioica, **STINGING NETTLE**

Deciduous/Evergreen: D/E   Zone: 4
Sun/shade preference: ◑
Shade tolerance: ◑
Performance rating: ✓✓✓
Fertility: SF
Cover: ✓✓   Flowers: Greenish-yellow

This is a well-known creeping perennial with stinging hairs on the leaves and stems. It is herbaceous, but ever-green in mild winter regions. You might not want to plant it, but it will probably be around anyway!

Size: Usually 70-100cm (2'4"-3'3") high, but up to 2m (6'6") high in fertile soils.
Cultivation: I suppose you can transplant some root cuttings in winter if you must! Most soils are fine, though it prefers rich soils.
Uses: The young shoots are briefly cooked and make a lovely spring vegetable.
Harvest and storage: Young shoots and leaves are harvested in early spring.
Cooking/processing: Young shoots can be steamed or fried. If the stems are getting a little tough, strip the leaves (using gloves of course!) and discard the stems before cooking.
Secondary uses: Beneficial insect plant. Nettles are high in nitrogen and can be soaked in water to make a liquid feed. Fibre plant – the stems used to make cloth, etc. Green dyes from the plant. Good mineral accumulator.
Propagation: By seed or division if you really need to.
Maintenance: Cut off flowering heads or young seedheads to stop it seeding around. You might need to stop it spreading – try pulling out all the stems you can see in summer, which will set it back enough.

Viola spp., **VIOLETS**

Deciduous/Evergreen: D/E   Zone: 4-8
Sun/shade preference: ◑
Shade tolerance: ◑
Performance rating: ✓✓
Fertility: SF
Cover: ✓-✓✓   Flowers: Various

Violets are small, mostly clump-forming plants. They need planting quite densely to make a ground cover. Some species, such as sweet violet (*Viola odorata*), spread via rhizomes and self-seed freely. Many are herbaceous; some are evergreen or semi-evergreen (e.g. sweet violet is evergreen in a favourable climate). They are a little slow to get established, and many are short-lived. Violets are very low-growing, so it can be a good idea to grow larger perennials amongst them. Evergreen species have a higher ground-cover rating; herbaceous or semi-evergreen ones a lower rating. They tolerate a little foot traffic.

All violet species can be used in the ways described below. Flowers, especially of yellow-flowered species, should be used in moderation. *V. odorata* is one of the best to eat.

Size: 15-20cm (6-8") high and 25-30cm (10-12") wide.
Cultivation: Transplant young plants in winter (they come early into growth). Like a well-drained but moist soil.
Uses: The flowers, flower buds and leaves are all edible in salads, and the leaves can be cooked.
Harvest and storage: Harvest flowers and flower buds in season; the leaves at any time.
Cooking/processing: The leaves are mucilaginous and thicken stews and soups.
Secondary uses: Bee plants.
Propagation: By seed, division in spring or autumn, or layering.
Maintenance: Some weeding is likely to be required, especially while establishing.

Perennials/covers with other edible parts

Plants in this category include perennial tuber crops, as well as those with other edible parts such as flowers or fleshy leaf stalks.

Armoracia rusticana, HORSERADISH

Deciduous/Evergreen: D   Zone: 5
Sun/shade preference: ◯
Shade tolerance: ◖
Performance rating: ✓✓✓
Fertility: SF
Cover: ✓✓   Flowers: White

This well-known spice is robust, deep-rooted and clump-forming. Plant at 45cm (1'6") spacing to form a good cover.

Size: 60-100cm (2-3'3") high.
Cultivation: Transplant pieces of root in winter (comes early into growth). Fine in any moist soil.
Uses: The roots are used as a hot flavouring.
Harvest and storage: Roots are harvested in winter. You won't be able to easily harvest an entire root, so just break of the top 10-15cm (4-6") and it will regrow from the remaining root. It is best to harvest a root and use it immediately rather than store roots.
Cooking/processing: The root is grated (will make you cry!) and used as a hot mustard-like flavouring in many savoury dishes. Preserved with vinegar, salt and sugar as horseradish sauce.
Secondary uses: The very young leaves are eaten lightly steamed – can be good, although the quality varies a lot between plants. They're too tough to eat raw.
Propagation: By seed or from pieces of root.
Maintenance: None required. Not easy to get rid of!

Camassia quamash, QUAMASH

Deciduous/Evergreen: D   Zone: 4
Sun/shade preference: ◯
Shade tolerance: ◖
Performance rating: ✓
Fertility: SF
Cover: ✗   Flowers: Blue

Quamash is a bulbous North American perennial. Although it can easily colonise large areas and produce masses of bulbs (2.5cm/1") diameter, the cooking process is not straightforward.

Size: 80cm (2'8") high, 20cm (8") wide.
Cultivation: Plant bulbs in winter or early spring into a moist but well-drained, humus-rich soil.
Uses: The bulbs are eaten roasted.
Harvest and storage: Harvest in winter, after the top has died down. The bulbs can be stored dry for months.
Cooking/processing: The bulbs need cooking for a long time at high temperature to make them palatable – they are traditionally steamed in pits for 2-3 days! After this they have a sweet, squash-like flavour.
Propagation: Bulbs are easily obtainable from ornamental flower bulb companies.
Maintenance: Little required once established.

Cardoon (*Cynara cardunculus*).

Cynara cardunculus, CARDOON & *C. cardunculus* Scolymus Group, GLOBE ARTICHOKE

Deciduous/Evergreen: E   Zone: 7
Sun/shade preference: ◯
Shade tolerance: ◖
Performance rating: ✓✓
Fertility: SF
Cover: ✓✓   Flowers: Blue

These are robust, grey-leaved Mediterranean perennials. They are now recognised to be the same species but simply different forms. Plant at 60cm (2') spacing to form a good (if rather tall) cover. Globe artichoke has been bred for larger flowerheads. In my experience cardoon is slightly hardier than globe artichoke.

Size: 80-210cm (2'8"-7') high and 50-100cm (1'8"-3'3") wide, occasionally more.

Cultivation: Raise young plants and transplant in late spring. Well-drained soil is essential. Wet winter soil conditions can kill them.

Uses: Edible young flowerheads and leaf ribs.

Harvest and storage: Harvest leaf stalks in spring (sometimes plants are covered to blanch the stalks); unopened flowerheads in summer and autumn.

Cooking/processing: Globe artichoke is one of the few well-known perennial vegetables: the unopened flowerheads can be cooked and the bracts and heart eaten. Cardoon flowerheads, which are slightly smaller, are eaten in the same way. With both, the leaf mid-ribs can also be cooked, peeled and eaten – rather like a bitter celery (though better blanched).

Secondary uses: Great bee plants if any flowers open.

Propagation: By seed or division.

Maintenance: Little required. After winter the clumps may be small enough to allow for weeds to come in, so some weeding is needed.

Filipendula ulmaria, MEADOWSWEET

Deciduous/Evergreen: D **Zone:** 2
Sun/shade preference: ◯
Shade tolerance: ◗
Performance rating: ✓✓✓
Fertility: SF
Cover: ✓ **Flowers:** White

Meadowsweet is a robust, deep-rooted, clump-forming perennial common in British hedgerows. Plant at 45cm (1'6") spacing to form a good cover.

Size: 1m (3') high and 60cm (2') wide.

Cultivation: Transplant young plants in winter, giving a moist or wet soil of reasonable fertility.

Uses: The flowers make lovely herb teas and wines.

Harvest and storage: Flowers are harvested in summer.

Secondary uses: it is a good mineral accumulator, and also attracts beneficial insects.

Propagation: By seed, or division in spring or autumn.

Maintenance: None required.

Glycyrrhiza echinata & G. glabra, RUSSIAN & COMMON LIQUORICE

Deciduous/Evergreen: D **Zone:** 6
Sun/shade preference: ◯
Shade tolerance: ◗
Performance rating: ✓✓
Fertility: SF
Cover: ✗ **Flowers:** Bluish-purple

The liquorices (or licorices) are very deep-rooted perennial plants that accumulate many minerals from deep in the subsoil.

Size: up to 1.5m (5') high.

Cultivation: Transplant seed-raised plants in winter. Deep topsoil is useful if you intend to harvest the roots. In any case the soil should be fairly well drained and not too acid.

Uses: The roots of liquorice have well-known edible and medicinal uses. They make great herb teas – dried roots can be chopped and boiled up in water for a few minutes.

Harvest and storage: Dig roots in winter. If you remove just the top section of root, the plant will normally regrow from the roots left in the ground. The roots can be dried and then store very well.

Secondary uses: Leguminous nitrogen fixers, mineral accumulators, and good bee plants.

Propagation: By seed (needs scarification) or root cuttings (each piece of root should have at least one bud).

Maintenance: Liquorices come into growth late in spring, so are susceptible to weed competition at this time. Best to grow through a low base-layer ground cover.

Jerusalem artichoke (*Helianthus tuberosus*).

Helianthus tuberosus, JERUSALEM ARTICHOKE / SUNCHOKE

Deciduous/Evergreen: D   **Zone:** 2
Sun/shade preference: ◯
Shade tolerance: ◖
Performance rating: ✓✓✓
Fertility: SF
Cover: ✗   **Flowers:** Yellow

A North American tuberous perennial, Jerusalem artichoke is clump-forming and slowly expands to form colonies.

Size: 2-3m (6'6"-10') high and 40cm (1'4") wide.
Cultivation: Plant tubers in winter or early spring into any moist, well-drained soil.
Uses: A well-known perennial tuber crop.
Harvest and storage: Tubers are dug in the winter, after frosts. Leave in the ground to store.
Cooking/processing: The tubers are cooked (boiled or roasted, etc.) and eaten. They are not as digestible as many tubers, with the inevitable flatulent results.
Secondary uses: The flowers are like small sunflowers and attract bees. The dead stems make good kindling. The plants also make a quick-growing summer screen or windbreak.
Propagation: By planting tubers or parts of tubers that have an eye.
Maintenance: They are best dug up each year otherwise plants will decline. You'll always miss a few tubers so some will come back again! In windy sites the tall plants

are susceptible to being blown over, so pinch out the tops when they are 80-100cm (2'8"-3'3") high to keep them bushy, or grow a dwarf variety.

Hemerocallis spp., DAY LILIES

Deciduous/Evergreen: D/E   **Zone:** 4
Sun/shade preference: ◯
Shade tolerance: ◖
Performance rating: ✓✓✓
Fertility: SF
Cover: ✓-✓✓   **Flowers:** Various

There are hundreds of cultivated varieties of day lilies, mostly clump-forming Asian perennials. Some are evergreen, and these make better ground cover than the deciduous cultivars. Plant at 45cm (1'6") spacing for good cover.

Size: 45-60cm (1'6"-2') high by 30-45cm (12-18") wide.
Cultivation: Transplant young plants in winter. Fine in any soil; protect from slugs when small.
Uses: The flowers make a substantial good addition to salads, and can also be cooked. The dried flower buds are sold in China as 'golden needles', used in soups and other dishes. The flowers and buds have a musky-sweet, earthy taste.
Harvest and storage: Pick flowers and flower buds in summer and autumn. The flower buds can be dried and stored.
Cooking/processing: To dry, pick flower buds early in the morning before the flowers open. Dried buds should be soaked for half an hour before using, usually in cooked dishes.
Secondary uses: Green, yellow and gold dyes are made from the flowers. Tubers and young shoots have been eaten but can cause digestive upsets.
Propagation: By seed, or division in spring or autumn.
Maintenance: Little necessary. Watch out for slug and snail damage on young plants.

Petasites japonicus, GIANT BUTTERBUR / FUKI / SWEET COLTSFOOT

Deciduous/Evergreen: D Zone: 4
Sun/shade preference: ◗
Shade tolerance: ●
Performance rating: ✓✓✓✓
Fertility: SF
Cover: ✓✓ Flowers: Greenish-yellow

Giant butterbur is a large, robust, creeping Asian woodland perennial, with huge basal leaves. It can spread to form large colonies.

Size: 1.1m (3'7") high and 1.5m (5') wide.
Cultivation: Transplant plants/divisions in spring or autumn to final positions in a moist, humus-rich soil.
Uses: The leaf stalks are used as a vegetable in Japan.
Harvest and storage: Harvest the leaf stalks (like giant celery) in spring.
Cooking/processing: The leaf stalks should be cut into 10-20cm (4-8") segments, boiled for 10 minutes, then dipped in cold water for a minute and the outer fibrous skin peeled off. The sections are then fried or added to soups, stews, etc. The flavour resembles celery.
Secondary uses: Bee plant. The large flower buds can also be eaten in spring but are somewhat bitter.
Propagation: Usually by division in spring or autumn.
Maintenance: None required unless it is spreading too fast for you! It is considered a weed by some.

Potentilla anserina, SILVERWEED

Deciduous/Evergreen: D Zone: 5
Sun/shade preference: ○
Shade tolerance: ◗
Performance rating: ✓✓✓
Fertility: SF
Cover: ✓✓ Flowers: Yellow

Silverweed is a low-growing European perennial, spreading vigorously via running roots. It was formerly cultivated for its roots in Britain and served as a staple for at least 20 hunter-gatherer peoples in North America.

Size: 30cm (1') high, spreading widely.
Cultivation: Plant in winter in any soil except very acid.
Uses: The storage roots are eaten raw or cooked.
Harvest and storage: Storage roots (as opposed to the thin, horizontal running roots) are harvested from early autumn through the winter. Each plant produces 1-6 of these, each 15-30cm (6-12") x 3-7mm (0.1-0.3") across. Although thin, they are crisp and full of starch, containing more starch per weight than potatoes. They can be dried and stored easily.
Cooking/processing: The roots can be roasted or boiled (for 10 minutes) and have a delicious nutty flavour.
Secondary uses: Bee plant.
Propagation: By seed or division.
Maintenance: None required. Tolerates foot traffic.

Primula vulgaris, PRIMROSE

Deciduous/Evergreen: D Zone: 6
Sun/shade preference: ◗
Shade tolerance: ●
Performance rating: ✓✓✓
Fertility: SF
Cover: ✓ Flowers: Yellow

A familiar clump-forming European perennial of woods and hedgerows, primrose may self-seed if happy. It comes very early into growth, in late winter. Plant at 30cm (1') spacing for a ground cover.

Size: 20cm (8") high and 30cm (1') wide.
Cultivation: Sow seed outside in autumn or transplant young plants in winter into a humus-rich soil.
Uses: The flowers make a welcome addition to salads at this early time of year. A favourite of mine, it also happens to be the county flower of Devon!
Harvest and storage: The flowers are harvested in early spring.
Cooking/processing: Use raw.
Secondary uses: Bee plants.
Propagation: By seed in autumn or division in autumn.
Maintenance: None required.

Turkish rhubarb (*Rheum palmatum*) 'Atrosanguineum'.

Rheum spp., RHUBARBS

Deciduous/Evergreen: D   Zone: 3/6
Sun/shade preference: ○
Shade tolerance: ◖
Performance rating: ✓✓✓✓
Fertility: SF
Cover: ✓✓✓   Flowers: Cream

Most, perhaps all, leaf stalks of *Rheum* can be eaten. My favourite species are *R. australe* (Himalayan rhubarb) and *R. palmatum* (Turkish rhubarb). *R. x hybridum* (garden rhubarb) is hardy to zone 3; *R. australe* and *R. palmatum* to zone 6.

Rhubarbs are large, sturdy perennials with deep roots and huge leaves. *R. palmatum* is one of the largest, with flower spikes reaching 2-2.5m (6'6"-8') high, and a width of 1-1.5m (3-5') – plant at 1.2m (4') spacing for a ground cover. *R. australe* is more the size of cultivated rhubarb, about 1.5m (5') high and 1m (3') wide – plant these at 80cm (2'8") spacing for a ground cover.

Size: 1-2.5m (3-8') high by 1-1.5m (3-5') wide.
Cultivation: Transplant pot-grown plants in winter (they come early into growth). Like a humus-rich soil.
Uses: The leaf stalks are eaten; usually cooked and sweetened. *R. australe* has apple-flavoured stalks; *R. palmatum* has gooseberry-flavoured stalks.
Harvest and storage: The leaf stalks are harvested, mainly before the end of June, as oxalic acid levels build up after that. The leaves are not edible, and indeed are toxic.
Cooking/processing: Chop leaf stalks into 2.5cm (1") sections and boil with a little water for 5-10 minutes. Sweeten to taste. They can also be baked in pies, etc.

Secondary uses: Mineral accumulators. Medicinal uses as a laxative.
Propagation: By seed or by division in early spring.
Maintenance: None required.

Sium sisarum, SKIRRET

Deciduous/Evergreen: D   Zone: 4
Sun/shade preference: ○
Shade tolerance: ◖
Performance rating: ✓✓✓
Fertility: SF
Cover: ✗   Flowers: White

Skirret is a clump-forming European perennial, formerly much grown in vegetable plots for its edible, sweet, bright white roots.

Size: 1.2m (4') high and 30cm (1') wide when flowering.
Cultivation: Raise plants from seed, transplanting in spring or winter. It crops best in a moist, fertile soil.
Uses: The roots are usually eaten cooked.
Harvest and storage: Dig the roots in winter. They look like a cluster of pencil-thick white parsnips.
Cooking/processing: Cook the roots by boiling or roasting – they have a lovely potato/parsnip flavour.
Secondary uses: Mineral accumulator.
Propagation: By seed or division. Plants divide very easily, just pulling apart, so when you dig them up you can replant a few.
Maintenance: It may need feeding to remain productive.

Stachys affinis, CHINESE ARTICHOKE

Deciduous/Evergreen: D   Zone: 5
Sun/shade preference: ○
Shade tolerance: ◖
Performance rating: ✓✓
Fertility: SF
Cover: ✗   Flowers: Purple, white

This is an Asian perennial, spreading via new tubers to form a carpet. Each plant forms a number of new tubers in the autumn.

Size: 45cm (1'6") high; spreading.

Cultivation: Plant tubers in winter or early spring (comes early into growth). Grows in most soils but crops best in fertile soils.

Uses: The tubers, white and 2.5-5cm (1-2") long by 1cm (0.4") wide, are crisp with a pleasant sweet flavour (resembling apple and pepper).

Harvest and storage: Harvest small tubers in winter – they will store in the ground in the UK.

Cooking/processing: The tubers are nice to eat raw or lightly cooked. Boil for 5-10 minutes or roast.

Secondary uses: Bee plant.

Propagation: By replanting some of the new tubers.

Maintenance: None required.

Medicinal perennials/covers

The medicinal plants listed here are just a few – fairly well-known – of the many possible perennial medicinal plants you can grow. As always with using plants medicinally, make sure you are confident of how to use them or consult a qualified herbalist.

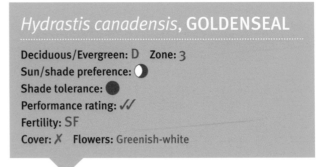

Echinacea angustifolia & *E. purpurea*, **CONEFLOWERS**

Deciduous/Evergreen: D   Zone: 3
Sun/shade preference: ◐
Shade tolerance: ◐
Performance rating: ✓✓
Fertility: SF
Cover: ✗   Flowers: Purple, pink, yellow

Coneflowers are clump-forming North American perennials, of dry sites.

Size: 1.2m (4') high and 45cm (1'6") wide when flowering.

Cultivation: Plant in winter or spring – protect from slugs. Give a well-drained soil. They like plenty of humus.

Uses: The roots and aerial parts are medicinal and widely used in herbal medicine as immune-system boosters.

Harvest and storage: Roots are dug in autumn or winter and can be dried.

Propagation: By seed or by root cuttings in late autumn to early winter.

Maintenance: Little required. Watch out for slug and snail damage on young plants.

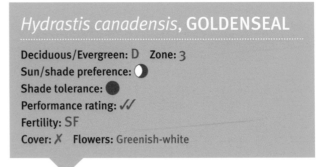

Hydrastis canadensis, **GOLDENSEAL**

Deciduous/Evergreen: D   Zone: 3
Sun/shade preference: ◐
Shade tolerance: ●
Performance rating: ✓✓
Fertility: SF
Cover: ✗   Flowers: Greenish-white

Goldenseal is a clump-forming North American woodland perennial. It can be difficult to establish.

Size: 50cm (1'8") high and 30cm (1') wide.

Cultivation: Transplant young plants in winter into a well-drained acid-to-neutral soil.

Uses: This is a well-known medicinal plant used in herbal medicine: it is anti-inflammatory and antibiotic.

Harvest and storage: Roots are harvested in late autumn and winter, and can be dried and stored.

Propagation: By seed is best.

Maintenance: Wait until your tree and shrub layers have semi-matured (10+ years) before you try to establish goldenseal beneath. Once established, little maintenance is required.

Hypericum perforatum, **ST JOHN'S WORT**

Deciduous/Evergreen: D   Zone: 3
Sun/shade preference: ◐
Shade tolerance: ◐
Performance rating: ✓✓✓
Fertility: SF
Cover: ✗   Flowers: Yellow

A lax, clump-forming perennial, St John's wort can self-seed here and there.

Size: 1m (3') high and 30cm (1') wide.

Cultivation: Broadcast seed in spring or transplant young plants in winter into any well-drained soil.

Uses: This is a well-known medicinal plant, used in herbal medicine as an antidepressant and astringent.

Harvest and storage: Flowering tops are harvested in summer.

Secondary uses: Good bee plant and dye plant (dyes red).
Propagation: By seed.
Maintenance: None required.

Panax ginseng, GINSENG

Deciduous/Evergreen: D   Zone: 6
Sun/shade preference: ◐
Shade tolerance: ●
Performance rating: ✓
Fertility: SF
Cover: ✗   Flowers: Yellow

Ginseng is a clump-formed Asian woodland perennial. American ginseng (*P. quinquefolius*) is similar and used similarly. They are tricky plants to grow and you have to wait a long time for a harvest!

Size: 30-50cm (1'-1'8") high and 30cm (1') wide.
Cultivation: Transplant young plants in spring into a humus-rich, moist, acid soil with good drainage. Protect from slugs and mice.
Uses: Ginseng is a well-known medicinal herb, much valued in Chinese medicine as an adaptogen.
Harvest and storage: Roots are harvested from plants that have grown for 6-10 years in wild or forest garden conditions, then are dried at warm temperatures.
Secondary uses: Mineral accumulator.
Propagation: By seed – deeply dormant: needs to go through a cold–warm–cold cycle over 18 months before germinating.
Maintenance: You might need to mollycoddle the plants a little, so maintenance is higher than for many other woodland plants. Mice and slugs are just two of the beasties that like to chomp on ginseng.

Solidago canadensis & *S. virgaurea*, GOLDENRODS

Deciduous/Evergreen: D   Zone: 5
Sun/shade preference: ◑
Shade tolerance: ◐
Performance rating: ✓✓✓
Fertility: SF
Cover: ✓✓   Flowers: Yellow

Goldenrod (*Solidago virgaurea*) and Canadian goldenrod (*S. canadensis*) are spreading perennials with woody rootstocks and bright yellow flowers.

Size: 1-2m (3'-6'6") high; spreading.
Cultivation: Transplant young plants in winter or early spring into any well-drained soil.
Uses: The leaves have long been used in herbal medicine as an anti-inflammatory.
Harvest and storage: Leaves are harvested in early summer, just before flowering.
Secondary uses: Attracts beneficial insects, especially lacewings. Mineral accumulator.
Propagation: By seed or by division in autumn or spring. May self-seed if happy.
Maintenance: Little required.

Tanacetum parthenium, FEVERFEW

Deciduous/Evergreen: D   Zone: 5
Sun/shade preference: ◑
Shade tolerance: ◐
Performance rating: ✓✓✓
Fertility: SF
Cover: ✓   Flowers: White & yellow

Feverfew is a well-known medicinal plant, long used to reduce fevers. It is also an attractive flowering plant but can self-seed widely where there is bare ground.

Size: 60cm (2') high and 25cm (10") wide.
Cultivation: Transplant young plants in winter into any reasonably well-drained soil.
Uses: The leaves and flowerheads are used medicinally, often in a herb tea.

Harvest and storage: Leaves and flowerheads are harvested in summer and dried to store.
Secondary uses: Attracts bees and beneficial insects.
Propagation: By seed or by division in spring.
Maintenance: Little required. You may want to remove seedheads before the seed ripens if you have bare ground nearby and do not want it to spread.

Perennials/covers for nitrogen fixation and mineral accumulation

Although nitrogen fixation is not as efficient in reduced light conditions, there are often ample opportunities to use N-fixers in the brighter parts of this layer. Some of the mineral accumulators work well in shady conditions and are well worth including beneath trees.

Milk vetch (*Astragalus glycyphyllos*).

Astragalus glycyphyllos, **MILK VETCH**

Deciduous/Evergreen: D   **Zone:** 5
Sun/shade preference: ◐
Shade tolerance: ◑
Performance rating: ✓✓✓
Fertility: SF
Cover: X   **Flowers:** Pale green

This is a loose trailing/scrambling perennial.

Size: 1m+ (3'+) long stems.
Cultivation: Transplant young plants in winter or early spring into any reasonably well-drained soil.

Uses: A useful nitrogen-fixing leguminous plant in this layer – doesn't interfere much with other plants.
Propagation: By seed; requires scarification.
Maintenance: Little required. It does not produce much shade so must be grown with other plants to form a good cover – easy to incorporate in mixtures.

Bird's foot trefoil (*Lotus corniculatus*).

Lotus corniculatus, **BIRD'S FOOT TREFOIL**

Deciduous/Evergreen: D   **Zone:** 5
Sun/shade preference: ○
Shade tolerance: ◑
Performance rating: ✓✓
Fertility: SF
Cover: ✓✓   **Flowers:** Yellow

Bird's foot trefoil is a clumping European perennial. The variety 'Plenus' (or 'Plena') is lower and trails over the ground better than the species. Bird's foot trefoil tolerates a little foot traffic.

Size: 40cm (1'4") high and wide, 'Plenus' up to 60cm (2') wide.
Cultivation: Broadcast seed in spring or transplant young plants in winter into a well-drained soil. Prefers neutral-to-alkaline pH.
Uses: A good nitrogen-fixing plant.
Secondary uses: Bee plant and attracts beneficial insects.
Propagation: By seed.
Maintenance: None required.

Lotus uliginosus, GREATER BIRD'S FOOT TREFOIL

Deciduous/Evergreen: D   Zone: 6
Sun/shade preference: ◔
Shade tolerance: ◐
Performance rating: ✓✓✓
Fertility: SF
Cover: ✓✓   Flowers: Yellow

This is a very similar though larger species than *L. corniculatus*. It is also clumping, but tolerates more moist soils than *L. corniculatus*.

Size: to 80cm (2'8") high and wide.
Cultivation: Transplant young plants in winter into a reasonably well-drained soil. Tolerates slightly acid soil.
Uses: A good nitrogen-fixing plant.
Secondary uses: Bee plant. Attracts beneficial insects.
Propagation: By seed.
Maintenance: None required.

Lupinus perennis, WILD LUPIN

Deciduous/Evergreen: D   Zone: 4
Sun/shade preference: ◔
Shade tolerance: ◑
Performance rating: ✓✓✓✓
Fertility: SF
Cover: ✓✓   Flowers: Blue

Wild lupin is the hardiest of a number of perennial lupins, which can be used as nitrogen fixers and mineral accumulators. They also make attractive flowering plants.

Size: Up to 70cm (2'4") high and wide.
Cultivation: Transplant young plants in winter. Likes an acid, reasonably well-drained soil.
Uses: Very good nitrogen-fixing plant. Note that the seeds of this lupin are not edible.
Secondary uses: Bee plant; mineral accumulator.
Propagation: By seed – requires scarification.
Maintenance: None required.

Lungwort (*Pulmonaria officinalis*).

Pulmonaria officinalis, LUNGWORT

Deciduous/Evergreen: E   Zone: 6
Sun/shade preference: ◑
Shade tolerance: ●
Performance rating: ✓✓✓✓
Fertility: SF
Cover: ✓✓   Flowers: Blue, purple

Lungwort is a mostly clump-forming evergreen European woodland perennial, with spotted leaves. It flowers in late winter and early spring. Plant at 40cm (1'4") spacing to make a ground cover. It tolerates sun if the soil is moist, and tolerates a little foot traffic.

Size: 25cm (10") high and 30-45cm (1'-1'6") wide.
Cultivation: Transplant young plants in early-to-mid winter (comes very early into growth). Likes a humus-rich soil.
Uses: A good mineral accumulating plant, which is also a very good early bee plant.
Secondary uses: The young leaves can be eaten but the texture is not pleasant so I do not recommend it. It has traditional medicinal uses for lung diseases.
Propagation: By seed, division in late spring or autumn, or root cuttings in winter.
Maintenance: None required.

Comfrey (*Symphytum officinale*).

Symphytum spp., COMFREYS

Deciduous/Evergreen: D/E **Zone:** 5
Sun/shade preference: ○
Shade tolerance: ◐
Performance rating: ✓✓✓✓
Fertility: SF
Cover: ✓✓✓ **Flowers:** White, blue, purple

Species include *Symphytum ibericum* (dwarf comfrey), *S. officinale* (medicinal comfrey), *S. orientale* (white comfrey), *S. tuberosum* (tuberous comfrey) and *S. x uplandicum* (Russian or Quaker comfrey). 'Bocking 14' is a variety of Russian comfrey.

Most comfreys are clump-forming herbaceous perennials that creep slowly via rhizomes. *S. ibericum* (to 40cm/1'4" high) is evergreen and spreads faster, with stems rooting as well, making a great low cover. *S. officinale* grows 1.2 to 1.5m (4'-5') high and 60-100cm (2'-3'3") wide; *S. orientale* 90cm (3') high and 50cm (1'8") wide, also evergreen; *S. tuberosum* 40-60cm (1'4"-2') high and wide; *S. x uplandicum* to 2m (6'6") high and 1m (3'3") wide. They tolerate foot traffic.

Size: Variable, as above.
Cultivation: Broadcast seed in late winter or transplant young plants in winter in any moist soil.
Uses: Fantastic mineral accumulating plants, particularly of potassium – very good beneath and around fruiting shrubs and trees. The larger species can be cut several times a year and the top growth used as a mulch.
Secondary uses: Great bee plants. The leaves and roots of *S. officinale* have long been used medicinally, for

example externally to aid bone setting after fractures amongst other things, but the roots are not now considered safe for internal use. The leaves of medicinal and Russian comfrey can be eaten raw or cooked, but raw they have an unpleasant texture and are not recommended.
Propagation: By seed, root cuttings in late winter or spring, or division in spring.
Maintenance: Little required. Some self-seeding is likely with all except Russian comfrey, which is sterile.

Dwarf comfrey (*Symphytum ibericum*).

Trifolium pratense, RED CLOVER

Deciduous/Evergreen: D **Zone:** 6
Sun/shade preference: ○
Shade tolerance: ◐
Performance rating: ✓✓✓
Fertility: SF
Cover: ✓✓ **Flowers:** Pinkish-red

Red clover is widely known through its use in agricultural grass/clover mixtures, and where light conditions are good it can make a useful soil-improving cover. It is more short-lived than white clover (*T. repens*, see right).

Size: to 60cm (2') high and wide
Cultivation: Broadcast seed in spring. Likes a well-drained soil, not too acid.
Uses: Primarily as a great nitrogen-fixing plant. It is also great for bees.
Secondary uses: Young shoots can be eaten in spring,

and flowers used in herb teas in late spring and summer.
Propagation: Can easily be bought as bulk seed and broadcast-sown.
Maintenance: Red clover can start to die out after 3-4 years and may need replacing with something else.

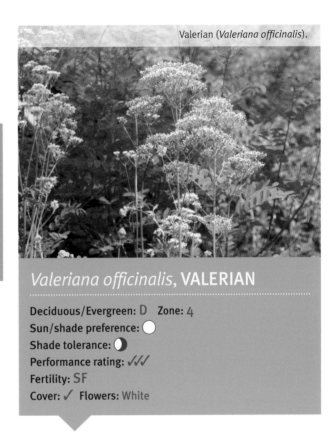
Valerian (*Valeriana officinalis*).

Trifolium repens, WHITE CLOVER

Deciduous/Evergreen: D   **Zone:** 4
Sun/shade preference: ◯
Shade tolerance: ◑
Performance rating: ✓✓✓
Fertility: SF
Cover: ✓✓   **Flowers:** White

White clover is a low-growing, herbaceous European perennial, spreading via rooting stems. Many clovers are excellent nitrogen fixers, but white clover is the most shade-tolerant. However, it is better as a ground cover in sun. It tolerates some foot traffic.

Size: 10-20cm (4-8") high; spreading.
Cultivation: Broadcast seed in spring. Likes a well-drained soil, not too acid.
Uses: Primarily as a great nitrogen-fixing plant. It is also great for bees.
Secondary uses: Young shoots can be eaten in spring, and flowers used in herb teas in late spring and summer.
Propagation: Can easily be bought as bulk seed and broadcast-sown.
Maintenance: None required.

Valeriana officinalis, VALERIAN

Deciduous/Evergreen: D   **Zone:** 4
Sun/shade preference: ◯
Shade tolerance: ◑
Performance rating: ✓✓✓
Fertility: SF
Cover: ✓   **Flowers:** White

A vigorous, sturdy, clump-forming European perennial, valerian self-seeds freely. Note that this plant is not the same as red valerian (*Centranthus ruber*, see page 217), which grows wild in walls in Britain.

Size: 1.2-2m (4'-6'6") high and 40-80cm (1'4"-2'8") wide.
Cultivation: Broadcast seed in spring or transplant young plants in winter. Fine in any soil.
Uses: Mainly as a mineral accumulator and attractor of beneficial insects.
Secondary uses: The roots have powerful medicinal properties (sedative). They are harvested in winter.
Propagation: By seed, or division in spring or autumn.
Maintenance: Little required. You might want to stop it seeding too much (by cutting the unripe seedheads), which it may do if conditions are to its liking.

Perennials/covers with other uses

Some of the other plants that can be used in this layer are listed below. They include efficient ground-covering species that may be valuable to bees or other beneficial insects but have no direct use for people – i.e. these are plants with system functions.

Acanthus mollis, BEAR'S BREECH

Deciduous/Evergreen: D Zone: 6
Sun/shade preference: ○
Shade tolerance: ◑
Performance rating: ✓✓
Fertility: SF
Cover: ✓✓ Flowers: Whitish-lilac

This is a mainly clump-forming perennial, although it can sucker. It is found in scrub in southern Europe and is deep-rooted. Plant at 90cm (3') spacing to form a good cover.

Size: 1-1.5m (3-5') high by 60-90cm (2-3') wide.
Cultivation: Transplant young plants in winter or spring. Tolerates any soil, though prefers a fertile loam. Slugs and snails can damage young plants.
Uses: Bee plant.
Propagation: Sow seed in spring, divide in spring or autumn, or take root cuttings in winter.
Maintenance: Little required. Very robust once established.

Bugle (*Ajuga reptans*).

Ajuga reptans, BUGLE

Deciduous/Evergreen: E Zone: 6
Sun/shade preference: ○
Shade tolerance: ●
Performance rating: ✓✓
Fertility: SF
Cover: ✓✓ Flowers: Purple

Bugle is a creeping and spreading perennial. Plant at 30cm (1') spacing to form a good cover.

Size: 10-30cm (4-12") high.
Cultivation: Transplant plants or rooted stems in winter (comes early into growth). Likes any moist soil.
Uses: Very good bee and butterfly plant.
Propagation: Separate rooted stems.
Maintenance: Little required.

Lady's mantle (*Alchemilla mollis*).

Asarabacca (*Asarum europaeum*).

Alchemilla mollis, **LADY'S MANTLE**

Deciduous/Evergreen: D   Zone: 5
Sun/shade preference: ◖
Shade tolerance: ●
Performance rating: ✓✓✓
Fertility: SF
Cover: ✓✓   Flowers: Lime green

Asarum europaeum, **ASARABACCA** & *A. canadense*, **WILD GINGER**

Deciduous/Evergreen: D/E   Zone: 2/4
Sun/shade preference: ◖
Shade tolerance: ●●
Performance rating: ✓✓✓
Fertility: SF
Cover: ✓✓   Flowers: Brownish-red

This is a clump-forming perennial of moist ground, and can self-seed freely. Plant at 40-60cm (1'4"-2') spacing to form a good cover. It tolerates a little foot traffic, and is drought-tolerant.

Size: 30-50cm (1'-1'8") high.
Cultivation: Transplant young plants in winter. Likes any moist, humus-rich soil – likely to do increasingly well as a forest garden establishes.
Uses: Good ground-cover plant.
Propagation: By seed or by division in spring or autumn.
Maintenance: Dies down completely in winter and often needs a weed in spring.

These are low-growing perennials of open woodland; evergreen in the case of *A. europaeum*. They creep via rhizomes. Plant at 30cm (1') spacing to form a ground cover. *A. canadense* is hardy to zone 2; *A. europaeum* to zone 4. They tolerate a little foot traffic.

Size: To 30cm (1') high.
Cultivation: Transplant young plants in winter. Likes a moist, humus-rich soil.
Uses: The roots have been used in the past as a ginger flavouring but there is some doubt about their safety, so this is not recommended. The plants form a good low ground cover in shade though.
Secondary uses: Green dyes from the leaves.
Propagation: By seed or by division in spring.
Maintenance: Often requires some weeding in spring.

Chrysogonum virginianum, GOLDEN STAR

Deciduous/Evergreen: SE   **Zone:** 5
Sun/shade preference: ◖
Shade tolerance: ◖
Performance rating: ✓✓✓
Fertility: SF
Cover: ✓✓   **Flowers:** Yellow

This is a low-growing, semi-evergreen North American perennial. Plant at 30cm (1') spacing to form a good cover. It tolerates a little foot traffic.

Size: 10cm (4") high (more when flowering), with creeping runners.
Cultivation: Transplant young plants in winter. It likes a moderately well-drained but moist soil.
Uses: A good ground-cover plant beneath other plants.
Secondary uses: Bee plant in spring.
Propagation: By seed, division, or layering of runners.
Maintenance: None required.

Geranium macrorrhizum, ROCK CRANESBILL

Deciduous/Evergreen: D   **Zone:** 3
Sun/shade preference: ◖
Shade tolerance: ●
Performance rating: ✓✓
Fertility: SF
Cover: ✓✓   **Flowers:** Pink

This is a robust, spreading European perennial, with rooting stems. Plant at 45cm (1'6") spacing for a good cover. It tolerates a little foot traffic.

Size: 30cm (1') high; spreading.
Cultivation: Transplant young plants in winter into any well-drained soil.
Uses: Good ground cover as a base-layer perennial.
Secondary uses: Bee plant. The leaves are a source of essential oils.
Propagation: Division in spring.
Maintenance: Little required.

Galax urceolata, WAND FLOWER

Deciduous/Evergreen: E   **Zone:** 4
Sun/shade preference: ◖
Shade tolerance: ●
Performance rating: ✓✓
Fertility: SF
Cover: ✓✓   **Flowers:** White

A low, spreading North American evergreen perennial with shiny leaves, this plant spreads via rhizomes. Plant at 30cm (1') spacing for a good cover. It tolerates some foot traffic.

Size: 25cm (10") high, spreading widely.
Cultivation: Transplant young plants in winter into a moist, acid but well-drained soil.
Uses: Use as a base-layer perennial for soil protection.
Propagation: By seed or by division in spring.
Maintenance: Little required. Good as a base-layer perennial.

Heuchera spp., ALUM ROOT / CORAL FLOWERS

Deciduous/Evergreen: E   **Zone:** 5
Sun/shade preference: ◖
Shade tolerance: ●
Performance rating: ✓✓✓
Fertility: SF
Cover: ✓✓   **Flowers:** Various

Species include *Heuchera americana, H. micrantha* var. *diversifolia, H. glabra, H. micrantha, H. sanguinea* and *H. versicolor.* They are evergreen or semi-evergreen clump-forming perennials. Plant at a spacing of 30-40cm (1'-1'4") for a ground cover. They tolerate some foot traffic.

Size: 45-100cm (1'6"-3'3") high and 30-40cm (1'-1'4") wide.
Cultivation: Transplant young plants in winter into a moist, well-drained soil.
Uses: The roots are used as a mordant in dyeing, hence the name alum root.

Harvest and storage: Roots are harvested in autumn.
Secondary uses: Great bee plants. *H. americana* is particularly good as a base-layer perennial.
Propagation: By seed or by division in autumn.
Maintenance: Little required. The woody rootstock pushes upwards but if there is leaf litter covering it each year then replanting should not be required.

Lysimachia nummularia, CREEPING JENNY

Deciduous/Evergreen: D   Zone: 4
Sun/shade preference: ◑
Shade tolerance: ◑
Performance rating: ✓✓
Fertility: SF
Cover: ✓✓   Flowers: Yellow

This is a very vigorous, low-growing, spreading perennial, with rooting stems. Plant at 60cm (2') spacing for a good cover. It is tolerant of foot traffic and good as a base-layer perennial.

Size: 5cm (2") high, spreading widely.
Cultivation: Plant young or divided plants in winter or early spring. Prefers moist soil but tolerates most soils.
Uses: Low, base-layer perennial.
Secondary uses: Bee plant.
Propagation: By division in spring, or layering.
Maintenance: Little required.

Mitchella repens, PARTRIDGE BERRY

Deciduous/Evergreen: E   Zone: 4
Sun/shade preference: ◑
Shade tolerance: ●
Performance rating: ✓✓
Fertility: SF
Cover: ✓✓   Flowers: White

This is a low, carpeting North American woodland shrub, spreading via rooting stems. Plant at 20cm (8") spacing for a good ground cover. It is tolerant of foot traffic.

Size: 5cm (2") high, spreading widely.
Cultivation: Plant young pot-grown plants in winter or spring. Likes a moist, acid but well-drained soil.
Uses: A very good base-layer perennial plant.
Secondary uses: Bee plant. The fruits are edible but tasteless.
Propagation: By seed, division in spring, or cuttings in summer.
Maintenance: Little required. Good as a base-layer perennial.

Sanguinaria canadensis, BLOODROOT

Deciduous/Evergreen: D   Zone: 3
Sun/shade preference: ◑
Shade tolerance: ●
Performance rating: ✓✓
Fertility: SF
Cover: ✓✓   Flowers: Yellow & white

This is a low, carpeting North American perennial of open woodland, spreading via rhizomes. Plant at 25cm (10") spacing for a ground cover.

Size: 20-50cm (8-20") high and 30cm (1') wide.
Cultivation: Transplant young plants in winter. Likes a humus-rich soil; tolerates wet soil.
Uses: The rhizomes can be used to make red dye.
Harvest and storage: Rhizomes are harvested in late autumn or winter. They exude red sap if cut.
Secondary uses: Bee plant. Medicinal – it is being investigated for its anti-cancer properties.
Propagation: By seed in autumn, or by division after flowering in spring.
Maintenance: None required.

Soapwort (*Saponaria officinalis*).

Saponaria officinalis, SOAPWORT

Deciduous/Evergreen: D **Zone:** 4
Sun/shade preference: ◐
Shade tolerance: ◐
Performance rating: ✓✓✓
Fertility: SF
Cover: ✓ **Flowers:** Pink, white

Soapwort is a spreading European perennial, with new stems arising from its rhizomes. Plant at 45cm (1'6") spacing for a reasonable cover, though it is best inter-planted with a lower plant. It tolerates a little foot traffic.

Size: 60cm (2') high, spreading widely.
Cultivation: Transplant young plants in early-to-mid winter (comes early into growth), in any well-drained, not-too-acid soil.
Uses: All parts contain saponins and can be used as a soap source. Soak and rub the leaves or roots in water, which you can use for washing clothes or yourself! The roots are still used as a mild cleanser on old tapestries, etc.
Harvest and storage: The aerial parts can be harvested throughout the season; the roots in winter.
Secondary uses: Bee and butterfly plant.
Propagation: By seed (needs 8 weeks' stratification), or division in spring or autumn.
Maintenance: None required.

Tiarella cordifolia, FOAM FLOWER

Deciduous/Evergreen: D **Zone:** 3
Sun/shade preference: ◐
Shade tolerance: ●
Performance rating: ✓✓
Fertility: SF
Cover: ✓✓ **Flowers:** Cream

Foam flower is a vigorous North American woodland perennial that spreads via rhizomes, forming a carpet. It is evergreen in mild winter regions. Plant at 35cm (1'2") spacing for a good ground cover. It tolerates some foot traffic.

Size: 30cm (1') high; spreading.
Cultivation: Transplant young plants in winter (comes early into growth). Most soils are tolerated, though it prefers a moist, humus-rich soil.
Uses: Attracts beneficial insects.
Propagation: By seed or by division in spring.
Maintenance: None required.

Greater periwinkle (*Vinca major*).

Vinca major & *V. minor*, PERIWINKLES

Deciduous/Evergreen: E **Zone:** 4/7
Sun/shade preference: ◐
Shade tolerance: ●●
Performance rating: ✓✓✓
Fertility: SF
Cover: ✓✓✓ **Flowers:** Violet, white

Periwinkles are prostrate evergreen European shrubs, spreading via rhizomes and rooting stems, forming carpets. There are many garden varieties. Plant at 40-45cm (1'4"-1'6") spacing to form a ground cover. They tolerate foot traffic. *Vinca major* is hardy to zone 7; *V. minor* to zone 4.

Size: *Vinca minor* grows 25-40cm (10-16") high; *V. major* 45-60cm (1'6"-2') high. They spread widely.
Cultivation: Transplant young shrubs in winter. Fine in any soil.
Uses: The stems are thin and flexible and are very good for fine basketry work. Good bee plants, flowering all year.
Harvest and storage: Harvest stems at any time of year.
Propagation: Division from autumn to spring; semi-ripe cuttings in summer.
Maintenance: Little required. You may need to stop it going where you don't want it.

Waldsteinia ternata, BARREN STRAWBERRY

Deciduous/Evergreen: E **Zone:** 4
Sun/shade preference: ◐
Shade tolerance: ●
Performance rating: ✓✓✓
Fertility: SF
Cover: ✓✓ **Flowers:** Yellow

This is a low, carpeting, evergreen Eurasian perennial, spreading by rooting stems. It has strawberry-like foliage and yellow flowers followed by tiny green non-edible fruit. *Waldsteinia fragarioides* (also called barren strawberry) is very similar. They tolerate some foot traffic.

Size: 10cm (4") high, spreading widely.
Cultivation: Transplant young plants in winter. Fine in any soil.
Uses: An excellent base-layer perennial plant. Bee plant.
Propagation: By division in spring.
Maintenance: Slugs can sometimes be a problem.

Sweet cicely (*Myrrhis odorata*) with green seeds ready for eating.

Chapter 16

Designing the perennial / ground-cover layer

Plant functions in the perennial layer

There are numerous plants that can be used in the low layer covering the ground and beneath shrubs. The plants used may comprise a mixture of herbaceous perennials (i.e. those that die down to the ground in winter), evergreen perennials, creeping or running perennials, bulbs, low shrubs and creeping shrubs. Scrambling or twining perennials may also feature, although they will climb where they can.

The intensity with which this layer is utilised very much depends on the size of the forest garden. Almost everyone will want a range of perennial vegetables or fruits here, but there are other very important functions that plants here can fulfil; the following in particular.

- Keeping the soil covered for as much of the year as possible, either with green growth or a dense mulch of dead stalks, etc. This is vitally important. It ensures that the soil is protected from drying sun, beating rain, etc., and thus maintains a loose friable soil texture that encourages maximum numbers of earthworms and other beneficial soil fauna. If the soil is maintained in good condition then everything else that grows in it will benefit.

- Plants in this layer can be mineral accumulators; for example comfreys (*Symphytum* spp.) or sorrels and docks (*Rumex* spp.) These are deep-rooted plants which tap into nutrient sources that other plants cannot reach, and as a result all parts of them are nutrient-rich. When the tops die back in winter, or are cut and left on the ground to rot down, nutrients are slowly released into the topsoil layers and enrich the soil for other nearby plants.

- Where light levels are not too low, plants here might also be nitrogen fixers, which also enrich the soil for other plants. Examples are sweet peas (*Lathyrus* spp.) and milk vetch (*Astragalus glycyphyllos*).

- The plants here can be very attractive for beneficial insects, which are the mainstay of the pest-control system of a forest garden.

- There is a theory – unproven because nobody has yet done the research – that growing highly aromatic plants underneath and around trees and shrubs improves their health. This would be because the aromatic plants, such as mints (*Mentha* spp.), lemon balm (*Melissa officinalis*) and oregano (*Origanum vulgare*) liberate large amounts of essential oils in the growing season. These essential oils are anti-bacterial and anti-fungal (there is plenty of mainstream research to prove this), and in theory these could 1) confuse pests and 2) have a protective effect on other nearby plants against bacterial and fungal diseases. Robert Hart was a great believer in this effect, and I have to say that from my experience I think there is a lot in it, and I deliberately plant a lot of aromatic plants in my forest garden for this reason. They are also very nice for people too!

Apple mint (*Mentha suaveolens*). Mints are excellent aromatic plants as well as beneficial insect attractants.

- By having a thick, largely self-sustaining cover of plants over the soil surface, very few weed seeds can grow and establish, thus minimising the work needed to maintain this layer.

Size of the forest garden and the perennial layer

A larger forest garden is likely to have a substantial part of the perennial/ground-cover layer filled with plants that are not directly harvested for food, medicine, etc. but are useful in the ways listed above. Don't think of these plants as unproductive, because they are doing just as important a job as a food plant.

A smaller forest garden is more likely to have most of the perennial/ground-cover layer filled with plants that are more directly harvested, simply because there is less space available. However, you will lose some of the benefits listed above if most of the low plants are directly harvested, and this will impact on the self-sustaining nature of the garden: it is more likely that fertility materials will need to be imported into the garden, for example, and you may get more pest problems.

No perennial layer

Of course, you could always plant the tree and shrub layers of a forest garden and then graze or mow a grass cover beneath. Indeed, many people do this as a temporary measure while they are underplanting over a number of years. However, a permanent grazing or mowing regime beneath trees can both damage the soil structure and deprive the whole system of the chance of much more diversity – thus reducing the overall health and success of the system.

Leaving the ground flora unmown, ungrazed and unplanted is not a good idea. What will happen is that, in the good light conditions prevalent at the start of a forest garden, weeds such as nettles and brambles will quickly dominate, and within a few years even access into the forest garden may be near impossible, through a 2m-high bramble patch. Whereas in new woodland plantings this can be acceptable, because the trees are densely planted and will out shade brambles in ten years or so, in a forest garden the trees are more widely spaced and you cannot rely on shade to control undesirable weeds.

How you start thinking about the perennial/ground-cover layer rather depends on what you are starting with, and how fast you want to achieve the planting.

Transitional ground-covers

You'll see from the table opposite that there are periods in the evolution of many forest gardens when you want the soil covered with plant growth (to keep the soil structure in good condition, etc.) but are not ready to plant out the final plants you want in this layer. In this case it is possible to sow a temporary, or transitional, ground cover in the meantime. If you start with pasture then this will suffice as the transitional cover, as long as it is mown at least once a year (though preferably two or three times). However, it still might be worth adding in other species, particularly if you have only grasses and little else. Legumes such as the clovers (see pages 258-259), and accumulator plants such as those on page 260 can be oversown into pasture – ideally when it is short after cutting – and rolled/trampled so the seeds touch the soil surface. Adding these can significantly increase soil fertility by the time you want to plant out your final perennial/ground-cover plants, and thus help them in the long term.

If you are starting with a bare-soil site, or have created bare soil by mulching out previous weed/plant growth and you cannot yet plant into this with your final plant choices, then you should not leave the soil bare for longer than you have to. As well as being an invitation for weed seeds to colonise, bare soil also allows nutrients to wash out easily and the soil structure can soon deteriorate.

Cardoon (*Cynara cardunculus*) undersown with poached egg plant (*Limnanthes douglasii*) as a transitional cover.

ROUTES TO CREATING THE PERENNIAL LAYER		
Starting with	**Planting perennial layer all in one go**	**Planting perennial layer over a number of years**
Clear site, pasture	Not possible immediately without the use of herbicides. The pasture grasses need to be killed off (preferably by mulching for a year) before a perennial layer can be planted.	Recommended – this is what the majority of people do. The existing pasture can be mulched section-by-section for replanting, with any remaining pasture cut or mown to stop it reverting to scrub.
Clear site, cultivated ground	Certainly possible, but likely to be feasible only on smaller sites because of the number of plants and work involved.	For larger sites this is recommended, planting the perennial layer in sections. Leaving bare soil for more than a few months is a bad option – weeds will soon colonise it. Therefore the area not to be underplanted in year one should be sown with a transitional ground-cover (see left).
Scrub	Not possible immediately (except on a very small site) without the use of herbicides. Not desirable because unwanted woody and perennial plants need to be cut and/or mulched out to ensure they are killed and won't regrow.	I recommend that no perennial-layer plants are planted in year one, allowing you to make sure that all undesirable species are dealt with. There is nothing worse than starting your underplanting in what you believe to be clean ground and then find a whole lot of perennial or scrubby weeds coming back up. Transitional covers (see left) may be appropriate.
Woodland	Probably not possible unless the ground layer is fairly clean. Existing trees will probably need thinning and removing to give space for forest garden species, and after that some ground-cover planting is possible.	Again, probably the best option. Allows time for brambles and other undesirables to be removed. Transitional covers (see left) may be appropriate.

Because transitional covers are often used over large areas, they are normally sown using cheap and easily available species – grasses and green manures. Some of these can persist for 2-4 years with no cutting or mowing before they start to get weedy. Any longer than this and they will need cutting to stop them reverting to scrub, and possibly replacing with another cover if they get thin. When you are finally ready to underplant with the perennial/ground-cover plants you want, then the transitional cover is killed off, preferably by mulching.

Single-species crops

Annual green manures can be used as short-term cover for up to a year, and some may overwinter. Unlike their mainstream use in agriculture and gardening, in a forest garden they are not usually dug into the soil but are left to die off after flowering. Some self-seeding may occur,

although shade and/or the perennial plants that will follow them will eventually remove them. These green manures can sometimes be underplanted with perennial plants before they die off (as they get leggier and allow more light through to the soil) – this is something I have done successfully with mustards (*Sinapsis* spp.).

The sowing rates given below are different (per unit area) for larger-scale sowings. Less seed per unit area is recommended on a large scale because there is usually a greater percentage of successful seeds germinating and growing into plants, owing to less predation by slugs, snails, etc., which do not have nearby cover to retreat to in larger-scale situations.

Borago officinalis, BORAGE
Deep taprooted; good at breaking soil pans.
Sowing time: April–May
Sowing rates: 3g/m2, 14kg/acre

Fagopyrum esculentum, BUCKWHEAT
Good on poor ground.
Sowing time: May–August
Sowing rates: 10g/m², 15kg/acre

Lupinus angustifolius, BLUE LUPIN
Legume; prefers acid soil. Deep-rooting; slow to get going.
Sowing time: March–July
Sowing rates: 10g/m², 20kg/acre

Medicago lupulina, BLACK MEDICK
Biennial legume, fine in most soils if not too acidic. Will tolerate shade.
Sowing time: March–August
Sowing rates: 3g/m², 10kg/acre

Phacelia tanacetifolia, PHACELIA
Bees love the flowers. Fine in any soil. Will overwinter in mild areas.
Sowing time: March–September.
Sowing rates: 3g/m², 15kg/acre
Duration: 2 years

Raphanus sativus, FODDER RADISH
Deep taprooted; good at breaking soil pans.
Sowing time: May–August
Sowing rates: 8g/m², 10kg/acre

Sinapsis alba, WHITE MUSTARD
Quick cover; fine in any soil. Will overwinter in mild areas if sown after August.
Sowing time: April–September.
Sowing rates: 5g/m², 10kg/acre

Trifolium incarnatum, CRIMSON CLOVER
Legume; fine in most soils that are not too acid.
Sowing time: March–August. Will overwinter until spring if sown July/August.
Sowing rates: 8g/m², 10kg/acre

Trifolium subterraneum, SUB CLOVER
Legume; tolerates more acid soils than other clovers. Can self-seed (it pushes the seeds under the ground itself) and persist in sunny locations. Rarely for a clover, it is not a good bee plant.
Sowing time: April–May
Sowing rates: 8g/m2, 10kg/acre

Vicia faba, FIELD BEAN
Legume; usually sown for overwintering until the following summer. Prefers heavier soils.
Sowing time: September–November
Sowing rates: 25g/m², 50kg/acre

Vicia sativa, VETCH / TARES
Legume; prefers heavier soils. Will overwinter until early summer if sown after July.
Sowing time: March–October
Sowing rates: 10g/m², 50kg/acre

Longer-term single-species green manures that are suitable as transitional covers are mostly legumes, such as those listed below. Bear in mind that legumes require good light conditions and will die out as shade increases. Of the species below, the most persistent and shade-tolerant is white clover (*Trifolium repens*).

Lotus corniculatus, BIRD'S FOOT TREFOIL
Prefers alkaline soils; good bee plant.
Sowing time: April–August
Sowing rates: 1g/m², 3kg/acre
Duration: 2 years

Medicago sativa, LUCERNE / ALFALFA
Very deep-rooting and an excellent accumulator of minerals. Needs to be sown with inoculant to ensure nitrogen fixation. Extremely drought-tolerant; requires pH 6.0 or more. Has edible shoots. Bee plant.
Sowing time: April–July
Sowing rates: 2-3g/m², 11kg/acre
Duration: 2 years

Onobrychis viciifolia, SAINFOIN
For alkaline soils. Varieties 'Giant' and 'Cotswold Common' recommended. Bee plant.
Sowing time: April–August
Sowing rates: 7-8g/m², 30kg/acre
Duration: 2-3 years

Trifolium pratense, RED CLOVER
An erect plant that establishes rapidly. The best varieties are the late-leafing 'Pawera' and 'Britta'. Edible leaves, flowers and seeds. Bee plant.
Sowing time: April–August
Sowing rates: 2-3g/m², 11kg/acre
Duration: 2 years

Trifolium repens, WHITE CLOVER
A prostrate, stoloniferous plant. This is the best species, both on its own and as a base, for long-term covers. Varieties 'Aran', 'Alice' and 'Donna' are recommended. Edible leaves and flowers. Bee plant.
Sowing time: April–August
Sowing rates: 2-3g/m², 11kg/acre
Duration: 3-4 years

METRIC TO IMPERIAL CONVERSIONS

1kg = 2lb 3oz; 10g = 0.35oz
1m² = 1.2 sq yards

Oregano (*Origanum vulgare*) undersown with mustards (*Sinapsis* spp.).

Species mixtures

Mown mixtures of grasses and legumes (and perhaps some mineral accumulators) are more robust and persistent than single-species covers. For example, lucerne and timothy persists for 4-5 years; white clover and dwarf perennial ryegrass persists for 10 or more years. The increasing shade as trees and shrubs mature might also affect the persistence of sown covers. Species mixtures based on white clover are the most persistent, and white clover is the most shade-tolerant of the legumes listed – this will be important for covers that need to last over 3-5 years because the increasing shade will deplete the population of other legumes.

By adding extra species (for example, the grasses listed below), the cover as a whole becomes more robust because the different species utilise different niches below and above ground. Bear in mind too that species used in sown covers need to be available relatively cheaply as seed, hence the use of mainly agricultural grasses.

Some recommended seeding mixtures are listed below.

Medicago sativa, LUCERNE / ALFALFA + *Phleum pratense*, TIMOTHY or *Festuca pratensis*, MEADOW FESCUE
Sowing time: April–July
Sowing rates: (2g+0.5g)/m², (7kg+1-2kg)/acre
Duration: 4-5 years

Trifolium pratense, RED CLOVER + *Lolium perenne*, DWARF PERENNIAL RYEGRASS
Sowing time: April–August
Sowing rates: (6-9g+0.5g)/m², (25-35kg+1-2kg)/acre
Duration: up to 3 years

Onobrychis viciifolia, SAINFOIN + *Phleum pratense*, TIMOTHY or *Festuca pratensis*, MEADOW FESCUE
Sowing time: April-August
Sowing rates: (6-9g+0.5g)/m², (25-35kg+1-2kg)/acre
Duration: 5-7 years

Trifolium repens, WHITE CLOVER + *Lolium perenne*, DWARF PERENNIAL RYEGRASS + *Festuca rubra* subsp. *rubra*, CREEPING RED FESCUE
Sowing time: April–August
Sowing rates: (1g+1-2g+1g)/m², (3kg+6kg+2kg)/acre
Duration: 10 years or more

Lotus corniculatus, BIRD'S FOOT TREFOIL + *Lolium perenne*, DWARF PERENNIAL RYEGRASS
Sowing time: April-August
Sowing rates: (1g+1-2g)/m², (3kg+6kg)/acre
Duration: 5+ years

Some recommended grass species to use in your own mixtures are as follows.

Festuca rubra subsp. *rubra*, CREEPING RED FESCUE
A low, rhizomatous grass; drought-tolerant. Combines well with white clover.

Festuca pratensis, MEADOW FESCUE
Combines well with lucerne and sainfoin.

Lolium perenne, PERENNIAL RYEGRASS
A persistent and hard-wearing grass. Many varieties are available; dwarf varieties (e.g. 'Manhattan', 'Numan') are best for ground-covers. Combines well with clovers.

Phleum pratense, TIMOTHY
Good in moist regions, combining well with lucerne and sainfoin.

Deep-rooting pasture herbs / mineral accumulators

Seed of some of these species, which accumulate minerals by sending deep roots down into the subsoil, can be added to sowing mixtures. The minerals are made available to other plants when the cover is cut or when plants die down in winter. All these species tolerate partial shade.

Bellis perennis, DAISY
Edible young leaves and flowers.

Cichorium intybus, CHICORY
All parts edible; bee plant; dye plant. Prefers neutral-to-alkaline soil.

Linaria vulgaris, TOADFLAX
Bee and butterfly plant; dye plant.

Ononis spinosa, RESTHARROW
Edible young shoots and roots. Nitrogen-fixing species; prefers alkaline soil.

Plantago spp. (e.g. *P. lanceolata*, *P. major*), PLANTAINS
Edible parts.

Sanguisorba minor & *S. officinalis*, BURNETS
Edible leaves and shoots; bee plants.

Valeriana officinalis, VALERIAN
Medicinal roots; butterfly plant. Can self-seed a lot!

Several other common species, such as docks and sorrels (*Rumex* spp.) and dandelion (*Taraxacum officinale*) are good accumulators. Often regarded as weeds, these will probably self-seed into the garden and don't need sowing deliberately!

Broadcast sowing

The seeds sown for a transitional cover should be sown on to clean soil before or after the main trees have been planted, and be rolled or treaded into the soil surface. Sow between March/April and August.

Transitional cover seeds should be broadcast evenly over the whole area prepared for sowing. On a small scale, the best way of doing this is to mix the seeds well with half a bucket of dry fine sand. The mixture can then be broadcast by hand: hold the bucket next to your body with your left arm (assuming you are right-handed), and grab handfuls of the mix with your right hand, throwing it to the left and right of your path as you walk forwards (reverse the directions if you are left-handed). Cover the whole area with parallel paths and then do it again at right angles if there is enough seed mix left.

On a larger scale, it may be worth your buying a small hand-cranked seed broadcasting machine, or 'seed fiddle'. These updated versions of the old-style seed fiddles are more controllable and adjustable. A hopper is filled with the seed, and the machine sits on your chest as you walk forward, turning the handle. You can adjust the rate at which seed is broadcast – always start on the cautious side so you don't run out of seed too soon!

Once the seed is broadcast, as long as the soil has been cultivated to a reasonable seedbed there is nothing else to do. Rolling or lightly trampling the seed can increase the germination rate, but I don't usually bother for bulk seeds.

See page 75, Chapter 7, for an example of transitional covers and succession planting.

Design and planting principles for the perennial layer

Getting this bit of the design right will save you lots of work in the long term, for these layers are where weeds can disrupt your plans most easily.

Ensure that undesirable species are killed off before planting

This is really important. As with all gardening, you can't plant into weedy ground and expect good results. Whole areas need to be prepared before planting these layers. Perennial grasses and deep-rooted weeds such as dandelions (assuming you don't want to eat them) and docks need substantial mulches for 6-12 months to kill them off. There is often a trade-off to be made here between ecological-mindedness and practicality. There is no doubt that plastic mulches are very efficient in doing the job, and I have used them a lot. The alternatives, such as several layers of thick card, require much more work to put in place and maintain. See pages 71-73, Chapter 7, for more details.

Aim to plant in drifts/patches of one or a few species

Don't start off trying to make things too complicated; it will only cause you a lot of work. The species complexity will increase naturally in time. In any one area (say a minimum of 3-4m²), don't try to mix more than a few different perennial/ground-cover species. If you do, then what is likely to happen is that because there are very small areas of individual species, some of these will get swamped by other species unless you put in a lot of effort to prevent it. Larger areas of individual species are more 'defendable' against some other plant overpowering them. If you want to grow polycultures of low-growing perennial species then there are some basic guidelines to follow to minimise this kind of problem – see page 267.

Design with different plant types

For the purposes of making the design of this layer easier, I find it convenient to split the plants used here into different categories. Different circumstances merit clump-forming plants, running or spreading plants, self-seeding plants, and mixtures of these.

Clump-forming plants

These are perennials that form a clump, or small woody shrubs. Neither spread by spreading roots, rhizomes or self-rooting shoots (although they may sometimes spread by seed). They are usually thought of as 'well-behaved'. To create areas of these species, many individual plants need to be planted at the appropriate planting distance. Examples include lemon balm (*Melissa officinalis*) and sweet cicely (*Myrrhis odorata*).

Sweet cicely (*Myrrhis odorata*) – a clump-forming plant.

Spreading or running plants

These are low perennial or woody plants that spread either by overground stems rooting where they touch the soil (e.g. strawberries, *Fragaria* spp.; and groundcover raspberries such as *Rubus nepalensis*, Nepalese raspberry), or by underground spreading roots/rhizomes (e.g. mints, *Mentha* spp.) In conventional gardening, these plants are often thought of as 'unruly', 'hard to control' or even 'invasive'. But in a forest garden they can be extremely useful, especially as many will grow successfully beneath taller perennials. In larger forest gardens they are likely to be an essential part of the perennial layer, keeping the soil well covered with desirable plant growth. You may need to design boundaries to stop them going too far – see page 265.

Comfrey (*Symphytum officinale*) – a self-seeding plant.

Nepalese raspberry (*Rubus nepalensis*) – a spreading plant.

Self-seeding plants

You'll find that, even with perennials that produce masses of seed, little self-seeding occurs unless there is bare soil or soil with little plant growth in spring. An example is the true medicinal comfrey (*Symphytum officinale*), which is often regarded as a self-seeding nuisance in conventional gardens. In forest gardens you are likely to get only the occasional plant springing up, and of course you can nearly always leave it to develop where it does, as it is an immensely beneficial plant. Some perennials do not make a good thick cover even when planted en masse but can still persist by occasionally managing to self-seed – an example is St John's wort (*Hypericum perforatum*). So you must expect such plants to appear in unexpected places and should usually try to value them wherever that is.

Nearly always include species that tolerate shade

Most forest gardens start from a fairly clear site, and in these situations light conditions change over time from fairly sunny to fairly shady. You don't have to plant all shade-tolerating or shade-loving perennial/ground-cover plants at the outset; you can certainly include plants that much prefer sunny or good light conditions. Over time, though, in most locations in the garden these are likely to decline and die out as shade increases. If this is going to happen then you have some choices – you can replant at a later date with more shade-loving species (which may involve mulching out an area that has become weedy because of a species decline), or indeed you can include shade-loving plants in a species mix at the outset. In the latter case, the ratio of sun lovers to shade lovers will change over time as the shade increases, and you can maintain a healthy ground-cover layer without having to replant. It has to be said, though, that there is experimentation involved here because little work has been done on perennial mixtures and how they change with increasing shade.

In areas of deep shade, think about using more spring ephemerals – plants that start into growth in late winter, flower in spring and die down to an underground bulb or tuber for the rest of the year. These plants, common in natural woodlands, take advantage of the extra light available before deciduous trees are fully in leaf.

Try to grow species that are easily propagated

You need a lot of plants in this layer. Typically you might need between 3 and 10 plants per square metre of planting, so even a fairly small forest garden of 100m² may need 300 to 1,000 plants here. Not too many people are going to buy in all those plants, and most will want to try to grow many of them themselves. Luckily, many perennials are easily propagated by seed, and for these you can source and buy seed each year (until you have your own seed perhaps), which is not difficult or expensive, or set up a propagation bed for vegetative propagation (see below).

Set up propagation beds for perennials

This is something you should think about in the early stages of a forest garden. I know I've said that you can leave the design of this layer until after the design of the tree and shrub layers, but it is really useful to set up propagation beds, especially for some of the spreading plants (if you are going to use them) in the first year or two, so they are productive as soon as you have the trees and shrubs planted. Basically, for rooting plants such as strawberries (*Fragaria* spp.) or groundcover raspberries (*Rubus* spp.) you need to plant one or more 'mother' plants, and each year you layer the stems to create extra new plants, which are removed and used. For rhizomatous plants such as mints (*Mentha* spp.), you can plant 'mother' plants which you allow to spread each year, digging up the new growth in winter to pot up; or plant out pieces of rhizome to create new plants.

Clumping perennials that can be propagated easily from cuttings, usually in summer, can also be placed in propagation beds if lots are required. A 'mother' plant is used as a source of cuttings only once in each season.

Wild strawberry (*Fragaria vesca*) is easy to layer.

Also worth including in a propagation bed are those perennials that are propagated by root cuttings, such as the comfreys (*Symphytum* spp.). For these, a 'mother' plant is planted, then each winter/spring it is dug up, many of the roots are cut off for propagation, and it is replanted.

White comfrey (*Symphytum orientale*) can easily be propagated from root cuttings.

See Appendix 1 for more details of perennial/ground-cover propagation methods.

Don't plant too close to young trees & shrubs

Competition (mostly for water in summer dry spells) is what kills most very young trees and shrubs. If there are woody plants less than a couple of years old in the midst of your ground-cover planting, take care not to plant nearer than 40-50cm (1'4"-1'8") to them to avoid excess competition. Most trees and shrubs can tolerate more competition when established, but smaller species may have yields affected by too much competition.

Use the 'expanding edge' technique

This is a technique used with spreading plants to expand their area into an unplanted area in a controlled way without having to do any planting. I have used this a lot for mints (horse mint, *Mentha longifolia*; apple mint, *M. suaveolens*) and groundcover raspberries (Nepalese raspberry, *Rubus nepalensis*; Chinese bramble, *R. tricolor*) with great results.

1. Clear an area, preferably long and narrow (1-2m/3'-6'6" wide), of perennial weeds and grasses by mulching, etc. for 6-12 months.

2. Plant individual plants out of the species you want to establish.

3. Immediately after planting the individual plants, mulch a parallel and adjacent area to the planted area. The width of this mulched area depends on the species you are using – 1m (3') for less-vigorous plants (e.g. Creeping bramble, *Rubus pentalobus*); 1.5m (5') for medium-vigour plants (e.g. *Mentha* spp., mints); 2m for more-vigorous plants (e.g. *Rubus nepalensis*; *R. tricolor*).

4. Leave this second area of mulch down for 12 months. During this time, as well as any weeds under the mulch being killed off, the spreading species will spread into the mulched area either underground (e.g. mints) or over the top (e.g. groundcover raspberries.) Remove the mulch and the spreading plant is immediately ready to colonise the new area.

5. Now mulch a further parallel and adjacent layer. If the mulch you used is not biodegradable, for example woven UV-stabilised plastic, you can move it and reuse it for the new area. Repeat this mulching process indefinitely until you have a large enough area of the species.

Sheet-mulching with landscape fabric parallel to a planted area of mint.

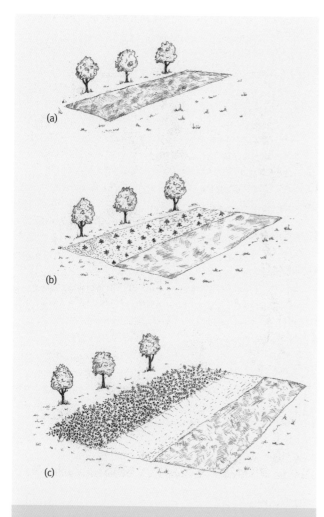

Expanding edge technique
(a) A sheet mulch is placed to kill off grasses, etc. (b) The sheet mulch is moved to a parallel adjacent area and an initial planting is made of a spreading plant, e.g. a groundcover raspberry. (c) A year later, the plants have established. The sheet mulch is moved to a new parallel area and the spreading plants can expand into the newly cleared area.

such as the groundcover raspberries *Rubus nepalensis* and *R. tricolor*.

- Design a path to be the boundary edge. The path should be mown or strimmed several times a year. This is good for perennial rhizomatous spreaders such as mints, which will not survive or cross mown areas.

- A very densely shaded area is a good boundary for most spreading species. Dense evergreen shrubs such as salal (*Gaultheria shallon*) or *Elaeagnus* x *ebbingei* are ideal for making the shady boundary.

Salal (*Gaultheria shallon*) makes an impenetrable boundary.

Design ground-cover boundaries

If you use spreading plants in this layer then some, notably the more vigorous, will probably need containing by some method, otherwise they might move almost everywhere. The following are easy methods you can use to do this.

- Patrol the boundary edge (this is a boundary that you define) on foot twice a year and simply cut off or bend back overground stems that are spreading out of the allowed area. This works well with woody spreaders

Take into account what is growing above

Obviously, plan for increased shade beneath trees compared with the space between trees. However, the density of tree canopies varies widely; a general rule is that trees with small leaves let more light through than those with large leaves.

One other consequence of trees with large leaves is that when the leaves fall in the autumn, they can smother less-rugged perennial plants. This may not matter if the perennials are herbaceous and already dying back for the winter, but evergreen perennials (e.g. *Bergenia* spp.) may get damaged. If the leaves do not rot down quickly (as the case with chestnuts, *Castanea* spp., for example) they may interfere with spring growth of all perennials. As well as chestnuts, many of the maples (*Acer* spp.) have large leaves. Beneath trees like this you need to make sure you use strong plants in the ground-cover layer, for example comfrey (*Symphytum* spp.).

Plant in a staggered pattern (not a square grid) for better coverage

When you come to actually do the planting of this layer, try to plant individual plants in a staggered pattern rather than square. It uses a few more plants but results in a better coverage of the area and thus of the soil, and leaves fewer gaps for weed seeds to exploit. It's a small thing but it makes a difference.

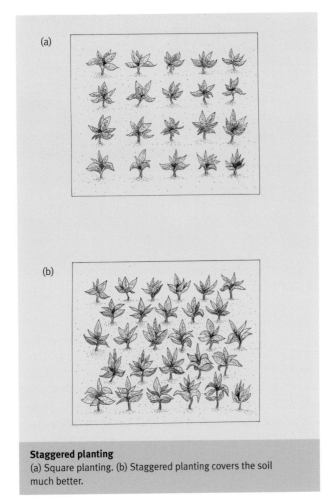

Staggered planting
(a) Square planting. (b) Staggered planting covers the soil much better.

Using polycultures (plant mixtures)

By 'polycultures' I mean using more intimate mixtures of different species than in a planting of several large clumps of various species. You don't have to do this – designing your perennial/ground-cover layer as a series of varying areas with one species per area is perfectly valid, and should give good results. If you look in the wild in shady areas, you rarely find numerous species all growing together in the ground-cover layer; more often there are either large areas of virtually single species, or a mixture of just a few species growing together.

Advantages of polycultures

- A plant mixture utilises the soil space and sunlight more efficiently. Every species has its own root and shoot characteristics, which never overlap completely. By using the soil and sunlight to maximum efficiency, you will maximise the overall functions of this layer, including soil protection and maintenance.

- Plant mixtures increase the resilience of the perennial/ground-cover layer. By having several species in the cover, the whole is less susceptible to major damage from pests and diseases – if one plant suffers, the others are still likely to be OK. Similarly, the cover will be less susceptible to extremes of climate or occasional events such as grazing (e.g. by deer) or foot-traffic damage.

Disadvantages of polycultures

- With a plant mixture the efficiency of harvesting may decline. If both species in a two-plant polyculture are harvested from time to time, the harvesting will probably be more time-consuming than from a single-species plot. You could avoid this by choosing the less-accessible species for its functions of soil improvement or pest prevention (for example), rather than for being directly harvestable.

- Rarely, one plant may be detrimental to another: this is known as allelopathy. Where this occurs it is usually caused by a strongly aromatic plant, owing to some of the aromatic chemicals in the leaves.

- Using polycultures makes the design of this layer more complex and time-consuming.

Guidelines for creating perennial polycultures

When mixing plants, consider the following factors for each species.

- Relative heights: a lower plant must be more shade-tolerant to survive in a mixture.

- if you want to grow 'islands' of one species in a 'sea' of another, then try to choose plants of similar vigour, otherwise one might quickly outcompete the other.

- Light requirements.

- Spread and planting distance.

- Planting time: do they need to be planted together or can one be added at a later date? (It would need to be shade-tolerant if so.)

- Planting pattern – where to plant species relative to one another.

Plant types

Clumping perennials, small shrubs and spreading shrubs and perennials can all be mixed in various ways. Evergreen plants, whether perennial or shrubby, are great in terms of being efficient at covering the soil all year round and reducing nutrient losses through winter leaching.

At least one spreading/running type added to a mixture makes it much more efficient. This is because if any gaps in the cover appear (for example, a perennial plant dies, as they are apt to do sometimes) then the spreading plant can rapidly move – within weeks or a couple of months – to fill the gap before something weedy and undesirable establishes there.

Seasonal variations

Across a season different plants have different growth patterns, and it could be that in some periods only one plant is visible. An example of this that works well for me is a mixture of ramsons (*Allium ursinum*) and ground ivy (*Glechoma hederacea*). In midwinter, ramsons starts growing from a bulb and there is no sign of the ground ivy. The ramsons itself makes a good cover. In spring the ground ivy starts up beneath the ramsons. The ramsons flowers in late spring and starts to die back, vanishing by midsummer, while the ground ivy gets stronger and takes over the ground cover completely for the summer and autumn, before dying down in early winter.

To minimise harvesting complications from two or more crops grown interplanted, firstly mix species that grow at distinct different heights. It is also helpful to combine crops (whether leaf, fruit or whatever) that are harvested at different times, so you don't damage one while harvesting another.

Growing two clumping species together

Two different species of clumping perennials or shrubs are rarely the same size and vigour. This means that it is not usually a very good idea to just interplant two species alternately, A–B–A–B–A–B etc; what usually happens in this instance is that the more vigorous, early-growing, taller or denser plant gradually outcompetes the other, leading to the die-off of the lesser plant.

Usually the taller species will be the one forming 'islands', which need not be regularly spaced. The smaller species should be a little more shade-tolerant. Both species are best planted at the same time, and of course more plants are needed of the smaller species. Either species can be evergreen or deciduous.

If one of the clumping plants is a small shrub, then it may be advantageous to plant this a year before interplanting the second species, especially if the shrub is slow-growing – you don't want it outcompeted while it still growing to its full size. If you do plant young shrubs a year earlier, keep the ground in between mulched so that weeds cannot get in.

The following are two examples of two clumping species grown together.

Salvia officinalis, SAGE + Rumex scutatus, FRENCH SORREL

Sage is an evergreen, grey-leaved aromatic shrub about 60cm (2') high. French sorrel is a perennial that dies down in winter but grows rapidly in spring, forming a trailing mass of stems that soon cover the ground between and underneath the sage bushes.

Cynara cardunculus, CARDOON + *Origanum vulgare*, OREGANO

Cardoon is an evergreen Mediterranean vegetable, closely related to globe artichoke, which likes reasonable light conditions. It grows large and throws lots of shade beneath, though it is smaller in winter. There is plenty of space beneath for perennials that are able to take advantage of good light conditions in winter and spring. Oregano is a surprisingly shade-tolerant herb that does well in this situation.

Growing a clumping plant with a spreading/running plant

Again, the idea to aim for here is 'islands' of the clumping plant in a 'sea' of the spreading plant. If the clumping species is strong and vigorous then individual plants of it can form the islands; if it is less so then each island can be formed of a group of plants.

Because spreading plants move to colonise bare ground, they are generally planted quite widely and so are economical in terms of numbers needed – indeed, as long as

Siberian purslane (*Claytonia sibirica*) growing with orpine (*Sedum telephium*) – two clumping plants.

A better rule of thumb is to position plants of the more-competitive species among a larger number of the less-competitive species – think of it as islands of the more-competitive plant in a sea of the less-competitive plant.

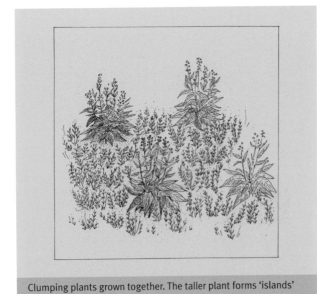

Clumping plants grown together. The taller plant forms 'islands' among the shorter one.

you can keep any bare ground mulched, you can pretty much vary the planting distance for these according to how many plants you have.

The two species can be planted at the same time, or the clumping species planted a year in advance (this may be necessary if the clumper is a slower-growing shrub).

Golden garlic (*Allium moly*), a clump-former, growing with strawberry (*Fragaria* x *biflora*), a runner.

A clumping plant interplanted with a widely spaced spreader.

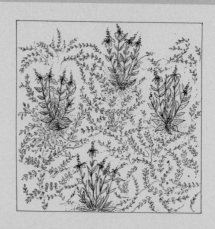

The spreader rapidly infills the gaps between the clumping plant.

Sweet cicely (*Myrrhis odorata*), a clumper, growing with a base cover of false strawberry (*Duchesnea indica*).

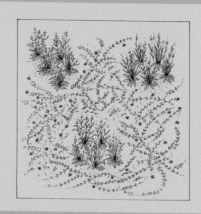

Narrower clumper planted with a runner. A group of the clumping plants are best planted together to make more substantial 'islands' within the runner.

Again, either can be deciduous or evergreen. The clumping species must be taller than the running one, otherwise it is likely to get outcompeted. The running species obviously needs to be more shade-tolerant then the clumper. Some examples are given below.

Angelica sylvestris, WILD ANGELICA + *Mentha suaveolens*, APPLE MINT
Angelica is a very tall perennial – 2.5m (8') – and is not worried about competition. The apple mint survives beneath it, thriving especially in late winter and spring when it is growing earlier than the angelica.

Claytonia sibirica, SIBERIAN PURSLANE + *Mentha* Bowles's mint, BOWLES'S MINT
Bowles's mint is the taller of these two, like all mints a spreader but not forming a thick cover; rather putting up sporadic stems each year. The Siberian purslane is very shade-tolerant and thrives beneath the mint, and in the UK is evergreen except in very dry or very cold conditions, when it dies back to a bulb.

Siberian purslane (*Claytonia sibirica*), a clumper, growing with Bowles's mint (*Mentha* Bowles's mint), a spreader.

Crambe maritime, SEA KALE + *Rubus tricolor*, CHINESE BRAMBLE
Most brassicas need lots of space to develop; however, this leaves a lot of potential bare ground beneath. Chinese bramble is the most vigorous groundcover raspberry, and perennials planted within it need to be tall and rugged to get through to the light each year. Comfreys (*Symphytum* spp.) also do well with Chinese bramble.

Phormium colensoi, MOUNTAIN FLAX + *Rubus nepalensis*, NEPALESE RASPBERRY
The lower-growing groundcover raspberry here makes a fine cover, and it is easy to grow through it perennials and small shrubs that are moderately vigorous. I have this mixture in a very shady spot.

Growing two spreading species together

There is more potential in this case for one species to dominate and outcompete the other, so this combination tends to work only when either the two species are very similar in vigour and habit, or when one is evergreen, shade-tolerant and less vigorous while the other is deciduous and more vigorous.

Plant both species at the same time – spacing is not terribly important as both will move. Two examples are given below.

Fragaria vesca, WILD STRAWBERRY + *Duchesnea indica*, FALSE STRAWBERRY
These are plants of similar habit: perennial plants with rooting runners. Both are semi-evergreen and grow to the same height.

Mentha x piperita, PEPPERMINT + *Rubus nepalensis*, NEPALESE RASPBERRY
Although peppermint is a spreading plant, it does not readily form a thick cover; more often a random sporadic scattering of stems arise later in spring. These easily come up through the low Nepalese raspberry, which, being evergreen, keeps the soil covered in good condition.

Annual squash patch surrounded by soapwort (*Saponaria officinalis*).

Chapter 17

Annuals, biennials and climbers

These plants need careful positioning to be able to thrive in forest gardens (see Chapter 18 for more information). Note that, although I use the terms annuals, biennials and perennials, in the real world the distinctions are sometimes a little less simple than that. Some annuals (known as hardy annuals) overwinter and thus live through parts of two growing seasons – but they live for no longer than a year. Some perennials may live for only a few years and occasionally be biennial. Nevertheless, one has to draw a line somewhere for practical design purposes.

Annuals and biennials

These groups of course include most of the 'conventional' vegetables that people grow, most of which I am not going to list here. Most conventional vegetables originate from sunny areas – seashore regions, the Mediterranean, Central America, etc. – and require full sun conditions to thrive. A number of the species listed here are well known as 'weeds' – but not everyone knows that some have good edible qualities.

Ground-cover ratings in this chapter refer to cover when the plants are growing strongly, but of course none of these species function as long-term ground-covers.

Note: The deciduous/evergreen ratings given here for hardy annuals and biennials should be interpreted as deciduous = bare over the single winter; evergreen = green over the single winter.

Alliaria petiolata, **GARLIC MUSTARD / JACK-BY-THE-HEDGE**

....

Deciduous/Evergreen: D **Zone:** 5
Sun/shade preference: ◗
Shade tolerance: ◗
Performance rating: ✓✓✓
Fertility: SF
Cover: ✓ **Flowers:** White

This is a European biennial, sometimes living longer than 2 years. The top dies back in the winter.

Size: 1-1.2m (3-4') high and 30cm (1') wide when flowering.
Cultivation: Broadcast seed in spring or transplant young plants in late spring. Most soils are fine – it tolerates some waterlogging.
Uses: The leaves have a garlic/mustard flavour, good in salads and soups. They get increasingly fiery as the season progresses. The seeds can be used as a fiery mustard-like spice.
Harvest and storage: Leaves in spring; seed in summer.
Cooking/processing: By late spring the leaves are too fiery to eat raw and are better cooked in soups, stews, etc.
Secondary uses: Attracts butterflies.
Propagation: By seed.
Maintenance: None required.

273

Amphicarpaea bracteata, HOG PEANUT

Deciduous/Evergreen: D   **Zone:** 5
Sun/shade preference: ◑
Shade tolerance: ◐
Performance rating: ✓✓✓
Fertility: SF
Cover: ✓   **Flowers:** Pinkish-white

This is a twining North American annual plant (often mistakenly classed as perennial). Interestingly, it forms two types of flowers, one type on the upper growth and one type low down. The low ones produce a pod that buries itself just below soil level.

Size: Up to 1.5m (5') high.
Cultivation: Raise young plants and transplant in late spring. Tolerates most soils, including acid ones.
Uses: Nitrogen fixer. Both the below- and above-ground seeds are edible. Below-ground seeds can be up to 15mm (0.6") diameter; above-ground seeds are smaller.
Harvest and storage: Harvest above-ground seeds in autumn and below-ground seeds in autumn and winter. Dry well to store.
Cooking/processing: Dried seeds, like all legumes, will require cooking. The underground seeds can be eaten raw (they are bean-flavoured) if soft enough.
Secondary uses: Bee plant.
Propagation: By seed.
Maintenance: Little required. Plant towards the southern side of shrubs that it can climb up.

Arctium lappa & A. minus, BURDOCKS

Deciduous/Evergreen: D   **Zone:** 3/5
Sun/shade preference: ○
Shade tolerance: ◐
Performance rating: ✓✓✓
Fertility: SF
Cover: ✓✓   **Flowers:** Pink

Burdocks are deep-rooted biennial plants from Europe and Asia. In some parts of the world, e.g. Japan, burdock is well know as a root vegetable and widely cultivated for

its one-year-old roots. The tops die back in winter. *A. lappa* is hardy to zone 3; *A. minus* to zone 5.

Size: 2m (6'6") high when flowering in their second year.
Cultivation: Sow seed in spring in situ or in pots and transplant in late spring in any reasonably well-drained soil.
Uses: The roots are cooked as a vegetable (of course, this makes it in effect an annual plant).
Harvest and storage: Roots dug in winter from one-year-old plants.
Cooking/processing: Roots are cooked by boiling or roasting.
Secondary uses: Bee and butterfly plant. Mineral accumulator.
Propagation: By seed (not dormant).
Maintenance: None required.

Barbarea verna, LAND CRESS

Deciduous/Evergreen: D   **Zone:** 6
Sun/shade preference: ○
Shade tolerance: ◐
Performance rating: ✓✓✓
Fertility: SF
Cover: ✗   **Flowers:** Yellow

This is a European biennial of the Brassicaceae family, quite often cultivated in vegetable gardens. The tops die back in winter.

Size: 60cm (2') high and 30cm (1') wide.
Cultivation: Sow outside in spring into any moist but well-drained soil.
Uses: Young leaves are peppery, used in salads; older leaves can be cooked.
Harvest and storage: Spring and summer.
Cooking/processing: The leaves take very little time to cook.
Secondary uses: Bee plant.
Propagation: By seed (not dormant) – can be sown thickly.
Maintenance: None required.

Beta vulgaris subsp. *cicla*, SPINACH BEET / SWISS CHARD

Deciduous/Evergreen: E **Zone:** 7
Sun/shade preference: ◯
Shade tolerance: ◐
Performance rating: ✓✓✓
Fertility: SF
Cover: ✓✓ **Flowers:** Green

Spinach beet (or perpetual spinach) and Swiss chard (or just 'chard') – *B. vulgaris* subsp. *cicla* var. *flavescens* – are familiar vegetables. If flowering is prevented, chard can be maintained as a perennial for a few years. The tops remain green over winter in mild areas where temperatures do not drop below about -6°C (21°F).

Size: 60cm (2') high and 40cm (1'4") wide; 1.2-1.5m (4-5') high or more when flowering in their second year.
Cultivation: Sow outside in spring or transplant potted seedlings in late spring into any well-drained soil.
Uses: The leaves, including their thick leaf stalks in the case of chard, are a fine cooked vegetable.
Harvest and storage: Harvest leaves at any time of year.
Cooking/processing: Steam the leaves and leaf stalks and serve with a sauce, or use in a lasagne, etc.
Propagation: By seed. Can self-seed easily.
Maintenance: None required.

Beta vulgaris subsp. *maritima*, SEA BEET

Sea beet has annual, biennial and perennial forms. For full details see page 214, Chapter 15 (Herbaceous perennial and ground-cover species).

Calendula officinalis, POT MARIGOLD

Deciduous/Evergreen: D **Zone:** 6
Sun/shade preference: ◯
Shade tolerance: ◐
Performance rating: ✓✓✓
Fertility: SF
Cover: ✓✓ **Flowers:** Yellow

This well-known European annual has long been used as a medicinal plant, though I use it a lot in salads. It is very easy to grow.

Size: 50-70cm (1'8"-2'4") high and 30cm (1') wide.
Cultivation: Sow seed outside in spring or transplant potted seedlings in late spring. Fine in any soil.
Uses: The aromatic leaves, and the flower petals, are very fine in salads.
Harvest and storage: Leaves can be harvested in spring and summer; flowers in summer and autumn.
Secondary uses: Bee plant; attracts hoverflies; medicinal antiseptic, anti-inflammatory, etc. A very useful plant!
Propagation: By seed. Self-seeds easily.
Maintenance: None required.

Campanula rapunculus, RAMPION

Deciduous/Evergreen: D **Zone:** 4
Sun/shade preference: ◯
Shade tolerance: ◐
Performance rating: ✓✓✓
Fertility: SF
Cover: ✓ **Flowers:** Blue

Rampion is a European biennial, once widely grown in England, Germany and other countries for its roots. The tops die down over winter.

Size: 30cm (1') high and wide in its first year; 1m (3') high when flowering in its second year.
Cultivation: Sow seed outside in spring or transplant potted seedlings late spring. Fine in any soil.
Uses: Mainly as a root crop: the roots are used after one year, before the plant flowers. Each plant forms a single large tap-root that can be up to 30cm (12")long and 2cm (0.8") wide.
Harvest and storage: Harvest roots at any time over winter.

Cooking/processing: The roots are cooked (boil or steam for 10-15 minutes), and have a sweet walnut flavour. They are bitter when raw.

Secondary uses: Bee plant. The young basal leaves are edible, like other *Campanula* leaves, in salads – nice, though older leaves can be tough. The young shoots in spring can be used as a cooked vegetable.

Propagation: By seed. If sowing outside, sow rows 22cm (9") apart and thin plants to 10cm (4") in the row.

Maintenance: Cut off any flowerheads that form in the first year, to maximise root size.

Cardamine flexuosa, WAVY BITTERCRESS & *C. hirsuta*, HAIRY BITTERCRESS

Deciduous/Evergreen: D **Zone:** 4
Sun/shade preference: ◯
Shade tolerance: ◖
Performance rating: ✓✓✓
Fertility: SF
Cover: ✗ **Flowers:** White

These European annuals flower and set seed very quickly. They are often a 'weed' in potted plants in nurseries, and will self-seed wherever there is bare soil.

Size: 30-45cm (1'-1'4") high and 20cm (8") wide.
Cultivation: Broadcast seed on bare soil from spring to autumn. Fine in any soil.
Uses: The leaves and stalks have a mustardy flavour and are good in salads.
Harvest and storage: Harvest leaves/stalks at any time of year.
Propagation: By seed. Self-seeds easily.
Maintenance: None required.

Claytonia perfoliata (syn. *Montia perfoliata*), WINTER PURSLANE / MINER'S LETTUCE

Deciduous/Evergreen: E **Zone:** 4
Sun/shade preference: ◯
Shade tolerance: ◖
Performance rating: ✓✓
Fertility: SF
Cover: ✓✓ **Flowers:** Pink

This is a hardy American annual that usually overwinters in the UK. The name 'miner's lettuce' comes from its being a staple green for the miners in the 1849 California gold rush.

Size: 30cm (1') high and wide.
Cultivation: Sow seed outside in spring or autumn in any moist soil.
Uses: The leaves and stems are good in salads, and can also be cooked.
Harvest and storage: Leaves are used in autumn, winter and spring.
Cooking/processing: The leaves are added to soups, stews, etc. and take only a few minutes to cook.
Propagation: By seed. Self-seeds readily.
Maintenance: None required.

Lathyrus odoratus, SWEET PEA

Deciduous/Evergreen: D **Zone:** 9
Sun/shade preference: ◯
Shade tolerance: ◖
Performance rating: ✓✓✓
Fertility: SF
Cover: ✗ **Flowers:** Purple; varieties various

The annual sweet pea is a well-known ornamental garden plant, with many cultivars selected for flowering characteristics.

Size: Up to 2-3m (6'6"-10') high; an annual tendril climber.
Cultivation: Sow in spring – protect from mice. Fine in any moist soil.

Uses: Nitrogen fixer.
Secondary uses: Bee plant. Like other *Lathyrus* species (see pages 283-284), the young seeds are a tasty snack in moderation (however, they contain a toxin that can accumulate and cause illness if a lot are eaten). Often used as a cut flower.
Propagation: By seed. Needs to be raised each year and planted out.
Maintenance: Little required once plants have started to climb.

Lunaria annua, **HONESTY**

Deciduous/Evergreen: E   Zone: 8
Sun/shade preference: ◐
Shade tolerance: ◑
Performance rating: ✓✓✓
Fertility: SF
Cover: ✓   Flowers: Blue

Honesty is a hardy Northern European biennial, often overwintering in a green state.

Size: 60cm (2') high and 30cm (1') wide.
Cultivation: Sow in spring and transplant when young into any soil, though it prefers neutral or alkaline soils. Fast-growing, drought-tolerant.
Uses: The leaves, flowers and taproots are eaten.
Harvest and storage: Leaves are harvested in late summer through to spring; flowers in late spring and summer; roots in winter.
Cooking/processing: The leaves and flowers are succulent and tender, with a mustard flavour – excellent in salads. The taproots, 6-10cm (2.5-4") x 1-1.5cm (0.4-0.6") are eaten raw or cooked, and taste like radish.
Secondary uses: Good bee and butterfly plant.
Propagation: By seed. Self-seeds readily.
Maintenance: None required.

Malva pusilla, **SMALL MALLOW &** *M. verticillata*, **CHINESE MALLOW**

Deciduous/Evergreen: D   Zone: 5
Sun/shade preference: ◐
Shade tolerance: ◑
Performance rating: ✓✓
Fertility: SF
Cover: ✓   Flowers: White & pink

These species are annuals, although *M. verticillata* has perennial forms too – see page 224, Chapter 15 (Herbaceous perennial and ground-cover species).

Size: 50-80cm (1'8"-2'8") high and 30cm (1') wide when flowering.
Cultivation: Sow outside in spring in any reasonable soil.
Uses: The leaves and flowers are good in salads.
Harvest and storage: Harvest leaves through the growing season; flowers in summer.
Cooking/processing: The leaves are mucilaginous and thicken soups, stews, etc.
Secondary uses: Bee plants.
Propagation: By seed.
Maintenance: None required.
Cultivars: *M. verticillata* 'Crispa' has leaves with curled edges.

Medicago lupulina, **BLACK MEDICK**

Deciduous/Evergreen: E   Zone: 5
Sun/shade preference: ◐
Shade tolerance: ◑
Performance rating: ✓✓✓
Fertility: SF
Cover: ✓✓   Flowers: Yellow

This legume is quite often used as a green manure crop. It can overwinter in milder areas and become biennial.

Size: 30cm (1') high and 20cm (8") wide.
Cultivation: Broadcast seed from spring to autumn into any reasonable well-drained soil.
Uses: Very good nitrogen fixer. The sprouted seeds are edible.
Harvest and storage: Harvest seed in autumn.

Cooking/processing: The seeds can be sprouted like other legume seeds.
Secondary uses: Bee plant.
Propagation: By seed – usually broadcast.
Maintenance: None required.

Oxalis tuberosa, OCA

Deciduous/Evergreen: D **Zone:** 9
Sun/shade preference: ◐
Shade tolerance: ◐
Performance rating: ✓
Fertility: SF
Cover: ✓✓ **Flowers:** Yellow

Oca is a tuberous, bushy, South American perennial. It is a very widely grown tuber crop in South America, but in all but the mildest regions in the UK it needs to be grown as a replanted annual rather than as a perennial, as the tubers are hardy to only about -5°C (23°F) soil temperature. It only starts forming tubers in late summer, so needs a long frost-free autumn to crop well.

Size: 30cm (1') high and wide.
Cultivation: Plant tubers in pots in early spring, transplanting outside after the last frosts. Likes a well-drained, fertile soil.
Uses: The tubers are excellent for eating raw or cooked. They have a sweet-acid flavour and crisp texture when raw, but lose the acidity – which is oxalic acid – if left out in the sun for a few days.
Harvest and storage: Harvest tubers carefully in autumn after the first frosts. They store well in a cool dark place.
Cooking/processing: Boil or roast for 10-15 minutes, when the tubers taste like slightly acid potatoes – very nice.
Propagation: By tubers – in spring, replant some of the tubers harvested in the autumn and stored over winter.
Maintenance: Usually dug up in autumn and replanted in spring, as the plants are tender.

Sisymbrium officinale, HEDGE MUSTARD

Deciduous/Evergreen: D **Zone:** 5
Sun/shade preference: ◑
Shade tolerance: ◐
Performance rating: ✓✓✓
Fertility: SF
Cover: ✓ **Flowers:** Yellow

An annual plant from Europe and North Africa, this is often regarded as a weed but has a long history of culinary use.

Size: 90cm (3') high and 30cm (1') wide.
Cultivation: Sow or broadcast seed in spring. Fine in any soil.
Uses: The young leaves and tops of young flowering shoots are mustardy and used in salads when young or cooked when older. The seed is used as a mustardy spice.
Harvest and storage: Harvest leaves and shoots in spring; seed in summer.
Cooking/processing: The leaves get hotter as they age. Older leaves can be too hot raw and are better cooked in soups, stews, etc.
Secondary uses: Bee plant.
Propagation: By seed.
Maintenance: None required.

Smallianthus sonchifolia (syn. Polymnia edulis, P. sonchifolia), YACON

Deciduous/Evergreen: D **Zone:** 9
Sun/shade preference: ◑
Shade tolerance: ◐
Performance rating: ✓
Fertility: SF
Cover: ✓✓ **Flowers:** Yellow

Yacon is another tuberous perennial that is very widely grown in South America, but in all but the mildest regions in the UK it needs to be grown as a replanted annual rather than as a perennial, as the tubers are hardy to only about -5°C (23°F) soil temperature. It prefers a hot, humid climate.

Size: 1-2m (3'-6'6") high by 40cm (1'4") wide.
Cultivation: Plant tubers in spring – protect from late frosts. Likes a well-drained, fertile soil.
Uses: The tubers are excellent for eating raw or cooked, being sweet and crisp like an apple. Their starch is in the form of inulin (as in Jerusalem artichokes), and so is indigestible by many people, causing flatulence.
Harvest and storage: Harvest tubers carefully in autumn after the first frosts. They store well in a cool dark place. They can reach the size of a large potato.
Cooking/processing: Cook like potatoes. They are likely to induce flatulence!
Secondary uses: The flowers attract beneficial insects.
Propagation: By tubers planted in the spring.
Maintenance: Usually dug up in autumn and replanted in spring.

Alexanders (*Smyrnium olusatrum*).

Smyrnium olusatrum,
ALEXANDERS / BLACK LOVAGE

Deciduous/Evergreen: D   **Zone:** 5
Sun/shade preference: ◑
Shade tolerance: ●
Performance rating: ✓✓✓
Fertility: SF
Cover: ✓✓   **Flowers:** Greenish-yellow

A strong-growing European biennial, Alexanders was brought to Britain by the Romans as a pot-herb.

Size: 1.5m (5') high and 80cm (2'8") wide when flowering.
Cultivation: Broadcast seed in autumn or raise plants to transplant in winter. Fine in any soil.
Uses: The leaves are good in salads (in small amounts

– the flavour is strong) or cooked in stews, etc. They have a lovage-like flavour. The seeds have a similar flavour and are used as a condiment.
Harvest and storage: Leaves are harvested in spring; seed in autumn.
Cooking/processing: Even cooked, you don't need many leaves to impart flavour. The seeds should be ground to use as a spice.
Secondary uses: Attracts beneficial insects. The roots of one-year-old plants are cooked as a vegetable.
Propagation: By seed – can be broadcast where you want it.
Maintenance: None required.

Stellaria media, **CHICKWEED**

Deciduous/Evergreen: D   **Zone:** 5
Sun/shade preference: ○
Shade tolerance: ◐
Performance rating: ✓✓✓
Fertility: SF
Cover: ✓   **Flowers:** White

This is a common annual weed of European and American gardens. Its name relates to the fact that chickens love to eat it – and it is pretty good for humans too!

Size: 40cm (1'4").
Cultivation: Broadcast seed any time if you really need to! Fine in most cultivated soils.
Uses: The leaves and stems are nice in salads when young, and can be cooked when older.
Harvest and storage: Harvest leaves and stems throughout the growing season.
Cooking/processing: The leaves and stems take only a few minutes to cook by steaming and are good added to soups and omelettes.
Secondary uses: Bee plant. Mineral accumulator.
Propagation: By seed. Self-seeds in cultivated soil.
Maintenance: None required.

Nasturtium (*Tropaeolum majus*).

Tropaeolum majus, **NASTURTIUM**

Deciduous/Evergreen: D   Zone: 5
Sun/shade preference: ◐
Shade tolerance: ◐
Performance rating: ✓✓✓
Fertility: SF
Cover: ✓✓   Flowers: Red, orange, yellow

Nasturtium is an annual South American climber/scrambler; perennial in warm climates. There are climbing and bush forms. I prefer to grow climbing forms, which are better able to seek out sunnier spots.

Size: 3m (10') high.
Cultivation: Sow seed in pots in spring, transplanting after last frosts into any reasonable soil.
Uses: The leaves and flowers are great in salads, with a peppery flavour. The young seeds are also peppery and used as a substitute for capers in cooking and preserves.
Harvest and storage: Leaves can be harvested throughout the season; flowers in summer and autumn; seeds in autumn.
Secondary uses: Bee plant. Attracts beneficial insects.
Propagation: By seed. I raise some of this plant from seed each year in case it doesn't self-seed much.
Maintenance: Little required. You might need to stop climbing forms from smothering lower plants.

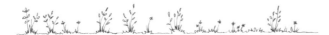

Ullucus tuberosus, **ULLUCO**

Deciduous/Evergreen: D   Zone: 9
Sun/shade preference: ○
Shade tolerance: ○
Performance rating: ✓
Fertility: SF
Cover: ✗   Flowers: Red

This tuberous South American perennial is a very widely grown tuber crop in its native region, but in all but the mildest regions in the UK it needs to be grown as a replanted annual rather than as a perennial, as the tubers are hardy to only about -5°C (23°F) soil temperature. It only starts forming tubers in early autumn, so needs a long frost-free autumn to crop well.

Size: 30cm (1') high and wide.
Cultivation: Start tubers in pots in spring, transplanting out after last frosts. Likes a well-drained, fertile soil.
Uses: The tubers, small-potato sized, are excellent for eating raw or cooked. They have a crisp, nutty flavour.
Harvest and storage: Harvest tubers carefully in autumn after the first frosts. They store well in a cool dark place.
Cooking/processing: Roast or boil the tubers like potatoes.
Secondary uses: The leaves are edible as a spinach.
Propagation: By tubers, like potatoes, planted in spring.
Maintenance: Usually dug up in autumn and replanted in spring, as the plants are tender.

Vicia sativa, **VETCH / TARES**

Deciduous/Evergreen: E   Zone: 5
Sun/shade preference: ○
Shade tolerance: ◐
Performance rating: ✓✓✓
Fertility: SF
Cover: ✓✓✓   Flowers: White & purple

Vetch, or tares, is an annual European scrambler. Most other vetches, some of which are perennial, can be used similarly. They like situations in hedges where they get some sun.

Size: Scrambling; can reach 1.2m (4') high, but is often much smaller.
Cultivation: Broadcast seed in spring and rake into soil. Fine in any reasonable soil.
Uses: The young shoots are eaten in moderation in salads or cooked. The green seeds are succulent and delicious. Like the sweet pea family (*Lathyrus* spp., see page 283), when eaten in large quantities as a famine food some health problems have ensued. However, in small quantities there is no problem.
Harvest and storage: Young shoots can be picked in early spring; green seeds in summer.
Cooking/processing: Steam young shoots for a few minutes. Green seeds can be eaten raw or steamed for a few minutes.
Secondary uses: Bee plant. Nitrogen fixing.
Propagation: By seed.
Maintenance: None required.

Herbaceous perennial climbers

These climbing plants die back to the ground each winter, although they may leave tough dead stems in place, which help them climb next season. If they don't have anything to climb they tend to form a thick mound and can be valuable ground-covering plants, hence the ground-cover ratings given in this section. Bear in mind, though, that if you are relying on them for ground cover and they do find a route to climb, they will soon put most of their energy into climbing and lose ground-cover value.

Most of these climbers are forest-edge plants, liking their roots in a moist humus-rich soil and preferring to climb or scramble upwards to find more light.

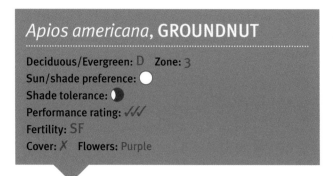

Apios americana, **GROUNDNUT**

Deciduous/Evergreen: D   Zone: 3
Sun/shade preference: ◯
Shade tolerance: ◖
Performance rating: ✓✓✓
Fertility: SF
Cover: ✗   Flowers: Purple

This is a twining, tuberous North American perennial vine (don't confuse it with peanut, *Arachis hypogaea,* which is also sometimes called groundnut). It produces strings of

tubers radiating underground from the mother plant; each tuber up to 5-6cm (2-2.5") in diameter, but often walnut-sized.

Size: 2.5m (8') high and 30cm (1') wide.
Cultivation: Plant tubers late winter or raise in pots and transplant in spring into any moist soil. Tolerates acid soils.
Uses: The tubers are eaten cooked.
Harvest and storage: Tubers can be harvested all year.
Cooking/processing: The starchy tubers are cooked much like potatoes – boil for 10-15 minutes. The flavour resembles peanut and potato.
Secondary uses: Bee plant and nitrogen-fixing plant.
Propagation: From tubers.
Maintenance: Little required. May take 2-3 years to establish. Plant towards the southern side of shrubs that it can climb up.

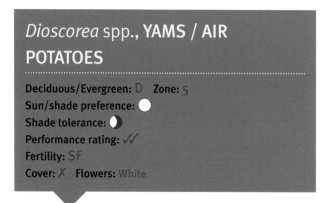

Dioscorea spp., **YAMS / AIR POTATOES**

Deciduous/Evergreen: D   Zone: 5
Sun/shade preference: ◯
Shade tolerance: ◖
Performance rating: ✓✓
Fertility: SF
Cover: ✗   Flowers: White

In temperate climes most people think of yams as tropical plants that we can't even consider here, but this is not true. There are several species that grow as perennial climbers in cooler climates, dying back in winter to an underground root or tuber, which is edible. Species for temperate regions include *D. batatas* (cinnamon vine / Chinese yam) and *D. japonica* (Japanese yam).

Some yams are also called air potatoes, because they form round aerial 'tubers', one from each leaf axil, which can easily be harvested. These mini-tubers (I call them yamlets) can be cooked and eaten in exactly the same way as the underground tuber, though they don't get as large. With *D. japonica* and *D. batatas* the aerial tubers grow to about 1cm (0.4") diameter, but the plants produce lots of them. *D. bulbifera* (air potato) forms larger aerial tubers, though I haven't grown this one yet and it may need warmer summers than we currently get in the UK. (It is considered a weed in parts of the southern USA.) Yams are twining vines, best planted on the southern side of large shrubs so that they can scramble up into better light conditions.

Size: 4m+ (13'+) in height and 30cm (1') wide.
Cultivation: Plant tubers in pots, planting out after the last frosts. Prefers a well-drained, humus-rich, moist soil.
Uses: Both the underground and aerial tubers can be eaten.
Harvest and storage: Harvest aerial tubers in late summer and autumn; underground tubers in winter. Tubers will store in a barely moist medium (sand, etc.) in cool temperatures through the winter. They will also store well loose in a fridge.
Cooking/processing: Both sorts of tubers can be boiled, fried or baked – they have a floury texture and a mild but very nice flavour.
Propagation: From aerial tubers.
Maintenance: None required.

Sweet tea vine (*Gynostemma pentaphyllum*).

Gynostemma pentaphyllum,
SWEET TEA VINE

Deciduous/Evergreen: D   Zone: 7
Sun/shade preference: ◗
Shade tolerance: ●
Performance rating: ✓✓✓✓
Fertility: M/F
Cover: ✓ Flowers: Unknown

Sweet tea vine is a Chinese perennial tendril climber, highly valued in China for its medicinal properties.

Size: 3m (10') high or more.
Cultivation: Plant pot-grown plants in winter or spring (comes quite late into growth). Likes any moist but well-drained soil and a position where it can clamber up a shrub or fence.
Uses: The leaves are harvested and used medicinally, being antioxidant and adaptogenic. They are usually made into herb teas. They have a 'woody' flavour, and are best mixed with other herbs to make a flavoursome tea.
Harvest and storage: The leaves can be harvested in summer and early autumn and dried for storage.
Propagation: Easiest by division or layering. Plants do not produce much seed, and both male and female plants are needed for fruiting.
Maintenance: Little required.

Hablitzia tamnoides,
CAUCASIAN SPINACH

Deciduous/Evergreen: D   Zone: 4
Sun/shade preference: ◖
Shade tolerance: ◖
Performance rating: ✓✓✓
Fertility: SF
Cover: ✗ Flowers: Pale yellow

This is a scrambling perennial climber from the Caucasus.

Size: 3m (10') high or more; 30cm (1') wide.
Cultivation: Transplant potted plants in winter or early spring into any moist, well-drained soil.
Uses: The steamed shoots make a nice spinach-like vegetable.
Harvest and storage: The leaves and young shoots are mainly harvested in the spring. The plant comes very early into growth and the shoots are frost-tolerant.
Propagation: By division, layering or seed. Plants do not produce much seed.
Maintenance: Little required.

Female flowers – 'cones' – of hop (*Humulus lupulus*).

Humulus lupulus, HOP

Deciduous/Evergreen: D **Zone:** 5
Sun/shade preference: ◯
Shade tolerance: ◐
Performance rating: ✓✓✓
Fertility: M/F
Cover: ✗ **Flowers:** Pale green

Hop (*Humulus lupulus*) 'Fuggle'.

Lathyrus latifolius & *L. sylvestris,* PERENNIAL SWEET PEAS

Deciduous/Evergreen: D **Zone:** 5
Sun/shade preference: ◯
Shade tolerance: ◐
Performance rating: ✓✓
Fertility: SF
Cover: ✗ **Flowers:** Pinkish-purple

Hop is a twining European perennial climber. Many full-size varieties, e.g. 'Fuggle' and 'Mathon', are selected for brewing. A good dwarf variety, growing 2.5m (8') high, is 'First Gold': this has the advantage that the crop is easily within reach, while the yield is almost the same as that of a traditional variety twice its height.

Size: Vigorous varieties can reach 6m (20') high.
Cultivation: Transplant pot-grown plants in winter (it comes into growth quite early). Likes any moist, well-drained soil.
Uses: The female flowers ('cones') are used in brewing beer.
Harvest and storage: Cones are harvested in early to mid-autumn.
Secondary uses: The young shoots can be cooked as a vegetable.
Propagation: By root cuttings, division or layering.
Maintenance: Little required. Old stems can be left in place for new ones to climb up.

Sweet peas are scrambling European tendril climbers. The perennial species interplant with other perennials very well, climbing up them to get at the light. *Lathyrus latifolius* (everlasting pea) and *L. sylvestris* (wood pea) are perennial.

Size: 1-3m (3-10') high and 15cm (6") wide.
Cultivation: Transplant potted plants in winter or early spring into any well-drained soil that is not too acid.
Uses: Mainly as a nitrogen-fixing interplant. The young peas inside the pods are delicious, tasting just like garden peas, *but should be eaten only in small quantities as they contain a toxin that can accumulate in the body, and in large amounts can cause serious illness* (this has occurred only in famine situations).
Harvest and storage: Pick pods in summer.
Cooking/processing: The young 'peas' are delicious raw, and could be cooked but it isn't really worth it for the quantities obtained.
Secondary uses: Bee plants. I like eating the seeds in the young pods, but see note above re toxicity.

Propagation: By seed; scarification helps.
Maintenance: None required.

Wood pea (*Lathyrus sylvestris*) interplanted with apple mint (*Mentha suaveolens*).

Lathyrus tuberosus, EARTHNUT PEA

Deciduous/Evergreen: D   **Zone:** 6
Sun/shade preference: ◐
Shade tolerance: ◖
Performance rating: ✓
Fertility: SF
Cover: ✗   **Flowers:** Pink

This is a scrambling European perennial tendril climber. The tubers are edible, though rather small. I have had trouble with mice eating the tubers in the ground.

Size: 1.2m (4') high and 15cm (6") wide.
Cultivation: Transplant potted plants in spring into any well-drained soil that is not too acid. Protect from mice.
Uses: The tubers are eaten cooked. They do not contain the toxic materials found in the seeds and foliage of *Lathyrus* species.
Harvest and storage: Tubers are harvested in winter when tops have died down. They are usually 2-3cm (about 1") in diameter.
Cooking/processing: Cook the tubers by boiling or roasting – they taste like sweet potatoes.
Secondary uses: Bee plant.
Propagation: By seed or tubers.
Maintenance: Watch out for slugs and mice eating the plants.

Passiflora incarnata, MAYPOP

Deciduous/Evergreen: D   **Zone:** 6
Sun/shade preference: ○
Shade tolerance: ◖
Performance rating: ✓✓
Fertility: SF
Cover: ✗   **Flowers:** Blue & white

This North American tendril perennial climber Is one of the passion fruit species. It is late to emerge in spring (hence the name).

Size: up to 5m (16') high and 40cm (1'4") wide.
Cultivation: Plant out potted plants in late spring after last frosts. Likes a well-drained soil; acid or neutral.
Flowering: Ornamental flowers appear in early summer; bee-pollinated.
Fruiting: Fruits ripen September to November.
Uses: The fruit pulp is edible with a nice flavour.
Harvest and storage: Fruit is harvested in autumn.
Secondary uses: Bee plant.
Propagation: By seed or layering.
Maintenance: None.

Tropaeolum tuberosum, MASHUA

Deciduous/Evergreen: D   **Zone:** 8
Sun/shade preference: ○
Shade tolerance: ◖
Performance rating: ✓
Fertility: SF
Cover: ✗   **Flowers:** Yellow

Mashua is a scrambling tuberous South American perennial climber. It needs a long summer season to produce good-sized tubers.

Size: 2m (6'6") high or more; 40cm (16") wide.
Cultivation: Plant tubers in late winter / early spring. Likes a moist, well-drained soil; acid or neutral.
Uses: The tubers are used as a cooked vegetable, and have a peppery flavour.
Harvest and storage: Tubers are dug in late autumn and winter.
Cooking/processing: Roast or boil the tubers like potatoes.

Secondary uses: Bee plant. Edible leaves and flowers like other nasturtiums.
Propagation: By seed or tubers.
Maintenance: In cold winter areas the tubers may die if left in the ground, so if this is a risk they should be lifted in autumn and stored in moist sand over winter before replanting in spring.

Vicia sylvatica, **WOOD VETCH**

Deciduous/Evergreen: D   **Zone:** 3
Sun/shade preference: ○
Shade tolerance: ◐
Performance rating: ✓✓✓
Fertility: SF
Cover: ✗   **Flowers:** White & purple

A tendril climber native to many parts of Europe and Asia, wood vetch is one of a large number of vetches that are all good nitrogen fixers. Some vetches are small and have trouble persisting in semi-shade, but wood vetch is tall enough that it can climb into better light conditions.

Size: Up to 2m (6'6") high.
Cultivation: Raise plants to transplant in late spring. Likes a moist, well-drained soil.
Uses: Nitrogen fixer. Edible seeds in small quantities (vetches, like *Lathyrus* species, contain toxins that can accumulate if you eat lots of them).
Harvest and storage: Seeds can be collected in autumn.
Cooking/processing: The seeds make a nice raw nibble. Dry seeds can be cooked.
Secondary uses: Bee plant.
Propagation: By seed.
Maintenance: Little required.

Woody climbers

All woody climbers can also be used for facade insulation: when they are grown against the wall of a building they will increase the insulation value of the wall, and so help keep the building warmer in winter and cooler in summer. Some tendril climbers (*Akebia*, *Parthenocissus*, *Vitis*) can also damage walls that have loose or old render, so should be avoided in such locations. All the climbers listed below can damage roof tiles if they are allowed to get to the top of a wall and start to grow in

between tiles, so they should be stopped before they get to the roof line.

As with the herbaceous perennial climbers, if they cannot climb then these woody climbers tend to make a mound and can function as ground-covers – hence the ground-cover ratings.

Purple hardy kiwi (*Actinidia arguta* var. *purpurea*).

Actinidia arguta, A. deliciosa &
A. kolomikta, **KIWIS**

Deciduous/Evergreen: D   **Zone:** 2/7
Sun/shade preference: ○
Shade tolerance: ◐
Performance rating: ✓✓✓
Fertility: M/F
Cover: ✗   **Flowers:** White

A. deliciosa is the well-known 'fuzzy' kiwi fruit. *A. arguta* and *A. kolomikta* are called the hardy kiwis. The hardy kiwis are, in my opinion, even nicer than the standard hairy kiwi fruits: the fruits are smaller, some 3.5cm (1.4") long, but are smooth-skinned with a tender skin and wonderful flavour. Hardy kiwis do not need as much summer heat to ripen the fruits as the fuzzy kiwi. They are all vigorous twining vines, and all native to Asian forests. The two hardy species will normally cross-pollinate. The details below cover all three species – the main difference is hardiness, with *A. deliciosa* hardy to zone 7 and the hardy kiwis to zone 2.

Size: 30m (100') into trees if you let them!
Cultivation: Plant pot-grown shrubs in winter; fine in any soil. Protect from frosts, slugs and cats.

Flowering: Flowers (not showy) appear in late spring. All kiwi species are dioecious – plants are male or female, and both sexes must be present for fruiting to occur.

Fruiting: Fruits ripen September to November.

Uses: The fruits are excellent eaten fresh.

Harvest and storage: Fruits are harvested in autumn.

Cooking/processing: There is good potential for making fruit leathers from the fruits – the whole fruits can be liquidised (the seeds are tiny).

Secondary uses: Edible sap.

Propagation: By layering or softwood cuttings. You need one male vine for up to eight or so females, although self-fertile varieties exist.

Maintenance: Protect young plants from cats (who are attracted by chemicals in the leaves) and slugs/snails. All species are susceptible to spring frost damage in the UK, so do not locate in frost pockets. They will need pruning to keep within a manageable size.

Cultivars:

A. arguta:
Females:
Anna
var. *cordifolia* (syn. *Cordifolia*)
Geneva
Geneva 2
Jumbo
Kens Red
MSU
var. *purpurea* Sadowa
Weiki female
Males:
Meader
74-32
Weiki male
Self-fertile:
Issai

A. deliciosa:
Female:
Hayward
Male:
Atlas
Self-fertile:
Boskoop
Jenny

A. kolomikta:
Females:
Arctic Beauty
Dr Szymanowski
Red Beauty
Sientiabrskeja
Tomoko
Male:
Adam

Kiwi vines (*Actinidia arguta*) being trained up a coppiced silver lime tree (*Tilia tomentosa*).

Akebia quinata & A. trifoliata, CHOCOLATE VINE / THREE-LEAF AKEBIA

Deciduous/Evergreen: E   **Zone:** 5
Sun/shade preference: ○
Shade tolerance: ◐
Performance rating: ✓
Fertility: SS
Cover: ✓✓   **Flowers:** Purple

These are evergreen or semi-evergreen Asian twining climbers. Fruits of the chocolate vine can still be found for sale in Japanese markets. The name 'chocolate vine' comes from the purple-brownish colour and spicy scent of the flowers. In some warm-climate regions they are regarded as a pest.

Size: 5-10m (16-33') high and 40cm (1'4") wide.

Cultivation: Plant bare-rooted or pot-grown plants in winter (comes very early into growth). Fine in most soils.

Flowering: Spring.

Fruiting: Pods ripen September/October.

Uses: The pulp from the pods is edible raw, with a sweet watermelon-like flavour. Eat or spit out the seeds.

Harvest and storage: Harvest the fruit pods in autumn and use immediately.

Secondary uses: The stems are excellent basketry material. Shoots of both plants are widely used in Chinese herbal medicine.
Propagation: By seed or layering.
Maintenance: May need pruning to keep within a manageable size.

Clematis vitalba, OLD MAN'S BEARD / TRAVELLER'S JOY

Deciduous/Evergreen: D   Zone: 4
Sun/shade preference: ◖
Shade tolerance: ●
Performance rating: ✓✓
Fertility: SF
Cover: ✗   Flowers: Greenish-white

This is a vigorous European twining climber that can self-seed rather a lot.

Size: 10m (33') high or more.
Cultivation: Plant fluffy seeds in autumn or transplant young plants in winter. Fine in any soil.
Uses: The stems are a good basketry material.
Harvest and storage: Stems are harvested in winter.
Secondary uses: Bee plant.
Propagation: By seed.
Maintenance: Little required.

Lonicera periclymenum, HONEYSUCKLE / WOODBINE

Deciduous/Evergreen: D   Zone: 5
Sun/shade preference: ◖
Shade tolerance: ◖
Performance rating: ✓✓
Fertility: SF
Cover: ✗   Flowers: White & yellow

A twining European deciduous climber, honeysuckle is well known as a wild woodland and hedge plant.

Size: 4m (13') high.
Cultivation: Transplant young plants in winter. Fine in any soil.

Uses: The stems are a good basketry material.
Harvest and storage: Stems are harvested in winter.
Secondary uses: Bee plant.
Propagation: By seed.
Maintenance: Little required.

Parthenocissus quinquefolia, VIRGINIA CREEPER & *P. tricuspidata*, BOSTON IVY

Deciduous/Evergreen: D   Zone: 3
Sun/shade preference: ○
Shade tolerance: ●
Performance rating: ✓✓✓
Fertility: SF
Cover: ✓✓   Flowers: Green

These very vigorous tendril climbers are often grown against walls for their amazing reddish autumn leaf colours. All too often they are unmanaged in such situations and can easily cause roof tile damage.

Size: 20-30m (66-100') high or more.
Cultivation: Transplant young plants in winter. Fine in any soil.
Uses: The stems are a good basketry material.
Harvest and storage: Stems are harvested in winter.
Secondary uses: Bee plants.
Propagation: By seed or layering.
Maintenance: Can be very vigorous and require regular control.

Schisandra chinensis, MAGNOLIA VINE

Deciduous/Evergreen: D Zone: 4
Sun/shade preference: ◯
Shade tolerance: ◑
Performance rating: ✓✓
Fertility: SS
Cover: ✗ Flowers: Cream-pink

A twining climber from northern China and eastern Russia, magnolia vine has long been valued for its medicinal properties.

Size: 7m (23') high or more.
Cultivation: Transplant pot-grown plants in winter (comes early into growth). Fine in most soils; protect from slugs.
Flowering: Spring. The species is dioecious – plants are male or female, and both are needed for fruiting unless you grow the self-fertile cultivar 'Eastern Prince'.
Fruiting: Fruits ripen August–October.
Uses: The fruits are edible, with a nice balanced flavour – they are about the size of redcurrants, borne in bunches.
Harvest and storage: Fruits are harvested in autumn.
Secondary uses: An important Chinese medicinal plant, used as an adaptogen.
Propagation: By seed, layering or division.
Maintenance: Might need pruning to keep within a manageable size.

Vitis spp., GRAPES

Deciduous/Evergreen: D Zone: 5
Sun/shade preference: ◯
Shade tolerance: ◑
Performance rating: ✓✓✓
Fertility: SF
Cover: ✓✓ Flowers: Green

Grape vines are very vigorous tendril climbers. *Vitis vinifera* is the true grape vine – hybrid varieties are hybrids of this and various American and Russian species, which tend to be healthier. There are hundreds of varieties; those listed on the right suit UK conditions.

Size: 30m (100') up into trees!
Cultivation: Plant bare-rooted or pot-grown plants in winter or early spring. Prefers a moist, well-drained soil.
Flowering and fruiting: Flowers in mid to late spring; fruits ripen September–October.
Uses: The fruits are eaten fresh and made into juice and wine. The leaves are used in cooking.
Harvest and storage: Fruits are harvested in autumn; leaves throughout the season.
Secondary uses: Edible sap. The seeds are used as a source of oil, etc.
Propagation: By hardwood cuttings in winter, or layering. Can also be grafted on to rootstocks.
Maintenance: Will need pruning to keep within a manageable size (see Chapter 18).
Cultivars: These have not been separated into different species because most are complex hybrids and also because people usually refer to edible grape vines all as one group. Where the species is not given here, the vine is a hybrid.
Eating cultivars:
Red:
[*vinifera*] Black Prince
Black Strawberry
Brandt (Brant)
Fragole (Fragola)
Gagarin (Gagarin Blue)
Glenora (Glenora Seedless)
Kempsey Black
Marshall Joffre (Maréchal Joffre)
Regent
Reliance (seedless)
Rembrant
Rondo
Saturn (seedless)
Schuyler
[*purpurea*] Spetchley Park
Tereshkova
White:
Aurora
[*vinifera*] Chasselas Rose (Chasselas Rosé)
[*vinifera*] Lakemont (seedless)
Phoenix (Phönix)
Precoce de Malingre (Précoce de Malingre)
[*vinifera*] Reichensteiner
Zalagyongye (Zalagyöngye)
Wine cultivars:
Red:
Baco (Baco Noir)
[*vinifera*] Black Prince

Kempsey Black
Leon Millot (Léon Millot)
Marshall Joffre (Maréchal Joffre)
Rembrant
Rondo
Siebel (syn. Siebel 13053)
[*purpurea*] Spetchley Park
Triomphe d'Alsace
White:
Aurora (syn. Siebel 5279)
[*vinifera*] Bacchus
[*vinifera*] Chardonnay
[*vinifera*] Chasselas Rose (Chasselas Rosé)
[*vinifera*] Reichensteiner
Zalagyongye (Zalagyöngye)

Wisteria spp., WISTERIAS

Deciduous/Evergreen: D   **Zone:** 4-6
Sun/shade preference: ◯
Shade tolerance: ◖
Performance rating: ✓✓✓
Fertility: SF
Cover: ✓✓   **Flowers:** White, violet, blue

Wisterias are well known as ornamental climbers, usually seen trained against a wall, but they are just as easy to train into large trees. They can grow into large sturdy plants, so make sure the tree you train into is also sturdy and large enough. Wisterias are some of the few woody climbing nitrogen fixers, and can in effect turn a non-nitrogen-fixing tree into a nitrogen-fixing one. Species include *W. floribunda* (Japanese wisteria) and *W. sinensis* (Chinese wisteria).

Size: 6-10m+ (20-33'+) up into trees.
Cultivation: Plant pot-grown shrubs in winter or early spring. They prefer moist, well-drained soil, and don't require very fertile soil.
Uses: Nitrogen fixing.
Secondary uses: Bee plants. Treat reports of edible parts with great caution.
Propagation: By seed or hardwood cuttings. Flowering cultivars are often grafted.
Maintenance: Little required when trained into trees. Wisterias trained on walls will need regular pruning. Wisteria scale, a Chinese pest that turned up in the UK in 2001, can damage plants by sucking the sap, but in a diverse ecosystem should not be a problem.

Hop (*Humulus lupulus*) 'Fuggle' growing up an Italian alder (*Alnus cordata*).

Chapter 18

Designing with annuals, biennials and climbers

Annuals and biennials

These short-lived plants tend to require disturbed ground and therefore will survive in a forest garden only if:

- they can self-seed in shaded or part-shaded conditions *and* the seeds fall where the soil is bare or thinly covered with plant growth in spring. One of the aims of forest gardens is to have the soil covered with plant growth, so there is little bare soil, even in winter – thus it becomes a challenge for short-lived plants to persist.

- they are sown and/or raised and planted out each year. This is certainly worth considering, especially for desirable annuals that cannot self-seed successfully in a forest garden. I always raise a few nasturtiums and calendulas each year, as I value them highly in the garden.

Either way, maintaining areas of short-lived plants is nearly always more work from the gardener's point of view – mainly in terms of weeding, because when the plants die the bare soil is prone to weed infestation.

Annuals and biennials of course include most of the conventional vegetables. Most of these originated from habitats such as the seashore, or from Mediterranean or Central/South American climates, and require sunny conditions. Apart from a few exceptions, they will perform poorly in shade. Some people keep their annual vegetable patch entirely separate from their forest garden, but it is quite possible to integrate annual vegetables, either in one larger clearing or several smaller patches, where there are good light conditions. See Chapter 19 for information about the design of such spaces.

Climbers

Nowadays most gardeners and horticulturalists are used to creating or using physical structures such as walls, fences and trellises for climbing plants, and if you already have such structures in your forest garden or at the edges, you can certainly make use of them. A trellis or pergola structure may fit in well with a 'living space' within the forest garden. However, I prefer to mainly use more natural methods to support climbers – i.e. other plants. This is the way climbers used to be supported before the era of post-and-wire trellises.

CLIMBERS LIKE TO CLIMB

Climbers such as grape vines and kiwi vines will climb 30m (100') high into trees given the chance, and in this situation most of their fruit will be way out of reach from the ground. I do not advise training climbers so high, unless you (or your children) enjoy climbing near to the outer edge of trees to harvest!

Unless you are happy for them to grow like lush ground-covering plants, climbing perennials or woody vines can of course be introduced into the forest garden only when there is something for them to climb up. This means you might need to wait for 5-8 years before you introduce them.

Most climbers are woodland edge plants, which means they like to have their roots in a cool forest soil, and be able to climb up the edge of trees and shrubs towards the sun.

Herbaceous perennial climbers

These plants die back to the ground each winter, so they can never get to the heights that some of the woody climbers can. Hops can grow 6m (20') high, which is about as high as herbaceous perennial climbers can go.

Perennial climbers are best planted to the southern side of a suitable-sized shrub or tree, and allowed (with the help of training if needed) to climb and clamber into it. Ideally the shrub/tree will not be a fruiting plant itself, otherwise the fruit crop will be reduced by the extra shade competition of the climber. However, if the climber is not too vigorous then you'll still get a fruit crop on the shrub/tree. So for hops, which are vigorous, I train them up the south side of one of my Italian alder trees, on which I have deliberately left some lower branches facing roughly south. The hop, a twining climber, may initially need a pole or canes to grow up, and then it uses the branches to cling on to. A similar tree arrangement is used for some woody climbers and is illustrated on the right.

Plant the climber a little distance from the stem of the shrub/tree it is to climb up, to minimise root competition – 1m (3') is adequate, but it could be more, especially if the shrub is round in shape and large in diameter.

An easy alternative is to provide an annual structure for the perennial to climb, made out of canes, poles, etc., similar to what you would use for runner or climbing French beans.

Woody climbers

Fruiting woody climbers such as grape vines and kiwi vines tend to bear their crops mainly on young wood – which is why those growing up tall trees will tend to fruit high up in the tree. Therefore a strategy is required to keep the fruiting wood low. I use two main methods for growing and training woody climbers.

In the first method, support is provided by a larger tree, generally Italian alder (*Alnus cordata*) in my garden, which is nitrogen-fixing. I usually raise its canopy by pruning off the lower side branches, but if the tree is to be used for training a climber up, a number of branches are left (though trimmed shorter) on the southern side of the trunk, between about 1.8m (6') and 3m (10') high. The climber is trained up to these branches and side

shoots trained along the branches to form a permanent framework. The leaves of the climber are mainly in sun. Short fruiting spurs are allowed to grow each year from the permanent framework, and replacement spurs are left in winter when excess wood is pruned off. The fruits hang from the alder/climber 'mixed' branches and are easy to harvest. I mainly use this technique with grape vines.

Growing a climber into a tree. This grape vine has been trained into the low branches left deliberately on an Italian alder.

Alternatively, I use a coppiced tree as support for the climber, usually a lime tree. I grow limes (*Tilia* spp.) as leaf crops, and they are treated as shrubs, growing to 3-4m (10-13') high and wide rather than into large trees. In the UK, after planting a young tree, the first coppicing is after 6-8 years and after that every 4-5 years. I coppice high (i.e. in fact pollarding), cutting off all growth at a height of about 1.5m (5'), which safeguards the new shoots from deer browsing. Other coppiced trees, e.g. a coppiced nitrogen-fixing tree (e.g. mimosa, *Acacia dealbata*), could be used similarly for climber supports.

- The woody climber (I mostly use kiwi fruits, mainly the hardy kiwi species – see page 285, Chapter 17) is planted at the same time as the tree is coppiced (it can be the first coppicing or later one). Plant it a short distance (1-2m/3'-6'6") from the trunk of its support tree.

- The climber is trained into the centre of the tree via a pole or cane.

- The coppiced tree and the climber grow together, with the climber automatically sending out shoots to the better light conditions at the outer edges of the canopy, where it fruits.

- When the tree is coppiced again, the climber is also coppiced (at the same height as the tree) and the cycle starts again.

- You will lose one year of fruiting after coppicing, but this is a small price to pay for an easy and sustainable training system.

Growing a climber into a coppiced tree
(a) Lime tree is planted. (b) Four to six years later the tree is large enough to coppice. (c) The tree is coppiced high and male and female kiwi vines planted. (d) The kiwi vines grow towards the outer surface of the lime canopy and fruit there. (e) When the tree is next coppiced, the kiwis are coppiced too.

Various ancient and traditional agroforestry systems in Europe used trees for supporting grape vines. These included poplars, but also trees such as mulberries. Be aware, though, that picking grapes borne on the outer surface of a large mulberry tree would be quite difficult and time-consuming, involving moving large ladders around the tree. Also, the shading of the mulberry by vine leaves could be significant enough to affect the mulberry crop.

Other methods for supporting climbers exist and can be

Hardy kiwi (*Actinidia arguta*) vines growing in a coppiced small-leaved lime tree (*Tilia cordata*).

devised. One that I haven't personally tried, but sounds feasible, is by using a sacrificial tree.

- Plant a tree with reasonably durable wood that does not coppice. This could be a pine (*Pinus* spp.) or other conifer such as western red cedar (*Thuja plicata*). Some species, such as pines, may be useful for 4-5 years in terms of herb teas from the needles.

- After 4-5 years, when the tree is 2-2.5m (6'6"-8') high, ring bark it at the base, so killing it, and plant your climber near it.

- The climber uses the tree as a support. You may need to help train it along the branches.

- Meanwhile you plant a new sacrificial tree, a metre or two away, to take over when the dead one finally rots.

- When the original tree rots, prune back the climber and retrain it to the newly killed new sacrificial tree. And so on.

Part 3
Extra design elements and maintenance

View over the pond in my forest garden in spring. The large trees coming into leaf are Italian alders (*Alnus cordata*). The shrub with catkins is green alder (*Alnus viridis*).

Chapter 19

Clearings

Designing clearings

Although this is a book about forest gardening, there are often special reasons for wanting a lighter gap between the trees somewhere – something akin to a clearing or glade in a natural wood. This may be because you want to:

- grow crops needing regular cultivation that also need extra light, such as conventional annual vegetable.

- grow shrub or tree crops that need extra light and warmth, for example peach trees in the UK

- grow shrub or tree crops that are of marginal viability, e.g. Japanese persimmon (*Diospyros kaki*) in the UK, by providing a sheltered and sunny location

- have a pond

- provide an open area for recreational uses – what I think of as living spaces. Spaces to rest in, eat in and play in are important and increase the functionality of your forest garden. Spending more time in the garden will benefit the garden too – you'll notice more and become more aware of how it works. Not all living spaces will be clearings, though: for example, some may be open areas beneath trees, the trees giving shade in summer.

If you decide you do want a clearing then you need to think about the design at an early stage, before you start to plant the canopy trees.

The climate inside a clearing is modified from that of the surrounding forest garden, mainly by the fact of increased direct solar radiation (sunlight). This means that generally there are higher temperatures during the day and near-normal temperatures at night. So marginal woody species have a better chance of having their wood ripen in the autumn, and thus avoid dieback due to winter cold. However, species sensitive to low temperatures may not necessarily perform better in a clearing – for example, those that leaf out early will still be susceptible to spring frost damage.

A pond is a type of clearing. The far side (to the south) of the pond has been kept open for good light.

Light

The critical factor to take account of when designing a clearing is the availability of light. An overly small or badly designed clearing will mean that the sun barely penetrates, and light-demanding species will not be happy.

Most of the energy available to a plant (70-90 per cent) comes from direct light from the sun; the rest from diffused light from the sky. Another way of putting this is that the energy plants can get from direct sun is three to ten times as much as that from diffuse radiation, whether it is diffuse because of cloudy conditions or a shady site.

Plants that are situated with a large hedge/forest edge to their north, but are still able to receive most direct sun, lose only 5-15 per cent of total energy (about half of the diffuse portion). This loss will normally be more than made up for by the extra shelter they receive, contributing to an advantageous microclimate that will allow them to grow as well or better than those in open sunlight in a less sheltered position.

This means that at the northern edge of a clearing, the height of hedge/edge plants is not an important limiting factor: these trees or shrubs should be of a height that protects any of the species used in the clearing from cold northerly winds.

Whatever is growing around the edges of the clearing has the potential to block direct sun from that direction, and you want to minimise such blocking from the east, west and south.

• Trees or shrubs to the east of the clearing block morning sunlight, when the sun is low and temperatures are cool.

• Trees or shrubs to the west of the clearing block late afternoon / evening sunlight, when the sun is low and temperatures are warm.

• Trees or shrubs to the south of the clearing block midday sunlight, when the sun is high.

• Trees or shrubs to the north of the clearing block hardly any sunlight.

Now you might think that morning sunlight and evening sunlight are of equal value to a plant that needs light for energy, but this is not so. Because air temperatures are cooler in the morning, photosynthesis is much less efficient then than in the late afternoon / evening, when temperatures are usually warmer. Afternoon/evening sun is much more valuable than morning sun, especially in a temperate climate like the UK's where mornings are cool. Your local microclimate may also affect how much morning and afternoon sun you get.

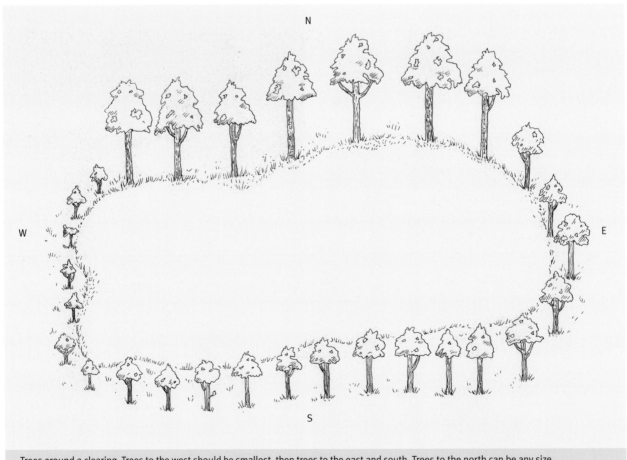

Trees around a clearing. Trees to the west should be smallest, then trees to the east and south. Trees to the north can be any size.

So, when thinking about the trees and shrubs around the edges of a clearing, use the following general rules.

- The height of plants at the eastern edge is not so critical, as long as they are not large trees. Not only is early morning eastern sun not so valuable to plants, but on frosty mornings the sun falling directly on frozen plant tissues can result in much greater damage.

- The height of plants along the western edge is very important. To maximise late-day sun these plants need to be quite low.

- The height of plants along the southern edge is also very important. But the sun is much higher as it moves near south, so these plants can be higher than west-edge plants, though should still be fairly low.

- The height of plants along the northern edge can be as large as desired, and in fact they should be at least as high as the highest tree to be used in the clearing, to give it maximum shelter from northerly winds.

Ideally, graduate the height of trees and shrubs near the edges (especially the southern and western edges) to maximise the amount of direct light in the clearing, as illustrated below.

Whatever the size of the clearing you are making, there will always be a strip near the southern edge that never gets direct sun, so you need to plan to use this for plants that can tolerate shade.

The width of the strip that gets no direct light, in UK latitudes, is about two-thirds of the height of the plants at the southern edge. So if there are shrubs 3m (10') high there, a strip about 2m (6'6") wide in the clearing will not get direct sun.

There is no perfect shape for a clearing, but in general try

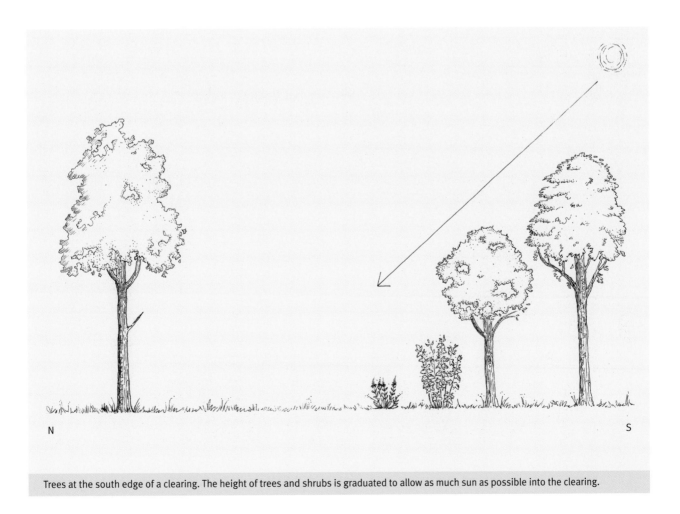

N

S

Trees at the south edge of a clearing. The height of trees and shrubs is graduated to allow as much sun as possible into the clearing.

to make the east–west width of the clearing larger than the north–south width, to maximise available sunlight. In practice, natural features and trees/shrubs around the edges will mean that the clearing edges are wavy.

In small gardens, clearings are practical only if species along the southern edge are small (say no more than about 2m/6'6" high in British latitudes).

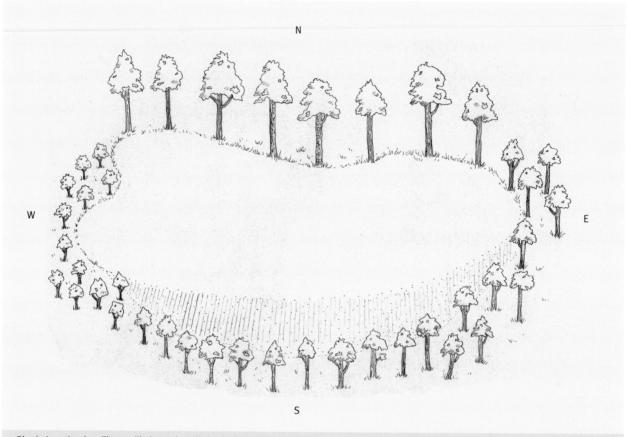

Shade in a clearing. There will always be a little shade on the southern edge, but shading at the east and west edges can be minimised by the size of plants used there.

Path bordered by Chinese bramble (*Rubus tricolor*) on the left and cardoon (*Cynara cardunculus*) with flax mulch mat on the right.

Chapter 20

Paths

Paths are always needed in a forest garden, but the number and density of permanent paths can vary a lot between small and large gardens. Usually, the larger the garden, the fewer paths are needed per unit area. This is because in a large garden there are likely to be areas that are not visited so often, and more areas of underplanting that are not used intensively, whereas in a small garden it is more likely that most of the space will be used intensively and therefore needs good access.

If anything, it's best to minimise the number of paths planned, because paths always require work to maintain them. I like to divide paths into two categories:

- main paths – used frequently to access distant parts of the garden, and to carry mulch and other materials

- minor paths – used to access specific areas for harvesting or other operations.

Main paths

Some main paths are always necessary. They should be planned at the start of your design so you can leave extra space between trees and shrubs. These paths should be at least 1m (3') wide, or perhaps more, especially if you want to get any machinery along them.

Main paths get heavy trampling in all weathers and they should be permanently covered, either with a living cover (mainly a mix of grasses), a mulch or (in small gardens) a solid surface. See 'Path surfaces', page 304.

The route of main paths can meander through your forest garden as you like. Bear in mind that you want all areas of the garden within a shortish distance of a main path (perhaps 5m/16'). Good places for main paths are next to hedges (where there is intense root competition and you

would have difficulty growing very much), and where they will form a boundary for species whose spread you want to control. Where slopes are steep, design paths to go across (zig-zagging if necessary) and at a shallow angle, to prevent soil erosion.

Main paths need to wide enough to transport materials and so you don't get soaked by wet foliage flopping over.

Minor paths

Minor paths are not always necessary, particularly in larger gardens, because the foot traffic is so diffuse in larger gardens that most ground-cover and perennial plants can cope with the occasional trampling. It is when ground-covers cannot cope with the amount of trampling that minor paths become necessary. In fact, when this happens minor paths tend to form themselves along 'desire lines' – where you walk most often – and any existing ground-covers on the route are likely to die off.

Thus to an extent, minor paths can be left unplanned until access is needed. The drawback of this technique is that they are likely to evolve from your initial planting of the perennial layer, and may comprise various weedy species you don't want too much (the foot traffic will kill off most existing plants – the ones you want – and leave bare areas of compressed soil that are colonised only by the plants that can tolerate those conditions). But really, the only plants that can tolerate lots of foot traffic are grasses, and you can always oversow an evolving minor path with suitable grass seed, which will come to dominate in time.

Minor paths might be quite narrow, and if they go through areas of overhanging perennials or shrubs then you might get soaked trousers walking through them after rain. So in these areas try to make the paths at least 60cm (2') wide.

If you have a small garden and are sure you know where your minor paths are going to be, then they can be designed at the outset. In confined areas they can even be made of 'stepping stones'.

Path surfaces

What your paths are made from may be determined by scale: larger forest gardens are likely, for reasons of cost and work involved, to have mainly living cover paths – i.e. grass mixes. For smaller gardens, solid and other surfaces are more of an option.

Shade-tolerant grass mixes

Grass paths will require mowing and perhaps weeding to stop invasion into the beds at either side. The grass cover will become very thin in deep shade.

To sow grass paths:

- use a high percentage of a dwarf perennial ryegrass, which is very tolerant of foot traffic

- include more shade-tolerant grasses such as creeping red fescue and browntop bentgrass

- white clover can be included as a nitrogen fixer. It is the most shade-tolerant of the clovers, especially the wild types

- sow early in the garden's life when there is still good light

- sow at a much higher rate than normal to ensure many small plants. This will mean that as shade increases there will still be enough plants to form a dense cover.

Some suitable mixtures for paths and hardwearing areas are listed below. Some seed companies sell mixtures; others sell individual grasses and you can mix the species yourself.

Standard forest garden path mix

	g/m² sowing rate
Lolium perenne, DWARF PERENNIAL RYEGRASS	35g
Festuca rubra subsp. *commutata*, CHEWINGS FESCUE	14g
Festuca rubra subsp. *rubra*, CREEPING RED FESCUE	14g
Agrostis capillaris, BROWNTOP BENTGRASS	2g
Poa pratensis, SMOOTH-STALKED MEADOWGRASS	3g
Total sowing rate: 68g/m²	

Mix without ryegrass but still fairly hardwearing

	g/m² sowing rate
Agrostis capillaris, BROWNTOP BENTGRASS	7g
Festuca rubra subsp. *commutata*, CHEWINGS FESCUE	25g
Festuca rubra subsp. *rubra*, CREEPING RED FESCUE	20g
Poa pratensis, SMOOTH-STALKED MEADOWGRASS	18g
Total sowing rate: 70g/m²	

Extra hardwearing mix for good winter cover

g/m² sowing rate

Lolium perenne,
DWARF PERENNIAL RYEGRASS 28g
(NB mix two or three varieties)

Festuca rubra subsp. *rubra,*
CREEPING RED FESCUE 7g

Total sowing rate: 35g/m²

Extra hardwearing mix for good summer cover

g/m² sowing rate

Lolium perenne,
DWARF PERENNIAL RYEGRASS 24g

Festuca rubra subsp. *commutata,*
CHEWINGS FESCUE 16g

Festuca rubra subsp. *rubra,*
CREEPING RED FESCUE 8g

Agrostis capillaris,
BROWNTOP BENTGRASS 5g

Total sowing rate: 53g/m²

White clover (*Trifolium repens*) seed ('Wild White' or similar) can be added to any of the above at a rate of 5-10g/m².

Recommended grass varieties for paths

Lolium perenne, DWARF PERENNIAL RYEGRASS:
Entrar, Manhattan, Numan, Troubadour

Agrostis capillaris, BROWNTOP BENTGRASS:
Highland

Festuca rubra subsp. *rubra,* CREEPING RED FESCUE:
Boreal, Estica

Festuca rubra subsp. *commutata,* CHEWINGS FESCUE:
Enjoy, Tatjana

Poa pratensis, SMOOTH-STALKED MEADOWGRASS:
Enprima

Solid materials for paths

Possible materials for solid paths include bricks, paving slabs, gravel, etc. These are suited only to small gardens,

Sow grass paths thickly.

as they involve a lot of initial work, though require very little maintenance afterwards. They are also quite expensive unless you can recycle waste materials. Gravel will require weeding after a while.

Organic mulches for paths

The most common materials used are straw and bark or wood chips. Both have pros and cons. Robert Hart used straw-mulched paths, but they do get slimy and slippery with age.

Any organic mulch used as a path material will get compressed and degraded quite fast, and will soon form a good seedbed for any seeds that are floating around. To avoid having to weed such paths very much, the materials must be topped up from time to time.

Straw-mulched paths

- These can last about 2 years before needing replacing.

- One small bale (about 30kg/66lb) covers about 2m² (2.4 sq yards). Many farmers no longer make small bales, so supply may be an issue.

- Costs depend on the price of straw, which fluctuates. A harvest price of £30/tonne gives a cost of about £25 per 100m² per year.

- They are quick and fairly easy to lay – straw comes off the bale in 10cm (4") wedges, which are laid directly.

- Non-organic straw will contain agrochemicals, though these usually biodegrade within a few months.

Bark- or woodchip-mulched paths

- These can last 3-5 years if large bark chips are used at 5cm (2") deep.
- 100 litres covers 4m² to a depth of 2.5cm (1"), or 2m² to 5cm (2").

- Costs for bagged bark are around £60 per 100m² per year. Bark and woodchip bought in bulk from a sawmill are much cheaper.

- Woodchip causes a nitrogen deficiency if used as a mulch around living plants, but as a path material it should cause little problem.

- Bark and woodchip are fairly quick and easy to lay.

Solid mulches for paths

Possible options for solid mulches for paths include plastic, carpet, card, etc. These are not recommended, as they will require weeding and replacement after a while.

Growing edible mushrooms on logs is the easiest way to turn wood into food.

Chapter 21

Fungi in forest gardens

Fungi will appear naturally in time in the forest garden, particularly mycorrhizal species forming associations with trees and shrubs, and decomposing fungi attacking live and dead wood. The fungal species mix can be manipulated through interventions to give crops of good edible mushrooms. This can be a particularly good way of using very shady moist areas, e.g. under trees with a dense canopy, where other plant crops are hard to grow or yield very little in terms of useful products.

The cultivation of mushrooms outdoors basically consists of preparing the substrate (i.e. what the fungi grow on), inoculating it with spores or spawn (material impregnated with mycelium – a fungal network of thread-like cells), and largely leaving it to the whims of nature, except for occasional watering if necessary.

There are three types of useful fungi that can be introduced into a forest garden.

- **Woodland mycorrhizal fungi.** These form a symbiotic association with tree/shrub roots. Most woodland fungi, e.g. boletus (*Boletus* spp.), chanterelle (*Cantharellus cibarius*), russula (*Russula* spp.) and truffle (*Tuber* spp.), are mycorrhizal.

- **Primary decomposing fungi.** These are wood-decomposing fungi, grown on stumps or logs. Examples are shiitake (*Lentinula edodes*, syn. *Tricholomopsis edodes*) and oyster mushroom (*Pleurotus ostreatus*).

- **Secondary decomposing fungi.** These are wood-decomposing fungi grown on woodchip, sawdust, or spent wood from log-cultivation of fungi. Examples are shaggy mane (*Coprinus comatus*), nameko (*Pholiota nameko*) and king stropharia (*Stropharia rugoso-annulata*).

Many of these types of fungi produce good edible mushrooms, and several produce medicinal anti-cancer compounds that are arousing great scientific interest.

Mycorrhizal fungi

Mycorrhizae are specialised structures that develop where certain fungi colonise the tissues of fine roots. The fungi help in the mineral nutrition of the plant in return for carbohydrates and other substances such as vitamins. This mutually beneficial relationship is called a symbiosis.

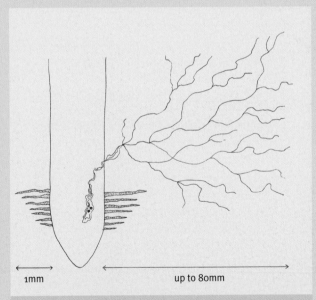

1mm   up to 80mm

A mycorrhizal root. Root hairs, up to 1mm long, exploit only a little soil space. The hyphae of the mycorrhizae exploit a much larger soil volume and can take up many more nutrients.

It has become evident over the last few decades that most woody species, and many herbaceous perennials and annuals as well (e.g. cereals, grasses and clovers), not only form mycorrhizal relationships with various species of fungi but also sometimes depend on them for healthy growth and survival. Some orchids and pines, for example, cannot grow normally without specific mycorrhizal fungi.

In the symbiosis the fungal threads (hyphae), which are much narrower than the finest plant roots, permeate the soil more intimately than plants' roots and take up nutrients and water, which they then transfer to the plant. Their main action is to improve mineral nutrient uptake, particularly of phosphorus but also of boron, copper, nitrogen, potassium, selenium, sulphur and zinc. Recently it has been found that mycorrhizae are critical in the sequestering of carbon in soils.

The mycorrhizal association can also reduce drought and temperature stress, increase root longevity, improve nitrogen fixation (in legumes and other N-fixing plants) and provide protection from some pathogens (e.g. pathogenic fungi). The hyphae can also directly transfer nitrogen and phosphorus from a plant rich in the mineral to one poor in it – up to some tens of metres away – thus forming a route for nitrogen-fixers and mineral accumulators to directly aid other plants. Growth of plants with mycorrhizae in ideal conditions can be 4-5 times as much as similar plants without. The rate of mineral soil weathering is also accelerated by a healthy mycorrhizal community.

Mycorrhizae tolerate a wide range of soil types and pH, but they are much reduced by soil disturbance, bare soils and excess nitrogen (hence many modern agricultural practices are detrimental). The turnover of hyphae is very rapid, so they can respond more quickly to changes in soil conditions than roots can. In a healthy forest garden ecosystem, mycorrhizal mats are formed of many species, covering virtually the whole of the topsoil volume and linking with many species of plants.

Most mycorrhizal fungi are not host-specific, i.e. they will form associations with many different plant species. Similarly, most plants are not too specific about which fungi they associate with.

SUMMARY: MYCORRHIZAL RELATIONSHIPS

- Most trees and shrubs form mycorrhizal relationships
- Many plants grow healthily only when suitable mycorrhizae are present
- The fungi improves plant mineral nutrient uptake
- The plant supplies sugars in return

The association:
- reduces drought/temperature stress
- improves nitrogen fixation
- protects from soil pathogens
- can transfer nitrogen and phosphorus from plant to plant
- is damaged by soil cultivation and excess fertilisation.

How to encourage mycorrhizal associations

If you do nothing, mycorrhizal fungi will appear in time. Their spores circulate in the air, particularly in autumn, and they may spread underground from nearby established sites. However, the process can be speeded up through various methods. None of these is 100-per-cent guaranteed to succeed, but I believe that some are worth doing: for little effort you may significantly increase the resilience of the forest garden system. Commercial dry spore mixtures are available that contain the spores of 15-20 species, though not usually any of the good edible types.

- Plant young tree seedlings near the root zones of proven mushroom-producing trees, then transplant them a few years later.

- Dip exposed roots of seedlings into water enriched with the spore mass of one or more mycorrhizal species. A spore mass solution can also be added to or watered on to compost. The spore mass can come from a commercial source of dry spores, or you can make it yourself by harvesting ripe mycorrhizal mushrooms from the forest floor and liquidising them – use 4-5 mushrooms for a bucketful of water, which can be used as a dip for 100-200 small trees/shrubs (such a mixture can be stored by mixing into a 15-per-cent glycerol solution and freezing).

- Broadcast spores on to the root zones of existing trees and shrubs, using spores in a water carrier. Success rates may be low, but little effort is required.

- Place a little soil from the root zone of proven mushroom-producing trees around seedlings, either in the nursery or soon after planting

- Inoculate the compost of pot-grown plants with a mix of dried spores of suitable species.

- When planting trees or shrubs, scatter a dry spore mixture into the planting hole.

The following table lists the most desirable edible mycorrhizal species and their likely candidate trees. As always when picking wild mushrooms to eat, make absolutely sure of the identification. The species with the best-quality mushrooms are highlighted in bold.

WOODLAND MYCORRHIZAL SPECIES WITH GOOD EDIBLE MUSHROOMS			
Species		**Candidates (habitats)**	**Origin**
Agaricus abruptibulbus	Woodland agaricus	Spruce	Europe
Agaricus augustus	The Prince	Deciduous/coniferous trees	Europe
Agaricus langei	Scaly wood mushroom	Deciduous/coniferous trees	Europe
Agaricus lanipes		Deciduous trees	Europe
Agaricus silvaticus	Red staining mushroom	Coniferous trees	Europe, N. America
Agaricus silvicola	Wood mushroom	Deciduous/coniferous trees	Europe, N. America
*Amanita solitaria**		Deciduous trees on chalk soil	Europe, N. America
*Amanita umbrinolutea**		Fir trees	Europe
*Amanita vaginata**	Grisette	Deciduous trees	Europe, N. America
Boletus aereus	Queen bolete	Deciduous trees (esp. beech, oak)	Europe
Boletus aestivalis	Summer king bolete	Deciduous trees (esp. beech, oak)	Europe
Boletus appendiculatus	Butter bolete	Deciduous trees (esp. oak)	Europe
Boletus badius	Bay bolete	Deciduous/coniferous trees	Europe, N. America
Boletus mirabilis	Velvet top	Coniferous trees	N. America
Boletus pinophilus	Pine bolete	Pine trees	Europe
Boletus pulverulentus	Inkstain bolete	Deciduous trees (esp. oak)	Europe
Boletus regius	King bolete	Deciduous trees (esp. oak, lime, birch)	Europe
Boletus spadiceus		Coniferous trees	Europe, N. America
Cantharellus cibarius	Chanterelle	Deciduous/coniferous trees (esp. Douglas fir, oak)	Europe, N. America
Cantharellus cinereus	Ashen chanterelle	Deciduous trees (esp. beech)	Europe
Cantharellus infundibuliformis	Trumpet chanterelle	Deciduous/coniferous trees	Europe, N. America
Cortinarius praestans	Goliath webcap	Birch, oak	Europe
Cortinarius varius		Coniferous trees	N. America
Gomphidius glutinosus	Slimy spike	Coniferous trees	Europe, N. America
Hygrophorus camarophyllus	Dusky waxy cap	Pine trees	Europe

* Take great care in identification – similar species in the genus are poisonous.

Continued overleaf

Species		Candidates (habitats)	Origin
Hygrophorus dichrous		Deciduous trees	Europe
Hygrophorus limacinus		Deciduous trees (esp. beech, hornbeam)	Europe
Hygrophorus poetarum		Beech	Europe
Lactarius deliciosus	Saffron milk cap	Pine, spruce	Europe, N. America
Lactarius deterrimus	False saffron milk cap	Pine, spruce	Europe
Lactarius sanguifluus		Coniferous trees	Europe
Lactarius volemus	Tawny milk cap	Deciduous/coniferous trees	Europe, N. America
Leccinum duriusculum	Slate bolete	Poplar	Europe, N. America
Leccinum quercinum	Orange oak bolete	Oak	Europe
Leccinum versipelle	Orange birch bolete	Birch	Europe, N. America
Russula alutacea	Yellow-gilled russula	Deciduous trees	Europe, N. America
Russula aurora	Dawn brittlegill	Deciduous trees	Europe
Russula brunneoviolacea		Deciduous trees (esp. oak)	Europe
Russula claroflava	Yellow swamp russula	Birch on wet ground	Europe
Russula cyanoxantha	The charcoal burner	Deciduous trees	Europe, N. America
Russula grisea		Beech	Europe
Russula heterophylla	Greasy green brittlegill	Deciduous trees	Europe, N. America
Russula ionochlora	Oilslick brittlegill	Beech	Europe
Russula lutea	Yellow-gilled russula	Deciduous trees	Europe, N. America
Russula melliolens		Deciduous trees	Europe
Russula obscura		Coniferous trees	N. Europe
Russula olivacea	Olive brittlegill	Beech	Europe, N. America
Russula paludosa		Coniferous trees	Europe
Russula polychroma		Coniferous trees	Europe, N. America
Russula vesca	Bare-toothed russula	Deciduous trees	Europe, N. America
Russula virescens	Quilted green russula	Deciduous trees (esp. beech)	Europe, N. America
Russula xerampelina	Shrimp russula	Deciduous trees (esp. beech, oak)	Europe
Tricholoma columbetta	Blue spot knight	Deciduous/coniferous trees	Europe, N. America
Tricholoma flavovirens	Man on horseback	Coniferous trees	Europe, N. America
Tricholoma matsutake	Matsutake	Pine trees	Japan
Tricholoma populinum	The sandy	Poplar	Europe
Tricholoma portentosum	Snow mushroom	Coniferous trees	Europe, N. America
Tuber aestivum	Summer truffle	Beech on chalk soil	Europe
Tuber gibbosum	Oregon white truffle	Douglas fir	W. and N. America
Tuber magnatum	White truffle	Deciduous trees	Europe
Tuber melanosporum	Perigord truffle	Beech	Europe

Growing primary decomposing fungi

These are the first fungi to capture a stump or log, and are typically fast-growing, sending out strands of mycelium that quickly attach to and decompose plant tissue. Some species of fungi are known to occur on both deciduous and coniferous stumps or logs: note that these are usually two separate strains, and the deciduous strain probably won't inoculate conifer wood, and vice versa. The species suitable for this type of culture can mostly be cultivated on both logs and stumps.

Stumps in the forest garden are a potential source of trouble, particularly from an invasive parasitic fungus such as honey fungus (*Armillaria* spp.), which may establish there and then spread to healthy trees and shrubs. Removal of stumps, often recommended in gardens and forestry, is difficult and involves a lot of work, and may be physically awkward in a forest garden without damaging other nearby plants. A better, easier and more productive method of dealing with stumps is to inoculate them with vigorous fungi that will colonise the stump before other more harmful species can do so (it is very much a case of first fungus in wins). If the fungi species used produces good edible mushrooms, a useful crop may emerge from the stump after some months or years.

Stumps with their roots intact are particularly good for mushroom cultivation, because water is continuously drawn via capillary action through the dead wood cells from the soil. Stumps in full or part shade (as most will be in a forest garden) are better than those in sun. The open face of a stump is highly susceptible to colonisation by wild mushrooms, so it is important to inoculate a stump within a few months and before the first season of wild mushrooms – old stumps are not worth inoculating, they will already have been colonised.

Log cultivation is a fast way to convert wood, for example from coppiced trees, into food. Using these fungi on stumps or logs will not seriously affect the health of other nearby trees.

The spawn for inoculation of stumps or logs is usually purchased from a commercial supplier, and usually comes with cheese wax for sealing. Note that spawn may need to be ordered up to 4-6 weeks before you inoculate, as it takes this long to grow it to order.

Stump inoculation

Stump inoculation is best undertaken in spring on to new stumps of trees cut in late winter or early spring. Deciduous tree stumps are generally easier to successfully inoculate than coniferous stumps. Oyster mushrooms (*Pleurotus* spp.) are one of the main species used on stumps. Inoculation is by one of the following methods.

- Using plug spawn: plugs or dowels of wood with grooves, which mycelium have fully colonised. These are inserted into the open face of the stump, either in holes specially drilled or in cracks in the face if they exist. Holes (a total of 30-60) should be drilled in a circle around the edge of the stump surface (a few centimetres from the bark), with a few scattered inside this circle across the face. The plugs are inserted by hand, hammered in with a mallet, and (optionally) the hole is then covered with cheese wax (melted and painted on) to protect the mycelium from insect or weather damage.

- By wedge or disc inoculation. Using a bow saw or chainsaw, a wedge is cut or a shallow disc is sliced from the open face of the stump; the newly cut faces are packed with sawdust spawn (i.e. mycelium grown in a sawdust substrate) and the cut wedge/disc replaced and secured with a few nails. The exposed areas of spawn at the edges need to be waxed to stop them drying out.

Small-diameter stumps rot faster and produce a crop of mushrooms sooner than bigger stumps, but they have a shorter mushroom-producing life. The speed of production depends partly on the speed of colonisation, which is itself dependent on a host of factors, including wood density in the stump (i.e. the species), moisture content, weather, etc. Chicken-of-the-woods (*Laetiporus sulphureus*) has been known to produce mushrooms 8 weeks after oak stump inoculation. Mushroom production in 12-36 months is more common. Stumps of species with less-dense wood, e.g. poplar and willow, will be colonised more quickly, but will crop for a lesser period than durable woods such as oak.

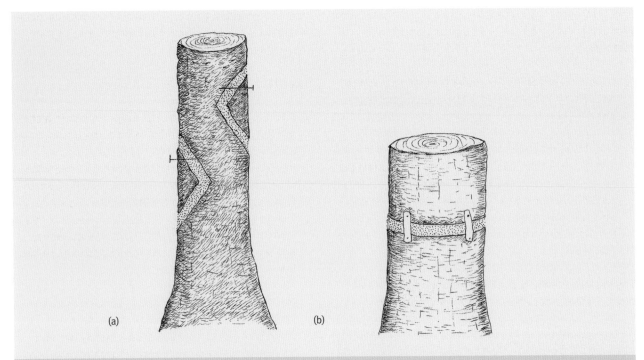

Stump culture of fungi. (a) Wedges are cut out, packed with spawn and replaced by nailing. (b) The top part of the stump is cut off, packed with spawn and replaced; nailed down with wooden strips.

Log inoculation

Logs for mushroom cultivation are usually cut from healthy trees in the winter or early spring before leafing, when the sapwood is rich in sugars, to a length of 50-120cm (1'8"-4') and diameter of 10-25cm (4-10"). Commercial growers use 10cm (4") diameter logs, and these are much easier to physically move and manage than larger logs.

Most hardwoods from deciduous trees can be used, but mushroom production will vary according to the density of the wood.

HISTORY OF LOG CULTIVATION

Mushrooms have been grown on logs for a long time in China and Japan – there are written records from the Song Dynasty one thousand years ago about the cultivation of shiitake. Shiitake in particular remains very popular in much of Asia, and increasingly so elsewhere as commercial production gains popularity.

A pine log inoculated with dowel spawn and waxed.

Logs with softer woods (e.g. alder, birch and poplar) start producing mushrooms very quickly, but production may last only 4-5 years.

- Logs with harder but non-durable wood (e.g. beech and cherry) take a little longer to start cropping, and last 5-8 years.

- Logs from trees with dense, durable, hard wood, such as oaks, may take 2 years to crop but will outlast the others, producing for 10 years. Commercial growers prefer these logs, with thick outer barks (necessary for good mushroom flushes), to the softer woods with thin bark, which are easily damaged by weather fluctuations.

The logs are ideally kept off the ground, and cool and moist, before inoculation, to prevent contamination.

Dowels ready to tap into a log.

Logs should be cut from healthy trees; bark should be undamaged and logs should have as few branches as possible – cut off any branches flush to the trunk. Inoculation must take place within 2 months of cutting, otherwise weed fungi will already have inoculated the log. I tend to

order spawn before I cut logs, and cut the logs only once the spawn is safely in the fridge (where it will store for several months).

Several inoculation methods can be used.

- Inserting sawdust or plug spawn (bought from a commercial supplier) into drilled holes along the log. Logs require 30-50 plugs, inserted into evenly spaced holes 10-15cm (4-6") apart in a diamond pattern (lines of holes 5cm/2" apart, because the mycelium grow faster along the wood grain than across the grain). The plugs are inserted by hand, hammered in with a mallet, and the holes are then covered with cheese wax (melted and painted on) to protect the mycelium from insect or weather damage.

- Placing newly cut logs near to logs already producing mushrooms, so that the spores are broadcast on to them. Less reliable in the UK, this method has long been used by Japanese cultivators with good rates of success. Logs showing no fungal growth after a year are removed from the production area.

- Similarly to stump inoculation (see page 313), wedges can be cut from the log, packed with sawdust spawn, and nailed back into position. A variation is to cut the log into 40-60cm (1'4"-2') sections, sandwich spawn between the sections, and nail them back together. A further variation is to pack the ends of the log with sawdust spawn and cap them with aluminium foil to hold the mycelium in place. Allow about 30-50g of sawdust spawn per log.

- Lastly, after years of trial and error I have discovered a way to inoculate logs without having to buy in spawn every year, and I now use this to produce shiitake logs. This method works only if you inoculate some logs every year. The very first year you will need to buy in spawn, and when you have inoculated logs with it, keep two logs separate. Place these in a heavy-duty plastic sack and fold over the end. Put the sack with the logs inside in a cool place. One year later, when you are ready to inoculate fresh logs, open the sack and you will find that the shiitake fungus has grown not only inside the two logs but all over the surface as well. Scrape off the white fungal growth on the surface and mix it with fresh sawdust: this is your inoculant for the new logs. When inoculated, put two of the logs into a plastic sack and repeat the process.

After inoculation, logs are stacked in ricks and covered with a tarpaulin, plastic or carpets, to keep them moist, for 6-12 months. If they are uncovered, keep them watered in dry weather. It may take up to 20 months for the fungus to completely colonise the log (though less time for light woods), at which point white mycelium will appear at both ends of the logs.

Shocking

Once the log is fully colonised, with some species such as shiitake (*Lentinula edodes*), you can make the log fruit when you want by 'shocking' it.

To shock a log:
- soak it in water for 24 hours or so
- after soaking, hit the end of the log with a wooden mallet a few times, or bang it on the ground a few times.

Hitting them really does help increase the fruiting. What you are simulating is a colonised branch falling to the ground, stimulating fruiting. With other fungi, such as oyster mushrooms, I have not managed to force logs to fruit but have to settle for them fruiting when conditions are right in late autumn.

Fruiting

Fruiting will occur only if temperatures are mild enough – spring to late autumn in the UK. In winter logs will not fruit outside, but if shocked and brought into a conservatory they can do.

After soaking and hitting, or in autumn if unshocked, the logs are then lined up vertically, either leaning against a fence or similar structure, or sunk into the ground by up to 25-30cm (10-12") – this is particularly useful when weather is very dry and where watering is a problem. They should be situated in permanent shade where there is some air movement. With shiitake, fruiting occurs 10-20 days after shocking, depending on air temperatures.

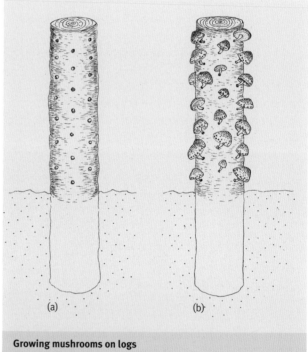

Growing mushrooms on logs
(a) Log drilled and inoculated, placed in soil after soaking.
(b) Log fruiting.

Shiitake mushrooms (*Lentinula edodes*) fruiting on oak logs.

Oyster mushrooms (*Pleurotus ostreatus*) fruiting on alder logs.

The total mushroom crop from a log over its lifetime can reach a third of the cut log weight. So a log weighing 15kg (33lb) and cropping over 5 years should produce about 1kg (2lb 3oz) of mushrooms per year. The species I most recommended are oyster mushrooms and shiitake.

The following table lists the majority of edible fungi suited to log and stump culture, and their likely candidate trees. The easiest of these to grow are the poplar fieldcap (*Agrocybe cylindracea*), the Indian oyster (*Pleurotus*

pulmonarius) and the shiitake (*Lentinula edodes*, syn. *Tricholomopsis edodes*).

Several species of fungi have long been used medicinally, particularly in China and other parts of Asia, often as adaptogens to stimulate the immune system. More recently, several species have been found to have anti-cancer properties, and there is a lot of research on them under way.

FUNGI WITH GOOD EDIBLE MUSHROOMS SUITED TO LOG AND STUMP CULTURE			
Species		**Candidates (habitats)**	**Origin**
Agrocybe cylindracea	Poplar fieldcap	Deciduous logs/stumps (esp. poplar, willow, maple)	Temp./subtropic. regions
Flammulina velutipes*	Enoki / velvet shank	Deciduous/coniferous logs/stumps	Temperate regions
Grifola frondosa	Hen-of-the-woods	Deciduous/coniferous logs/stumps	N. temperate regions
Hericium coralloides	Coral tooth	Deciduous/coniferous logs/stumps	Europe
Hericium erinaceus	Lion's mane	Deciduous logs/stumps (logs part-buried)	Temperate regions
Hericium ramosum		Deciduous logs/stumps (esp. beech)	Europe
Hypholoma capnoides	Conifer tuft	Deciduous/coniferous stumps	Europe, N. America
Hypholoma sublateritium	Brick cap	Deciduous logs/stumps	N. America, Europe, Asia
Hypsizygus tessulatus	Beech mushroom	Deciduous logs/stumps	Temperate regions
Hypsizygus ulmarius	Elm oyster	Deciduous/coniferous logs/stumps	Temperate regions
Laetiporus sulphureus	Chicken-of-the-woods	Deciduous/coniferous logs/stumps	Europe, N. America
Lentinula edodes (syn. *Tricholomopsis edodes*)	Shiitake	Deciduous logs (esp. oak)	Japan, China, Korea
Pholiota nameko	Nameko	Deciduous logs, part-buried	Japan, China, Taiwan
Pleurotus cornucopiae	Golden oyster	Deciduous logs/stumps	Temp./subtropic. regions
Pleurotus cystidiosus	Abalone mushroom	Deciduous stumps	Temperate regions
Pleurotus eryngii	King oyster	Deciduous/coniferous logs/stumps	Mediterranean, Asia
Pleurotus euosmus	Tarragon oyster	Deciduous logs/stumps (esp. elm)	Britain only
Pleurotus ostreatus	Oyster mushroom	Deciduous/coniferous logs/stumps	Temperate regions
Pleurotus pulmonarius	Indian oyster	Deciduous/coniferous logs/stumps	Europe, N. America
Pleurotus sajor-caju	Phoenix oyster	Deciduous/coniferous logs/stumps	Subtrop. Himalaya
Pluteus petasatus		Deciduous logs/stumps	Europe
Sparassis crispa	Cauliflower mushroom	Coniferous logs/stumps	Europe, N. America
Volvariella bombycina	Silky rosegill	Deciduous logs/stumps (esp. elm)	Europe, N. America

* Be careful not to confuse this with the poisonous *Galerina autumnalis*.

MEDICINAL FUNGI SUITED TO LOG AND STUMP CULTURE			
Species		**Candidates (habitats)**	**Origin**
Auricularia auricula-judae*	Jew's ear / wood ear	Deciduous logs	Europe, N. America
Auricularia polytricha†	Wood ear / tree ear	Deciduous/coniferous logs	Temperate regions
Ganoderma lucidum*	Reishi	Deciduous/coniferous logs/ stumps	Temperate regions
Oudemansiella mucida*	Porcelain fungus	Deciduous logs (esp. beech)	Europe, N. America

* Also edible, though poor quality.
† Also edible, though not flavourful, but highly prized in Asia.

Growing secondary decomposing fungi

These fungi can also be grown in a dark corner of the garden, where a layer of mixed spawn-inoculated sawdust/ woodchip is laid on the ground.

In a forest garden, piles of sawdust or woodchip may be freely available (or may be free from a local sawmill) and can be used as a substrate in which to grow fungi. It is important that the sawdust/woodchip is fresh. The best substrate of this kind is a mixture of 50:50 sawdust and woodchip (by volume). Alternatively, the crumbly decomposed log remains from growing primary decomposers such as shiitake can be used.

Spring is the best time for inoculation. Before inoculation, the sawdust or woodchip is moistened to near-saturation. The spawn is then thoroughly mixed in. There is a high risk of competition from wild species using this type of substrate, and a relatively high rate of inoculation is necessary.

- A ratio (by volume) of 3:1 substrate:spawn minimises competition from other fungi.

- A ratio (by volume) as low as 10:1 or 20:1 substrate:spawn allows some competition.

Sawdust spawn (a commercial sawdust and spawn mix) is best, though you can try using collected mushrooms (as for mycorrhizal species, see page 310); or you can try using collected mycelium from soil 5-15cm (2-6")

deep beneath established mushroom-fruiting patches. The mixture is laid in a layer on the soil surface and again watered, then covered with cloth, cardboard or carpet to protect the mycelium from dehydration and sun exposure.

Colonisation can take from a few weeks to several months. After the new mycelial mat has established (you will be able to see the white growth on the soil surface), the patch can be triggered into fruiting by frequent watering; the covers should be left off but the bed should be in shade. After the second year, more substrate can be added and mixed in. Such a woodchip/sawdust bed should be productive for 3-4 years.

Pest problems with growing mushrooms

Mushrooms are rarely affected by diseases – fungi are good at fighting off other fungi – but there are a few pests that can cause problems.

Slugs

Slugs can devastate young mushrooms. With log culture, the logs can be temporarily moved to a drier site while they fruit, or could maybe be placed on a mulch of sand, hair, shell or other slug-deterrent substance. With stumps, woodchip beds and ground fungi, there aren't many options – pick mushrooms early and carry out general slug-deterring practices.

FUNGI WITH GOOD EDIBLE MUSHROOMS SUITED TO SAWDUST OR WOODCHIP CULTURE			
Species		**Recommended substrate**	**Origin**
Agrocybe cylindracea	Poplar fieldcap	Woodchip	Temp./subtrop. regions
Coprinus comatus	Shaggy mane / shaggy ink cap	Hardwood sawdust	Temperate regions
Flammulina velutipes*	Enoki / velvet shank	Deciduous/coniferous sawdust	Temperate regions
Hypsizygus tessulatus	Beech mushroom	Woodchip	Temperate regions
Lentinula edodes (syn. Tricholomopsis edodes)	Shiitake	Hardwood sawdust (esp. oak)	Japan, China, Korea
Pholiota nameko	Nameko	Hardwood sawdust	Japan, China, Taiwan
Pleurotus cornucopiae	Golden oyster	Hardwood sawdust	Temp./subtropic. regions
Pleurotus cystidiosus	Abalone mushroom	Hardwood sawdust	Temperate regions
Pleurotus eryngii	King oyster	Deciduous/coniferous sawdust	Mediterranean, Asia
Pleurotus euosmus	Tarragon oyster	Hardwood sawdust	Britain only
Pleurotus ostreatus	Oyster mushroom	Deciduous/coniferous sawdust	Temperate regions
Pleurotus pulmonarius	Indian oyster	Deciduous/coniferous sawdust	Europe, N. America
Pleurotus sajor-caju	Phoenix oyster	Deciduous/coniferous sawdust	Subtrop. Himalaya
Pluteus petasatus		Deciduous woodchip/sawdust	Europe
Stropharia rugoso-annulata	King stropharia	Woodchip/sawdust	Temperate regions

* Be careful not to confuse this with the poisonous *Galerina autumnalis*.

Fungus fly larvae

These are the tiny 'worms' that are often found in wild fungi that have 'gone over'. Harvest mushrooms young, before the flies get to them. Mushrooms fruiting in cool weather are less prone to damage. Remove wormy mushrooms to some distance away and compost them. If you have a big problem then consider other measures (e.g. placing wormy mushrooms in a container of water, as you might do for pernicious weeds) to break the pest cycle.

Chinese dogwood (*Cornus kousa* var. *chinensis*) in flower.

Chapter 22

Harvesting and preserving

Once a forest garden is established, you might find that, because maintenance is so minimal, harvesting takes most of the time you spend in the garden. How much time you spend harvesting of course depends on your garden, and every garden is different. Many of the techniques and tips in this section are not unique to forest gardens, though some are.

This chapter does not aim to give a complete guide to food-preserving techniques – there are plenty of other books which cover that in detail – but I do pay particular attention to food drying, which is still rare in the UK and deserves to be better understood.

Food plants

Most forest gardens have a preponderance of food plants, both for eating fresh and for storage. Although in mild parts of the UK there are fresh foods available all winter, most folk will want or need to preserve food from the summer and autumn for the lean winter months.

Salad crops

Picking a forest garden salad is much more interesting than going to a vegetable patch and picking a lettuce. It can also take more time, depending on the number of ingredients you want. To pick a 20-ingredient salad from my forest garden takes about 40 minutes (2 minutes per person-portion).

When I'm picking a salad I tend to think in terms of 'base' ingredients (which are usually mild in flavour and you can pick in bulk) and more flavourful 'aromatic' ingredients. I try to have at least two or three base ingredients and a dozen or more aromatics. I also always try to pick two or more types of flower, either to go into the mix or be sprinkled on top of the salad for decoration.

Larger leaves I usually chop, while smaller ones can be left whole. A mixed forest garden salad is more than just the sum of its parts. It takes on a character of its own, with mild ingredients 'pepped up' and very strong ingredients diluted down. I rarely bother to put in more than about 30 ingredients, though my friend and fellow forest gardener Justin West has made salads with over 100 ingredients when he was at the Schumacher College in Dartington.

Try not to pick salad leaves in the heat of the day, when they will quickly wilt – better to pick early in the morning and keep them cold, or pick in the evening.

Preserving raw leafy crops is not usually a high priority in climates where leafy crops are available all through the winter. Some options are to preserve them in oils, e.g. make a pesto; or preserve in lactic acid via wild fermentation (the process that makes sauerkraut) – see Sandor Katz's book *Wild Fermentation* for more information.

Perennial vegetables

It is often best to grow patches or drifts of one species of perennial vegetable to make a larger contiguous area, rather than dot them around here and there, to make harvesting that much quicker and efficient (single plants of most perennial vegetables do not provide enough crop in a picking, so you need to crop several plants).

The plants themselves will often determine what you eat when. Bamboo shoots, for instance, have to be picked within days of appearing otherwise it is too late. You'll soon learn what is ready when – but it is a learning process, because many of the perennial vegetables in this book will be unfamiliar.

All the usual preservation techniques for annual vegetables

can be used, e.g. blanching and freezing, making chutneys and pickles, lactic acid preservation, etc.

FOOD PALATABILITY

Many plants are processed – even if that just means cooking – to improve their palatability. Food palatability is experienced as a mixture of the following tastes.

- Sweetness: this is easily assimilated and naturally craved by people. Sweetness is often bound up in fruits and is released only by cooking, crushing or exposure to frost.

- Sourness: this balances the sweetness so it is not cloying.

- Bitterness: often a sign that a food is poisonous, in moderate levels bitterness does not usually cause a problem. Bitter foods can stimulate digestion.

- Astringency: this is caused by tannins, which dry the mouth up, and make proteins less digestible. Heating can sometime remove astringency, as can crushing an astringent fruit and exposing the pulp to air for 1-2 days.

- Saltiness.

Tubers

In a temperate climate where the ground does not freeze too much in winter, and does not get waterlogged, the best place to store tubers is usually in the ground. Where winter temperatures do get colder, then dig non-hardy tubers (e.g. yams, *Dioscorea* spp.) in autumn and store in sand, compost, etc. in a cool place or in a root cellar. Replant tubers in spring to grow the next season's crop. If you are in a region where the ground freezes hard for long periods then you'll probably want to harvest all your tubers in the same way.

Small fruits

Small fruit on bushes – currants, blueberries, salal, etc. – can be picked by hand as usual. A minimal pruning

regime will lead to higher bushes than 'normal', resulting in less stress on your back from picking fruits. Alternatively, you can put down a sheet or tarpaulin on the ground, then pick and drop the fruits. Fruits borne on a reasonably long stem free of leaves can also be harvested quickly using a harvesting 'comb' (much-used in Scandinavia to harvest bilberries and lingonberries).

Small fruits on both bushes and trees (e.g. mulberry) can be harvested quite efficiently by beating or shaking the branches; a basket or similar container on a handle can be held beneath the branch that is beaten.

Small fruits on trees with good access beneath are best harvested by laying down a sheet or tarp beneath the tree and shaking the branches and/or picking and dropping the fruit. I use this for species like hawthorns (*Crataegus* spp.) and autumn olives (*Elaeagnus umbellata*). Ripe fruits often fall very well. Of course you will end up with some leaves, spiders, etc., which will need sorting out.

Fruits can be preserved by freezing, bottling, jamming, etc., although my favourite method is drying, described opposite, under 'Larger fruits'. If I don't have time to process fruits into jams, leathers and so on immediately, I put them in the freezer and remove them at a later date to process.

Autumn olive (*Elaeagnus umbellata*) fruits make great jam and leathers.

Larger fruits

These usually have to be hand-picked (as opposed to beating/shaking, etc.). For larger trees, if you don't want to be bothered with ladders (which, incidentally, can easily cause damage to trees), then invest in a decent long-handled fruit picker: the telescopic sort are best – there is nothing more comical than trying to pick fruits with a picker that is way too long. Using these pickers is not fast; having a second person to empty them helps.

As mentioned in Chapter 9 (page 92), you don't have to harvest all the fruits from a tree. Whatever is not harvested will get recycled into the forest garden system. However, with 'improved fruits' – apples, pears, plums, peaches and apricots – it is important not to leave mummified or mouldy fruits on the tree over winter, as these can re-infect the tree the following season. 'Unimproved' fruits rarely have similar problems.

Some fruits – late apples, pears, etc. – store well in a cool place for several months over the winter, though it can now sometimes be a problem keeping fruit stores cool enough during winters in the UK.

With plums, I often put some in the freezer so I can mix them with more acid fruits to make leathers (see page 324) later in the season.

There are many conventional ways of preserving fruits – making jams, chutneys, etc., but I am very keen on drying fruits, which I do in two main ways:

* by cutting fruits into slices or quarters and drying

* by making a fruit pulp and drying this to make a fruit leather.

I highly recommend electric dehydrators for drying – I use the excellent 'Excalibur' model, which loads at the front and has a good capacity. Although these machines use electricity, the drying is fast and efficient. When you are drying fruits, time is of the essence, and although you can sometimes succeed using low-temperature ovens or drying above Aga-type ranges, the product is never as good-quality and won't keep as long. To dry efficiently you need both warm controllable temperatures and the correct airflow, and you don't usually get that in ovens.

In sunny climes solar drying is possible and to be recommended, but my experiments with solar drying in the UK have not been very successful – we just don't get enough sun, especially in autumn when you are doing most of the drying.

Apples are easily dried by peeling, coring and cutting into 6-8mm (0.25-0.3")-thick circular slices (there is a nifty hand-cranked machine that does all this one operation – do a web search for apple peeler/corer/slicer), then drying in a dehydrator at 55°C (131°F) for about 12 hours. Pears are better quartered, with any core pieces cut out, but left with their skins on. They can take 16-20 hours in a dehydrator at 55°C. Plums and other pulpy fruits are best halved and dried, taking 20-24 hours at 55°C.

Dried fruit or leathers will store for 1-2 years in plastic bags at ambient air temperatures. They will store for twice as long if vacuum packed – there are small home-scale vacuum-packing machines available. Separate the layers of leather with non-stick sheet before vacuum packing, otherwise they will bond together so tightly you might never get them apart again. (I know – it happened to me!)

Medlar (*Mespilus germanica*) 'Nottingham' fruits are lovely raw or made into jam.

MAKING FRUIT LEATHERS

Making a fruit pulp for drying to a leather enables you to dry not just single-species fruit pulps but interesting mixtures too. It is good to mix acid fruit pulp with a sweeter pulp (an acid fruit when dried tastes very acid) – I often use plum pulp as a sweeter pulp and mix in acid pulps such as those from blackcurrant or sea buckthorn.

- You may need to lightly cook firm fruits for a few minutes to soften the flesh enough to liquidise well.

- De-seed fruits with unappetisingly large seeds, either before or after liquidising.

- Liquidise (don't add any water).

- The pulp you end up with should be thick enough that you can spread a layer of it 4-6mm (about 0.2") thick without it spreading. If your pulp is too thin, you can always thicken it by adding a thicker pulp, or ground nuts, or oatmeal, etc. There are lots of possibilities.

- Spread the pulp in a layer on a flexible non-stick baking sheet and dry it in a dehydrator at 55°C for 24 hours or so. It may need turning over for the last few hours of drying. It will then peel off cleanly and have a leathery consistency similar to that of the fruit bars than you can buy.

Nuts

Assuming you have outwitted the squirrels (see Chapter 23 for details!) then nuts are usually harvested from the ground, because they are borne on medium-to-large trees. When ripe, the nuts will usually fall loose from their husks or burrs (though some, like chestnuts, can sometimes fall in-burr) – you can help them considerably by shaking the branches before each harvest.

Try to harvest nuts daily, to prevent predation from birds, squirrels and other rodents, and to stop the nuts picking up moulds from the soil.

If you have plants growing under the nut trees then you will probably need to lay out nets over the low plants to catch the nuts. A two-person team is invaluable to handle the nets and gather/pour the nuts from them into containers.

If you can cut plants down under the nut trees or have cut grasses beneath them, then you can collect from the ground, which is quicker than using nets. You can hand-harvest a few trees easily enough. I highly recommend some hand-held harvesters called 'Nut Wizards'. These are made in the USA (see Resources section) and consist of a handle with a rotating head that you roll over the ground; it picks up nuts inside the head, which you empty into a bucket from time to time. These great small machines make harvesting hazels a delight! Different versions do walnuts and chestnuts, though with chestnuts some of the spiny burrs fall with nuts still inside and must be opened by hand. The walnut version will also pick up medium-sized apples – well suited to cider apples, for example.

In the UK, no nuts will store for long without drying – they all contain too much moisture. They store much longer if dried in-shell, rather than being shelled first and just the kernels dried. Oily nuts such as hazels and walnuts should be dried at 35-40°C (95-104°F) (no hotter or else the oils will go rancid) for 24 hours, after which they will store for 2-3 years at ambient air temperatures. Starchy nuts such as chestnuts contain much more water and take much longer to dry – 3-5 days at 40-50°C (104-122°F). Dried chestnuts store for years, and after shelling can be ground into chestnut flour.

Cracking nuts by hand, particularly the smaller nuts such as hazels, is tiresome. There are no small-scale nut-cracking machines suitable for people with just a few nut trees. I have built a nut-cracking machine that works really well and is quite simple to build if you have some engineering skills. See *Agroforestry News*, Vol 13 No 3 for plans.

Mushrooms

If you are growing mushrooms on logs, then with the easier fungi, such as shiitake, you can try to stagger cropping over a long period. There are still likely to be times, however, when you have a glut. Drying is again the best way to preserve mushrooms – they dry quickly at 40-50°C (104-122°F). Dried mushrooms are easily rehydrated by soaking in water for a few hours before cooking.

Oyster mushrooms (*Pleurotus* spp.) and others are easy to dry.

Logs for fuel and mushroom cultivation

Most coppicing is best undertaken in winter. If you delay – by accident or design – until late winter, then the tree may not put forth new shoots until late May or even June, which will restrict its growth that season. If the new shoots are particularly tasty (e.g. from Chinese cedar, *Toona sinensis*) then delayed coppicing may be used as a deliberate technique to spread the cropping season. Otherwise, aim to coppice by February at the latest.

Harvesting logs to use for growing mushrooms should take place only once you have the inoculant ready – so if you are buying inoculant, order it first, in early winter. Logs need inoculating very quickly otherwise spores of weed fungi will get in first.

Medicinal plants

For specific processing of medicinal plants please refer to an authoritative text (e.g. *The Encyclopedia of Medicinal Plants* – see Resources section). Very often the quantities of the substances with medicinal properties reach a maximum just before the plant flowers, so this is the optimum harvesting time. Time is of the essence when processing medicinal plants so as not to lose vital substances.

Poles and canes

Poles from plants such as coppiced hazel should be cut in winter when dormant, when you can see better what is going on. Most poles are not very durable and will last only a year, possibly two.

Bamboo canes can be cut at any time of year. Assuming they are of the right age (see pages 186-187, Chapter 13) then they need to be dried for several months after cutting to harden off and be of maximum durability.

Arrow bamboo (*Pseudosasa japonica*) has very straight canes.

Turkish rhubarb (*Rheum palmatum*).

Chapter 23

Maintenance

Irrigation and water use

Most plants in a temperate forest garden should not need irrigation, even in hot dry spells in summer (though this may change in decades to come). However, in very dry spells the yields of heavily fruiting trees in particular are likely to be affected, and it might be worth thinking ahead to what you will do in such a situation. After all, climate change science predicts that the UK is going to experience hotter and drier summers in future.

No irrigation at all

This is obviously the least work! And it is best-suited to loamy and clay soils. If you have a well-drained sandy soil then you need to either seriously think about irrigation or plant only drought-resistant crops – which excludes many fruit plants.

In dry spells, yields of late-summer- and autumn-fruiting trees and shrubs will suffer. Typically, fruit drop in June (when some natural fruit thinning always occurs) can be more severe, and fruit size will be reduced. The same applies to nut crops.

Selective irrigation of valued/fruiting trees

This is likely to be necessary on well-drained sandy soils.

Depending on the size of the garden, irrigation may require a network of pipes to be established – ideally at the outset, before you have planted much. Ordinary 20mm MDPE plastic water pipe should be adequate in most situations, buried 30cm (1') deep or so in trenches. Regular connection points or taps can be established to connect to mobile sections of pipe or hose, for watering specific plants.

You may want to water very young valuable trees or shrubs if they appear to be suffering from drought. These young plants, before they are properly established, are obviously at greater risk of drought damage than are established plants.

Otherwise, in a very dry spell you should aim to water only those trees and shrubs with significant crops of fruits or nuts, from July until September, when the fruits are swelling.

Water sources

Ideally, one should use naturally sourced water, grey water or rainwater. Grey water (water used once already by a household) will suffice only for a very small garden, and probably needs to be used quickly as problems may arise when it is stored. Similarly, water collected in butts will not go very far. For example, a medium-sized heavily fruiting tree (e.g. apple or plum, 4m/13' wide and high) might require in the region of 2.5cm (1") of irrigation water per week in a drought, which works out as some 400 litres per week.

Taking water from streams or rivers usually requires an abstraction licence and may not be reliable in droughts anyway.

Making a reservoir
The alternative, especially for larger gardens, is rain harvesting on a larger scale. 1m² of roof, reservoir area or collector will collect 700-1,000 litres of water per year in the UK. It does not take much effort or expense to dig a large hole and line it to create a reservoir. I have made several, the most recent a 50m³ (50,000-litre) reservoir measuring roughly 16m x 3m x 1m depth (53' x 10' x 3').

- Digging reservoirs in some areas may require planning permission, so check that out first.

- Ideally, create water storage at the highest point of your garden, so you can run water by siphon and gravity to wherever it is needed. On a gentle slope you can use the material dug out to form the lower retaining wall. Steeper slopes can be trickier and I would suggest getting professional advice.

- If you create a reservoir that is not very deep then you don't need to worry too much about retaining walls/dams or maintenance problems; also the deeper you dig, the more problems you may get with large rocks.

- A mini-digger in amateur hands can dig about 50m³ per day.

- As you dig, keep checking the levels of the top of the retaining walls (using a water-filled hose is easiest – the water levels at both ends of the hose will be level even though the hose dips into the hole and out again).

- Unless you have very clayey subsoil to use as a puddled liner, you will need a plastic or rubber liner. Before you put the liner in the hole, cover the whole of the sides and bottom of the hole with some sort of under-liner to protect the liner from rocks and stones. Old plastic sacks are ideal as an under-liner; you can also use turves if they are fairly stone-free.

- You may want to consider covering the reservoir to stop leaves, etc. getting in and potentially clogging filters and so on – I use green windbreak netting stretched over the top, which lets the rain through.

Irrigation methods

Avoid using sprinklers, which are very wasteful of water and may encourage diseases through wetting of foliage. On a small scale you can just use a hose directed beneath a tree, but by far the best method (from the point of view of the plant and soil) is micro-irrigation – low volume, slow, trickle or drip irrigation. Basically this is the frequent, slow application of water at specified points along water lines through emitters or applicators. It is a highly efficient way of delivering water directly to the root zone of the target plant. The delivery pipes and lines are usually 13-25mm (0.5-1") in diameter and can be above ground or below ground, as can the emitters themselves – in a forest garden it is unlikely you will need a permanent underground system, and you can use portable sections of pipe with drippers attached.

In small forest gardens a watering can and hose may the only methods of watering available. For very small and young plants a watering can is OK – use about 2-3 canfuls (around 20-30 litres) per square metre in a drought. If using a hose, measure out how long it takes for this quantity to run, and try to time the watering accordingly.

For larger forest gardens there are numerous types of delivery systems, including the following.

- 'Leaky' rubber or plastic pipes, which slowly leak water along their length. Some of these are low-pressure systems.

- Individual drippers (sometimes with adjustable flow rates) that drip typically at 1-4 litres/hour each. 'Compensating' drippers have a fixed flow rate whatever the water pressure; 'non-compensating' ones have a variable rate depending on the pressure. The drippers either plug into holes in the delivery pipe or can be fitted into small (typically 5mm) PVC pipes up to 1-2m (3'-6'6") long, which themselves plug into the delivery pipe. Drippers can be placed over small holes in the ground and covered with an upturned tin or similar to minimise evaporation losses. This system requires good water pressure.

- Micro-jets or micro-sprinklers, which have a higher flow rate (16-200 litres/hour) and larger orifices, and thus are less susceptible to cloggage problems. They can sprinkle water over an area of up to diameter 6m (20'). They require good water pressure and can sometimes lead to fungal problems from wetting of foliage.

Advantages of micro-irrigation

- Less water is used, reducing costs and conserving water resources.

- Weed growth is reduced because less soil surface is wetted.

- With leaky pipe or dripper systems, foliar diseases are reduced because foliage is not wetted.

- The uniform water application prevents plant stresses and enhances yield.

- It is easy to mix growth enhancers (e.g. seaweed solution) or fertilisers (e.g. nettle and comfrey liquid) with the water.

- Water is directed where it is needed most.

Disadvantages of micro-irrigation

- Initial costs for systems can be high.

- Above-ground systems have lines, tubes, etc. where they may get in the way of other operations.

- Below-ground systems are difficult to observe and repair.

- High-quality water supply is essential. Clogging of emitters, etc. can be a serious problem. Particles in the water must be eliminated by efficient filters.

- Damage to delivery lines and tubes by rodents and other animals can be a problem.

Where to irrigate

In terms of tree crops, most trees have roots that extend slightly beyond the drip line (i.e. the edge of the canopy where rain would drip down to the ground), with the concentration of roots highest at the drip line itself, although there will be feeder roots through the whole circular area that the drip line defines. So you should aim to irrigate this whole area and, if possible, apply more water in the drip line region than in the central region near the tree trunk. Thus a large fruit tree with drip irrigation may have four to eight drip emitters around it, and a fruiting bush one or two emitters.

Water spread from a drip irrigation system very much depends on the soil characteristics and length of time for which the dripper is dripping. Water tends to spread outwards underground in an inverted cone shape. Surface layers of soil are often irrigated to a diameter (centred on the dripper) of 60-100cm (2'-3'3"), whereas deeper layers are often irrigated to a diameter of 2m (6'6") or more.

Micro-irrigation systems can be operated at night, when there is minimum evaporation of water from the soil surface. Irrigation at night will wet a larger volume of soil than daytime irrigation.

Weeding

Apart from harvesting, weeding is the main job that takes any length of time in a forest garden. There is no such thing as a no-weed garden, and forest gardens must be weeded, otherwise they will turn back into forest dominated by whichever tree species are close by and are able to seed themselves there.

Having said that, compared with 'conventional' gardens, weeding in a forest garden does not take long. The aim in weeding should not be to remove every small plant that you don't want to be there – this is just a waste of effort! Instead, concentrate on controlling weeds that would become a real nuisance if not controlled – for example, brambles and tree weeds. When I weed my forest garden my main tool is a pair of garden shears. I very rarely dig up weeds, and only occasionally pull them up (I will pull up very small weed trees, for example); instead I just chop them off at soil level. Remember, weeds are often doing a tremendous job of bringing up nutrients into their top layers – many, such as docks (*Rumex* spp.) are mineral accumulators, and by cutting them and letting them regrow you will be increasing soil fertility for other plants – and the weeds will eventually give up after repeated cutting.

I do a weed round from spring until late summer, every 3-4 weeks. In April, the first weeding of the year takes the longest (2 days for my 2 acres). By June it takes one day and in August half a day. After that I don't bother as there as so few weeds left. The reason this works is that most of my ground-cover layer consists of plants that can outcompete pesky low weeds such as creeping buttercup (which likes Devon conditions), so with a bit of selective weeding (cutting) you can encourage the more desirable plants to dominate.

As well as tree weeds (ash and willow mainly) and brambles, I usually cut back docks and dandelions – both good accumulators – and cut or pull out nettles (for I have plenty around the edges of my forest garden); I also pull out cleavers, especially from around young plants, which they can damage. Smaller weeds such as buttercups, grasses, etc. may get cut occasionally but are usually swamped by plant growth by the summer.

To stop areas of herbaceous perennials, which die back down to the ground each winter, getting weedy – especially in mild areas where weeds might carry on growing in the winter – you can place a temporary sheet mulch over the top in the winter. Use something that is easily removed in early spring (a sheet of plastic, old carpet or cloth mulch) and make sure you remove it before the perennials start into growth.

If a patch in your forest garden gets excessively weedy and time-consuming to manage, consider replacing the existing perennial layer with another. This may necessitate sheet-mulching to kill off the existing plants first. When you are thinking about what to replant with, think about the niche(s) that the weedy species were exploiting and try to replant using desirable species that fill the same niche.

Pruning and coppicing

Cutting back trees and branches is a small but important part of forest garden maintenance. The diameter of the material being cut is usually small, and good hand tools (a bow saw and good pruning saw) are quite adequate.

Pruning

As I've mentioned previously, I try to keep pruning to a minimum. However, there is always some pruning to be done. I try to do most woody pruning in late winter – on dry sunny days in January and February, which is after the peak season for disease spores in the air. Most fruit trees, excepting the *Prunus* family and canopy trees such as alders, are best pruned at this time. Prune to remove dead wood and diseased wood, to raise canopies, and to stimulate new fruiting wood if needed. Deciduous hedges can also be trimmed now.

The *Prunus* family (plums, apricots, peaches, almonds, etc.) are best pruned from late spring to summer (May to August), to reduce the risk of silverleaf infection of branch cuts.

Unless diseased, prunings are best left on the ground to decay in their own time into the soil. There is no advantage in trying to compost them. You may need to cut them into smaller sections so they lie flatter and so don't impede foot traffic. You may also need to place them where the existing perennial layers of plants can cope with a mass of prunings – so not on your small tender plants! This is

an aspect of forest gardening that really distinguishes it from the 'conventional'.

Coppicing

Coppicing of most deciduous trees (including hazels for poles and willows for basketry materials, etc.) is best undertaken over the winter too. If you leave it until late in the winter you will delay the appearance of new shoots in spring (although this can be useful sometimes, if you want to spread the cropping season of new shoots).

Strictly speaking, coppicing means cutting all stems off low to the ground – as low as possible usually. This is fine if you do not have problems with deer or rabbits. I prefer to pollard, which is basically coppicing higher, at 1-2m (3'-6'6") high, which keeps young shoots out of reach of deer. Pollarding also lets more side light through to the ground under the tree and so gives you a wider choice of what to grow there.

Evergreen trees are best coppiced in late spring. This includes eucalypts, which are also susceptible to silver-leaf disease. Evergreen hedges are also best trimmed in late spring if required.

Other maintenance

Other tasks include path maintenance and propagating. How much work is needed will vary from garden to garden – for example, in the early years of a garden you are likely to be doing a lot more propagating than in later years when it is fully established.

Paths

Path maintenance will depend on your garden and design (see Chapter 20). Very often grass paths will be used, and these need scything, mowing or strimming through the garden season to maintain accessibility and stop the seeding of grasses into the garden beds.

Propagating

Spring is obviously the time for starting off seeds and root cuttings, and perhaps for doing some grafting.

Remember to save seeds from your plants through the growing season, especially of herbaceous perennials that you may well want more of to extend ground-layer plantings. In early summer you can start to take softwood cuttings of many plants, and later in the summer semi-ripe cuttings. Hardwood cuttings are best taken in late autumn, but they can be taken through the winter too. Trailing species can be layered in summer. See Chapter 8 for details of propagation techniques.

Pests

Although insect pests tend to be minimal – they get eaten by predators – larger animals can be a problem. In town gardens, rabbits and deer are unlikely to be a problem, although slugs, snails and rabbits can sometimes be more trouble in urban areas than in rural ones.

Slugs and snails

The permanent perennial cover in a forest garden encourages large numbers of slug predators such as ground beetles, but these molluscs can still be troublesome at times. Particularly susceptible perennials include hostas – so expect these to have holes in them. Mulberry trees when young are also susceptible to snails, which graze the bark off. Try to attract other predators, such as frogs by providing a pond. For small areas (e.g. an annuals vegetable patch), biological controls can work against slugs and organic slug pellets seem to work well.

Rabbits

You really need to keep rabbits out if you want to grow a productive perennial layer. If they are nearby then I strongly advise that you fence them out. Posts and 2.5cm (1") mesh netting do not cost too much in the grand scheme of things. One hint – rather than dig a trench for the fence as in traditional methods, just lay a portion of the netting outwards from the garden on the soil and peg or weigh down (see diagram). This works just as well and is a lot less effort.

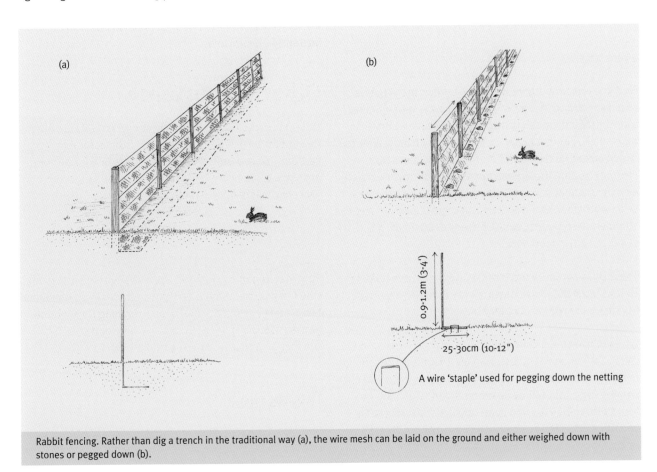

(a)

(b)

0.9-1.2m (3-4')

25-30cm (10-12")

A wire 'staple' used for pegging down the netting

Rabbit fencing. Rather than dig a trench in the traditional way (a), the wire mesh can be laid on the ground and either weighed down with stones or pegged down (b).

Deer

Deer are unlikely to come into a forest garden too much in the early years, when it is relatively open with only small trees. However, if they are nearby then as the garden matures they will come in more and more. A deer fence can be an expensive undertaking. Instead you can protect the most vulnerable trees – those of the apple family, for instance – with net guards to prevent browsing. Spiral rabbit guards will prevent bark-rubbing damage to small-diameter vulnerable trees or shrubs.

Squirrels

Red squirrels are protected in Britain, Ireland and much of mainland Europe, so in these areas the following applies only to grey squirrels. In North America both grey and red squirrels can be troublesome and may need controlling.

On a small scale deterrents can work, but not for long. Most sprays sold contain cayenne pepper and have to be renewed after rain. I have used plastic blow-up snakes to scare off squirrels from nut trees – they work for a week or so, but squirrels get used to anything quite soon.

Sweet chestnut fruits are too spiny for most squirrels, but if you have many other large nut trees and want nuts, then you can protect the trees by pruning them to form a 2.1m (7') straight trunk, and enclosing this each year with a strong smooth sheet of some hard material 1.2m (4') wide – tree guard plastic works for a year or two – starting at a height of 90cm (3'), so that the guard lies between the heights of 0.9m (3') and 2.1m (7'). The squirrels can't jump over it and it is too smooth to climb. Note that this only works if the squirrels can't jump from another tree into the canopy of the nut tree.

Apart from that the only controls that work are lethal ones. The best is live trapping, using cage traps baited with whole dried maize. If you do catch a grey squirrel in Britain you are legally obliged to kill it.

Birds

You will get a lot of birds in a forest garden, and some predation on fruits is inevitable. But you will also get the benefits of insect pest control and the influx of bird manures, which can be considerable.

Birds have a colour preference system for what fruits they go for: red or purple comes top, then orange and blue. White, yellow, green and black fruits have a much lower priority, so one thing you can do is deliberately choose fruit varieties with these unusually coloured fruits – such as yellow cherries, green elderberries and white strawberries. These will often be left untouched.

Also consider later-ripening varieties. The worst bird predation occurs when mothers still have young in the nests, from June to mid-August. After this the same type of fruit may be untouched. My late-ripening redcurrants, for example, are rarely bothered by birds.

You can also treat some crops, e.g. rowan and barberry, as sacrificial, knowing that the birds will go for these while your more valuable fruits are less troubled. It can work but is not altogether reliable – the birds may just take both crops!

Birds are not fooled for long by any one technique, so the thing to do is wait until fruits are nearly ripe before starting, then use a series of techniques, each one for no longer than 5 days or so – less if the birds become a problem. Solid plastic owls and snakes placed in trees are very effective for a few days. You can also use flashing tape (e.g. old audio tape strung between trees), foil strips, humming line (a commercial repellent that hums in the wind) or CDs hung up.

INSECT PEST CONTROL

Insect pests should not be a significant problem in a diverse forest garden system: there should be plenty of predators around to keep their numbers down. In my forest garden, aphids often turn up in spring on a few of their favourite plants, but within a week or two they have all vanished, eaten by hoverflies and other predators. Bats eat any codling moths, so I have no maggoty apples. I can basically stop thinking about insect pests and let the system do all the work for me – this works because I dedicate quite a lot of the ground-cover layer to beneficial insect plants.

Moths

Fruit tree moths are often problematical to fruit growers. Good control can be achieved through the use of two techniques together. Firstly, use pheromone traps for apple, pear and plum moths. These will trap male moths in summer and reduce fertilisation. Commercial organic growers often use these same pheromone chemicals to flood the air in an orchard and completely confuse moths.

Secondly, try to attract bats by putting up bat boxes. Bats are fantastic moth predators: one bat can eat 500 moths per night. That's a lot of potential fruit maggots!

Diseases

In the moist atmosphere of a forest garden, conditions are great for fungal diseases – for example scab, canker and mildew. When choosing varieties of the common top fruit species, make sure you choose those that are resistant, or at least not susceptible, to these diseases.

If you do get fungal problems on some trees, the first thing to do is see if you can improve soil conditions: a stressed tree is always more susceptible to diseases. Improve the soil by adding organic matter of any kind and the tree health might improve. You can also prune to make the tree more open, to improve air flow through it.

Avoid encouraging parasitic fungi (e.g. honey fungus) by treating with fungal inoculant any cut stumps that are not being left for coppice regrowth.

Garlic mustard (*Alliaria petiolata*).

Chapter 24

Ongoing tasks

So, you've planted out your forest garden – which may have taken several years, to fully underplant the trees and shrubs you've used. Now what?

Well, no garden, including a forest garden, should be set in stone. Plants do not live forever, and every now and then a tree or shrub may die, or a pest or disease may suddenly appear and affect the growth of, say, one of your herbaceous perennials so that it loses vigour and starts to get weedy.

So it is useful to keep a list of those trees and shrubs that you may have considered in your initial design, but decided you didn't have space for after all.

If something dies, do not replace it with the same type of plant – this is unwise because of the risk of replant disease. This is where soil pests and diseases attack the same species, which can suffer because it is small, whereas the original larger plant could tolerate these organisms. Instead, look back at your list and choose something new to try – or, if something is doing particularly well in your garden and you want more of it, then plant more.

Don't forget that forest gardens should be fun and enjoyable places to be in. In time you, the gardener, can become integrated into the garden too as part of its interconnected web of life. Experiment, play around, try new things – it all makes life more interesting.

As shade increases in the garden you might also find that the ground-covering effectiveness of some of the species you have planted suffers. If patches start to become weedy and are requiring a lot of maintenance then you should do something about it. You can mulch out failing areas of herbaceous perennials with a sheet mulch for a season, and replant with new shade-tolerant plants.

As your garden matures, environmental conditions will also be changing as a result of climate change. Summers in the UK are likely to get hotter and drier, winters will be wetter, storms will be more powerful, and new pests and diseases will arrive more and more frequently. Some plants are bound to suffer.

But the strength of the forest garden system is resilience through diversity – diversity of species and diversity of structure. When fields are turning brown in summer and gardeners are desperate to water their annual plants with diminishing water supplies, you will be able to forage in the cool shade of your forest garden, using and eating healthy plants grown in a system that mirrors the strength and beauty of natural ecosystems.

The forest garden bursting with new growth in spring.

Glossary

Accumulator: See *Mineral accumulator.*

Acid soil: Soil with a pH of less than 7.0; acid is the opposite of alkaline.

Actinorhizal: A group of nitrogen-fixing plants in which *Frankia* bacteria form the symbiosis to enable nitrogen fixation.

Adaptogen: A non-toxic herb that increases the body's resistance to stress, trauma, anxiety and fatigue.

Agro-ecosystem: A spatially and functionally coherent agricultural system, including the living and non-living components as well as their interactions.

Alkaline soil: Soil with a pH greater than 7.0; alkaline is the opposite of acid.

Allelopathy: A biological phenomenon that is characteristic of some plants, algae, bacteria, coral and fungi, by which they produce certain biochemicals that influence the growth and development of other organisms.

Annual: A plant that completes its life cycle in one year.

Aspect: The orientation of a slope – north, south, east, west, etc.

Berry picker: A hand-held harvesting tool with comb-like teeth to facilitate the harvesting of small fruits.

Biennial: A plant that completes its life cycle in two years.

Canopy tree: A tree in the highest layer of trees in a forest garden.

Chilling hours: For a particular perennial species, the number of hours of temperatures under 7.2°C (45°F) from when it becomes dormant for the winter. After a specific number of chilling hours, the plant is then ready to resume active growth when conditions are favourable.

Climax vegetation: The mix of species that will eventually grow at a given site if left undisturbed for a long time.

Closed canopy: The situation in a forest where the tree canopies are meeting.

Coppicing: Cutting a tree or shrub down low to the ground and allowing it to regrow.

Cultivar: A distinct genetic individual within a species, also called 'variety'.

Deciduous: Woody plants (trees and shrubs) that lose their leaves in winter.

Dormancy (in seeds): Dormant seeds are those where characteristics of the embryo prevent germination in favourable conditions until it has experienced a period of cold, moist conditions.

Dormancy (in trees and shrubs): Woody plants that exhibit dormancy require a certain number of 'chilling hours' (see left) over winter to allow normal growth to resume in spring.

Ecosystem: An ecological community together with its environment, functioning as a unit.

*Frankia***:** A genus of bacteria that associates with the actinorhizal plants in nitrogen-fixing symbiosis.

Fruit leather: Fruit pulp that has been dried to form a thin leathery preserve.

Graftwood: Scions of a cultivar to be used for grafting on to a rootstock.

Green manure: A plant that is deliberately grown to improve soil conditions.

Guild: A group of plant species that support each other in beneficial ways, aiding self-maintenance.

Harvesting comb: see *Berry picker.*

Herbaceous: A plant with no woody parts.

Hyphae: long, branching filamentous cells of a fungus; the main mode of its vegetative growth.

Improved fruit/cultivar/variety: A fruit species that has been bred for increased fruit size and/or yield.

Leather: See *Fruit leather.*

Legume: A family of nitrogen-fixing plants in which *Rhizobium* bacteria form the symbiosis to enable nitrogen fixation.

Mineral accumulator: A plant that is particularly good at extracting certain minerals from the soil (or especially the subsoil) and concentrating them in the top growth and ultimately the topsoil.

Mineralisation: The process of minerals being made available from the soil for plants by the action of various soil fauna.

Mycorrhiza: A fungus that forms a symbiotic association with plant roots.

Nitrogen fixer: A plant with symbiotic bacteria living attached to its roots, which can take nitrogen from the air in the soil and make it available to the plant.

Niche: The place or function of a given or potential organism within its ecosystem.

Nut Wizard harvester: A hand tool to aid the harvest of nuts from the ground (see Resources section).

Nutrient cycling: The process by which nutrients are recycled from the soil through plants and back to the soil.

Perennial: A plant that lives for three or more years.

pH: A scale of 0-14, measuring acidity and alkalinity. pH 7.0 is neutral; less than 7 is increasingly acid; more than 7 is increasingly alkaline.

Pioneer species: Species that colonise previously uncolonised land, or land that has been cleared either by people or natural events such as forest fires.

Pollarding: Cutting a tree or shrub down to 1-2+m (3'-6'6"+) from the ground and allowing it to regrow.

Rhizobial: A plant of the legume family.

Rhizobium: A genus of bacteria that associates with the leguminous plants in nitrogen-fixing symbiosis.

Rhizome: A root-like structure of herbaceous plants that runs horizontally under the soil surface.

Root turnover: The process, in perennial and woody plants, of fine roots growing and dying off each year.

Rootstock: The part of a grafted fruit tree that forms the roots and very low part of the trunk.

Scarify: Seed treatment to soften a hard shell and improve germination.

Scion: The part of a grafted fruit tree that forms the branches and bears fruits or nuts.

Species: A distinct and closely related group of plants that can interbreed with each other.

Spp.: Abbreviation of species (plural).

Stool: A living stump of a tree or shrub capable of producing shoots or cuttings.

Stratification: A period of cold moist conditions, sometimes preceded by warm moist conditions, that dormant seeds must undergo before they will germinate.

Succession: The gradual process of change in an ecosystem brought about by the progressive replacement of one species community by another.

Symbiosis: A close and often long-term interaction between different biological species, from which both organisms benefit.

Transpiration: The process of water absorption by plant roots, the movement of water through the plant, and the loss of water to the air through small openings on the underside of leaves called stomata.

Unimproved fruit/cultivar/variety: A fruit species that has not been bred for increased fruit size and/or yield.

Variety: Often used to mean 'cultivar' (see above); however, the two words are not synonymous because 'variety' as a botanical term (usually abbreviated to 'var.') is a taxonomic rank. 'Variety' also has a legal meaning with respect to plant breeders' rights. This is why I have used the term 'cultivar' through this book.

Wake zone: The area to the lee of a windbreak where turbulent winds can cause damage.

Propagation tables

Tree and shrub propagation by seed

The majority of tree and shrub seeds need some sort of pre-treatment before they will germinate properly.

Tree or shrub species		Treatment (weeks of stratification)	Comments
Acacia spp.	Wattles	Scarify	
Acer spp.	Maples / sycamore	Most need 13 weeks	
Actinidia arguta	Hardy kiwi	13 weeks	
Actinidia deliciosa	Kiwi	8-13 weeks	
Actinidia kolomikta	Hardy kiwi	26 weeks, start in summer in warm	
Alnus spp.	Alders	8 weeks	Very fast-growing
Amelanchier alnifolia	Saskatoon	20 weeks, start in early autumn in warm	Most seedlings true to type, i.e. very close genetically to parent
Amorpha fruticosa	False indigo	Scarify	
Araucaria araucana	Monkey puzzle	Not dormant	Slow to germinate
Arbutus unedo	Strawberry tree	Not dormant	
Aronia spp.	Chokeberries	13 weeks	
Asimina triloba	Pawpaw	13 weeks	Slow to germinate
Atriplex spp.	Saltbushes	Not dormant	
Berberis spp.	Barberries	8-13 weeks	
Betula spp.	Birches	Not dormant	Needs light to germinate
Calycanthus spp.	American allspice	13 weeks	
Caragana arborescens	Siberian pea tree	Scarify	
Carya spp.	Hickories	13 weeks	
Carya illinoinensis	Pecan	Not dormant	
Castanea spp.	Chestnuts	Not dormant	Sow immediately in autumn
Ceanothus americanus	New Jersey tea	Scarify	
Cephalotaxus spp.	Plum yews	13 weeks	Slow to germinate
Cercis spp.	Redbuds	Scarify then 8 weeks	
Chaenomeles spp.	Flowering quinces	13 weeks	

Tree or shrub species		Treatment (weeks of stratification)	Comments
Citrus spp.	Citrus	Not dormant	
Clematis vitalba	Old man's beard	12 weeks	
Cornus capitata	Bentham's cornel	8 weeks	
Cornus kousa	Chinese dogwood	14 weeks	
Cornus mas	Cornelian cherry	23 weeks	Slow to germinate, may take a second year
Cornus stolonifera	Red osier	13 weeks	
Corylus spp.	Hazels	16 weeks	
Crataegus spp.	Hawthorns	13 weeks, often require a preceding 26 weeks of warmth	Slow to germinate, may take a second year
Cydonia oblonga	Quince	13 weeks	Cultivars usually grafted
Cytisus scoparius	Broom	Scarify	
Decaisnea fargesii	Blue bean	Scarify	Seedlings prone to damping off
Diospyros kaki	Japanese persimmon	4 weeks	
Diospyros lotus	Date plum	4 weeks	
Diospyros virginiana	American persimmon	13 weeks	
Drimys lanceolata	Mountain pepper	Not dormant	
Elaeagnus angustifolia	Oleaster	Not dormant	
Elaeagnus x *ebbingei*		Not dormant	Fresh seed in spring may not germinate for a year
Elaeagnus multiflora	Goumi	8 weeks	
Elaeagnus umbellata	Autumn olive	13 weeks, start in early autumn in warm	
Eucalyptus spp.	Eucalyptus	Not dormant	Seed very small
Fagus sylvatica	Beech	16 weeks	
Ficus carica	Fig	Not dormant	Cultivars usually propagated via cuttings
Fraxinus excelsior	Ash	34 weeks	
Fuchsia spp.	Fuchsias	Not dormant	
Garrya spp.	Fever bush	13 weeks	
Gaultheria procumbens	Wintergreen	13 weeks	
Gaultheria shallon	Salal	17 weeks	Very small seed, ericaceous
Genista tinctoria	Dyer's greenweed	Scarify	
Ginkgo biloba	Maidenhair tree	Not dormant	
Halesia carolina	Snowbell tree	13 weeks	
Hippophae rhamnoides	Sea buckthorn	17 weeks	
Juglans spp.	Walnut / heartnut / butternut	13 weeks	Cultivars usually grafted
Juniperus communis	Juniper	26 weeks, start in summer in warm	
Laurus nobilis	Bay	Not dormant	
Lavandula spp.	Lavenders	Not dormant	

Tree or shrub species		Treatment (weeks of stratification)	Comments
Lespedeza bicolor	Bush clover	Scarify	
Lonicera caerulea	Blue honeysuckle	13 weeks	
Lonicera periclymenum	Honeysuckle	13 weeks	
Lupinus spp.	Lupins	Scarify	
Lycium barbarum	Goji berry	Not dormant	
Maackia amurensis	Amur maackia	Scarify	
Mahonia spp.	Oregon grapes	17 weeks	
Malus spp.	Crab apples	16 weeks	Can be used as an apple rootstock. Apple cultivars usually grafted
Mitchella repens	Partridge berry	22-26 weeks	
Morus spp.	Mulberries	13-16 weeks	
Myrica spp.	Bayberries	8-13 weeks	Fruits need dewaxing first by rubbing between two sheets of sandpaper
Myrtus communis	Myrtle	Not dormant	
Myrtus ugni	Chilean guava	Not dormant	
Parthenocissus spp.	Virginia creeper / Boston ivy	12 weeks	
Philadelphus spp.	Mock orange	8-17 weeks	
Phormium tenax	New Zealand flax	Not dormant	
Phyllostachys spp.	Bamboos	Not dormant	
Pinus armandii	Chinese white pine	13 weeks	
Pinus cembra	Arolla pine	26 weeks, start in summer in warm	
Pinus cembroides / P. edulis / P. monophylla	Piñon pines	Not dormant	
Pinus gerardiana	Nepal nut pine	13 weeks	
Pinus koraiensis	Korean nut pine	13 weeks	
Pinus nigra var. *maritima*	Corsican pine	4 weeks	
Pinus pinea	Stone pine	Not dormant	
Pinus radiata	Monterey pine	4 weeks	
Pinus sibirica	Siberian nut pine	13 weeks	
Pleioblastus simonii	Simon bamboo	Not dormant	
Populus spp.	Poplars	Not dormant	
Poncirus trifoliata	Trifoliate orange	Not dormant	
Prunus armeniaca	Apricot	13 weeks	Cultivars usually grafted
Prunus avium / P. cerasus	Sweet / sour cherry	13-16 weeks	Cultivars usually grafted
Prunus cerasifera	Cherry plum	24 weeks, start in late summer in warm	Can be a useful plum rootstock. Cultivars usually grafted
Prunus domestica / P. insititia	Plum / gage / damson / bullace	13 weeks	Cultivars usually grafted
Prunus dulcis	Almond	13 weeks	Cultivars usually grafted

Tree or shrub species		Treatment (weeks of stratification)	Comments
Prunus persica	Peach / nectarine	29 weeks, start in summer in warm	Not as highly bred as apples – you may be lucky! Cultivars usually grafted
Prunus spinosa	Blackthorn	13 weeks	
Prunus tomentosa	Nanking cherry	13 weeks	
Pseudosasa japonica	Arrow bamboo	Not dormant	
Pyrus communis	Wild (European) pear	16 weeks	Can be a vigorous pear rootstock. Cultivars usually grafted
Quercus spp.	Oaks	Not dormant	Sow immediately in the autumn
Rhus spp.	Sumachs	8-13 weeks	
Ribes spp.	Currants / gooseberry	13 weeks	Cultivars usually propagated from cuttings
Robinia pseudoacacia	Black locust	Scarify	
Rosa rugosa	Apple rose	17 weeks	
Rosmarinus officinalis	Rosemary	Not dormant	
Rubus spp.	Blackberries / raspberries	16 weeks	Cultivars usually propagated from cuttings
Salix spp.	Willows	Not dormant	
Salvia officinalis	Sage	Not dormant	
Sambucus spp.	Elders	39 weeks, start in summer in warm	
Semiarundinaria fastuosa	Narihira bamboo	Not dormant	
Shepherdia spp.	Buffalo berries	13 weeks	
Sorbus spp.	Rowans / whitebeams / service trees	16 weeks	
Staphylea spp.	Bladdernuts	35 weeks, start in summer in warm	
Symphoricarpos spp.	Snowberries	13 weeks warm + 26 weeks cold	
Thuja plicata	Western red cedar	4 weeks	
Tilia spp.	Limes, lindens	39 weeks, start in summer in warm	
Toona sinensis	Chinese cedar	8 weeks	
Ulex europaeus	Gorse	Scarify	
Vaccinium spp.	Blueberries / cranberries	13-16 weeks	Ericaceous, very small seed. Cultivars usually propagated from cuttings
Viburnum opulus var. *americanum*	Highbush cranberry	26 weeks, start in summer in warm	
Vinca spp.	Periwinkles	12 weeks	
Vitex agnus-castus	Chaste tree	Not dormant	
Vitis spp.	Grapes	13 weeks	Cultivars usually grafted or taken from cuttings
Wisteria spp.	Wisterias	Scarify	

Tree or shrub species		Treatment (weeks of stratification)	Comments
Xanthoceras sorbifolium	Yellowhorn	Not dormant	
Yushania spp.	Bamboos	Not dormant	
Zanthoxylum spp.	Pepper trees	13-17 weeks	

Herbaceous perennial propagation by seed

Seeds of many herbaceous perennials also need some sort of pre-treatment before they will germinate properly. Note that *Gaultheria*, *Mitchella*, *Rubus*, *Vaccinium* and *Vinca* are in the tree and shrub table on the preceding pages.

Herbaceous perennial species		Treatment (weeks of stratification)	Comments
Acanthus mollis	Bear's breech	Not dormant	
Aegopodium podagraria	Ground elder	Not dormant	
Agastache foeniculum / A. rugosa	Anise hyssop / Korean mint	Not dormant	
Ajuga reptans	Bugle	Not dormant	
Alchemilla mollis	Lady's mantle	4 weeks	
Alliaria petiolata	Garlic mustard	Not dormant	
Allium ampeloprasum var. *babingtonii*	Babington's leek		Does not produce seed, propagate from bulbils (not dormant)
Allium cepa	Multiplier onions / Egyptian onion		Does not produce seed, propagate from bulbils (not dormant)
Allium fistulosum	Welsh onion	Not dormant	
Allium neapolitanum	Daffodil garlic	Not dormant	
Allium tricoccum	Ramps	15 weeks	
Allium tuberosum	Garlic chives	Not dormant	
Allium ursinum	Ramsons	15 weeks	
Althaea officinalis	Marsh mallow	Not dormant	
Amphicarpaea bracteata	Hog peanut	Scarify	
Angelica sylvestris	Wild angelica	Not dormant	
Apios americana	Groundnut	Scarify	
Aquilegia vulgaris	Columbine	Not dormant	
Armoracia rusticana	Horseradish	Not dormant	Seed rarely produced
Asarum spp.	Wild ginger / asarabacca	18 weeks, 10 weeks warm + 8 weeks cold	
Asparagus officinalis	Asparagus	Not dormant	
Asphodeline lutea	Yellow asphodel	Not dormant	
Astragalus glycyphyllos	Milk vetch	Scarify	

Herbaceous perennial species		Treatment (weeks of stratification)	Comments
Beta vulgaris subsp. *maritima*	Sea beet	Not dormant	
Brassica oleracea	Perennial broccoli / collards / kale	Not dormant	
Bunias orientalis	Turkish rocket	Not dormant	
Bunium bulbocastanum	Pig nut	Not dormant	
Camassia quamash	Quamash	4 weeks	Slow to germinate
Campanula spp.	Bellflowers	Not dormant	
Cardamine spp.	Bittercresses	Not dormant	
Centranthus ruber	Red valerian	Not dormant	
Chenopodium bonus-henricus	Good King Henry	Not dormant	
Chrysogonum virginianum	Golden star	Not dormant	
Chrysosplenium spp.	Golden saxifrages	Not dormant	
Cichorium intybus	Chicory	Not dormant	
Claytonia sibirica	Siberian purslane	Not dormant	
Cornus canadensis	Creeping dogwood	26 weeks, start in summer in warm	
Crambe spp.	Colewort / sea kale / Tartar bread plant	Not dormant	
Cryptotaenia japonica	Mitsuba	Not dormant	
Cynara spp.	Cardoon / globe artichoke	Not dormant	
Duchesnea indica	False strawberry	Not dormant	
Echinacea spp.	Coneflowers	Not dormant	
Epilobium angustifolium	Rosebay willowherb	Not dormant	
Filipendula ulmaria	Meadowsweet	13 weeks	
Foeniculum vulgare	Fennel	Not dormant	
Fragaria spp.	Strawberries	4-8 weeks	
Galax urceolata	Wand flower	Not dormant	
Galium odoratum	Sweet woodruff	10 weeks, 4 weeks warm + 6 weeks cold	
Geranium macrorrhizum	Rock cranesbill	Not dormant	
Glechoma hederacea	Ground ivy	Not dormant	
Glycyrrhiza spp.	Liquorices	Scarify	
Hablitzia tamnoides	Caucasian spinach	13 weeks	Slow to germinate
Helianthus tuberosus	Jerusalem artichoke		Grown from tubers
Hemerocallis spp.	Day lilies	Not dormant	
Heuchera spp.	Alum roots	Not dormant	
Hosta spp.	Hostas	Not dormant	
Humulus lupulus	Hop	10 weeks, 4 weeks warm + 6 weeks cold	
Hydrastis canadensis	Goldenseal	Not dormant	Sow fresh seed if possible

Herbaceous perennial species		Treatment (weeks of stratification)	Comments
Hypericum perforatum	St John's wort	Not dormant	
Lathyrus spp.	Sweet peas	Scarify	
Levisticum officinale	Lovage	Not dormant	
Lotus spp.	Bird's foot trefoils	Scarify	
Lupinus spp.	Lupins	Scarify	
Lysimachia nummularia	Creeping jenny	Not dormant	Seed rarely produced
Malva spp.	Mallows	Not dormant	
Matteuccia struthiopteris	Ostrich fern		Propagate from spores – very small (not dormant)
Medicago sativa	Lucerne	Not dormant	
Melissa officinalis	Lemon balm	Not dormant	
Mentha spp.	Mints	Not dormant	
Myrrhis odorata	Sweet cicely	20-24 weeks	
Nasturtium officinale	Watercress	Not dormant	
Origanum vulgare	Oregano	Not dormant	
Oxalis acetosella / O. oregana	Wood sorrel / redwood sorrel	15 weeks	Usually grown from division
Oxyria digyna	Mountain sorrel	Not dormant	
Panax spp.	Ginseng	18 months	
Passiflora incarnata	Maypop	Not dormant	
Peltaria alliacea	Garlic cress	Not dormant	
Petasites japonicus	Giant butterbur	Not dormant	Usually grown from division
Phytolacca americana	Poke root	13 weeks	
Plantago spp.	Plantains	Not dormant	
Polygonatum spp.	Solomon's seals	Not dormant	
Potentilla anserina	Silverweed	10 weeks, 4 weeks warm + 6 weeks cold	
Primula vulgaris	Primrose	Not dormant	
Pulmonaria officinalis	Lungwort	8 weeks	
Reichardia picroides	French scorzonera	Not dormant	
Rheum spp.	Rhubarbs	Not dormant	
Rumex spp.	Sorrels	Not dormant	
Sanguinaria canadensis	Bloodroot	8 weeks	
Sanguisorba minor	Salad burnet	Not dormant	
Saponaria officinalis	Soapwort	8 weeks, 4 weeks warm + 4 weeks cold	
Scorzonera hispanica	Scorzonera	Not dormant	
Sedum spp.	Sedums / orpine	Not dormant	
Sium sisarum	Skirret	Not dormant	
Smilacina racemosa	False spikenard	16 weeks, 8 weeks warm + 8 weeks cold	

Herbaceous perennial species		Treatment (weeks of stratification)	Comments
Solidago spp.	Goldenrods	Not dormant	
Stachys affinis	Chinese artichoke		Grown from tubers
Stellaria graminea	Lesser stitchwort	Not dormant	
Symphytum spp.	Comfreys	Not dormant	
Tanacetum parthenium / T. vulgare	Feverfew / tansy	Not dormant	
Taraxacum officinale	Dandelion	Not dormant	
Tiarella cordifolia	Foam flower	Not dormant	
Trifolium spp.	Clovers	Not dormant	
Urtica dioica	Stinging nettle	Not dormant	
Valeriana officinalis	Valerian	Not dormant	
Vicia spp.	Vetches	Scarify	
Viola spp.	Violets	Not dormant	
Waldsteinia ternata	Barren strawberry	15 weeks	

Propagation by cuttings

TREES & SHRUBS SUITABLE FOR HARDWOOD CUTTINGS		
Species		**Comments**
Berberis spp.	Barberries	Some species only
Cornus stolonifera	Red osier	
Elaeagnus angustifolia	Oleaster	
Elaeagnus umbellata	Autumn olive	
Hippophae rhamnoides	Sea buckthorn	
Hippophae salicifolia	Himalayan sea buckthorn	
Lonicera caerulea	Blue honeysuckle	
Ribes x *culverwellii*	Jostaberry	
Ribes divaricatum / R. odoratum	Worcesterberry / buffalo currant	
Ribes nigrum	Blackcurrant	
Ribes rubrum	Redcurrant	
Ribes uva-crispa	Gooseberry	Not quite so easy as other *Ribes* spp.
Rubus fruticosus	Blackberry	Cut off green leaves if necessary
Rubus x *loganobaccus*	Loganberry	
Salix spp.	Willows	
Sambucus canadensis	American elder	Elders come into leaf very early, so take cuttings no later than January
Sambucus nigra	European elder	
Sambucus racemosa	Red elder	

TREES & SHRUBS SUITABLE FOR HARDWOOD CUTTINGS		
Species		**Comments**
Viburnum opulus var. *americanum*	Highbush cranberry	
Vitis spp.	Grapes	Late to leaf out

TREES & SHRUBS SUITABLE FOR SUMMER CUTTINGS		
Species		**Comments**
Actinidia spp.	Kiwis	Semi-ripe
Akebia spp.	Chocolate vine	Semi-ripe
Aronia spp.	Chokeberries	Semi-ripe
Atriplex spp.	Saltbushes	Semi-ripe
Berberis spp.	Barberries	Semi-ripe
Cephalotaxus spp.	Plum yews	Semi-ripe, autumn
Chaenomeles spp.	Flowering quinces	Semi-ripe with heel
Cornus kousa	Chinese dogwood	Softwood
Cytisus scoparius	Broom	Semi-ripe with heel
Drimys lanceolata	Mountain pepper	Semi-ripe
Elaeagnus spp.	Elaeagnus	Semi-ripe. Good for evergreen spp.
Ficus carica	Fig	Softwood or semi-ripe
Fuchsia spp.	Fuchsias	Softwood or semi-ripe
Gaultheria spp.	Wintergreen / salal	Semi-ripe
Juniperus spp.	Junipers	Semi-ripe or take in spring
Laurus nobilis	Bay	Semi-ripe
Lonicera caerulea	Blue honeysuckle	Semi-ripe
Lycium barbarum	Goji berry	Semi-ripe
Morus spp.	Mulberries	Softwood, can be difficult to overwinter
Myrica spp.	Bayberries	Semi-ripe with heel
Poncirus trifoliata	Trifoliate orange	Semi-ripe
Rosmarinus officinalis	Rosemary	Semi-ripe
Salix spp.	Willows	Any time
Schisandra chinensis	Magnolia vine	Semi-ripe
Staphylea spp.	Bladdernuts	Semi-ripe with heel
Vaccinium spp.	Blueberries / cranberries	Semi-ripe
Vinca spp.	Periwinkles	Semi-ripe

Propagation by layering

All the species in this table are suitable for setting up in propagation beds, and will produce rooted plants within a few months. Many other woody plants can also be layered but may take 1-2 years to produce a rooted plant.

SHRUBS SUITABLE FOR LAYERING		
Species		**Comment**
Actinidia spp.	Kiwis	Spring, slow
Akebia spp.	Chocolate vine	Layer into pots, easy
Rubus 'Betty Ashburner'	Groundcover raspberry	Layer into pots, easy
Rubus nepalensis	Nepalese raspberry	Layer into pots, easy
Rubus pentalobus	Creeping bramble	Layer into pots, easy
Rubus phoenicolasius	Japanese wineberry	Layer on to ground
Rubus tricolor	Chinese bramble	Layer into pots, easy
Schisandra chinensis	Magnolia vine	Spring and summer
Vitis spp.	Grapes	Layer into pots, easy

Vegetative propagation of herbaceous perennials

Herbaceous perennial species		Cuttings	Division	Layering
Acanthus mollis	Bear's breech	Root cuttings, early winter	Spring or autumn	
Aegopodium podagraria	Ground elder	Rhizome cuttings	Spring	
Agastache foeniculum / A. rugosa	Anise hyssop / Korean mint		Spring	
Ajuga reptans	Bugle			Spring and summer
Alchemilla mollis	Lady's mantle		Spring or autumn	
Allium fistulosum	Welsh onion		Spring	
Allium neapolitanum	Daffodil garlic		Spring	
Allium tuberosum	Garlic chives		Spring	
Apios americana	Groundnut		Spring	
Aquilegia vulgaris	Columbine		Spring	
Armoracia rusticana	Horseradish		Spring	
Asarum spp.	Wild ginger / asarabacca		Spring	
Asparagus officinalis	Asparagus		Winter	
Asphodeline lutea	Yellow asphodel		Spring	
Astragalus glycyphyllos	Milk vetch		Spring	
Bamboos			Spring	

Herbaceous perennial species		Cuttings	Division	Layering
Brassica oleracea	Perennial broccoli / collards / kale	Soft basal cuttings, spring		
Bunias orientalis	Turkish rocket		Spring	
Campanula spp.	Bellflowers	Soft basal cuttings, spring	Spring	
Centranthus ruber	Red valerian	Softwood cuttings		
Chrysogonum virginianum	Golden star		Spring	Summer
Chrysosplenium spp.	Golden saxifrages		Spring	
Claytonia sibirica	Siberian purslane		Spring	
Cornus canadensis	Creeping dogwood		Spring	
Crambe spp.	Colewort / sea kale / Tartar bread plant	Root cuttings, winter	Spring	
Cynara spp.	Cardoon / globe artichoke		Spring	
Duchesnea indica	False strawberry			Spring and summer
Echinacea spp.	Coneflower	Root cuttings, winter	Spring	
Epilobium angustifolium	Rosebay willowherb		Spring or autumn	
Filipendula ulmaria	Meadowsweet		Spring or autumn	
Foeniculum vulgare	Fennel		Spring	
Fragaria spp.	Strawberries			Spring and summer
Galax urceolata	Wand flower		Spring	
Galium odoratum	Sweet woodruff	Softwood, late spring	Spring	
Geranium macrorrhizum	Rock cranesbill		Spring	
Glechoma hederacea	Ground ivy	Softwood, any time	Spring	Spring and summer
Glycyrrhiza spp.	Liquorices		Spring	
Gunnera spp.	Gunneras		Spring	
Gymnostemma pentaphyllum	Sweet tea vine		Spring	Summer
Hablitzia tamnoides	Caucasian spinach		Spring or autumn	Summer
Helianthus tuberosus	Jerusalem artichoke		Spring	
Hemerocallis spp.	Day lilies		Spring	
Heuchera americana	Alum root		Spring or autumn	
Hosta spp.	Hostas		Spring	
Humulus lupulus	Hop		Spring	
Lathyrus spp.	Sweet peas		Spring	
Levisticum officinale	Lovage	Root cuttings with bud(s), spring	Spring	
Lupinus spp.	Lupins	Soft basal cuttings, spring		
Lysimachia nummularia	Creeping jenny		Spring	Any time
Malva spp.	Mallows	Soft basal cuttings, spring		

Herbaceous perennial species		Cuttings	Division	Layering
Matteuccia struthiopteris	Ostrich fern		Spring	
Melissa officinalis	Lemon balm		Spring	
Mentha spp.	Mints	Summer, will root in water; also root cuttings	Spring	
Mitchella repens	Partridge berry	Summer	Spring	
Myrrhis odorata	Sweet cicely	Root cuttings with bud(s), autumn & winter	Spring or autumn	
Origanum vulgare	Oregano	Soft basal cuttings, spring	Spring	
Oxalis acetosella / O. oregana	Wood sorrel / redwood sorrel		Spring	
Passiflora incarnata	Maypop			Spring and summer
Peltaria alliacea	Garlic cress		Spring or autumn	
Petasites japonicus	Giant butterbur		All year	
Phytolacca americana	Poke root		Spring	
Polygonatum spp.	Solomon's seals	Rhizomes with buds, spring	Spring	
Potentilla anserina	Silverweed		Spring	
Primula vulgaris	Primrose		Autumn	
Pulmonaria officinalis	Lungwort	Root cuttings, winter	Spring or autumn	
Rheum spp.	Rhubarbs		Spring	
Rumex spp.	Sorrels		Spring	
Sanguinaria canadensis	Bloodroot		Late spring	
Sanguisorba minor	Salad burnet		Spring	
Saponaria officinalis	Soapwort		Spring or autumn	
Sedum spp.	Sedums	Soft and leaf cuttings, summer	Spring	
Sedum telephium	Orpine	Soft and leaf cuttings, summer	Spring	
Smilacina racemosa	False spikenard		Spring	
Solidago spp.	Goldenrods		Spring or autumn	
Stachys affinis	Chinese artichoke		Winter and spring	
Symphytum spp.	Comfreys	Root cuttings, winter and spring	Spring	
Tanacetum parthenium / T. vulgare	Feverfew / tansy	Soft basal cuttings, spring	Spring	
Tiarella cordifolia	Foam flower		Spring	
Trifolium spp.	Clovers		Spring	
Urtica dioica	Stinging nettle		Winter	
Valeriana officinalis	Valerian	Soft basal cuttings, spring	Spring or autumn	
Viola odorata	Sweet violet	Basal shoots, late summer	Spring	Summer
Waldsteinia ternata	Barren strawberry		Spring	

Appendix 2

Trees and shrubs for hedging and fencing

Trees and shrubs for windbreak hedges

These are trees and shrubs which can primarily be used for their windbreak ability, but which also have other uses.

SMALL SHRUBS – 0.6-3m (2-10') HIGH					
Species		**Evergreen**	**N-fixer**	**Edible**	**Main other use**
Alnus viridis	Green alder		✓		
Amelanchier alnifolia	Saskatoon			Fruit	Bee plant
Aronia spp.	Chokeberries			Fruit	Bee plant
Atriplex spp.	Saltbushes	✓		Leaves	
Berberis spp.	Barberries	✓some		Fruit	Bee plant
Caragana arborescens	Siberian pea tree		✓	Seed	Bee plant
Cornus stolonifera	Red osier				Basketry
Corylus spp.	Hazels			Nut	
Cytisus scoparius	Broom		✓		Bee plant
Elaeagnus multiflora	Goumi	✓some	✓	Fruit	Bee plant
Garrya elliptica	Fever bush	✓			Medicinal
Gaultheria shallon	Salal	✓		Fruit	Bee plant
Juniperus communis	Juniper	✓		Fruit	
Mahonia spp., e.g. *M. aquifolium*	Oregon grapes	✓		Fruit	
Phormium tenax	New Zealand flax	✓			Fibre, twine
Poncirus trifoliata	Trifoliate orange			Fruit	
Ribes spp., e.g. *R. nigrum*	Currants			Fruit	Leaves for teas
Rosa spp., e.g. *R. rugosa*	Roses			Fruit	Flowers in salads
Rubus tricolor	Chinese bramble	✓		Fruit	Ground cover
Salix spp.	Willows				Basketry, bee plant
Symphoricarpos spp.	Snowberries				Bee plant
Ulex europaeus	Gorse		✓		Bee plant

LARGE SHRUBS – 3-8m (10-26') HIGH

Species		Evergreen	N-fixer	Edible	Main other use
Alnus spp.	Alders		✓		
Amelanchier spp.	Juneberries			Fruit	Bee plant
Arbutus unedo	Strawberry tree	✓		Fruit	Bee plant
Berberis spp.	Barberries	✓some		Fruit	Bee plant
Cornus spp., e.g. *C. kousa*	Dogwoods			Fruit	
Corylus spp., e.g. *C. avellana*	Hazels			Nut	
Elaeagnus x *ebbingei*		✓	✓	Fruit	Bee plant
Elaeagnus umbellata	Autumn olive		✓	Fruit	Bee plant
Pseudosasa japonica	Arrow bamboo	✓			Bamboo shoots/ canes
Rosa spp.	Roses			Fruit	
Salix spp.	Willows				Basketry, bee plant
Sambucus spp., e.g. *S. canadensis*	Elders			Fruit	Edible flowers
Viburnum opulus var. *americanum*	Highbush cranberry			Fruit	Bee plant

SMALL TREES – UNDER 10m (33') HIGH

Species		Evergreen	N-fixer	Edible	Main other use
Crataegus spp.	Hawthorns			Fruit	Bee plant
Hippophae rhamnoides	Sea buckthorn		✓	Fruit	Bee plant
Malus spp.	Crab apples			Fruit	Bee plant
Pinus spp.	Pines	✓		Seed	Medicinal
Prunus cerasifera	Cherry plum			Fruit	Bee plant
Prunus insititia	Damson / bullace			Fruit	Bee plant
Salix spp.	Willows				Basketry, bee plant
Sambucus nigra	European elder			Fruit	Edible flowers
Sorbus spp., e.g *S. aucuparia*	Rowans / whitebeams / service trees			Fruit	Only some edible

LARGE TREES – OVER 10m (33') HIGH					
Species		Evergreen	N-fixer	Edible	Main other use
Alnus cordata	Italian alder		✓		
Alnus rubra	Red alder		✓		
Hippophae salicifolia	Himalayan sea buckthorn			Fruit	Bee plant
Pinus radiata	Monterey pine	✓			
Pinus nigra var. *maritima*	Corsican pine	✓			

Trees suitable for short-rotation (5 years) coppice within hedge

Note that not all these species have their own detailed entry in the book.

Tree species		Evergreen	N-fixer	Edible	Main other use
Alnus glutinosa	Common alder		✓		For firewood or as mushroom logs for growing shiitake or oyster mushrooms, etc.
Betula pendula	Silver birch				
Betula pubescens	Downy birch				
Castanea sativa	Sweet chestnut			Seed	
Fraxinus excelsior	Ash				
Populus hybrids	Poplars				
Populus x *canadensis*	Canadian poplar				
Populus nigra	Black poplar				
Salix spp., e.g. *S. viminalis*	Willows				

Climbers/scramblers for utilising wire fences

Note that not all these species have their own detailed entry in the book.

Climber/scrambler species		Evergreen	N-fixer	Edible	Main other use
Actinidia spp., e.g. *A. arguta*	Kiwis			Fruit	
Clematis vitalba	Old man's beard				Basketry, bee plant
Hedera helix	Ivy	✓			Bee plant
Parthenocissus spp.	Virginia creeper / Boston ivy				Bee plant
Rosa spp., e.g. *R. banksiae*	Roses			Fruit	Flowers in salads
Rubus spp.	Blackberries			Fruit	Bee plant
Vitis spp.	Grape vines			Fruit	Edible leaves

Tree species for use as pioneers

Of the conifer species listed in the second table below, those that have durable timber can be used, when harvested, for fencing or other outdoor uses. Note that not all these species have their own detailed entry in the book.

DECIDUOUS PIONEERS		Evergreen	N-fixer	Edible	Main other use
Species					
Alnus cordata	Italian alder		✓		
Alnus rubra	Red alder		✓		
Populus spp.	Poplars				

CONIFER PIONEERS		
Species		**Main other use**
Abies grandis	Grand fir	
Chamaecyparis lawsoniana	Lawson's cypress	Durable timber
Chamaecyparis nootkatensis	Nootka cypress	Durable timber
Chamaecyparis obtusa	Hinoki cypress	Durable timber
Chamaecyparis pisifera	Sawara cypress	Durable timber
Cryptomeria japonica	Japanese cedar	Durable timber
x Cupressocyparis leylandii	Leyland cypress	Durable timber
Cupressus macrocarpa	Monterey cypress	Durable timber
Larix decidua	European larch	Durable timber
Larix eurolepis	Dunkeld larch	Durable timber
Larix kaempferi	Japanese larch	Durable timber
Picea abies	Norway spruce	
Picea sitchensis	Sitka spruce	
Pinus nigra var. maritima	Corsican pine	
Pinus radiata	Monterey pine	
Pinus sylvestris	Scots pine	
Pseudotsuga menziesii	Douglas fir	
Thuja plicata	Western red cedar	Durable timber
Tsuga canadensis	Eastern hemlock	

Plants to attract beneficial insects and bees

A healthy population of beneficial insects is a vitally important part of any resilient agro-ecosystem. Beneficial insect predator and parasite numbers can be boosted by planting species of plants that are attractive to them for some of their feeding stages. Bees, especially wild bees, are extremely important for pollination and their numbers should also be encouraged, especially as the gregarious nature and narrow genetic variability of hive bees makes the latter susceptible to disease and parasite problems.

Beneficial insect predators

There are many types of insect that can help control populations of potential pests. Rather than wait for a pest to arrive, then try to do something about it, as most gardeners and farmers do, if you have attracted a wide diversity of predators then large pest populations should never build up.

Anthocorid bugs

The adults and nymphs of the Anthocoridae family are general predators of small invertebrates, including caterpillars, weevil larvae and pupae, and red spider mites and eggs. Adults hibernate over winter and lay their eggs on the fruit tree in spring.

Capsid or mirid bugs

Most of these are important predators, with both adults and nymphs very active voracious carnivores. Adults either hibernate over the winter and lay their eggs in the young wood in spring, or lay eggs in summer/autumn, which overwinter to hatch in spring.

Damsel bugs

This is a group of agile and ferocious carnivores.

Earwigs

Earwigs are important predators of fruit and hop insects, including aphids, mites and insect eggs. Feeding is usually at night, and during the day earwigs hide under loose bark, leaves, etc.

Ground beetles

Many species of ground beetles are useful predators of soil pests, and also feed on the pupae of winter moths and other pests that spend part of their life cycle in or on the ground. They are generally dark, shiny black, and live under stones and decaying vegetation; they vary widely in size, from 1.5-25mm (up to 1"), and feed mainly at night. Adults may climb plants in search of prey, but few species of ground beetle occur regularly on trees or shrubs. Their prey includes slugs, vine weevils, moth pupae and red spider mites.

Hoverflies (syrphids)

Adult hoverflies visit fruit blossom and many other flowers, especially Compositae, Rosaceae and Umbelliferae, in large numbers, feeding on nectar and pollen. Their larvae are predators of aphids and other insects. One larva can eat up to 50 aphids a day (1,000 in a lifetime).

Lacewings

Several species of lacewing are important predators of fruit pests. There are three groups – green, brown and powdery lacewings – and all are useful. Some species overwinter as adults; others as prepupae. The adults devour their prey, but feed mainly on nectar; the larvae are voracious predators that suck the contents out of their prey, leaving a 'shell'. Their prey includes aphids, red spider mites, scale insects and small caterpillars.

Ladybirds

Ladybird larvae feed voraciously on aphids, spider mites, small caterpillars, scale insects, etc; a single larva can eat several hundred aphids during its development. Adults usually hibernate over the winter in suitable locations, e.g. beneath loose bark.

Midges

Midges are common predators of aphids and their larvae are often present amongst aphid and mite colonies.

Rove beetles

This is a large group of active, often predatory beetles, which are most abundant in moss and decaying vegetation. They feed mainly at night. Their prey includes slugs, vine weevils, moth pupae and red spider mites.

Beneficial insect parasites

Some insects are parasitic on other invertebrates, and can be just as important as the predators described above in keeping pest populations at a low level.

Braconid wasps

This is a huge family – one of the richest in the insect kingdom – and most are parasites on other insects. They are important enemies of moth caterpillars.

Chalcid wasps

These small or minute insects (most under 3mm/0.1" long) parasitise many insect pests, particularly aphids, moth larvae and scale insects.

Harvestmen

Harvestmen look very similar to spiders, having a small round body balanced on very long, thin, delicate legs. They are common on fruit crops as predators of aphids, caterpillars and other small insects.

Ichneumon wasps

Another huge family of insects mainly parasitic on other insects. They attack fruit pests, especially moth caterpillars, and various species are deliberately used as biological control agents.

Mites

Several mites are predators of other mites, aphids and small insects. Some overwinter on dead leaves on the ground.

Money spiders

These are very small (usually under 2.5mm/0.1" long) with shiny black abdomens; they are abundant, particularly in the autumn, on fruit crops as predators of spider mites, small aphids and other small insects. Money spiders like shady, damp sites.

Parasitic flies (tachinids)

Tachinid larvae are internal parasites of other insects, particularly moth caterpillars.

Parasitic wasps

These tiny wasps generally lay their eggs in the bodies of other insects, which then become the food source for the developing wasp larvae. The adults are rarely noticed except on a sunny day, when they can be found feeding on umbelliferous flowers.

Social wasps

Social wasps (e.g. *Vespula germanica* and *V. vulgaris*) are of value as predators of harmful insects, including aphids and caterpillars; this prey is fed to the wasp larvae, which require a diet of animal protein. Predatory activity is maintained through brood-rearing, but in late summer and autumn the workers can be a nuisance on fruits.

Spiders

Many species of spider are found on fruit trees and shrubs. Their prey includes aphids, codling moth adults and larvae.

Useful perennials for attracting beneficial insects

Herbaceous perennials that are useful in attracting beneficial insects include all of:

- the Compositae (attracts hoverflies)
- the Umbelliferae (attracts hoverflies and parasitic wasps).

INSECT ATTRACTANTS	
Achillea spp.	Yarrows
Agastache spp.	Anise hyssop, etc.
Alcea rosea	Hollyhock
Angelica spp.	Angelicas
Antennaria spp.	Catsfoot, etc.
Anthemis tinctoria	Golden marguerite
Apios americana	Groundnut
Arctium spp.	Burdocks
Artemisia spp.	Tarragon / wormwood
Aster spp.	Asters
Astragalus glycyphyllos	Milk vetch

INSECT ATTRACTANTS	
Baptisia spp.	Wild indigo, etc.
Bellis perennis	Daisy
Borago officinalis	Borage
Brassica spp.	Cabbage, etc.
Bunium bulbocastanum	Pig nut
Centaurea spp.	Knapweeds
Chamaemelum nobile	Chamomile
Cichorium intybus	Chicory
Conopodium majus	Pignut
Convolvulus spp.	Bindweed, etc.
Coreopsis spp.	Tickseeds, etc.
Cryptotaenia japonica	Mitsuba
Cytisus scoparius	Broom
Echinacea spp.	Coneflowers
Eryngium spp.	Sea hollies
Eupatorium cannabinum	Hemp agrimony
Ferula spp.	Giant fennels
Foeniculum vulgare	Fennel
Fragaria vesca	Wild strawberry
Glycyrrhiza spp.	Liquorices
Hedysarum spp.	Sweet vetches
Helianthus spp.	Sunflowers
Heracleum spp.	Cow parsnips
Lathyrus spp.	Sweet peas
Levisticum officinale	Lovage
Ligusticum spp.	Scots lovage, etc.
Lupinus spp.	Lupins
Malva moschata	Musk mallow
Medicago sativa	Lucerne
Melissa officinalis	Lemon balm
Mentha spp.	Mints
Monarda spp.	Bee balms
Myrrhis odorata	Sweet cicely
Origanum vulgare	Oregano
Osmorhiza spp.	Sweet roots

INSECT ATTRACTANTS	
Petasites spp.	Butterburs
Phaseolus spp.	Beans
Pimpinella saxifraga	Burnet saxifrage
Psoralea esculenta	Breadroot
Pycnanthemum spp.	Mountain mints
Rosmarinus officinalis	Rosemary
Salvia officinalis	Sage
Sanguisorba spp.	Burnets
Satureja spp.	Savorys
Scorzonera hispanica	Scorzonera
Silphium lanciniatum	Pilotweed
Sium sisarum	Skirret

INSECT ATTRACTANTS	
Solidago spp.	Goldenrods
Stachys officinalis	Betony
Stellaria media	Chickweed
Symphytum spp.	Comfreys
Tanacetum spp.	Feverfew / tansy, etc.
Taraxacum officinale	Dandelion
Thaspium spp.	Meadow parsnips
Thermopsis spp.	False lupins
Thymus spp.	Thymes
Trifolium spp.	Clovers
Urtica dioica	Stinging nettle
Vicia spp.	Vetches

Wild/bumble bee nectar and pollen plants

To maximise bee populations, aim to plant to cover the whole flowering season, especially late winter / early spring.

The following table cannot possibly list all bee plants – very often whole families of the same genus are valuable to bees – but it gives a good indication of which plants mentioned in this book are valuable, as well as a number of others.

Nec indicates a particularly good nectar source for wild bees. **Pol** indicates a particularly good pollen source for wild bees. ■ indicates that the plant is usually in flower that month.

BEE PLANTS															
Species		Nec	Pol	Jan	Feb	Mar	Apr	May	Jun	Jul	Aug	Sep	Oct	Nov	Dec
Acanthus mollis	Bear's breech	✓								■	■				
Achillea millefolium	Yarrow	✓								■	■				
Agastache foeniculum	Anise hyssop	✓								■	■	■	■		
Agastache rugosa	Korean mint	✓							■	■	■	■			
Alcea rosea	Hollyhock	✓	✓							■	■	■			
Anchusa azurea	Garden anchusa	✓							■	■	■				
Anemone blanda	winter wandflower		✓		■	■	■								
Anemone nemorosa	Wood anemone		✓			■	■	■							
Anthemis tinctoria	Golden marguerite	✓							■	■	■				
Antirrhinum majus	Snapdragon	✓								■	■	■	■		

BEE PLANTS															
Species		Nec	Pol	Jan	Feb	Mar	Apr	May	Jun	Jul	Aug	Sep	Oct	Nov	Dec
Arctium spp.	Burdocks	✓	✓							■	■	■			
Armeria maritima	Sea pink (thrift)	✓	✓					■	■	■	■				
Asparagus officinalis	Asparagus	✓	✓						■	■	■				
Aubretia deltoidea	Rock cress	✓	✓			■	■								
Barbarea vulgaris	Winter cress	✓	✓					■	■						
Berberis darwinii	Darwin's barberry	✓	✓				■	■							
Berberis vulgaris	Common barberry	✓	✓					■							
Berberis wilsoniae	Wilson's barberry	✓	✓							■					
Borago officinalis	Borage	✓	✓					■	■	■	■				
Brachyglottis greyi	Daisy bush		✓						■						
Buddleja spp.	Buddleias	✓						■	■	■	■				
Calendula officinalis	Pot marigold	✓	✓					■	■	■	■	■	■		
Calluna vulgaris	Heather (ling)	✓	✓								■	■			
Caltha palustris	Marsh marigold	✓	✓	■	■	■	■	■	■	■	■	■	■	■	■
Campanula carpatica	Tussock bellflower	✓	✓						■						
Centaurea spp.	Knapweeds	✓	✓							■	■	■			
Centaurea cyanus	Cornflower	✓	✓						■	■	■	■			
Centaurea montana	Perennial cornflower	✓							■						
Chaenomeles speciosa	Flowering quince	✓	✓			■	■								
Chrysogonum virginianum	Golden star	✓				■	■	■							
Cichorium intybus	Chicory	✓	✓							■	■	■	■		
Cirsium arvense	Creeping thistle	✓	✓						■	■	■	■			
Clematis vitalba	Old man's beard	✓	✓							■					
Colchicum autumnale	Meadow saffron	✓	✓								■	■			
Convolvulus tricolor	Morning glory	✓	✓							■	■	■			
Cotoneaster conspicuus		✓	✓						■						
Cotoneaster dammeri	Bearberry cotoneaster	✓	✓						■						
Cotoneaster franchettii		3	3							■					
Cotoneaster frigidus	Tree cotoneaster	✓	✓						■	■					
Cotoneaster horizontalis	Rockspray cotoneaster	✓	✓					■							

BEE PLANTS																
Species		Nec	Pol	Jan	Feb	Mar	Apr	May	Jun	Jul	Aug	Sep	Oct	Nov	Dec
Cotoneaster multiflorus		✓	✓						■						
Cotoneaster purpurascens		✓	✓					■	■						
Cotoneaster salicifolius	Willow-leaved cotoneaster	✓	✓						■						
Cotoneaster simonsii	Himalayan cotoneaster	✓	✓						■						
Cucurbita ficifolia	Fig-leaf gourd	✓	✓							■	■	■			
Cynara cardunculus	Cardoon	✓								■	■	■	■		
Cynoglossum officinale	Hound's tongue	✓	✓							■	■	■			
Cytisus scoparius	Broom	✓	✓					■	■						
Dahlia pinnata	Garden dahlia	✓	✓							■	■	■	■		
Dianthus barbatus	Sweet william	✓							■	■					
Digitalis purpurea	Foxglove	✓							■	■		■			
Dipsacus fullonum	Teasel	✓								■	■	■			
Doronicum plantagineum	Leopard's bane	✓	✓			■	■								
Eccremocarpus scaber	Glory vine	✓								■	■	■			
Echinops ritro	Small globe thistle	✓									■				
Echium vulgare	Viper's bugloss	✓	✓						■	■	■	■			
Elaeagnus x ebbingei		✓											■	■	
Elaeagnus umbellata	Autumn olive	✓				■	■								
Epilobium angustifolium	Rosebay willowherb	✓	✓							■	■	■			
Epilobium hirsutum	Great hairy willowherb	✓	✓							■	■				
Erica carnea	Winter heath	✓	✓	■	■	■	■							■	■
Erica erigena	Irish heath	✓	✓			■	■								
Erica tetralix	Cross-leaved heath	✓	✓						■	■	■	■	■		
Erica vagans	Cornish heath	✓	✓									■	■	■	
Eryngium maritimum	Sea holly	✓								■	■	■			
Eryngium x tripartitum	Sea holly	✓								■	■	■			
Eschscholzia californica	California poppy	✓	✓						■	■	■	■	■		
Fritillaria imperialis	Crown imperial	✓					■								
Fuchsia excorticata	Tree fuchsia	✓	✓						■	■	■	■	■		

BEE PLANTS															
Species		Nec	Pol	Jan	Feb	Mar	Apr	May	Jun	Jul	Aug	Sep	Oct	Nov	Dec
Fuchsia magellanica	Hardy fuchsia	✓	✓						■	■	■	■	■		
Genista aetnensis	Mount Etna broom	✓								■					
Genista hispanica	Spanish gorse	✓						■	■						
Genista lydia	Lydian broom	✓						■	■						
Genista tinctoria	Dyer's greenweed	✓								■					
Glechoma hederacea	Ground ivy	✓	✓			■	■	■	■						
Hebe pinguifolia 'Pagei'			✓					■	■						
Hedera helix	Ivy	✓	✓									■	■	■	■
Helenium spp.	Sneezeweeds	✓	✓							■	■				
Helianthemum nummularium	Rock rose		✓						■	■					
Helianthus annuus	Sunflower	✓	✓							■	■	■			
Heracleum sphondylium	Hogweed	✓	✓						■	■	■				
Hippophae rhamnoides	Sea buckthorn	✓					■								
Hyacinthoides non-scripta	Bluebell	✓	✓				■	■	■						
Hypericum spp.			✓						■	■	■				
Impatiens noli-tangere	Touch-me-not balsam	✓	✓								■	■			
Knautia arvensis	Field scabious	✓	✓						■						
Lamium album	White deadnettle					■	■	■	■	■	■	■	■	■	
Lamium purpureum	Purple deadnettle	✓	✓	■	■	■	■	■	■	■	■	■	■	■	■
Laurus nobilis	Bay	✓						■	■						
Lavandula spp.	Lavenders	✓	✓							■	■				
Leontodon autumnalis	Autumn hawkbit	✓	✓						■	■	■	■			
Leucanthemum x *superbum*	Shasta daisy	✓							■	■	■				
Ligustrum ovalifolium	Privet	✓	✓							■	■				
Limnanthes douglasii	Poached egg plant	✓	✓						■	■	■				
Linaria vulgaris	Toadflax	✓	✓							■	■	■	■		
Lobelia cardinalis	Cardinal flower	✓								■	■				
Lotus corniculatus	Bird's foot trefoil	✓	✓					■	■	■	■	■			
Lysimachia vulgaris	Yellow loosestrife		✓							■	■	■			
Lythrum salicaria	Purple loosestrife	✓	✓						■	■	■	■			

		Nec	Pol	Jan	Feb	Mar	Apr	May	Jun	Jul	Aug	Sep	Oct	Nov	Dec
BEE PLANTS															
Species		Nec	Pol	Jan	Feb	Mar	Apr	May	Jun	Jul	Aug	Sep	Oct	Nov	Dec
Mahonia aquifolium	Oregon grape	✓	✓		■	■	■	■							
Mahonia japonica	Mahonia	✓	✓		■	■									
Mahonia nervosa	Dwarf oregon grape	✓	✓		■	■	■	■							
Malus domestica	Apple	✓	✓				■	■							
Malva spp.	Mallows	✓	✓						■	■	■				
Melilotus spp.	Sweet clovers	✓	✓						■	■	■	■			
Mespilus germanica	Medlar	✓	✓					■	■						
Monarda spp.	Bee balms	✓							■	■	■	■			
Myosotis spp.	Forget-me-nots	✓	✓				■	■							
Nicotiana tabacum	Common tobacco	✓	✓						■	■	■	■			
Olearia x *haastii*	Daisy bush	✓	✓							■	■				
Origanum vulgare	Oregano	✓	✓							■	■	■			
Papaver orientale	Oriental poppy		✓					■	■						
Papaver rhoeas	Field poppy	✓	✓						■	■	■				
Parthenocissus quinquefolia	Virginia creeper	✓	✓								■				
Penstemon spp.	Bearded tongues	✓							■	■					
Polygonatum spp.	Solomon's seals	✓						■	■						
Primula elatior	Oxlip	✓					■	■							
Primula vulgaris	Primrose	✓					■	■							
Prunus avium	Wild (sweet) cherry	✓	✓				■								
Prunus cerasifera	Cherry plum	✓	✓		■	■									
Prunus dulcis	Almond	✓	✓		■	■									
Prunus persica	Peach / nectarine	✓	✓				■	■							
Pulmonaria officinalis	Lungwort	✓			■	■	■								
Pulmonaria saccharata	Bethlehem sage	✓					■	■							
Reseda odorata	Mignonette	✓	✓						■	■	■	■	■		
Ribes nigrum	Blackcurrant	✓	✓				■	■							
Ribes sanguineum	Flowering currant	✓	✓			■	■								
Ribes speciosum	Fuchsia-flowered currant	✓	✓					■	■						
Robinia pseudoacacia	Black locust	✓	✓						■						
Rosa rugosa	Apple rose		✓						■	■					

BEE PLANTS														
Species		**Nec**	**Pol**	**Jan**	**Feb**	**Mar**	**Apr**	**May**	**Jun**	**Jul**	**Aug**	**Sep**	**Oct**	**Nov**	**Dec**
Rosmarinus officinalis	Rosemary	✓	✓				■	■	■	■					
Rubus deliciosus	Boulder raspberry	✓	✓					■	■						
Rubus fruticosus	Blackberry	✓							■	■					
Salix aegyptiaca	Musk willow	✓	✓	■	■										
Salix alba	White willow	✓	✓				■	■							
Salix alba var. *caerulea*	Cricket bat willow	✓	✓				■	■							
Salix caprea	Goat willow	✓	✓		■	■	■								
Salix fragilis	Crack willow	✓	✓			■	■								
Salix purpurea	Purple willow	✓	✓					■							
Salix repens	Creeping willow	✓	✓				■								
Salix x *smithiana*	Silky-leaved osier	✓	✓			■	■								
Salvia viridis	Clary	✓							■	■	■	■			
Satureja spp.	Savory	✓								■	■	■	■		
Scrophularia auriculata	Water figwort	✓	✓						■	■	■	■			
Scrophularia nodosa	Figwort	✓	✓						■	■	■				
Sedum pulchellum	Stonecrop	✓	✓					■	■	■					
Sinapis arvensis	Charlock	✓	✓					■	■						
Solidago spp.	Goldenrods	✓	✓								■	■	■	■	
Sorbus aucuparia	Rowan	✓	✓					■	■						
Stachys annua	Annual woundwort	✓								■	■	■			
Stachys germanica	Downy woundwort	✓								■	■	■			
Stachys recta	Yellow woundwort	✓								■	■	■			
Symphytum caucasicum	Blue comfrey	✓	✓						■	■	■	■			
Symphytum ibericum	Dwarf comfrey	✓	✓					■	■	■	■				
Symphytum officinale	Comfrey	✓	✓					■	■	■					
Symphytum tuberosum	Tuberous comfrey	✓	✓					■	■	■					
Symphytum x *uplandicum*	Russian comfrey	✓	✓						■	■	■				
Tanacetum parthenium	Feverfew	✓	✓							■	■	■			
Tanacetum vulgare	Tansy	✓	✓							■	■	■			
Taraxacum officinale	Dandelion	✓	✓			■	■	■	■	■	■	■	■		
Thymus spp.	Thymes	✓							■						

BEE PLANTS															
Species		**Nec**	**Pol**	**Jan**	**Feb**	**Mar**	**Apr**	**May**	**Jun**	**Jul**	**Aug**	**Sep**	**Oct**	**Nov**	**Dec**
Tilia x *euchlora*	Crimean lime	✓	✓						■	■	■				
Trifolium pratense	Red clover	✓	✓					■	■	■	■	■			
Trifolium repens	White clover	✓	✓					■	■	■	■	■	■		
Tulipa kaufmanniana	Water lily tulip		✓			■									
Tussilago farfara	Coltsfoot	✓	✓		■	■									
Ulex europaeus	Gorse	✓	✓	■	■	■	■	■	■	■	■	■	■	■	■
Verbascum thapsus	Great mullein	✓	✓						■	■	■	■			
Vicia cracca	Tufted vetch	✓							■	■	■				
Vicia faba	Broad bean / field bean	✓							■	■					
Vicia sativa	Vetch (tares)	✓					■	■	■	■	■	■			
Vicia sativa subsp. *nigra*	Blackpod vetch	✓					■	■	■	■	■	■			
Vicia sylvatica	Wood vetch	✓							■	■	■				
Vicia tenuifolia	Fine-leaved vetch	✓							■	■					
Vicia villosa	Hairy vetch	✓							■	■	■	■	■	■	
Weigela florida	Weigela	✓						■	■						
Wisteria sinensis	Chinese wisteria	✓	✓					■	■	■	■				
Yucca filamentosa	Adam's needle		✓									■			

Appendix 4

Edible crops by month of use

The following tables show when the plants described in this book are available to use fresh during the year in UK conditions. Many of these can of course be stored for many months, or sometimes for longer in the right conditions.

FRUITS														
Species		**Jan**	**Feb**	**Mar**	**Apr**	**May**	**Jun**	**Jul**	**Aug**	**Sep**	**Oct**	**Nov**	**Dec**
Actinidia spp.	Kiwis									■	■		
Akebia spp.	Chocolate vine										■		
Amelanchier spp.	Juneberries							■					
Arbutus unedo	Strawberry tree										■	■	■
Aronia spp.	Chokeberries									■	■		
Asimina triloba	Pawpaw									■	■		
Berberis spp.	Barberries									■	■	■	
Cephalotaxus spp.	Plum yews											■	
Chaenomeles spp.	Flowering quinces								■	■	■	■	
Cornus canadensis	Creeping dogwood									■	■		
Cornus capitata	Bentham's cornel											■	■
Cornus kousa	Chinese dogwood										■		
Cornus mas	Cornelian cherry								■	■			
Crataegus spp.	Hawthorns									■	■		
Cydonia oblonga	Quince										■	■	
Decaisnea fargesii	Blue bean										■		
Diospyros kaki	Japanese persimmon										■	■	
Diospyros lotus	Date plum										■	■	
Diospyros virginiana	American persimmon										■	■	■
Elaeagnus x *ebbingei*					■	■							
Elaeagnus multiflora	Goumi							■	■				

FRUITS

Species		Jan	Feb	Mar	Apr	May	Jun	Jul	Aug	Sep	Oct	Nov	Dec
Elaeagnus umbellata	Autumn olive									■	■		
Ficus carica	Fig								■	■	■		
Fragaria spp.	Strawberries						■	■	■	■	■		
Fuchsia spp.	Fuchsias							■	■	■	■		
Gaultheria shallon	Salal							■	■				
Hippophae spp.	Sea buckthorns								■	■	■		
Juniperus communis	Juniper										■	■	
Lonicera caerulea	Blue honeysuckle								■				
Lycium barbarum	Goji berry								■	■	■		
Mahonia spp.	Oregon grapes							■	■	■			
Malus domestica	Apple	■	■	■	■	■		■	■	■	■	■	■
Mespilus germanica	Medlar										■	■	
Morus spp.	Mulberries								■	■			
Myrtus ugni	Chilean guava											■	■
Passiflora incarnata	Maypop									■	■		
Poncirus trifoliata	Trifoliate orange										■		
Prunus armeniaca	Apricot								■	■			
Prunus avium	Sweet cherry							■	■	■			
Prunus cerasifera	Cherry plum							■	■				
Prunus cerasus	Sour cherry								■	■			
Prunus domestica	Plum / gage							■	■	■	■		
Prunus insititia	Damson / bullace							■	■				
Prunus persica	Peach / nectarine								■	■			
Prunus salicina	Japanese plum							■	■	■			
Prunus spinosa	Blackthorn										■	■	■
Prunus tomentosa	Nanking cherry							■	■				
Pyrus spp.	Pears	■	■					■	■	■	■	■	■
Ribes x *culverwellii*	Jostaberry							■	■				
Ribes divaricatum	Worcesterberry							■	■				
Ribes nigrum	Blackcurrant							■	■	■			

FRUITS														
Species		**Jan**	**Feb**	**Mar**	**Apr**	**May**	**Jun**	**Jul**	**Aug**	**Sep**	**Oct**	**Nov**	**Dec**
Ribes odoratum	Buffalo currant							■	■				
Ribes rubrum	Redcurrant						■	■	■	■			
Ribes uva-crispa	Gooseberry					■	■	■	■				
Rosa rugosa	Apple rose									■	■		
Rubus spp.	Rubus hybrids							■	■	■			
Rubus 'Betty Ashburner'	Groundcover raspberry							■	■				
Rubus fruticosus	Blackberry							■	■	■	■		
Rubus idaeus	Raspberry							■	■	■	■		
Rubux x loganobaccus	Loganberry							■	■	■			
Rubus nepalensis	Nepalese raspberry							■	■	■			
Rubus pentalobus	Creeping bramble							■	■				
Rubus phoenicolasius	Japanese wineberry								■				
Rubus tricolor	Chinese bramble							■	■	■			
Sambucus nigra	European elder								■	■	■		
Sambucus racemosa	Red elder							■	■	■			
Schisandra chinensis	Magnolia vine										■		
Sorbus devoniensis	Devon sorb apple										■		
Sorbus domestica	Service tree									■	■		
Sorbus thibetica	Tibetan whitebeam										■		
Vaccinium spp.	Blueberries							■	■	■			
Vaccinium arctostaphylos	Caucasian whortleberry							■	■				
Vaccinium macrocarpon	American cranberry									■	■	■	
Vaccinium vitis-idaea	Lingonberry									■	■	■	
Viburnum opulus var. *americanum*	Highbush cranberry										■	■	
Vitis spp.	Grapes										■		

NUTS AND SEEDS

Species		Jan	Feb	Mar	Apr	May	Jun	Jul	Aug	Sep	Oct	Nov	Dec
Amphicarpaea bracteata	Hog peanut	■	■	■						■	■	■	■
Araucaria araucana	Monkey puzzle									■			
Caragana arborescens	Siberian pea tree									■			
Carya spp.	Hickories / pecan										■		
Castanea spp.	Chestnuts									■	■	■	
Castanea pumila	Chinkapin									■	■		
Cephalotaxus spp.	Plum yews											■	
Corylus spp.	Hazels									■			
Ginkgo biloba	Maidenhair tree									■			
Juglans ailantifolia var. *cordiformis*	Heartnut									■	■		
Juglans nigra	Black walnut										■		
Juglans regia	Walnut										■		
Lathyrus spp.	Sweet peas							■	■	■			
Pinus spp.	Pines										■	■	■
Prunus dulcis	Almond										■		
Quercus spp.	Oaks										■	■	
Staphylea spp.	Bladdernuts									■	■	■	
Vicia spp.	Vetches								■	■	■		
Xanthoceras sorbifolium	Yellowhorn										■		

SALAD LEAVES, VEGETABLES AND FLOWERS

Species		Jan	Feb	Mar	Apr	May	Jun	Jul	Aug	Sep	Oct	Nov	Dec
Aegopodium podagraria	Ground elder				■	■	■	■	■	■	■		
Agastache foeniculum / *A. rugosa*	Anise hyssop / Korean mint					■	■	■	■	■			
Alliaria petiolata	Garlic mustard			■	■								
Allium ampeloprasum var. *babingtonii*	Babington's leek	■	■	■	■	■					■	■	■
Allium fistulosum	Welsh onion				■	■	■	■	■	■	■		
Allium neapolitanum	Daffodil garlic	■	■	■	■						■	■	■
Allium tuberosum	Garlic chives				■	■	■	■	■	■			
Allium ursinum	Ramsons		■	■	■	■	■						
Althaea officinalis	Marsh mallow				■	■	■	■	■	■			
Angelica sylvestris	Wild angelica				■	■	■	■	■	■			

SALAD LEAVES, VEGETABLES AND FLOWERS														
Species		Jan	Feb	Mar	Apr	May	Jun	Jul	Aug	Sep	Oct	Nov	Dec
Aquilegia vulgaris	Columbine				■	■	■	■	■	■			
Armoracia rusticana	Horseradish				■	■							
Asparagus officinalis	Asparagus					■	■						
Asphodeline lutea	Yellow asphodel				■	■							
Atriplex spp.	Saltbushes	■	■		■	■	■	■	■	■	■	■	■
Bamboos					■	■	■	■					
Barbarea verna	Land cress				■	■	■	■	■	■	■		
Beta vulgaris subsp. *cicla*	Spinach beet / Swiss chard	■	■	■						■	■	■	■
Beta vulgaris subsp. *maritima*	Sea beet						■	■	■	■	■		
Brassica oleracea	Perennial brassicas	■	■							■	■	■	■
Bunias orientalis	Turkish rocket				■	■	■	■	■	■			
Bunium bulbocastanum	Pig nut				■	■	■	■	■	■	■		
Calendula officinalis	Pot marigold						■	■	■	■	■		
Campanula spp.	Bellflowers				■	■	■	■	■				
Caragana arborescens	Siberian pea tree							■	■				
Cardamine flexuosa / *C. hirsuta*	Bittercresses	■	■	■	■	■	■	■	■	■	■	■	■
Cardamine pratensis	Lady's smock	■	■	■	■	■						■	■
Centranthus ruber	Red valerian			■	■	■	■	■	■	■	■		
Chenopodium bonus-henricus	Good King Henry						■	■	■	■	■		
Chrysosplenium spp.	Golden saxifrages			■	■	■	■	■	■	■	■		
Cichorium intybus	Chicory						■	■	■	■	■		
Claytonia perfoliata	Winter purslane	■	■	■	■						■	■	■
Claytonia sibirica	Siberian purslane	■	■	■	■	■	■	■	■	■	■	■	■
Crambe maritima	Sea kale				■	■	■						
Cryptotaenia japonica	Mitsuba				■	■	■	■	■	■			
Cynara spp.	Cardoon / globe artichoke				■	■	■	■	■	■	■		
Duchesnea indica	False strawberry	■	■	■	■	■	■	■	■	■	■	■	■
Epilobium angustifolium	Rosebay willowherb					■	■						
Fagus sylvatica	Beech					■							
Foeniculum vulgare	Fennel						■	■	■	■	■		
Fragaria spp. (leaves)	Strawberries				■	■	■	■	■	■			
Hablitzia tamnoides	Caucasian spinach				■	■	■						
Halesia carolina	Snowbell tree							■					
Hemerocallis spp.	Day lilies						■	■	■	■			

SALAD LEAVES, VEGETABLES AND FLOWERS													
Species		Jan	Feb	Mar	Apr	May	Jun	Jul	Aug	Sep	Oct	Nov	Dec
Hosta spp.	Hostas				■	■							
Humulus lupulus	Hop				■								
Levisticum officinale	Lovage				■	■	■	■	■	■	■		
Lunaria annua	Honesty	■	■	■	■	■	■	■		■	■	■	■
Lycium barbarum	Goji berry				■	■	■						
Malva spp.	Mallows	■	■	■	■	■	■	■	■	■	■	■	■
Matteuccia struthiopteris	Ostrich fern				■	■							
Melissa officinalis	Lemon balm				■	■	■	■	■	■	■	■	
Mentha spp.	Mints				■	■	■	■	■	■	■		
Myrrhis odorata	Sweet cicely				■	■	■	■	■	■	■		
Nasturtium officinale	Watercress	■	■	■	■	■	■	■	■	■	■	■	■
Origanum vulgare	Oregano				■	■	■	■	■	■	■		
Oxalis acetosella / O. oregana	Wood sorrel / redwood sorrel				■	■	■	■	■	■	■		
Oxyria digyna	Mountain sorrel			■	■	■	■	■	■	■	■		
Peltaria alliacea	Garlic cress		■	■	■	■							
Petasites japonicus	Giant butterbur				■	■							
Phytolacca americana	Poke root				■	■							
Plantago spp.	Plantains				■	■	■	■	■				
Polygonatum spp.	Solomon's seals				■	■							
Primula vulgaris	Primrose				■								
Reichardia picroides	French scorzonera				■	■	■	■	■	■	■		
Rumex spp.	Sorrels				■	■	■	■	■	■	■		
Rumex acetosa 'Schavel'	Sorrel	■	■	■	■	■	■	■	■	■	■	■	■
Sanguisorba minor	Salad burnet				■	■							
Scorzonera hispanica	Scorzonera				■	■							
Sedum spectabile	Ice plant				■	■	■	■	■	■			
Sedum telephium	Orpine						■	■	■	■	■		
Sisymbrium officinale	Hedge mustard			■	■	■							
Smilacina racemosa	False spikenard				■	■							
Smyrnium olusatrum	Alexanders			■	■	■	■						
Stellaria graminea	Lesser stitchwort				■	■	■	■					
Stellaria media	Chickweed				■	■	■	■	■	■	■		
Taraxacum officinale	Dandelion		■	■	■								
Tilia spp.	Limes					■	■	■	■	■	■		
Toona sinensis	Chinese cedar					■	■						

SALAD LEAVES, VEGETABLES AND FLOWERS

Species		Jan	Feb	Mar	Apr	May	Jun	Jul	Aug	Sep	Oct	Nov	Dec
Tropaeolum majus	Nasturtium					■	■	■	■	■	■		
Urtica dioica	Stinging nettle			■	■	■							
Viola spp. (herbaceous)	Violets			■	■	■	■	■	■	■	■		
Viola spp. (evergreen)	Violets	■	■	■	■	■	■	■	■	■	■	■	■

BULBS, ROOTS AND TUBERS

Species		Jan	Feb	Mar	Apr	May	Jun	Jul	Aug	Sep	Oct	Nov	Dec
Allium ampeloprasum var. *babingtonii*	Babington's leek								■	■	■		
Allium fistulosum / *A. cepa* Aggregatum Group / *A. cepa* Proliferum Group	Welsh onion / multiplier onions / Egyptian onion									■	■		
Allium neapolitanum	Daffodil garlic							■	■	■	■		
Althaea officinalis	Marsh mallow	■	■	■							■	■	■
Apios americana	Groundnut	■	■								■	■	■
Arctium lappa / *A. minus*	Burdock	■	■								■	■	■
Armoracia rusticana	Horseradish	■	■									■	■
Asphodeline lutea	Yellow asphodel	■	■	■							■	■	■
Beta vulgaris subsp. *maritima*	Sea beet	■	■	■							■	■	■
Bunium bulbocastanum	Pig nut	■	■	■							■	■	■
Camassia quamash	Quamash	■	■	■							■	■	■
Campanula rapunculus	Rampion	■	■	■							■	■	■
Cichorium intybus	Chicory	■	■	■							■	■	■
Claytonia sibirica	Siberian purslane	■	■	■	■	■	■	■	■	■	■	■	■
Crambe maritima	Sea kale	■	■	■								■	■
Dioscorea spp.	Yams	■	■	■	■							■	■
Glycyrrhiza spp.	Liquorices	■	■	■	■							■	■
Helianthus tuberosus	Jerusalem artichoke	■	■	■								■	■
Lathyrus tuberosus	Earthnut pea	■	■	■								■	■
Lunaria annua	Honesty	■	■	■								■	■
Myrrhis odorata	Sweet cicely	■										■	■
Oxalis tuberosa	Oca										■	■	■
Potentilla anserina	Silverweed	■								■	■	■	■
Scorzonera hispanica	Scorzonera	■	■	■							■	■	■
Sium sisarum	Skirret	■	■	■							■	■	■
Smallianthus sonchifolia	Yacon										■	■	■

BULBS, ROOTS AND TUBERS

Species		Jan	Feb	Mar	Apr	May	Jun	Jul	Aug	Sep	Oct	Nov	Dec
Stachys affinis	Chinese artichoke	■	■	■							■	■	■
Taraxacum officinale	Dandelion	■	■									■	■
Tropaeolum tuberosum (tubers)	Mashua	■	■	■								■	■
Ullucus tuberosus	Ulluco										■	■	■

MISCELLANEOUS EDIBLES, SPICES AND FLAVOURINGS

Species		Jan	Feb	Mar	Apr	May	Jun	Jul	Aug	Sep	Oct	Nov	Dec
Acer spp. (for sap)	Maples		■	■									
Betula spp. (for sap)	Birches		■	■									
Calycanthus spp. (bark)	American allspices							■	■				
Ceanothus americanus (leaves)	New Jersey tea						■						
Drimys lanceolata (seed)	Mountain pepper										■		
Filipendula ulmaria (flowers)	Meadowsweet							■	■				
Glechoma hederacea (leaves)	Ground ivy				■	■	■	■	■	■	■		
Laurus nobilis (leaves)	Bay	■	■	■	■	■	■	■	■	■	■	■	■
Medicago lupulina (sprouted seeds)	Black medick	■	■	■	■	■	■	■	■	■	■	■	■
Myrica spp. (leaves)	Bayberries	■	■	■	■	■	■	■	■	■	■	■	■
Myrica spp. (seed)	Bayberries									■	■		
Myrtus communis (leaves)	Myrtle					■	■	■	■	■			
Rheum spp. (leaf stalks)	Rhubarbs		■	■	■	■	■						
Rhus spp. (flowers)	Sumachs							■	■	■	■		
Rosa rugosa (flowers)	Apple rose					■	■	■	■				
Rosmarinus officinalis (leaves)	Rosemary	■	■	■	■	■	■	■	■	■	■	■	■
Salvia officinalis (leaves)	Sage	■	■	■	■	■	■	■	■	■	■	■	■
Sambucus canadensis (flowers)	American elder							■	■	■	■	■	
Tropaeolum majus (seed)	Nasturtium									■	■		
Vitex agnus-castus (leaves)	Chaste tree					■	■	■	■	■			
Zanthoxylum spp. (leaves)	Pepper trees					■							
Zanthoxylum spp. (seed)	Pepper trees									■	■		

Useful organisations, suppliers and publications

Organisations and websites

Agroforestry Research Trust
46 Hunters Moon, Dartington, Totnes, Devon TQ9 6JT
Fax: 01803 840776
www.agroforestry.co.uk
mail@agroforestry.co.uk
Researches and publishes leaflets, articles, booklets, etc. on many aspects of forest gardening. Also runs courses based in Martin Crawford's forest garden.

Agroforestry and Forest Garden Network
www.agroforestry.co.uk/fgnetwork.html
Informal network of agroforestry practitioners, which aims to facilitate visits to forest gardens in the UK and beyond.

Apios institute
www.apiosinstitute.org
US-based network that builds communities of practitioners to research and demonstrate temperate agroforestry systems. Hosts an Edible Forest Garden wiki.

Edible Forest Gardens
www.edibleforestgardens.com
Site set up to support forest gardeners (particularly in North America). Includes design consultancy and relevant course listings.

Forest gardening discussion group
http://tech.groups.yahoo.com/group/ForestGardening

Plants for a Future
www.pfaf.org
UK resource centre for rare and unusual plants, particularly those with edible, medicinal or other uses. The PFAF online plant database is a great resource.

Regenerative Ecology
www.regenerativeecology.com

Consultancy, research, design and implementation of residential and commercial regenerative edible land-scapes, throughout North America and elsewhere.

Suppliers

UK and Europe

If you have trouble finding a particular plant you can search for a UK supplier on the RHS website (www.rhs.org.uk).

Agroforestry Research Trust
Details as left.
Supplies seeds and plants of common and rare species for forest gardens, as well as information sheets and books on the subject.

Ann Miller's Speciality Mushrooms
Greenbank, Meikle Wartle
Inverurie, Aberdeenshire AB51 5AA
Tel/fax: 01467 671315
www.annforfungi.co.uk
ann@annforfungi.co.uk
Supplies inoculant for log- and woodchip-grown fungi.

Ascott Smallholding Supplies
The Old Creamery, Four Crosses, Llanymynech SY22 6LP
Tel: 0845 130 6285
Fax: 0870 774 0140
www.ascott.biz
sales@ascott.biz
Supplies seed fiddles and useful small-scale farming equipment.

B & T World Seeds
Paguignan, 34210 Olonzac, France
Tel: (+33) 468 912963
Fax: (+33) 468 913039

www.b-and-t-world-seeds.com
le@b-and-t-world-seeds.com
The largest commercial seed list I have come across, with many rare items.

Chiltern Seeds
Bortree Stile, Ulverston
Cumbria LA12 7PB
Tel: 01229 581137
Fax: 01229 584549
www.chilternseeds.co.uk
info@chilternseeds.co.uk
Stocks a good selection of tree, shrub and perennial seeds.

Cool Temperate
45 Stamford Street, Awsworth
Nottingham NG16 2QL
Tel/fax: 0115 916 2673
http://cooltemperate.co.uk/index.shtml
phil.corbett@cooltemperate.co.uk
Stocks a good range of trees and shrubs.

Edulis
Flowers Piece, Ashampstead
Reading, Berks RG8 8SG
Tel/fax: 01635 578113
www.edulis.co.uk
edulis.nursery@virgin.net
Nursery specialising in unusual useful plants.

Future Forests
Kealkill, Bantry, Co. Cork, Ireland
Tel: (+353) 27 66176
Fax: (+353) 27 66939
www.futureforests.net
futureforests@eircom.net
The best selection of useful trees and shrubs in Ireland.

Ray Mears Bushcraft
Woodlore Ltd, PO Box 3, Etchingham
East Sussex TN19 7ZE
Tel/fax: 01580 819668
www.raymears.com
info@raymears.com
Sells the Scandinavian berry picker (harvesting comb).

Silky Fox
Foxley Estate Offices, Mansel Lacy
Hereford HR4 7HQ
Tel: 01981 590224
Fax: 01981 590355
www.silkyfox.co.uk
sales.silkyfox@virgin.net
Sells high-quality pruning saws.

UK Juicers Ltd
Unit 5 Harrier Court, Airfield Business Park
Elvington, York YO41 4EA
Tel: 01904 757070
Fax: 01904 757071
www.ukjuicers.com/dehydrators
enquiries@ukjuicers.com
Sells a good range of dehydrators, including the Excalibur.

North America

Edible Landscaping
361 Spirit Ridge Ln, Afton, VA 22920, USA
Tel: (+1) 800 524 4156
Fax: (+1) 434 361 1916
www.ediblelandscaping.com
info@ediblelandscaping.com
Stocks a good range of fruiting and other edible plants.

Fungi Perfecti
PO Box 7634, Olympia, WA 98507, USA
Tel: (+1) 800 780 9126
Fax: (+1) 360 426 9377
www.fungi.com
info@fungi.com
Supplies all things fungi-related.

Grimo Nut Nursery
979 Lakeshore Rd, R.R.3, Niagara-on-the-Lake
Ontario LOS 1J0, Canada
Tel: (+1) 905 934 6887
Fax: (+1) 905 935 6887
www.grimonut.com
nuttrees@grimonut.com
Stocks a great range of the less common nut trees as well as some fruit trees.

Hartmann's Plant Company
PO Box 100, Lacota, MI 49063-0100, USA
Tel: (+1) 269 253 4281
Fax: (+1) 269 253 4457
www.hartmannsplantcompany.com
info@hartmannsplantcompany.com
Stocks a good range of bush and climbing fruits.

The Nut Wizard

PO Box 81, Bedford, IN 47421, USA

Tel: (+1) 314 838 5467

www.thenutwizard.com

dick@thenutwizard.com

Supplies Nut Wizard nut harvesters.

One Green World

28696 S. Cramer Rd, Molalla, OR 97038, USA

Tel: (+1) 877 353 4028

www.onegreenworld.com

info@onegreenworld.com

Stocks a large selection of the more unusual tree and shrub crops.

Prairie Moon Nursery

32115 Prairie Lane, Winona, MN 55987, USA

www.prairiemoon.com

info@prairiemoon.com

Tel: (+1) 866 417 8156

Fax: (+1) 507 454 5238

Offers a large range of native North American seeds.

Richters Herbs

357 Highway 47, Goodwood, ON L0C 1A0, Canada

www.richters.com

Tel: (+1) 905 640 6677

Fax: (+1) 905 640 6641

Offers a great range of seeds, mainly perennials.

Publications

Forest gardening

Crawford, M. (2009) *A Forest Garden Year* DVD. Green Books.

Hart, R. (1996) *Forest Gardening*. Green Books.

Jacke, D. & Toensmeier, E. (2005) *Edible Forest Gardens* Vols 1 & 2. Chelsea Green.

Whitefield, P. (2002) *How to Make a Forest Garden*. Permanent Publications.

Useful plants

Chevallier, A. (1996) *The Encyclopedia of Medicinal Plants*. Dorling Kindersley.

Crawford, M. (2001) *Directory of Apple Cultivars*. Agroforestry Research Trust.

Crawford, M. (2005) 'Food Value of Annual and Perennial Vegetables'. In *Agroforestry News*, Vol 13 No 4. (Compares nutrient values of annual and perennial vegetables.)

Crawford, M. (1998) *Nitrogen-Fixing Plants for Temperate Climates*. Agroforestry Research Trust.

Crawford, M. (1993) *Useful Plants for Temperate Climates*. Agroforestry Research Trust.

Fern, K. *Plants for a Future*. (1997) Permanent Publications.

Irving, M. (2009) *The Forager Handbook*. Ebury Press.

Mears, R. (2008) *Wild Food*. Hodder & Stoughton.

Ocean, Suellen. *Acorns and eat 'em*. www.californiaoaks. org/ExtAssets/acorns_and_eatem.pdf (Recipe book in pdf form.)

Toensmeier, E. (2007) *Perennial Vegetables*. Chelsea Green.

History of forest gardening

Kumar, B. & Nair, P. (2006) *Tropical Homegardens: A Time-Tested Example of Sustainable Agroforestry*. Springer.

Reijntjes, C., Haverkort, B. & Waters-Bayer, A. (1992) *Farming for the Future: An Introduction to Low External-Input and Sustainable Agriculture*. MacMillan Press. (These two books give a good background on the origins and history of forest gardening in warmer climates.)

Fungi

Mukerji, K., Chamola, B. & Singh, J. (2000) *Mycorrhizal Biology*. Kluwer.

Read, D., Lewis, D. Fitter, A. & Alexander, I. (1992) *Mycorrhizas in Ecosystems*. CABI. (The above two books include a lot of scientific information on how mycorrhizae move nutrients around.)

Steineck, H. (1984) *Mushrooms in the Garden*. Mad River Press.

Stamets, P. (2000, 2nd edn) *Growing Gourmet and Medicinal Mushrooms*. Ten Speed Press.

Other books

Altieri, M. (1995) *Agroecology*. IT Publications / Westview Press.

Katz, S. (2003) *Wild Fermentation: the flavour, nutrition, and craft of live-culture foods*. Chelsea Green.

Burke S. (1998) *Windbreaks*. Inkata Press.

Russel Smith, J. (1987) *Tree Crops: A Permanent Agriculture*. Island Press.

Journals

Agroforestry News. Quarterly journal published by the Agroforestry Research Trust. www.agroforestry.co.uk.

Permaculture Magazine. Quarterly journal from Permanent Publications. www.permaculture-magazine.co.uk.

The Permaculture Activist. North American quarterly journal. www.permacultureactivist.net.

Index